ORTHODOX VISIONS OF ECUMENISM

ORTHODOX VISIONS OF ECUMENISM

STATEMENTS, MESSAGES AND REPORTS
ON THE ECUMENICAL MOVEMENT
1902 - 1992

COMPILED BY GENNADIOS LIMOURIS

WCC Publications, Geneva

Cover design: Edwin Hassink

ISBN 2-8254-1080-2

Printed in Switzerland

Table of Contents

Foreword

The Orthodox have indeed spoken to the ecumenical movement! Throughout the years, they have given much and have received much in return. Orthodox commitment to the common journey of Christians, sisters and brothers belonging to different traditions and coming from various parts of the world, was manifest from the very beginning and Orthodox views and positions on the ecumenical movement have always been formulated *from within*.

This new anthology — which includes official statements, encyclicals, messages and reports of inter-Orthodox consultations, as well as articles on subjects pertaining to the ecumenical movement — illustrates the level and quality of this sustained commitment. At the same time it is an integral part of contemporary ecumenical history.

Much has been said about the significance of Orthodox contribution to the ecumenical movement. Not to reiterate here what has already been affirmed, I would simply point to some areas in which Orthodox insights have become sources of precious inspiration in our past and present work.

Orthodox ecclesiological sensitivity enabled the ecumenical community to take seriously the ecclesiological nature of our being together in the ecumenical movement and in the World Council of Churches; especially, it constantly reminded that the ecumenical problem is not the *unity of the Church*, which is a gift of God, but the *disunity of Christendom and humankind*. Orthodox affirmation of the Trinitarian nature of our faith has contributed in widening the earlier Christocentric orientation of the ecumenical movement and in indicating the need to embrace an understanding of eschatological fulfilment in the light of the working of God's Spirit in nature and history. Orthodox theological tradition has reinforced the understanding of *oikoumene* which had to overcome its anthropocentric character and include the dimension of time as well, incorporating the historical past and an eschatological future. The centrality of eucharist in Orthodox life and thought has nurtured the "eucharistic vision" within the ecumenical movement, which binds together the spiritual and the secular, eschatology and history, liturgy and diakonia, icon and action. Finally, Orthodox liturgical and spiritual experience strengthened an ecologically conscious theology of creation, drawing on the recognition in biblical-patristic thought of the relational, interdependent character of all life which is sustained by the life-giving power of the Holy Spirit.

Of course, many difficulties have regularly appeared and still emerge. Most of the documents in the present collection make evident the difficulties of overcoming through dialogue centuries-old theological problems, of envisaging together contemporary challenges arising from the encounter of distinct traditions and cultures, of facing in common new sources of tension. Orthodox churches, participating fully in the life of the WCC, feel the need to review again and again their participation in the ecumenical movement. They feel the need constantly to challenge the others and to re-examine their own involvement. This mutual questioning is probably the most eloquent confirmation that the history of the ecumenical endeavour is now a common history.

There is much reason for gratitude. The present volume is dedicated to the Heads of Eastern and Oriental Orthodox churches for their contribution to the vision of unity in the ecumenical movement. Undoubtedly, this dedication is extended to their numerous representatives, to generations of committed ecumenical workers, clergy and lay, men and women, old and young, who faithfully served their churches and the ecumenical movement, witnessing to the new reality of a profound fellowship with each other while remaining rooted in their tradition.

The spirit and contents of the present publication indicate hope for the future of our ecumenical work together against the background of many contemporary challenges facing both the churches and the WCC. In commending it to the wider ecumenical community and the younger Orthodox generation, I look forward to a continued and deepened Orthodox contribution in the years to come.

Konrad Raiser
General Secretary
World Council of Churches

Preface

This volume follows the two excellent publications on *The Orthodox Church* (1978)[1] and *Orthodox Thought* (1983),[2] which have served for many years as reference books and have been much used in ecumenical gatherings and pan-Orthodox conferences and meetings.

This collection of Orthodox statements, declarations and reports of inter-Orthodox consultations, supplemented by several pertinent theological articles,[3] shows the fruitful contribution and active participation of the Eastern and Oriental Orthodox churches and theologians in the World Council of Churches and in the ecumenical endeavour in general.

Most of the texts here come from the period since 1982. This past decade has been one of the most important and active periods in the history of the World Council of Churches. The assemblies in Vancouver and Canberra, six world conferences,[4] hundreds of ecumenical consultations and meetings, involving thousands of people from different Christian churches and denominations, have marked the life of the Council and its member churches. A considerable number of ecumenical statements, reports and publications have also been produced.

During these years enormous efforts have been undertaken to seek the *unity of the Church.* Yet many today would say that ecumenism is undergoing a crisis of *identity, purpose and goal* — and of this there is no doubt. Because of the divisions that have occurred during the past two millennia, the sin of the rent in "the seamless robe of Christ" is so great that it is beyond the power of human beings to expiate it and to heal the wounds which our separations have inflicted on the Church.

People are strong enough to destroy the unity of Christ's Church, but are not capable of restoring it. We can only believe in it and pray for it.

It is time for the ecumenical movement to break free from earlier dreams of bringing about the visible unity of the churches in one fell swoop. We must be clear-sighted and realistic: it is easier to destroy than to create!

Having lost its original unity and failed to take account of the separatist tendencies of race, language, culture, etc., the Church in medieval and modern times has been faced by an almost insurmountable problem: that of returning to the state of being one and undivided.

It is impossible to turn back to those early prophetic days. History does not repeat itself. The past belongs to the past, and we must accept the new reality which the ecumenical movement is facing and experiencing. Today, after centuries of growing

---

• The texts in this volume have been reprinted in their original form.

further apart, there is only one hope left for the Christian churches: not to achieve uniformity, but gradually to come nearer to each other by together spreading the Christian message all over the world.

Orthodox theology believes that its own teaching and its hierarchical structure are based on the unbroken Tradition which was transmitted by Christ to the apostles and was experienced through the conciliar period and the fathers of the Church.

The present volume offers the ecumenical family the opportunity of discovering the richness of Orthodox tradition and teaching, and of understanding how Orthodoxy sees the unity of the churches for today.

I would like to express my thanks to all those who have contributed to this publication: colleagues in the Office of Communication, Renate Sbeghen for her valuable assistance in preparing the manuscript, and members of the Orthodox task force for their advice and encouragement.

Phanar

Gennadios Limouris
Coordinator of the Synodical Committee
on Inter-Church Affairs
Ecumenical Patriarchate

NOTES

[1] C. Patelos ed., *The Orthodox Church in the Ecumenical Movement*, Geneva, WCC, 1978.

[2] G. Tsetsis ed., *Orthodox Thought: Reports of Orthodox Consultations Organized by the WCC, 1975-1982*, Geneva, WCC, 1983.

[3] Published in *The Ecumenical Review*, the *Greek Orthodox Theological Review* and *One World*. We express our gratitude and thanks to the authors and journals.

[4] Cf. "Diakonia 2000: Called to Be Neighbours", Larnaca, Cyprus, 1986; "Koinonia: Sharing Life in a World Community", El Escorial, Spain, 1987; "Your Will Be Done — Mission in Christ's Way", San Antonio, USA, 1989; "Justice, Peace and the Integrity of Creation", Seoul, South Korea, 1990; the Ecumenical Global Gathering of Youth and Students, Mendes, Brazil, 1993; "Towards Koinonia in Faith, Life and Witness", Santiago de Compostela, Spain 1993.

Patriarchal and Synodical Encyclical of 1902

To their Beatitudes and Holinesses the Patriarchs of Alexandria and Jerusalem, and to the most holy autocephalous sister-Churches in Christ, in Cyprus, Russia, Greece, Romania, Serbia and Montenegro.

Whereas the most holy presidents of the venerable autocephalous Orthodox Churches have written to us in Irenical Letters in reply to our announcement of our election (by God's pleasure) and elevation to the most holy apostolic and patriarchal Ecumenical Throne, we are happy to observe the ancient and unbreakable bond, manifested with all haste and great warmth, and the words of evangelical love so warmly expressed and the ardent prayers addressed to God on behalf of this senior holy and Great Church of Christ, their sister most ready in faith and hope and love.

This appearance of brethren praying together in Christ and united in a sacred harmony, stirs our soul and warms us to a more continuous effectual fellowship; and it has excited in us greater hopes of a more fruitful cultivation of mutual relations among Churches sharing in the same opinion, with a view to a more splendid and abundant religious harvest. We declare ourselves full of most excellent intentions and we gladly take up the sincere assurances of the holy Churches, among whom our most holy sister who bears the honours among the Churches in Orthodox States (we speak of the Orthodox Church of All the Russias) has brought us great consolation by addressing herself as follows:

"The summons to peace and fraternal love and lively mutual fellowship, which you addressed to us and to the other autocephalous Churches, will find an echo and a sympathy in the hearts of all Orthodox Christians, who are sincerely devoted to their mother Church. Divided by reasons of history and differences of language and nationality, the local holy Churches of God find their unity in mutual love and their courage in close fellowship with one another; and they derive power to make progress in faith and devotion, rejecting the crafts of hostility and proclaiming the Gospel universally." The

---

● H.H. Joachim III, Patriarch of Constantinople, informed all local Orthodox Churches of his election as Ecumenical Patriarch in his "Irenical Letter", in which he also stressed the need for cooperation between them. In response to their congratulations he addressed them the Encyclical of 12 June 1902 in which he deals, for example, with the relations of Orthodox Churches with Roman Catholics and Protestants; relations with the ancient oriental Churches; and the question of the calendar. Two years later, when the replies of the local Orthodox Churches had been received, the Patriarch issued another Encyclical (dated 12 May 1904). He strongly criticized the fact that the canons established by the Councils were being neglected, and emphasized the danger this represented for the unity of the Orthodox Church. He then referred indirectly to the current troubled situation of the Orthodox Churches of Cyprus and Antioch, and finally brought up once again the question of relations with non-Orthodox Churches.

same spirit of brotherly love and unity derived from the divine source of the Gospel breathes vitally through similar words and expressions in the esteemed letters from all the other sister-Churches: they give us courage and strength, and they afford happy opportunities for us, following the good custom (which dates from time immemorial) of exchanging fraternal greetings and love, to seek also their wise counsel on matters on which both common study and judgment could be considered opportune by the Churches and also the successful achievement of good works to the benefit of the local Churches as well as of the whole Church, whose head is Christ.

Happily encouraged, then, by such brotherly support and having in mind the advice of the Apostle Paul to the Corinthians and to all in all ages who believe in Christ: "I beseech you, brethren, through the name of our Lord Jesus Christ, that you all speak the same thing, and there be no division among you; but that you be perfected together in the same mind and in the same judgment", we decided to suggest to our Holy Synod for deliberation a plan which we judged to be right and holy and worthy of serious consideration. With a view to a clearer formulation and easier study of certain topics of a religious nature and of great importance, we communicated that plan to our venerable and dear synodical brothers in Christ; and we asked them whether our holy and Great Church of Christ considered it opportune to seek an exchange of views with the holy patriarchs and most reverend presidents of the autocephalous Churches on these topics.

After expert study and preparation, they have agreed by a unanimous synodical resolution of our dear brother-bishops gathered around us in the Holy Synod; but standing firm to the custom prevailing in the primitive Church (according to which the bishops and pious guardians of the Churches acquainted each other by letter of their problems and of their solutions, diligently and fraternally being careful to seek after a common mind in word and deed), we are proceeding to outline the questions which have been approved synodically: they do not raise any new matters, but put forward matters which have for some time been the subjects of common study, with the object of mutual enlightenment of the local holy Orthodox Churches of God. They, motivated (of course) by similar intentions for the general good, will gladly (we believe) accept and judge opportune such research into the cycle of spiritual intercommunion in overseeing: it is not only to be perceived pragmatically but is also commanded by the calling with which all of us who have been called in Christ, by the favour and grace of God, to guard His holy Churches by giving heed to themselves and to be concerned for the salvation of all men.

It is, indeed, necessary that those who are set over the faithful for their spiritual government should pay attention to the greater good of all Christians, in order that the most precious crown of love might be enabled to bear more fruit according to the divine will. Wherefore, we consider that what should first of all be examined is whatever the venerable presidents of the holy autocephalous Orthodox Churches deem would be beneficial to do but which is not being done; and what henceforward should and could be done, towards bringing together the Orthodox peoples in the unity of faith and in mutual love and common purpose; and what thereafter should be done to strengthen further our holy and Orthodox faith, and to defend more strongly the holy Churches of God against the assault of the contrary spirit of these days.

It is, moreover, pleasing to God, and in accordance with the Gospel, to seek the mind of the most holy autocephalous Churches on the subject of our present and future relations with the two great growths of Christianity, viz. the Western Church and the Church of the Protestants. Of course, the union of them and of all who believe in Christ with us in the Orthodox faith is the pious and heart-felt desire of our Church and of all genuine Christians who stand firm in the evangelical doctrine of unity, and it is the subject of constant prayer and supplication; but at the same time we are not unaware that this pious desire comes up against the unbroken persistence of these Churches in doctrines on which, having taken their stand as on a base hardened by the passage of time, they seem quite disinclined to join a road to union, such as is pointed out by evangelical and historical truth; nor do they evince any readiness to do so, except on terms and bases on which the desired dogmatic unity and fellowship is unacceptable to us. It is a truism that the holy catholic and apostolic Church is founded upon the Apostles and preserved by the divine and inspired Fathers in the Ecumenical Councils, and that her head is Christ the great shepherd, who bought her with his own blood; and that according to the inspired and heaven-bound Apostle she is the pillar and ground of the truth and the body of Christ: this holy Church is indeed one in identity of faith and similarity of manners and customs, in unison with the decisions of the seven Ecumenical Councils, and she must be one and not many, differing from each other in dogmas and fundamental institutions of ecclesiastical government. If, as in every matter which is impossible with men but possible with God, we cannot yet hope for the union of all as ever being a possibility, yet because divine grace is constantly active and men are being guided in paths of evangelical love and peace, one must consider very carefully whether it might be possible to prepare the (at present) anomalous way which leads to such a goal and to find points of encounter and contact, or even to turn a blind eye to certain irregularities until the completion in due course of the whole task, whereby might be fulfilled to our joint satisfaction and benefit our Lord and God and Saviour Jesus Christ's saying about one flock and one shepherd. Wherefore, if it might be acceptable to the holy brethren to follow up this suggestion, we are bold to add this fraternal question: whether the present is judged to be the right time for preliminary conference on this, to prepare a level ground for a fraternal approach and to determine, by common agreement of members of the whole of the Orthodox Church, what might be considered the best bases, ways and means.

Clearly relevant to Christian unity are the questions concerning those Western Christians who recently separated from the Roman Church and call themselves Old Catholics, and who say that they accept the teachings of the undivided Church down to the ninth century and the decrees of the seven holy Ecumenical Councils: they claim that they are already in the Orthodox Church as a whole, and they seek union and communion with her as the remaining task of formal regularization. The impetuous zeal for Christian truth and evangelical love on the part of these pious Christians is all together praiseworthy, and in their fine struggle they proved themselves to be filled with it. Their conferences' resolutions and acts are well known to the Christian world, as are their dogmatic and liturgical teaching through their catechetical and symbolical books.

A clear and agreed opinion as to their professed confession of faith does not yet prevail among us, but various opinions about it are expressed by our churchmen, both by those who have known them at close quarters and also by those who have studied them at a distance: some of them have decided that on important dogmatic points this confession is still far from perfect Orthodoxy, and others on the contrary consider it not to contain essential differences which would preclude unity of faith and ecclesiastical communion but to be a well-nigh complete acceptance by them of the complete healthy Orthodox teaching and tradition. We think it good, therefore, to invite the pious and fraternal views of the holy Orthodox sister-Churches on this important matter, as to whether they deem it opportune (and what way would be good and acceptable) to facilitate the realization of the desire of these Christians for complete union with us, as an auspicious first-fruit of the hoped-for and longed-for unity of all Christians.

Worthy of no less attention, in our opinion, is the question of a common calendar, already for some time spoken and written about, especially the proposed methods of reforming the Julian Calendar which has prevailed in the Orthodox Church for centuries, or the acceptance of the Gregorian: the former is more defective scientifically, the latter more exact, considering also the change of our ecclesiastical Easter after the necessary agreement. In the studies on this topic, we see that the opinions which are held by Orthodox who have made a special investigation of it are divided. Some of them consider our ancient inheritance as alone fitting in the Church, having been handed down from the fathers and always having had the Church's authority; not only do they think that there is very little need for change, but they would rather avoid it, for the reasons which they elaborate. Others, champions of the Westerners' calendar and its introduction by us, suggest the greatest possible chronometric accuracy, or even the new usage of uniformity; and they advocate the practice of the Western Church as being reasonable, perhaps in expectation of possible religious benefits, in their own opinion. So, in our times, the discussion has been intensified, various and stimulating assertions being propounded by either side, both of a scientific and of a religious nature, on both of which in some Orthodox countries a certain inclination is evident of adherence to the notion of changing our Orthodox calendar or of some reform of it; and, inasmuch as this question (for all its obvious scientific form) has an ecclesiastical importance, it seems right to us to exchange with the other Orthodox Churches the relevant information in order that on this too a common mind might be reached among them, and a single opinion and decision of the whole Orthodox Church expressed. For, to her alone belongs the judgment on this matter and the research (if necessary) for a way of uniting (so far as is possible) the hoped-for scientific accuracy with the desired maintenance of hallowed ecclesiastical decrees.

So, then, our Great Church of Christ considers this exchange of views on the above-mentioned points to be a simple indication of spiritual and practical intercommunion, and as cementing the unity which should be maintained on all common questions and which is most effective in Orthodoxy; and she cherishes high hopes that her fraternal concern in this matter, and her earnest prayer for holy and evangelical conclusions, will find a sympathetic echo in the hearts of the venerable sister-Churches in Christ and have the approval of their brotherly love, so that on each matter the views of those who reverently preside over the Churches may be made known. We think, too, that as well as the common benefits expected from the mutual exchanges the great moral strength of the holy Orthodox Church of Christ may be demonstrated once again to the world; for its source is her possession of the unchanging truth, and its strong lever is the unbreakable unity of the local Churches. With such hopes and convictions, which we base upon the inspired zeal of those venerable presidents who govern the holy Churches of God and of the Holy Synods, that their Churches may be glorious and steadfast, we pray to the Lord with all our heart that all the Orthodox faithful may be preserved and sheltered by His invincible shield, and that He will vouchsafe great happiness and health and long life to Your Beatitude and Holiness, who are much beloved and cherished by us.

JOACHIM OF CONSTANTINOPLE

Joachim of Ephesus	Joachim of Xanthi
Nathanael of Proussa	Nicodemus of Vodena
Alexander of Neocaesarea	Nicephoros of Lititsa
Basil of Smyrna	Tarasios of Helioupolis
Constantine of Chios	Hieronymos of Kallioupolis
Polycarpos of Vrna	

Response to the Reactions
of the Local Orthodox Churches

Blessed be the God and Father of our Lord Jesus Christ, the Father of compassion and the God of all comfort, who always pours out richly His mercy upon us, and who lately bestowed upon us the great and consoling grace of receiving and reading the most welcome and esteemed fraternal letters of the Holy Churches of God: His Beatitude the Patriarch of the Holy City Jerusalem and All Palestine; the most reverend Presidents of the Holy Synods of the sister-Autocephalous Churches of Russia, Greece, Romania and Serbia; and the reverend pastor of the Holy Church of Montenegro. His Beatitude the Pope and Patriarch of the Great City of Alexandria and All Egypt, for reasons unknown to us, has not yet replied; and the affairs of the Apostolic and Patriarchal Church in Antioch, and of the holy Church of New Justinian in Cyprus, make it difficult to maintain ecclesiastical correspondence with them, for canonical reasons in the former case and because of the loss of a canonical Archbishop and President in the latter case.

To these Churches we send our best wishes; and to our dear brothers and co-ministers in Christ, who graciously and fraternally replied to our Patriarchal and Synodical letter of 12 June 1902, we express the dutiful thanks of our holy Great Church of Christ and the indescribable joy with which unanimously they declare and confess the good done, even by proxy, to the Church of God by the more frequent intercourse among the local Churches through correspondence, especially in recent days when ambitions and calculations have a more secular and nationalist character and are opposed to the holy Apostolic and Conciliar canons: they are foreign to the holy Churches of God and to their godly pastors, and they are pursued under the guise of a zealous provision for and protection of the interests of Orthodoxy, and by stirring up proselytizing societies among her suffering children. These things are done in open breach and violation of the rights of the local Churches which have pertained since time immemorial and which were ratified by ecumenical canons; and they create misunderstandings and suspicions among the sister-Churches, to the confusion and incalculable harm of Christian people and to the disruption and fragmentation of the one Catholic Church of Christ into parts and sections recognizable by national

---

● This is the text of the response to the replies from the local Orthodox Churches (12 May 1904); it has been translated by the WCC Language Service. The Greek text of the two letters can be found in B. Stavridis, *Historia tis Ikoumenikis Kiniseos*, Athens, 1964, pp. 116-127.

traditions and linguistic peculiarities. They forget usually their kinship in faith and provoke one another for the sake of worldly goods, and envy one another.

For how can those who follow carefully the events of our times avoid noticing, outside the confines of the Universal Church, that fecund and strange and cunning spirit, which fatally influences both the uneducated and those who are educated only in the wisdom of this world? It makes excuses for anything and defiles everything by any ways and means, in the service of worldly tendencies; and within the compass of the Church of God it infiltrates its seeds, through the actions of lay domination over ecclesiastical matters and affairs, not sparing even the Lord's venerable dwellings and our holy fathers' sacred objects; and it strives to make the Church of Christ nothing but a handmaid and instrument of worldly ambitions and political programmes.

This spirit, which is quite foreign to the Church and threatens the peace and health of the holy Churches of God, seems to us as much as any to require the fraternal consultation and counsel of our most revered fellow-priests in accordance with the clear arrangements and salutary instructions of hoary and venerable antiquity. For this is the most fundamental feature of Orthodoxy, the basis of her whole canonical and administrative structure, "not to move eternal boundaries which our Fathers fixed". This alone will enable us to repulse the more recent tendencies and activities which are advancing (in the Apostle's words) "with a wisdom earthly, sensual and devilish".

How is it not right to venerate, to treat gently and to keep henceforward those things which have been set in order for so many centuries? How is it not without danger to shake violently and to disturb the decorous and sacred system of the holy Patriarchal Churches, originating from the Ecumenical Councils and the Rules of the Fathers, whose apostolic foundations and nineteen centuries of life have been wrought with unsparing pains and troubles and indescribable sufferings and martyrs' blood, and whose theological services to the whole Church are universally acknowledged and greatly valued? They ought, therefore, to be inviolate and respected; and anything which (even from afar) could lessen their reputation and power should be avoided. Every assistance and aid to their advantage, every restoration of the fallen or help for the helpless, or treatment of the wounded and rescue of the persecuted and those in danger, should not be done in any other way than in accordance with God's will and in a spirit of brotherly love and through the local canonical pastors of the Church.

A neglecting of the aforesaid decrees and definitions of the Fathers has produced, with no good result, grievous (indeed lamentable) breaches more recently in the fabric of the Orthodox Church. And as they were produced by the neglect of these things, so also by their observation will come, by God's help, better things for the sister-Churches and salvation for those who will hear, although with difficulty are those who set worldly goods and their own glory above the authority of ecclesiastical and canonical order and doctrine persuaded by the word of truth and righteousness. That the satisfactory solution of the other questions put forward for consideration in our former letters presents many (and perhaps very many) difficulties has not escaped our notice; and we too know and admit to our revered brethren in Christ that the difficulties are increased by the manifold attempts of the Roman Church and of many Protestants to poach and proselytize in the domestic folds of the Orthodox Church. It is indeed very dangerous, and quite contrary to the Christian calling, for Christians to attack Christians or to suborn and foment trouble among the faithful: as Scripture has it, "traversing land and sea to make one proselyte" (Mt 23:15). We all feel pain and are deeply wounded when we see and hear the souls of the sick in mind and the lukewarm in faith, or children of the defenceless and neglected, or widows of those who have been overwhelmed by suffering, seduced and led astray; and when we see characters so besmirched that religion is practised for gain, parents rising against children, or brothers against brothers, or communities against the local pastors, and everywhere quarrels and discord being created in blasphemy against the honoured Christian name among the nations. Such being the case, it is obvious that we ought certainly "to take heed to ourselves and to all the flock in which the Holy Spirit has made us bishops, to tend the Church of God which he purchased with his own blood", and to keep watch day and night, and to guard and preserve from any adverse influence the flock which has been entrusted to us. But besides being watchful for our own defence, we ought also to look to the concerns of others and pray with all our soul for the union of all, not adding to the difficulties nor holding that the matter does not bear discussion or is quite impossible, but considering the possible ways of progress in the good work of the union of all: walking in wisdom and in the spirit of gentleness towards those who disagree with us, and remembering that they too believe in the All-Holy Trinity and glory in the name of our Lord Jesus Christ and hope to be saved by the grace of God.

Having greater and better hopes, we ought to pay more attention both to the so-called Old Catholics and to those of the Anglican Church, since they show more respect and regard to the holy Orthodox Church of Christ. Although there are divisions of opinion among the theologians as to the difference between the doctrine of the Old Catholic Church and that of the Apostolic and Catholic Orthodox Church, yet one would not be wrong in saying that of the Christians in the West they are the closest to the Orthodox Church. Because of this it is right to help them as much as possible to fight the good fight, in order that, inclining neither to right nor left, they may seek after the way which leads directly to the Orthodox Church. Lest we be charged with indifference for our brethren who are seeking what is right and God-given and who long for ecclesiastical intercommunion and union with us, let us not be misunderstood as doing them an injustice by judging them on rumours and reports rather than on authentic and official confessions: it might be worth while to ask them the reason for their hope in these matters, i.e. for a clear and precise and official confession of their faith, published and subscribed by their bishops and pastors in council, that so it might be possible to have a discussion and clarification and an understanding and (with God's help) fulfilment of our common desire.

We also consider those of the Anglican Church who have turned towards the Orthodox Church to be worthy of no least sympathy and feelings of reciprocity; and on not a few occasions they have furnished tokens of their fraternal attitude towards us. It is self-evident that those Eastern Christians, too, who are closer to us both in forms and customs as well as in their whole doctrine and ecclesiastical administration and worship, deserve similar sympathy and support.

It is opportune, we believe, here to remind our revered brothers in Christ that the other holy local Churches of God follow another opinion and practice on certain points, and this is no mere chance: on baptism and holy orders they are separated from the Orthodox Church. On such matters, at least, it seems desirable (or rather, essential) to define a common mind and a common practice in accordance with the spirit and the decrees of the Universal Church. These and suchlike matters can be investigated through fraternal letters: certainly they might be examined more exactly and more carefully if, as some of our brothers in Christ have suggested, during the next three years theologians sent by the holy Churches of God were to come together and their carefully considered opinions were to be notified to the other Churches by the first in order, the Archbishop of Constantinople, for their final decision.

As to our calendar, this is our opinion: the venerable tradition of Easter has been firmly established for centuries, and ratified by the Church's constant practice, according to which we are instructed to celebrate the Lord's Light-bearing Resurrection on the first Sunday after the full moon of the spring equinox, whether these coincide or follow one another, and it is not right to make innovations in this matter; and those who keep the Julian calendar and our immovable Feasts overleap only thirteen days, so that it is absurd and pointless to try to reconcile our Menologies and the Menologies of those who follow the other calendar, since there is no reason (ecclesiastical or scientific) to omit so many days and this reconciliation of the Menologies would be temporary, until the year 2100, when again the difference of a day will begin. But the reform of the Julian calendar, as being allegedly inexact, and the establishment of the common civil year as being more consistent with the solstice, we consider to be premature and quite superfluous at present; for from an ecclesiastical point of view we are not at all obliged to alter the calendar and, as experts have assured us, science has not yet declared itself definitely as to the precision with which the solar year is calculated.

Replying thus to you and disclosing our own views on the questions and suggestions that have been aired, dear brothers and fellow-pastors in Christ, we rejoice in the Lord; and we are in hope, nay rather we know, that in effect we shall be ready protectors and sincere counsellors to one another in all our thoughts and doubts, communicating liberally as each has been given grace "for the perfecting of the saints unto the work of ministering, unto the building up of the body of Christ". Thus making good each other's deficiencies, we shall be worthy and unashamed ministers of the will of our Great God and Saviour Jesus Christ, confident that He who has begun a good work in us will perform it even to the praise of His glory, by whose saving grace we have health and length of days, setting forth rightly the word of truth and adorning the Church.

JOACHIM OF CONSTANTINOPLE

Joachim of Ephesus	Prokopios of Dyrrachion
Philotheos of Nicomedia	Basile of Belgrade
Joachim of Rhodes	Constantine of Servia and Kozani
Gregory of Serrai	Panaretus of Eleftheroupolis
Cyril of Mytilene	Theokletos of Krini
Philaret of Didymotheichou	

Encyclical of the
Ecumenical Patriarchate, 1920

"Unto the Churches of Christ Everywhere"

"Love one another earnestly from the heart."
1 Peter 1:22

Our own church holds that rapprochement[2] between the various Christian Churches and fellowship[1] between them is not excluded by the doctrinal differences which exist between them. In our opinion such a rapprochement[1] is highly desirable and necessary. It would be useful in many ways for the real interest of each particular church and of the whole Christian body, and also for the preparation and advancement of that blessed union which will be completed in the future in accordance with the will of God. We therefore consider that the present time is most favourable for bringing forward this important question and studying it together.

Even if in this case, owing to antiquated prejudices, practices or pretensions, the difficulties which have so often jeopardized attempts at reunion in the past may arise or be brought up, nevertheless, in our view, since we are concerned at this initial stage only with contacts[3] and rapprochement,[2] these difficulties are of less importance. If there is good will and intention, they cannot and should not create an invincible and insuperable obstacle.

Wherefore, considering such an endeavour to be not possible and timely, especially in view of the hopeful establishment of the League[1] of Nations, we venture to express below in brief our thoughts and our opinion regarding the way in which we understand this rapprochement[2] and contact[3] and how we consider it to be realizable; we earnestly ask and invite the judgment and the opinion of the other sister churches in the East and of the venerable Christian churches in the West and everywhere in the world.

We believe that the two following measures would greatly contribute to the rapprochement[2] which is so much to be desired and which would be so useful, and we believe that they would be both successful and fruitful:

First, we consider as necessary and indispensable the removal and abolition of all the mutual mistrust and bitterness between the different churches which arise from the tendency of some of them to entice and proselytize adherents of other confessions. For nobody ignores what is unfortunately happening today in many places, disturbing the internal peace of the churches, especially in the East. So many troubles and sufferings

---

• This Encyclical, issued in January 1920 by the Ecumenical Patriarchate, is a call to overcome the spirit of mistrust and bitterness and to demonstrate the power of love between the churches. To achieve this, the churches should establish a koinonia of churches. The Encyclical should also be seen in the context of the relations being established at that time with the Church of Sweden (Lutheran) and the visits to the Ecumenical Patriarchate in 1919 by representatives of the Episcopal Church in the USA. Greek text by B. Stavridis, *Historia tis Ikoumenikis Kiniseos*, Athens, 1964, pp. 127-131. English translation in *The Ecumenical Review*, Vol. XII, October 1959, No. 1, pp. 79-82.

are caused by other Christians and great hatred and enmity are aroused, with such insignificant results, by this tendency of some to proselytize and entice the followers of other Christian confessions.

After this essential re-establishment of sincerity and confidence between the churches, we consider,

Secondly, that above all, love should be rekindled and strengthened among the churches, so that they should no more consider one another as strangers and foreigners, but as relatives, and as being a part of the household of Christ and "fellow heirs, members of the same body and partakers of the promise of God in Christ" (Eph. 3:6).

For if the different churches are inspired by love, and place it before everything else in their judgment of others and their relationships with them, instead of increasing and widening the existing dissensions, they should be enabled to reduce and diminish them. By stirring up a right brotherly interest in the condition, the well-being and stability of the other churches; by readiness to take an interest in what is happening in those churches and to obtain a better knowledge of them, and by willingness to offer mutual aid and help, many good things will be achieved for the glory and the benefit both of themselves and of the Christian body. In our opinion, such a friendship and kindly disposition towards each other can be shown and demonstrated particularly in the following ways:

a) By the acceptance of a uniform calendar for the celebration of the great Christian feasts at the same time by all the churches.

b) By the exchange of brotherly letters on the occasion of the great feasts of the churches' year as is customary, and on other exceptional occasions.

c) By close relationships between the representatives of all churches wherever they may be.

d) By relationships between the theological schools and the professors of theology; by the exchange of theological and ecclesiastic reviews, and of other works published in each church.

e) By exchanging students for further training between the seminaries of the different churches.

f) By convoking pan-Christian[4] conferences in order to examine questions of common interest to all the churches.

g) By impartial and deeper historical study of doctrinal differences both by the seminaries and in books.

h) By mutual respect for the customs and practices in different churches.

i) By allowing each other the use of chapels and cemeteries for the funerals and burials of believers of other confessions dying in foreign lands.

j) By the settlement of the question of mixed marriages between the confessions.

k) Lastly, by whole-hearted mutual assistance for the churches in their endeavours for religious advancement, charity and so on.

Such a sincere and close contact between the churches will be all the more useful and profitable for the whole body of the Church, because manifold dangers threaten not only particular churches, but all of them. These dangers attack the very foundations of the Christian faith and the essence of Christian life and society. For the terrible world war which has just finished brought to light many unhealthy symptoms in the life of the Christian peoples, and often revealed great lack of respect even for the elementary principles of justice and charity. Thus it worsened already existing wounds and opened other new ones of a more material kind, which demand the attention and care of all the churches. Alcoholism, which is increasing daily; the increase of unnecessary luxury under the pretext of bettering life and enjoying it; the voluptuousness and lust hardly covered by the cloak of freedom and emancipation of the flesh; the prevailing unchecked licentiousness and indecency in literature, painting, the theatre, and in music, under the respectable name of the development of good taste and cultivation of fine art; the deification of wealth and the contempt of higher ideals; all these and the like, as they threaten the very essence of Christian societies are also timely topics requiring and indeed necessitating common study and cooperation by the Christian churches.

Finally, it is the duty of the churches which bear the sacred name of Christ not to forget or neglect any longer his new and great commandment of love. Nor should they continue to fall piteously behind the political authorities, who, truly applying the spirit of the Gospel and of the teaching of Christ, have under happy auspices already set-up the so-called League[2] of Nations in order to defend justice and cultivate charity and agreement between the nations.

For all these reasons, being ourselves convinced of the necessity for establishing a contact[3] and league (fellowship[1]) between the churches and believing that the other churches share our conviction as stated above, at least as beginning we request each one of them to send us in reply a statement of its own judgment and opinion on this matter so that common agreement or resolution having been reached, we may proceed together to its realization, and thus "speaking the truth in love, may grow up into Him in all things, which is the head, even Christ; from whom the whole body fitly joined together and compacted by that which every joint supplieth, according to the effectual working in the measure of every part, maketh increase of the body unto the edifying of itself in love" (Eph. 4:15,16).

In the Patriarchate of Constantinople
in the month of January in the year of grace 1920

NOTES

[1] The same historic word Κοινωνία (Koinonia) is used in these four places. In the first sentence of the message the content shows that it is used in the New Testament meaning of partnership or fellowship and not in the sense of "league" (société in French) which is the primary meaning in modern Greek. But in the last paragraph but one of the document the League (Koinonia) of Nations is used as an example for the relationship which the churches should have among themselves and in the last paragraph *Koinonia* carries therefore both the meaning of "fellowship" and of "league". The covering letter sent with the message makes this point even more clearly when it speaks of the formation of a "League of Churches" according to the example of the happy establishment of the League of Nations. Archbishop Germanos often referred to the message as proposing a "League of Churches".

[2] προσέγγισις (Proseggisis).

[3] συνάφεια (Synapheia).

[4] This word παγχριστιανικῶν simply means "embracing all Christians". It was used in the Papal Encyclical *Mortalium Animos* of 1928 to designate all the ecumenical movement.

First World Conference on Faith and Order

Lausanne, Switzerland, 1927

Brethren, on receiving the invitation of the Organizing Committee of the World Conference on Faith and Order seven years ago, the Orthodox Church answered readily by sending representatives from her particular Orthodox Churches to the preliminary Conference in 1920 at Geneva. That delegation of the Orthodox Church put before the Conference a united declaration in general terms of the teaching of their Church in the matter of faith and order, and at the conclusion recommended that before any discussion of the reunion of the Church in faith and order, a League of Churches should be established for their mutual co-operation in regard to the social and moral principles of Christendom. Further, when the Orthodox Church was invited a short time ago to take part through her representatives in the present Conference, although many of her particular Churches are in distress so grave as to threaten their very existence, she has hastened to send her delegates to it.

Accordingly, we, the undersigned, delegates of the Orthodox Church, being inspired by a sincere feeling of love and by a desire to achieve an understanding, have taken part in every meeting held here for the purpose of promulgating closer brotherhood and fellowship between the representatives of the different Churches and for the general good and welfare of the whole body of Christians. But while sharing the general labours of the Conference both in delivering addresses as arranged in the programme and in taking part in the open debates, as also in the work of the Sections, we have concluded with regret that the bases assumed for the foundation of the Reports, which are to be submitted to the vote of the Conference, are inconsistent with the principles of the Orthodox Church we represent.

Therefore, we judge it to be a matter of conscience that with the exception of the first we must abstain from voting in favour of the two Reports which are now ready. Although both in papers read, in speeches, in debate and in statements made in the three Sections, we Orthodox have already made plain and clear what are the points of view and the conceptions of the Orthodox Church in regard to the subjects under discussion, we hold it to be of importance that we should specify here certain points in order to make manifest the differences which separate us from other members of the Conference. For example, while the Report on the Message of the Church, since it is drafted on the basis of the teaching of the Holy Scripture, is in accordance with the

---

● This statement was read to the conference by one of the great promoters of the ecumenical movement, Metropolitan Germanos of Thyateira, delegate of the Ecumenical Patriarchate of Constantinople. Greek text in Stavridis, *op. cit.*, pp. 134-137. English in R.G. Stephanopoulos, *Guidelines for Orthodox Christians in Ecumenical Relations*, New York, Standing Conference of Canonical Orthodox Bishops in America, 1974, pp. 30-34.

Orthodox conception and can be accepted by us, it is otherwise with the two other Reports, on the Nature of the Church. The drafting of these two latter was carried out on a basis of compromise between what in our understanding are conflicting ideas and meanings, in order to arrive at an external agreement in the letter alone: whereas, as has often at times been emphasized in statements by representatives of the Orthodox Church, in matters of faith and conscience there is no room for compromising. For us, two different meanings cannot be covered by, and two different concepts cannot be deduced from, the same word of a generally agreed statement. Nor can we Orthodox hope that an agreement reached upon such statements would remain lasting.

That the drafting committees have realized the existence of this disagreement is apparent from many of the notes which they have placed in the Reports and which leave full liberty upon matters at least we Orthodox hold to be fundamental. Thus, for example, we Orthodox cannot conceive of a united Church in which some of its members would hold that there is only one source of divine revelation, namely Holy Scripture alone; but others would affirm that apostolic tradition is the necessary completion of Holy Scripture. While the full freedom so accorded in the Report to each Church to use its own confession of faith would make these confessions of indifferent value in themselves, on the other hand, nothing but confusion as to the one common conception of *the* Faith of the so united single Church could arise.

The Orthodox Church adheres fixedly to the principle that the limits of individual liberty of belief are determined by the definitions made by the whole Church, which definitions we maintain to be obligatory on each individual. This principle holds good for us not only as to the present members of the Orthodox Church, but also as to those who, in the future, may become united with it in faith and order. Moreover, the symbols which would be accepted by the united Church acquire their importance (in our conception as Orthodox) not only from the fact of their being historical witnesses of the faith of the primitive Church, but above all because the Church has affirmed their validity in her Ecumenical Councils. It should be unnecessary for us to add that the Orthodox Church recognizes and accepts as an Ecumenical Symbol only the Creed of Nicea-Constantinople.

That which holds good for us in regard to the Ecumenical Symbol holds good also in regard to the dogmatic definitions of the Seven Ecumenical Councils, the authority of which no Orthodox would be justified in shaking.

Therefore the mind of the Orthodox Church is that reunion can take place only on the basis of the common faith and confession of the ancient, undivided Church of the seven Ecumenical Councils and of the first eight centuries.

Although the Reports of the other three Sections are not yet to hand, the process of debate on them makes it evident that agreement on them can be reached only by vague phrases, or by a compromise of antithetical opinions. Thus, for example, we cannot conceive how agreement can be made possible between two conceptions which agree that the existence of the ministry of the Church is by the will of Christ, but differ as to whether that ministry was instituted by Christ Himself in its three degrees of bishop, priest, and deacon. In the same way we judge there to be no practical value in an agreed formula as to the necessity of the sacraments in the Church, when there is a fundamental difference between the Churches not only in regard to their number but also to their particular efforts.

This being so, we cannot entertain the idea of a reunion which is confined to a few common points of verbal statements, for according to the Orthodox Church where the totality of faith is absent there can be no *communio in sacris*.

Nor can we here apply that principle of *economy* which in the past the Orthodox Church has applied under quite other circumstances in the case of those who came to her with a view to union with her.

In consequence, while we, the undersigned Orthodox representatives, must refrain from agreeing to any Reports other than that upon the Message of the Church, which we accept and are ready to vote upon, we desire to declare that in our own judgment the most which we can now do is to enter into co-operation with other Churches in the social and moral sphere on a basis of Christian love. Further, we desire to add that as Orthodox Delegates we should view a partial reunion of those Churches which share the same principles with satisfaction as a precedent to general union, inasmuch as it would thus be easier for our Orthodox Church to discuss reunion with the Churches which had so united into a single Church and had a single faith, than with many Churches with different faiths.

In making it plain that we have arrived at our decision only in obedience to the dictates of our conscience we beg to assure the Conference that we have derived much comfort here from the experience that, although divided by dogmatic differences, we are one with our brethren here in faith in our Lord and Saviour Lord Jesus Christ. Declaring that in the future we shall not cease to devote ourselves to labour for the closer approach of the Churches, we add that we shall pray to God without ceasing that by the operation of His Holy Spirit He will take away all existing hindrances and will guide us to that unity for which the Founder and Ruler of the Church prayed to His Heavenly Father "that they all may be one as we are one".

We close with the intercession that our Lord will richly give His blessing to one and all who labour in sincerity and in His fear for the establishment of His kingdom among men.

Second World Conference on Faith and Order

Edinburgh, Scotland, 1937

On behalf of the Orthodox representatives here present I have the honour to make the following declaration:

I. The Orthodox representatives who have been appointed by their respective autocephalous Churches to take part in the Second World Conference on Faith and Order desire to begin by expressing their satisfaction and joy at coming together in Conference for the time with you their brethren, who represent other Churches of Christ.

The Orthodox delegates are present here in comparatively small numbers. This is due not only to geographic distance, but also to the distressed situation in which some of the Orthodox Churches — first among them the martyred Church of Russia — find themselves. In spite of this the Orthodox not only have shown much activity in the general and sectional discussions here, but have also taken an active part in the preparatory work for this Conference.

We desire to make grateful acknowledgement of the fact that we have had every opportunity to give expression to our religious convictions in statements and discussions. But we ask pardon for saying quite frankly that sometimes, indeed often, the form in which the final statements of the Reports came to be cast was not congenial to us. Generalising and the use of somewhat abstract language does not appeal to the Orthodox mind.

We hold firmly that in religious discussions the truth is better served by making points of difference clear. When an agreement is achieved on such a basis its value is very great.

II. A careful study of the Reports which are now before the Conference will show that they express many fundamental agreements which exist between us and our Christian brethren on many important points. On the other hand, they contain a long series of statements in regard to which significant differences exist of such weight that we found it necessary to formulate the Orthodox standpoint upon them in a series of short footnotes. I now proceed to offer you our comments on the four Reports and to specify some of the most outstanding divergences from the Orthodox position.

In Report I, on the Grace of Jesus Christ, fundamental agreement has been reached as to the meaning of Grace and as to its primary importance in the work of our salvation.

● This statement was read by Metropolitan Germanos of Thyateira, delegate of the Ecumenical Patriarchate of Constantinople. Greek text in Stavridis, *op. cit.*, pp. 137-141. Also published in Stephanopoulos, *op. cit.*, pp. 35-38.

While being in agreement with this report on the whole, we desire to draw your attention to the term "co-operation" *(synergia)*, by which term the theology of the Fathers is accustomed to designate the active participation of man's will in the process of his sanctification. We wish that the Report had dealt with this term.

Report II expresses a satisfactory agreement as to the inspired character of the Holy Scriptures, but with regard to the importance of tradition the Orthodox doctrine has been formulated according to what the Orthodox supported at Lausanne and elsewhere.

On the other hand, there are most important points on which we cannot agree with Part II of this Report. We consider the Church and not the "Word" (i.e. the written and preached Word) as primary in the work of our salvation. It is by the Church that the Scriptures are given to us. They are God's gift to her; they are the means of grace which she uses in the work of our salvation. Further, we must point out with reference to the discussions about an "invisible" Church that the Orthodox Church believes that, by its essential characteristic, the Church on earth is visible and that only one true Church can be visible and exist on earth.

In Report III the agreement achieved is much more limited than in the two former Reports. This will be evident from the great number of footnotes provided by the Orthodox members of the Section. Moreover, disagreement on points of capital and fundamental importance is very plain, for example, upon the nature of the Sacred Ministry and of Holy Orders, upon the Apostolic Succession, upon the nature and the number of the Sacraments, upon the problem of validity and lastly upon some points touching the doctrine of Baptism and of the Eucharist, which are the only Sacraments that have received detailed consideration. It being impossible to enter into details here, we desire to emphasize the great importance which the Orthodox Church has from the very beginning attached to the Sacrament of Order upon which, from the Orthodox point of view, depends, of necessity, the valid rendering of all the other Sacraments, Baptism only being excepted. We would remind you that this conception of the Orthodox Church is shared by all those who, calling themselves Catholics, insist on faithfulness to the doctrine and practice of the undivided Church.

Passing to Report IV we desire to state here once more that we hold that intercommunion must be considered as the crowning act of a real and true Reunion which has already been fully achieved by fundamental agreement in the realm of Faith and Order and is not to be regarded as an instrument for Reunion. As to the other and extremely important subject of this Report, i.e. the Communion of the Saints, we recognize that in discussion of the veneration of the Holy Virgin, the Theotokos, and of the saints, a very valuable advance has been achieved. None the less essential differences remain, and we Orthodox have felt obliged to mention our divergent points of view in separate footnotes.

III. We Orthodox delegates, faithful to the tradition of the ancient undivided Church of the seven ecumenical Synods and of the first eight centuries, cherish the conviction that only the dogmatic teaching of the ancient Church as it is found in the Holy Scriptures, the Creed, the decisions of the ecumenical Synods and the teaching of the Fathers and in the worship and whole life of the undivided Church, can form a solid basis for dealing successfully and rightly with the new problems of doctrine and theology which have arisen in recent times. We Orthodox delegates further stress the necessity of accuracy and concreteness in the formulation of the faith and are convinced that ambiguous expressions and comprehensive expressions of the faith are of no real value. We are opposed to vague and abstract terms which are used to identify conceptions and tenets that are really different from one another. We Orthodox therefore consider it our duty both to our Church and to our conscience, to declare in all sincerity and humility that while the reports in which such vague and abstract language is used may perhaps contribute to the advancement of reunion between churches of the same essential characteristics, they are altogether profiles for the larger end for which they have been used, especially in regard to the Orthodox Church.

It is inevitable therefore that in this matter we Orthodox should remember what was said by the Orthodox delegates to the World Conference in Lausanne, namely, that the general reunion of Christian Churches may possibly be hastened if union is first achieved between those Churches which present features of great similarity with one another. In such a way the gradual drawing together of the Christian Churches may be helped and promoted. The happy results which have now been reached in different parts of Christendom, namely, that Churches akin to one another have recovered or are on the way to recovering their union and that others by friendly intercourse are drawing nearer together, fills us with hope and gives us encouragement to continue our efforts in the direction of an ultimate reunion of all Christians.

Brethren! After having made this declaration in order to satisfy our consciences, we are constrained and rejoice to utter a few words by which to emphasize the great spiritual profit which we have drawn from our daily intercourse with you, the representatives of other Christian Churches. With you we bewail the rending asunder of the seamless robe of Christ. We desire, as you, that the members of the one Body of Christ may again be reunited, and we pray, as you, day by day in our congregations for the union of all mankind.

It is a spiritual solace and a spiritual edification which have been granted to us in and through the intercourse with you and therein we have been strengthened in our faith; inasmuch as we have known with you the inspiration of "looking unto Jesus the Author and Finisher of our Faith; who for the joy that was set before him endured the cross, despising the shame, and is set down at the right hand of the throne of God". We have felt here with renewed strength the great importance which our Church attaches to mutual love as the presupposition which enables us to look to a common confession of faith: "Let us love one another in order that we may with one mind confess the Father, the Son and the Holy Ghost".

With you we realize that to be uplifted into participation in the Cross and the death and the risen life of our Lord Jesus Christ is the true way to union. For in spite of all our differences, our common Master and Lord is One — Jesus Christ who will lead us to a more and more close collaboration for the edifying of the body of Christ: "Till all come in the unity of the faith, and of the knowledge of the Son of God, unto a perfect man, unto the measure of the stature of the fullness of Christ" (Eph. 4:12-13).

Resolution on the Ecumenical Question

Moscow, USSR, 1948

We have come to a complete and joint understanding that at the present time influence is being exerted on the Orthodox Church by other confessions from at least two directions.

On the one hand the Papacy, as the head of the Roman Catholic Church, as though it had lost the sense of saving faith that the gates of hell shall not prevail against the Church of Christ, and anxious to preserve its worldly authority, carried on by means of its political relations with the powerful of this world, is trying to tempt the Orthodox Church into agreement with it. For this purpose the Papacy has set up various kinds of "union" organisations.

On the other hand, Protestantism in all its vast diversity and its divisions into sects and cults, having lost faith in the eternity and unshakability of Christ's ideals, proud in its scorn of the statutes of the Apostles and the Early Fathers, is trying to organise a counter-campaign against Popery. Protestantism is trying to win the Orthodox Church as its ally in its conflict, in order to obtain for itself the importance of an influential international force.

And here Orthodoxy faces a still greater temptation — to turn aside from its seeking the Kingdom of God and enter a political arena which is foreign to its purpose. This is the practical aim of the ecumenical movement today.

In addition of the Orthodox Church, this same influence is being exerted upon the Armenian, Georgian, the Syrian Jacobite, the Abyssinian, the Coptic and the Syrian Chaldean, among the non-Roman Churches, and also upon the Old Catholic Church, so nearly related to Orthodoxy.

Whereas:

a) The purpose of the ecumenical movement expressed in the formation of a "World Council of Churches" with its consequent aim of organising an "Ecumenical Church" is not in accord with the ideals of Christianity and the aims of the Church of Christ as they are understood by the Orthodox Church;

b) Effort by means of social and political activity for the creation of an Ecumenical Church as an international influence is comparable to falling into the temptation which Christ refused in the desert, and a diversion of the Church's labours towards the taking of human souls in the net of Christ by non-Christian means;

c) The ecumenical movement in its present scheme, the "World Council of Churches", contrary to the interest of Christ's Church, has too early lost faith in the

---

• This text was adopted by the Church Conference of Heads and Representatives of Orthodox Autocephalic Churches, 8-17 July 1948, in Moscow. It appeared in *The Ecumenical Review*, Vol. I, No. 2, Winter 1949, pp. 189-191.

possibility of union in one Holy, Catholic and Apostolic Church. The overwhelmingly Protestant composition of the Edinburgh Conference of 1937, having either suffered failure or merely foreseen it, hastily abandoned its efforts for a union of the Churches in Christ, and in order to assure the self-protection of Protestantism, has come along the line of least resistance in the way of abstract unionism on social, economic and even political grounds. This movement has based its further plans on the theory of setting up a new external apparatus, the "Ecumenical Church", as an institution within the State, bound to it in one way or another, and possessing worldly influence;

d) During all the past ten years (1937-1947) there has been no further discussion, based on documents, of the idea of union of the Churches on dogmatic and confessional grounds: this idea is considered as having a secondary, merely pedagogical importance for future generations. Thus the present ecumenical movement offers no assurance for the work of uniting the Churches by the ways and means of grace;

e) The reduction of requirements and conditions for unity to the simple recognition of Christ as our Lord lowers the Christian faith to such a degree as to be accessible even to the devils (James 11:19; Matt. 8:29; Mk. 5:7). Taking account of this present situation, our Conference of heads and representatives of Autocephalic Orthodox Churches, having prayerfully invoked the presence of the Holy Spirit, has decided:

> To inform the "World Council of Churches", in reply to the invitation we have all received to participate in the Amsterdam Assembly as members, that all the national Orthodox Churches taking part in the present Conference are obliged to decline participation in the ecumenical movement, in its present form.

Encyclical of the Ecumenical Patriarchate

Phanar, 1952

Subsequent to the amalgamation in one single organisation (the present World Council of Churches) of the great Christian organisations "Life and Work" and "Faith and Order", which formerly existed and operated separately and independently, the question arose whether our Most Holy Orthodox Church should or should not participate in the work and conferences of the World Council. Upon this question the opinion of the revered Presiding-Hierarchs of the Orthodox Autocephalous Churches, our sister Churches, was sought in encyclical letters dated February 4, 1945, with the Protocol No. 45.

We have submitted to the consideration of the Holy and Sacred Synod from time to time the replies of our sister Churches and the declarations concerning the First Assembly of the World Council of Churches called together at Amsterdam in 1948 which were afterwards made by them, as well as by the delegates of the Orthodox Church who participated. We have made this matter the subject of special study in the framework of the aims and activities of the whole pan-Christian movement up to the present time, in order to clarify our future attitude to the World Council of Churches and the appropriate mode of our participation in its work and its Assemblies. We are, therefore, now writing to you on the occasion of the impending third World Conference of Faith and Order at Lund, Sweden, making known to your revered and well-beloved Beatitude the views on this most important question of our Most Holy Oecumenical Throne, asking you also to be good enough to communicate to us, in due course, your views and those of your Most Holy Church.

In an epoch in which the peoples and nations of the world are working intensely for some kind of rapprochement in order to confront the great problems which face humanity today, and when the need for some manifestation of the unity of the Christian world in opposition to the anti-Christian tendencies in the world has acquired particular importance, the task of rapprochement and cooperation between all the Christian confessions and organisations is a sacred obligation and a holy duty, derived from their own function and mission. According to the Constitution of the World Council of Churches, it is its function to facilitate common action by the churches, to promote cooperation in the study of the Christian spirit, to promote the growth of the ecumenical consciousness in the members of all the churches, to support the distribu-

---

• This Encyclical, dated 31 January 1952 and sent to patriarchs and heads of the Orthodox Autocephalous Churches, was issued by the Ecumenical Patriarchate in view of the Third World Conference on Faith and Order in Lund. It reflected the great debate within the Orthodox Churches, following the Inaugural Assembly of the WCC in Amsterdam in 1948, on the nature of Orthodox participation in the World Council of Churches. Greek text in Stavridis, *op. cit.*, pp. 131-134. English translation in *The Ecumenical Review*, Vol. V, January 1953, No. 2, pp. 167-169.

tion of the sacred Gospel, and to preserve, uplift and cause to prevail the spiritual values of man, in the most general Christian context. It is, therefore, quite clear that the principal aim of the Council is a practical one and that its task is pleasing to God as an attempt and a manifestation of a noble desire, that the churches of Christ should face together the great problems of humanity.

Because this is the aim of the World Council of Churches, and also because the Orthodox Church, in her past participation in the pan-Christian movement, has sought to make known and to impart to the heterodox the riches of her faith, worship and order and her religious and ascetic experience, as well as to inform herself about their new methods and their conceptions of church life and activity (things of great value that the Orthodox Church could not possess and foster, on account of the particular conditions in which she lived), we consider that, in many ways, the future participation and cooperation of the Orthodox Church with the World Council of Churches is necessary.

However, in the light of the experience of the Orthodox Church in her past participation in the pan-Christian Movement, and having regard to what was ascertained in this participation, we think that future participation should be carried out with the following limitations:

a) Although the principal aim of the World Council of Churches continues to be the cooperation of the Churches on the plane of social and practical issues, nevertheless the "Faith and Order" organisation still exists as a special Commission of the Council which is occupied exclusively with dogmatic questions. It is meet that any participation by the Orthodox Church in the discussions and operations of this Commission should be avoided, inasmuch as this Commission has for its aim the union (of Churches) by means of dogmatic discussions between delegates of Churches separated from one another by the deepest issues; this should be plainly and categorically stated to the Central Committee of the Council. But it is also necessary that our Orthodox Church should also inform the heterodox about the content of her faith and teaching and it is meet that this should be done through books written for this special purpose, inasmuch as the Handbooks of Dogmatics and Symbolics used among us, not having been compiled with this object in view, cannot serve the Church in this particular task.

b) Because the participation of our Orthodox Church in the operations of the World Council of Churches is an event of great importance in her life, it is meet that she should be represented by delegates of all the local Orthodox Autocephalous Churches; this would give the appropriate authority prestige to her participation. The individual sister Churches should cooperate appropriately in the common study and preparation of the subjects to be considered in the Assemblies of the World Council of Churches, so that our Church should not appear in pan-Christian conferences in an inferior position, but with the strength and authority appropriate to her position and to her historic mission in the world of inter-Christian relationships. For this purpose it is necessary that permanent Synodical Commissions on the Ecumenical Movement should be formed in the Orthodox Churches, in order to study, in cooperation with the professors of the Theological Schools, the different problems involved, and in order to clarify beforehand the point of view of the Orthodox Church about them and the attitude she should adopt.

c) It is meet that Orthodox Clerics who are Delegates (of their Church) should be as careful as possible about services of worship in which they join with the heterodox, as these are contrary to the sacred canons and make less acute the confessional sensitiveness of the Orthodox. They should aim at celebrating, if possible, purely

Orthodox liturgical services and rites, that they may thereby manifest, before the eyes of the heterodox, the splendour and majesty of Orthodox adoration.

We shall await the definite opinion of your venerable Beatitude and of your Most Holy Church about the above, that we may give a timely reply to the invitation extended to us by the Central Committee of the World Council of Churches, to the Assembly gathered together in Lund. We greet your Beatitude with an embrace and again with a holy kiss we are with brotherly love the beloved brother in Christ of your revered Beatitude.

Athenagoras of Constantinople
January 31, 1952

Third World Conference on Faith and Order

Lund, Sweden, 1952

Most Reverend President:

Although I have the honour to be one of the Vice-Presidents of the Commission on Faith and Order, I present myself to the honourable members of this Conference preferably for these moments in the capacity of a Prelate of the Greek Orthodox Church who happens to be Exarch of the Ecumenical Patriarchate of Constantinople.

The capacity of a Greek Orthodox Prelate is not at all in contrast to the capacity of any officer of this Commission. On the contrary, I believe that the two offices are in full harmony and helpful to each other in the sacred endeavour in search of the unity of Christendom, in which the World Council of Churches and the Greek Orthodox Church are engaged. This being the case I may as well speak on behalf of the two offices at the same time. But I am appointed as the leader of the Patriarchal delegation to this conference composed of Greek and Russian theologians and the plenipotentiary delegate of the Patriarchate of Antioch and of the autonomous and autocephalous Church of Cyprus.

In these various capacities I have the honour to address this Conference and I hope that I will be allowed to use a little time of its very congested programme.

The Greek Orthodox Church comprises over two hundred million members; but the well known temporary political reasons prevent the Orthodox national Churches behind the iron curtain from participating as delegates to this Conference. So we may say that the delegation of the Ecumenical Patriarchate under my leadership has to represent the whole Greek Orthodox, or Eastern Orthodox Church, if you prefer this title.

By his appointment of me as the leader of the Patriarchal delegation to the conference, His All Holiness the Oecumenical Patriarch Athenagoras entrusted me also to convey to this Conference his greetings and his paternal blessings and the expression of his sincere admiration for the enthusiasm and efforts of the Christian groups for the great and sacred ideal of the unity of Christendom in the one Holy Church of Christ. The unity of all Christendom is the ideal of the Greek Orthodox Church and in all her prayers she constantly prays "for the peace of the whole world, for the stability of the Holy Church of God and for the union of all".

The Ecumenical Patriarchate has full knowledge of the great obstacles and difficulties that the ecumenical movement confronts in pursuing the realisation of its

---

● This statement was read to the conference by Archbishop Athenagoras of Thyateira, delegate of the Ecumenical Patriarchate of Constantinople. It seeks to explain the spirit and the content of the Encyclical letter published at the beginning of the same year. Greek text in Stavridis, *op. cit.*, pp. 141-144. Also published in *The Third World Conference on Faith and Order, Lund, 1952,* Oliver Tomkins (ed.), London, 1953, pp. 123-126.

ideal, especially in its Faith and Order department. The Patriarchate follows and studies all the relevant reports which are issued by the various committees. It appreciates the value of many conclusions which after deep and long research the reports bring out to light. It judges with affection and understanding the resolutions which they make, regardless of the fact that some of them are not correct according to the Orthodox understanding of the Faith. We attribute it to the brief space of time that has elapsed since the ecumenical movement started its colossal work.

It is for this reason and with the same attitude that the Patriarchate, in spite of the adverse circumstances which it confronts, has sent a delegation to this Conference as it did to the previous conferences in Edinburgh, Lausanne and Stockholm.

This year's delegation consists of well-educated Greek professors at the Halki Theological School, Chrysostom Constantinides, Maximos Repanellis, Emmanuel Photiades, Emilian Timiades and, well known for many good reasons, the Russian professors and authors George Florovsky and Leo Zander.

This decision of the Ecumenical Patriarchate to participate through this delegation in this Conference and its sincere desire to see realised the goal of the World Council of Churches, honours its Holy Synod and its entire Hierarchy. Nevertheless His All Holiness has as usual given instructions to the delegation not to be involved in dogmatical disputes.

This instruction is not at all an inimical act or a sign of indifferent attitude on the part of the Orthodox Church to the work of this Conference. On the contrary, she is more than ever its sincere friend. This fact is also seen from the letter of His Beatitude Spyridon, Archbishop of the Church of Greece to the Secretary of the Faith and Order Conference, the Rev. Oliver Tomkins.

"I wish to assure you that the absence of a delegation from the Church of Greece to the Lund Conference means in no way a change in the policies of our Church or its participation as a member of the World Council of Churches and of the several committees to which members from Greece have been appointed: neither does it mean that our co-operation has lessened. We have had a long and effective mutual contact with the co-operating Churches in the World Council and through this contact we have become closer in knowledge of the co-operating Churches and the Greek Church has become known and esteemed among the several church members."

The reason for the above mentioned instruction is a natural product of the Orthodox Church's dogmatical and administrative policy during the nineteen centuries of its life, which is as follows: In the Greek Orthodox Church the individual theological opinions have no value whatsoever in themselves. It is the whole Church, clergy and laity, and above all her Hierarchy, the totality of her Bishops, not as individuals but in Holy Synods, that expresses the teaching of her faith.

This being the case the Hierarchy of the entire Greek Orthodox Church reserves for itself only the right to decide what is wrong in religious matters and to pronounce what is compatible or incompatible with her faith.

That is why she allows her theologians, professors of theology in the Orthodox theological schools and above all her representatives at conferences to make only positive and definite statements about our faith without being involved in sterile disputes or voting for resolutions on matters of faith, worship and order which cannot be settled in this way.

That is not a new thing; it has always been so, because the Greek Orthodox Church knows and proclaims that she is not dealing with human teaching and human precepts but with divine ones and no one has the right to confuse these with individual opinions about them. She is the whole and only Church, the Body of Christ, the only mandatory agent of the Apostles. So she only can define the faith. And we are sure that this is a proof of her uniqueness.

So the delegates of the Greek Orthodox Church to the conference will be present in all its sections. They will follow the discussions with an undiminished interest and will be ready to give information on questions relative to the teaching of our Church but not to express their opinions or even the opinion of our Church on the teaching of your Churches. We do not come to criticise other Churches but to help them, to illumine their mind in a brotherly manner by informing them about the teaching of the One Holy, Catholic and Apostolic Church which is the Greek Orthodox Church, unchanged since the apostolic era.

The only thing I take the liberty of recommending to all of you is to be kind enough to have the same friendly attitude towards us here and everywhere else, to respect our Church and, above all, to condemn in your conscience the tendency of any Protestant group to exercise proselytism in the bosom of the Greek Orthodox country, and to resist it. Such proselytising, if not stopped, might cause enmity amongst the Orthodox people against all the Protestants and this would be disastrous to any ecumenical movement.

Let us all be brothers in Christ and pray together and show to unbelievers everywhere that Christianity is the religion of love, the religion of every noble consideration of men to men, the heavenly religion of the Son of God our Lord Jesus Christ, so that they also will accept Him for their salvation and to the glory of God.

Second Assembly
of the World Council of Churches

Evanston, USA, 1954

a) General statement on the main theme of the Assembly "Christ, the Hope of the World"

Being entrusted with the responsibility of representing the Orthodox member churches at this Assembly of the World Council of Churches, we are in duty bound to present the following comments on the Report of the Advisory Commission on the Main Theme: "Christ, the Hope of the World".

(1) We are happy to express our general agreement with the Report of the Advisory Committee. Ever since Pentecost, the Orthodox Church has been proclaiming to the world that Christ is the Hope and especially in our time she is persistently re-affirming that all human hopes must be interpreted and judged, condemned, or amended, in the light of this hope. That at this decisive moment in its life the World Council of Churches unanimously felt that Christians should proclaim this hope to the world, and should alert themselves of their responsibilities in a world full of distress and suffering, makes us rejoice exceedingly.

(2) But this general statement makes it even more necessary to state clearly, on the one hand, what we regard as not fully acceptable from the standpoint of the Orthodox Church, and, on the other hand, what we consider as requiring further development in the Report, and formally draw attention to certain points that were not touched upon in the report at all. Obviously, in these few remarks we cannot give a full confession of the Orthodox conception of the Christian Church. It must be affirmed, to begin with, in stronger terms, that the Christian Hope is grounded on Christian Faith. It is grounded on the belief that God takes a personal interest in human life and human history. God so loved the world as to give His only begotten Son. The Christian Hope is grounded in the belief that Jesus Christ, Incarnate Lord, came down from Heaven to save men. He accomplished the work of salvation on the Tree of the Cross and He manifested the new life for humanity in His glorious resurrection. He established upon earth His Holy Church which is His Body in which by the power of the Holy Spirit He abides with man for ever. The Church of Christ is one loving Body of Christ in which all generations of believers are united in the new life of Christ.

It is misleading to describe the Church simply as "the pilgrim people of God" and to forget that the Church Triumphant and the Church Militant are but One Body. It is precisely in this unity that the Christian Hope is grounded. The Church is the great

---

● This statement was read to the conference by Archbishop Michael of North and South America, delegate of the Ecumenical Patriarchate of Constantinople. Greek text in Stavridis, *op. cit.*, pp. 144-147 and 147-150. Also published in Stephanopoulos, *op. cit.*, pp. 42-44 and 45-47.

Communion of Saints. We upon earth live and strive in communion with the glorious "cloud of witnesses" revealed through the ages and are strengthened by the intercessions of the Theotokos and the Saints within whom we join in adoration of Christ our Redeemer.

(3) The Report justly stresses the importance of the belief in the second coming of Christ for the Christian Hope. However, we strongly believe that it is necessary to place an adequate emphasis on the actual presence of the Kingdom of God in the Church. The Kingdom has been founded by God through the incarnation of His Son, the Redemption, the Resurrection, the Ascension of Christ in glory and the descent of the Holy Spirit. It has been existing on earth since the Pentecost and is open to all men, bestowing to all who enter the power transforming and renewing human existence now on earth. Life eternal is not only an object of future realization, it is given to those who were called by the Word of God in the Sacrament of Baptism (Rom. 6) and is continuously renewed through the participation in the Holy Eucharist. Nothing has been left undone by God for our salvation and for the immediate transformation of human existence. Thus our participation in the renewed life of the Kingdom of God is a present reality as well as a future fulfilment.

(4) The hope in Christ is itself a gift of the Holy Spirit and no one can confess Him as Lord and Saviour except by the Holy Spirit. It would be in vain to preach Christ as the Hope of the World without mentioning divine action and acknowledging the reality of grace which is the sole source of this hope. The tragedy of the fallen world consists precisely in its inability to hope in Christ without the help of grace. Moreover, this hope is meaningful and fruitful only inasmuch as it leads man into the real life in Christ which presupposes the continuous action of the Holy Spirit within us.

(5) The paragraphs of the Report dealing with the unity of the Church raise serious doubts. This subject will be treated in full in the Section on Faith and Order, but it should be noted that some of the ideas expressed in the Report lead to interpretations that cannot be accepted from the standpoint of the Orthodox Church.

The power of God is operating in the midst of human weakness. We never can fulfil all the demands which Christ makes upon us and in humility and repentance we must acknowledge our limitations and shortcomings, apply steadfastly for an increase of our faith and strength. And yet it is in the Church that we find this strength. The reality of the New Life is never compromised or annulled by our failures. Thus, the Church of Christ, as the realized Kingdom of God, lies beyond Judgment, whereas her members being liable to sin and error are subject to Judgment.

(6) In proclaiming that Christ is the Hope of the world, we must not lose sight of the reality that Christ is not separated from His Father and the Holy Spirit. Hope in Christ cannot be separated from the Hope in God, the Father, and God, the Holy Spirit. Of all the promises of Christ, the most precious is when He asserts that the Holy Trinity will abide in us (John 14:23; 15:26; 16:13-17; 17:21-26). Life eternal is but fellowship with the Divine Trinity.

(7) Hope in Christ must be interpreted in its true content. We place our hope in the Incarnate Son of God, in Whom we also have become sons of God, the Father, and co-heirs with Christ. This sonship constitutes the foundation, the content, and the aim of our Christian Hope. Adoption by the Father renders man a "new creation". In Christ the Fatherhood of God has been revealed to us and communion with him has been given. Through Jesus Christ, the Son of God, the Father bestows on us the knowledge of truth, divine love, sanctification, eternal life, and ultimately participation in the divine nature (theosis).

(8) Hope in Christ means hope in the Blessed Trinity. The Orthodox Church gives clear expression to this truth in one of her prayers: "My Hope is in the Father, my Refuge is the Son; my Shelter is the Holy Spirit: Holy Trinity, glory to Thee."

(9) Finally, we do not believe that the analysis of false hopes given in the Report is adequate and complete. False doctrines, which are mentioned in the Report, especially that of communism, threaten the whole of human existence, threaten human personality as such. All of these de-humanize life. It is this aspect of false hopes with which the Church is primarily concerned. The danger to man which these false doctrines present appears to be sorely underestimated in the Report. If we seek at the present time in our troubled and distorted world, a true basis for human hope, we must profess emphatically that it is only in the Church of God, Holy, Catholic, and Apostolic, that this basis can be found, since the Church is the "pillar and ground of the Truth".

b) Statement concerning Faith and Order

As delegates of the Orthodox Church participating at this Assembly of the World Council of Churches, we submit the following statement concerning the report of Section I.

1. We have studied the document with considerable interest. It falls into three parts: the first contains an able exposition of the New Testament doctrine of the Church. The organic character of the Church and her indissoluble unity with Christ are adequately stressed in the document. We feel that this at least provides fruitful ground for further theological elaboration. The second and third parts of the document deal with the divided state of Christendom and suggest practical steps toward union. It is our conviction that it does not follow logically from the first part and indeed if we do actually accept the New Testament doctrine of the Church we should come to write different practical conclusions which have been familiar to us Orthodox for centuries. The whole approach to the problem of reunion is entirely unacceptable from the standpoint of the Orthodox Church.

2. The Orthodox conception of church unity implies a twofold agreement.

(a) The whole of the Christian Faith should be regarded as one indivisible unity. It is not enough to accept just certain particular doctrines, basic as they may be in themselves, e.g. that Christ is God and Saviour. It is compelling that all doctrines formulated by the Ecumenical Councils, as well as the totality of the teaching of the early, undivided Church, should be accepted. One cannot be satisfied with formulas which are isolated from the life and experiences of the Church. They must be assessed and understood within the context of the Church's life. From the Orthodox viewpoint, re-union of Christendom with which the World Council of Churches is concerned can be achieved solely on the basis of the total, dogmatic Faith of the early, undivided Church without either subtraction or alteration. We cannot accept a rigid distinction between essential and non-essential doctrines, and there is not room for comprehensiveness in the Faith. On the other hand, the Orthodox Church cannot accept that the Holy Spirit speaks to us only through the Bible. The Holy Spirit abides and witnesses through the totality of the Church's life and experience. The Bible is given to us within the context of Apostolic Tradition in which in turn we possess the authentic interpretation and explication of the Word of God. Loyalty to the Apostolic Tradition safeguards the reality and continuity of church unity.

(b) It is through the Apostolic Ministry that the mystery of the Pentecost is perpetuated in the Church. The Episcopal Succession from the Apostles constitutes a historical reality in the life and structure of the Church and one of the presuppositions of unity throughout the ages. The unity of the Church is preserved through the unity of the Episcopate. The Church is one Body whose historical continuity and unity is also safeguarded by the common faith arising spontaneously out of the fullness (pleroma) of the Church.

3. Thus when we are considering the problem of Church unity we cannot envisage it in any other way than as the complete restoration of the total faith and the total episcopal structure of the Church which is basic to the sacramental life of the Church. We would not pass judgment upon those of the separated communions. However, it is our conviction that in these communions certain basic elements are lacking which constitute the reality of the fullness of the Church. We believe that the return of the communions to the Faith of the ancient, united, and indivisible Church of the Seven Ecumenical Councils, namely to the pure and unchanged and common heritage of the forefathers of all divided Christians, shall alone produce the desired reunion of all separated Christians. For, only the unity and the fellowship of Christians in a common Faith shall have as a necessary result their fellowship in the sacraments and their indissoluble unity in love, as members of one and the same Body of the one Church of Christ.

4. The "perfect unity" of Christians must not be interpreted exclusively as a realization at the Second Coming of Christ. We must acknowledge that even at the present age the Holy Spirit dwelling in the Church continues to breathe in the world, guiding all Christians to unity. The unity of the Church must not be understood only eschatologically, but as a present reality which is to receive the consummation in the Last Day.

5. It is suggested in the report of the section that the road which the Church must take in restoring unity is that of repentance. We must recognize that there have been and there are imperfections and failures within the life and witness of Christian believers, but we reject the notion that the Church herself, being the Body of Christ and the repository of revealed Truth and the "whole operation of the Holy Spirit", could be affected by human sin. Therefore, we cannot speak of the repentance of the Church which is intrinsically holy and unerring. For, "Christ loved the Church and gave himself for it, that He might present it to Himself as a glorious Church, not having spot or wrinkle or blemish or any such thing, but that it should be holy and without blemish" (Eph. 5:26-27).

Thus the Lord, the only Holy One, sanctified His Church for ever and ordered that her task be the "edification of the saints and the building of the body of Christ". Her holiness is not vitiated by the sins and failures of her members. They cannot in any way lessen or exhaust the inexhaustible holiness of the divine life which from the Head of the Church is diffused throughout all the body.

6. In conclusion, we are bound to declare our profound conviction that the Holy Orthodox Church alone has preserved in full and intact "the faith once delivered unto the saints". It is not because of our human merit, but because it pleases God to preserve "his treasure in earthen vessels, that the excellency of the power may be of God" (2 Cor. 4:7).

Third Assembly
of the World Council of Churches

New Delhi, India, 1961

Representatives of the Orthodox Church in the Section on Unity welcome the Report of the Faith and Order Commission adopted at St Andrews, Scotland, in August, 1960, as an important and stimulating ecumenical document. The ecumenical movement, as is now embodied in the World Council of Churches, has begun by Protestant initiative, but was not meant, from the very beginning, to be a Protestant endeavour, nor should it be regarded as such. This must be especially emphasized now, when almost all churches of the Orthodox Communion have entered the membership of the World Council. In this situation the Orthodox Representatives feel themselves obliged to underline the basic difference between their own approach to the ecumenical problem and that which is implied in the document of St Andrews. The ecumenical problem, as it is understood in the current ecumenical movement, is primarily a problem of the Protestant world. The main question, in this setting, is that of "Denominationalism". Accordingly, the problem of Christian unity, or of Christian Reunion, is usually regarded in terms of an interdenominational agreement or Reconciliation. In the Protestant universe of discourse such approach is quite natural. But for the Orthodox it is uncongenial. For the Orthodox the basic ecumenical problem is that of schism. The Orthodox cannot accept the idea of a "parity of denomination" and cannot visualize Christian Reunion just as an interdenominational adjustment. The unity has been broken and must be recovered. The Orthodox Church is not a confession, one of many, one among the many. For the Orthodox, the Orthodox Church is just the Church. The Orthodox Church is aware and conscious of the identity of her inner structure and of her teaching with the Apostolic message (kerygma) and the tradition of the ancient undivided Church. She finds herself in an unbroken and continuous succession of sacramental ministry, sacramental life, and faith. Indeed, for the Orthodox the apostolic succession of episcopacy and sacramental priesthood is an essential and constitutive, and therefore obligatory element of the Church's very existence. The Orthodox Church, by her inner conviction and consciousness, has a special and exceptional position in the divided Christendom, as the bearer of, and the witness to, the tradition of the ancient undivided Church, from which all existing denominations stem, by the way of reduction and separation. From the Orthodox point of view, the current ecumenical endeavour can be characterized as "ecumenism in space", aiming at agreement between various denominations, as they exist at present. This endeavour is, from the Orthodox point of view, quite inadequate and incomplete.

• This text was submitted as a contribution to the Section of the Assembly dealing with the unity of the Church. It was the last statement of its kind. Greek text in Stavridis, *op. cit.*, pp. 150-152. Also published in Stephanopoulos, *op. cit.*, pp. 50-51.

The common ground, or rather the common background of existing denominations, can be found, and must be sought, in the past in their common history, in that common ancient and apostolic tradition, from which all of them derive their existence. This kind of ecumenical endeavour can be properly denoted as "ecumenism in time". The report of Faith and Order itself mentions "agreement (in faith) with all ages" as one of the normative prerequisites of unity. Orthodox theologians suggest this new method of ecumenical inquiry, and this new criterion of ecumenical evaluation, as a kingly rock, with the hope that unity may be recovered by the divided denominations by their return to their common past. By this way divergent denominations may meet each other on the unity of common tradition. The Orthodox Church is willing to participate in this common work as the witness which had preserved continuously the deposit of apostolic faith and tradition. No static restoration of old forms is anticipated, but rather a dynamic recovery of perennial ethos, which only can secure the true agreement "of all ages". Nor should there be a rigid uniformity, since the same faith, mysterious in its essence and unfathomable adequately in the formulas of human reason, can be expressed accurately in different manners. The immediate objective of the ecumenical search is, according to the Orthodox understanding, a reintegration of Christian mind, a recovery of apostolic tradition, a fullness of Christian vision and belief, in agreement with all ages.

First Pan-Orthodox Conference

Rhodes, Greece, 1961

I. Study of ways of bringing closer and uniting the Churches in a Pan-Orthodox perspective.

II. Orthodoxy and the Lesser Ancient Oriental Churches:

   a) Cultivation of friendly relations with a view to establishing a union with them:
      1. Exchange of visits
      2. Exchange of teachers and students
      3. Contacts of a theological character
   b) Study of history, faith, worship and administration of these Churches.
   c) Cooperation with them:
      1. In Conferences of an ecumenical character
      2. In practical matters

III. Orthodoxy and the Roman Catholic Church:

   a) Study of the positive and negative points between the two Churches:
      1. In faith
      2. In administration
      3. In church activities (especially propaganda, proselytising, the Uniates).
   b) Cultivation of relations in the spirit of Christian love, with particular reference to the points anticipated in the Patriarchal Encyclical of 1920.

IV. Orthodoxy and the Churches and Confessions emanating from the Reformation:

   a) Confessions lying further from Orthodoxy:
      1. Lutheranism
      2. Calvinism
      3. Methodism
      4. Other Protestant Confessions
   b) Confessions lying nearer to Orthodoxy:
      1. Anglican Church
      2. Episcopalians in general.

● The Orthodox Churches met in Rhodes in 1961 to prepare for a Great and Holy Pan-Orthodox Synod. The conference drew up a list of themes to be dealt with at the Synod, giving special attention to the relations of the Orthodox Church with the rest of the Christian world. Greek text in *I Proti Panorthodoxos Diaskepsis*, 24 September-1 October 1961, Ecumenical Patriarchate 1967, pp. 130-140. Translation by the Language Service of the WCC.

Study of the best relations to cultivate and of drawing them closer, especially the Episcopalian and Anglican Churches, to the Orthodox Church, in the light of existing definite assumptions.

V.   Orthodoxy and Old Catholicism:

Advancement of relations with them in the spirit of former theological discussions and their stated intentions and inclinations to unite with the Orthodox Church.

VI. Orthodoxy and the Ecumenical Movement:

a) The presence and participation of the Orthodox Church in the ecumenical movement, in the spirit of the Patriarchal Encyclical of 1920.

b) Study of theological and other subjects related to the assumptions of the Orthodox Church's participation in the ecumenical movement.

c) The importance and the contributions of the Orthodox participation as a whole in the direction of ecumenical thinking and action.

Address by His All Holiness Athenagoras I, Ecumenical Patriarch

On the Occasion of His Visit to WCC Headquarters, 1967

Most Reverend General Secretary, Gentlemen,

We thank Your Most Beloved Reverence from our inmost heart for the greetings which you have addressed to us on behalf of the beloved World Council of Churches and those who render such valuable services therein.

We consider it as a gift of grace, granted to us by our Lord, that He has bestowed His blessing on the sacred desire which we had long nourished in our hearts, namely, that of visiting and paying honour to this renowned Centre where the Christians of the world work together in unity.

We greatly rejoice that today this desire received its fulfilment, and above all that our visit falls nearly half a century after the publication of the well-known Encyclical Letter of our Apostolic and Patriarchal See of 1920, and almost 20 years after the founding of the World Council of Churches.

These two chronological landmarks in the historical journey travelled thus far by the Council constitute the starting-point of a new period in the life of this interchurch organisation — a period on the one hand of more complete understanding between its member churches and, on the other hand, of closer collaboration between them, so that they may the better promote the spirit of Christian unity and of service to mankind.

Brothers and beloved children in Christ, we have come to you along with the honoured persons who accompany us, to bring you the greetings, good wishes and blessings of our Holy Ecumenical See and of ourselves. We come not as strangers to strangers, but as members of the same family, to this our common home, in witness of our Church's profound awareness that it is one of the founding Churches of this Council and — along with the other sister Orthodox Churches — a deeply engaged and active member of it in the inter-Christian dialogue of love and unity. But, at the same time, we come to bear witness to the fact that our Ecumenical Patriarchate is conscious of how much it has owed in the past, owes now, and will also owe in the future to the World Council of Churches — and most rightly so, for this Council is destined to act in all things against the sin of division within the Christian Church, and to serve the holy purpose of Christian unity by bringing closer together the various denominations. At this moment, some relevant and appropriate words of a 14th century Byzantine theologian come to my mind:

> How fruitful and pleasing a thing it is for brothers to live together, and how joyful
> and profitable a thing for them to struggle with unanimity towards deep spirituality; and

● Responding to the address of welcome made by Dr Eugene Carson Blake on 6 November 1967, the Ecumenical Patriarch outlined the basic principles of the work of the Ecumenical Patriarchate in the service of the Ecumenical Movement. The response was published in *The Ecumenical Review*, Vol. XX, January 1968, No. 1, pp. 86-88.

how miserable and fruitless it is for those who are united in the Spirit to be in conflict with one another.

If it is true that where two or three are gathered together in Christ, He is directly present in the midst of them, then how much more so, when two or three or more nations are gathered in Him, is He there present to bestow all goodness upon them. That is why we are torn asunder in our hearts on account of the division of the Churches; for, being members of Christ, having access to and communion with One and the Same Head, and being fitly framed together, we nevertheless do not think in harmony, nor move forward to the same goal.

We are happy to be able to confirm to all of you that now, as always, such is the thinking of Our holy and great Church of Christ, and of the Orthodox Church in general.

The Orthodox Church, suffering on account of the divisions in the one flock of Christ, has ever longed for sincere and understanding collaboration between the Christian Churches and denominations, and has prayed and prays daily to the Lord, "for the peace of the whole world, the stability of the Holy Churches of God, and the union of all."

The Orthodox Church does this so much the more because it believes that today, more than ever, the Christian world has had enough of sterile verbal exchanges. The Kingdom of Christ is a kingdom of love, and we must return to that love if we are to be able to bind up the wounds of the past, wounds which were inflicted upon the Church of Christ by a spirit that distorted the truth, or by human deviations, or the flames of discord. No Christian Church has the right to remain in isolation, to proclaim that it has no need to be in contact with other Christian brothers, and that those who live outside its frontiers are deprived of bonds which link them with Christ. On the contrary, the more a Church has the consciousness that it alone possesses the truth, and remains faithful to the word of Christ, the tradition and the mission of the One Ancient and Undivided Church, so much the more must it, and has it the obligation to, enter into dialogue and collaboration with all the other Christian denominations. It must do this in a spirit of love, humility and service, in accordance with the example of Christ, so as to advance the victory of truth and the building-up of the Body of Christ. Christendom must feel anew the impetus of this Spirit of Christ, which is rooted in Christian unity and, in its turn, is established on the foundation of love, so that it may spread its beneficent influence to the world and to all mankind.

Our collaboration in the World Council of Churches has as its goal an increase in love and the common study — undertaken in a spirit of total fidelity to the truth — of the differences which separate the Christian Churches, in order that we may build up Christian unity. In collaborating within the World Council of Churches, we do not aim at setting aside our theological differences, nor at achieving superficial understanding, nor disregarding the points that divide us. But we do aim at a spirit of reciprocal and sincere understanding, in the authentic spirit of Christ, and at directing ourselves towards the preparation of the way that will one day make it possible for the Holy Spirit to enable all members of the Body of Christ to receive Communion with the same Bread and from the same Chalice. In a world that is torn asunder, full of suffering, and threatened with dire catastrophe; in a world that is plunged into unparalleled and hitherto unheard-of spiritual and moral confusion; in a world that lacks guidance and a sense of orientation, this collaboration of the Christian Churches and denominations is an urgent need of the times, and an obligation that we have to history.

Our Ecumenical Patriarchate — in the position that it took from the very beginning, in its historic Encyclical of 1920 on the formation of a League of Churches, and in its subsequent collaboration in the Ecumenical Movement — has undoubtedly been, and still is, an ardent preacher of the true ecumenical ideal, and true ecumenical dialogue to foster Christian unity. For this reason, so as to encourage the ecumenical spirit, it has taken initiatives in Christian reconciliation in all directions. And for this reason a new era in relations between the Roman Catholic Church and the Orthodox Church has opened up into one of sincere collaboration with His Holiness Pope Paul VI. For this reason it cultivates and promotes bi-lateral relations with member churches of the World Council of Churches, such as the Anglican, Old Catholic and Post-Chalcedonian Churches, and the Lutheran Church.

The Ecumenical Patriarchate, in working in these directions, is firmly convinced that it is also promoting the work of the World Council of Churches. Therefore we greatly rejoice when we see communication and cooperation constantly increasing between our World Council of Churches and the great Roman Catholic Church.

As we examine the present position of the movement of ecumenism towards Christian unity, we can observe that the Spirit of God has led it to an important point, to a point that is one of increasing maturity and, simultaneously — as always happens in things divine — one also of crisis.

Today we find ourselves facing the temptation to content ourselves with what has already been achieved, thus allowing the ecumenical movement — narcissistically and in total contradiction of itself — to stagnate; on the other hand is the possibility of the ecumenical movement's being inspired to new dynamic action, and thus justifying itself as a movement that leads to its own renewal and to the task of the renewal of the churches, a renewal which is a fundamental presupposition for their meeting on the one divine road that leads to unity.

The renewal of churches, of Christians and Christian Unity are mutually linked. Thus the Fourth Assembly of our World Council of Churches is awaited by everyone with great hopes and most anxious expectations. The eschatological watchword of this Assembly — "Behold, I make all things new" — most accurately formulates the anguishing demands of the Church of our times.

We hope and pray that He who can make all things new, the common and only Father of all Christians, He who is and was and always will be, may make our Fourth Assembly His instrument, an instrument that will renew the ecumenical movement and the member churches.

Looking to the future and seeking for that which is best in Jesus Christ, the Light and Hope of the world, we cannot ignore, and fail to honour, the past. It is therefore with a profound sense of gratitude and a desire to pay tribute of honour, that we recall at this moment the inestimable services rendered by the champions of the ecumenical movement who have passed on: the never-forgotten John Mott, Archbishop Nathan Söderblom of Uppsala, Archbishop William Temple, Bishop Bell and Metropolitan Germanos of Thyatheira who, as all acknowledge, have left indelible footprints of their passing and have set the seal of their personalities on the work and orientation of the ecumenical movement. Nor can we fail to mention at this moment two significant events in the life of the World Council of Churches, namely, the retirement of the Rev. Dr W.A. Visser 't Hooft from the high responsibility of the General Secretaryship, and the assumption of it by the Rev. Dr Eugene Carson Blake. It is not our intention to analyse the personalities and work of these two eminent and distinguished labourers in the ecumenical movement, for we believe, as St John Chrysostom says, that "the voice of the work itself speaks more dazzlingly". The work of both in the ecumenical movement is known to all and speaks for itself, so that further talk is superfluous. But we wish to express to both of them the profound love, honour and appreciation that we bear to them. May glory and honour and peace be given to all who work for the good of the ecumenical movement.

Filled with such thoughts and feelings, we extend from this common Centre of ours an embrace of love and peace to all the member churches of the World Council of Churches. We pray that its task may be accomplished by the realization of the only purpose for which it exists: the unity of all in the One Church of Christ, so that His will may be done, and the world may believe that God did indeed send Him.

Fourth Pan-Orthodox Conference

Chambésy, Switzerland, 1968

Resolution

1. The Inter-Orthodox Committee gathered in Geneva expresses the common mind of the Orthodox Church, that she is an organic member of the World Council of Churches (WCC), and her firm resolve, with all the means at her disposal, theological and other, to contribute to the advancement and the success of all the WCC's work.
2. To this end it considers it essential that WCC, in cooperation with the local Orthodox Churches, should appoint more Orthodox to its staff, whether theologians or not.
3. All the Representatives of the Orthodox Churches serving the WCC, either as staff of this Conference or as Permanent Representatives of their Churches, ought to have regular contacts with one another.
4. It gives voice to its desire that on the "Faith and Order" Committee there should be a permanent position for an Orthodox Secretary or Assistant Secretary, who would also ensure a continuous contact between his department and member Orthodox Churches.
5. Whenever the "Faith and Order" Committee sets up a local study-group, specialist Orthodox representatives should be invited to take part.
6. There is need to organize carefully prepared Orthodox acts of worship, as an organic part of the WCC's programme of services.
7. It expresses the wish that the appropriate publications staff of WCC might include among the papers published in the periodical *The Ecumenical Review* (and in other publications) a reasonable number of contributions from Orthodox theologians, to facilitate a better reciprocal awareness of theological positions.
8. It is necessary that competent Orthodox staff should be prepared and designated for the ecumenical movement, to be used in various ways (e.g. establishing special chairs in Theological Schools, special seminaries, etc.); and this need should be brought to the attention of the local Churches.

● Following the first Pan-Orthodox conference in Rhodes in 1961, two further Pan-Orthodox conferences were held there in 1963 and 1964. The Fourth Conference was held in Chambésy, Geneva, from 8-15 June 1968. Relations with other Churches, and especially Orthodox participation in the World Council of Churches, were again under discussion. Greek text in *I Diorthodoxos Epitropi i sinelthousa en Genevi en to Orthodoxo Kentro tou Ikoumenikou Patriarchiou* (8-15 June 1968), Ecumenical Patriarchate 1968 (mimeographed text), pp. 105f. Translation by the Language Service of the WCC.

9. More particularly, as regards the role of Orthodoxy during the Fourth Assembly of WCC at Uppsala, it is considered necessary to ensure a more effective Orthodox contribution at the Assembly by bringing together the Orthodox delegates (or at least one plenipotentiary from each) during the Conference itself: this would ensure the sharing of information about the discussions of theological matters of prime importance in the various Sections.

The Russian Orthodox Church and the Ecumenical Movement

Metropolitan Nikodim

In 1961 the Russian Orthodox Church joined the World Council of Churches, namely a *fellowship of churches* (see Constitution of the WCC, Art. 1) whose primary aims are to contribute as much as possible to the unity of all Christians and to give joint Christian service to mankind in the spirit of the Gospel's commandments to love and to be loyal to God's will.

It is a well-known fact that, while maintaining a positive attitude towards the ideas of ecumenism, the Russian Orthodox Church was formerly extremely cautious about expressing ecumenism in concrete form. For many years after the First Assembly of the WCC at Amsterdam in 1948 the Russian Orthodox Church studied the activity of this new ecumenical body in order to see what possibility might exist to collaborate with it without prejudicing the principles of Orthodoxy.

Moreover, from the very outset it was clear to the Orthodox that collaboration with the World Council of Churches, still more membership of it, would inevitably mean plunging into the Protestant element or, if you prefer, undergoing a sort of *kenosis*, because the voice of Orthodox witness at ecumenical meetings and in the WCC documents would always be submerged by a chorus of diverse, but essentially Protestant, opinions.

It is only by increasing the number of representatives of the Orthodox Churches, so as to reflect the real importance of Orthodoxy in Christendom (and at the same time to improve the quality of that representation) that a balance can be created between the two confessional groups or systems, and their forces equalized. But that does not always guarantee a maximum of mutual understanding. I must frankly say that this situation will not disappear until all the Christian Churches have attained unanimity in their confession of faith, i.e. until all the Churches belonging to the World Council of Churches hold the faith which was the faith of the ancient undivided Church. It is clear that this confession of the true faith, or Orthodoxy if you like, does not necessitate resembling the form in which Orthodoxy expresses itself today in this or that local church, including the Russian Church. We Orthodox avoid the kind of statement made at ecumenical meetings, because we do not think that constant reference to the difference between Orthodoxy and Protestantism is conducive to "peace and mutual

● At the time of writing this paper, Metropolitan Nikodim of Leningrad and Novgorod, of the Patriarchate of Moscow and All Russia, was chairman of the Synodal Commission for the Unity of Christians and Relations between Churches. He was elected one of the six presidents of the World Council of Churches at the Nairobi Assembly of the WCC in 1975. The Metropolitan delivered this speech during the visitors' programme at the Uppsala Assembly. The text, translated from the French, was published in *The Ecumenical Review*, Vol. XXI, April 1969, No. 2, pp. 116-119.

upbuilding" (Rom. 14:19). However, at a moment as responsible as the present when, as leader of the delegation from the Moscow Patriarchate, I have to explain to the Assembly of the World Council of Churches the point of view of my own Church concerning the ecumenical movement, I feel it is my duty before God and before my conscience to do so with all the frankness and all the sincerity of a witness who does not adapt his remarks to the liking of his audience (2 Tim. 4:3) because he knows that he would then be deceiving them as well as himself (2 Tim. 3:13).

In order to show that that is not simply my personal opinion I will quote what a very eminent Russian Orthodox theologian said on this subject: His Holiness Patriarch Sergius. In his well-known work "The Church of Christ and the Dissident Communities" he wrote:

> Among educated Christians one avoids bluntly raising the question of the true Church. One prefers to affect "wider" views by affirming, for instance, that "the divisions between the confessions do not reach up to heaven". The divisions within the Church are imputed to the ambitions of the hierarchies and to the intransigence of theologians. It does not matter much whether a man is Orthodox, Roman Catholic or Protestant; as long as he leads a Christian life he need not worry... But this broadness of view, which is so convenient in daily relationships and so reassuring, cannot satisfy those who are really children of the Church and who are fully aware of their own beliefs and convictions. They feel that this "broadness of view" really conceals scepticism, a lukewarm faith and indifference about the salvation of the soul.[1]

What was it then which incited the Russian Orthodox Church to join the World Council of Churches? My answer is this: firstly, the love of brethren who feel how baneful are the divisions between Christians, and who declare their desire to eliminate the obstacles to fulfilling the will of our Lord Jesus Christ "that they may all be one" (John 17:21). Secondly, awareness of the importance of coordinating the efforts of all Christians, in their witness and service to men in the complex conditions of the secularized world of today, subject to rapid changes, divided, but aspiring to unity.

The fact that the Russian Orthodox Church has joined the World Council of Churches cannot be regarded as an ecclesial act in the ecclesiological sense. It is connected with those aspects of its own life and activity whose free expression does not impose direct responsibility on all the local Orthodox Churches — that responsibility which is incumbent upon every part of the sacred Body of Christ in face of the plenitude of the Holy, Catholic, Apostolic Church as a whole. This really is a fact, as is shown by the way in which the Russian Orthodox Church joined the World Council of Churches. All the local Orthodox churches declared their desire for membership of the WCC without any preliminary pan-Orthodox consultation. The Conference of representatives of some of the autocephalous Orthodox Churches held at Moscow in 1948 was not pan-Orthodox, nor were the consultations which followed with the Churches which had attended that Conference. (During those consultations the Russian Orthodox Church reversed its decision and informed them that it intended shortly to join the WCC, as the result of modifications in the WCC's activities.)

The question of joining the WCC was studied successively by the Holy Synod, then by the Council of Bishops of the Russian Orthodox Church, so that the local church was not called upon to give a formal consent through its hierarchy, its clergy and its members, because they were represented in the local Council. This is significant if one takes account of the firm conviction in Orthodoxy as a whole, that it is the actual body of the Church, namely the people (including of course the hierarchy and the clergy) who are the guardians of piety, always in the hope of preserving their faith unchanged in accordance with the faith of their forefathers (see Circular Letter of the Eastern Patriarchs, 6 May 1848).

These limitations in the official sanction of the Russian Orthodox Church's entry into the World Council of Churches do not mean, however, that any doubt exists about the legitimacy of this act. Not only the decisions of the hierarchical power meeting in Council, but also those of the Synod, enjoy complete authority and confidence in our Church. However, I repeat, the way in which the Russian Orthodox Church took the decision to join the WCC clearly indicates that this act was never considered as having an ecclesiologically obligatory meaning for the Orthodox conscience. It would be more exact not to speak of the Russian Orthodox Church "joining" the WCC, still less "being admitted" to the WCC, but rather of an agreement between the leaders of the Russian Orthodox Church and those of the World Council of Churches for representatives of the Russian Orthodox Church to enter into permanent collaboration with representatives of other Churches belonging to an association called the World Council of Churches. The Assembly held at New Delhi in 1961 gave its consent to a collaboration of this kind. In speaking of the World Council of Churches I must point out that, from the very outset, there has been a certain confusion or ambiguity in the definition of the nature of that body.

The "Committee of Thirty-Five" which met in London on the 8th July, 1938, was convinced that the time had come to form a World Council of Churches, namely a permanent organ whereby those Churches could accomplish their common ecumenical tasks. This Council was defined as an association of church-representatives pursuing the interests of the "Life and Work" and "Faith and Order" movements.

The Conferences held at Oxford and Edinburgh shortly afterwards approved the suggestion and decided to merge the two movements ("Life and Work" and "Faith and Order").

The Conference which met at Utrecht in May 1938 approved and adopted the following *Basis* for the World Council of Churches, which was afterwards confirmed at its first Assembly at Amsterdam in 1948:

> The World Council of Churches is a fellowship of churches which accept our Lord Jesus Christ as God and Saviour.[2]

It is absolutely evident that an organ set up by Churches, an association of their representatives, is not at all the same thing as an association (or society) of the Churches themselves. Just as the United Nations Organization is not at all the same thing as the united nations themselves.

The decision concerning the Authority of the Council, adopted by the Amsterdam Assembly in 1948, is somewhat equivocal in character. It says:

> The World Council of Churches is composed of churches which acknowledge Jesus Christ as God and Saviour. They find their unity in Him. They have not to create their unity; it is the gift of God. But they know that it is their duty to make common cause in the search for the expression of that unity in work and in life. The Council desires to serve the churches, which are its constituent members, as an instrument whereby they may bear witness together to their common allegiance to Jesus Christ, and co-operate in matters requiring united action... Moreover, while earnestly seeking fellowship in thought and action for all its members, the Council disavows any thought of becoming a single unified church structure independent of the churches which have joined in constituting the Council, or a structure dominated by a centralized administrative authority.

> The purpose of the Council is to express its unity in another way. Unity arises out of the love of God in Jesus Christ which, binding the constituent churches to Him, binds them to one another. It is the earnest desire of the Council that the churches may be bound closer to Christ and therefore closer to one another. In the bond of His love, they will desire continually to pray for one another and to strengthen one another, in worship and in witness, bearing one another's burdens and so fulfilling the law of Christ.[3]

This text shows that the World Council is a fellowship of Churches which realize their unity to be incomplete, and which have begun to seek a way of expressing this unity more fully. For this purpose they have formed themselves into a fellowship with common tasks, common activities and a common life.

On the other hand, however, the World Council is an instrument created by the Churches which have joined it, in order to express their unity, an instrument whose task is to serve the Church which formed it in order to witness... collaborate... and unite between themselves. In this sense the World Council of Churches is a unified ecclesial structure (although not "special" nor "independent") of the united Churches, a structure which is not "directed by a centralized administrative power" but which is served by a special, centralized controlling machinery.

At the meeting of the Central Committee of the WCC at Rochester in 1963, Dr Visser 't Hooft presented a report on the "Meaning of Membership in the World Council of Churches", in which he pointed out that some confusion exists about the definition of the World Council of Churches. He said, the time seemed to have come to draw a clear distinction between the World Council of Churches and the new ecumenical reality.

> Now it would seem that we must carefully distinguish between the World Council of Churches and this new ecumenical reality... to transfer the description of the emerging ecumenical reality to the World Council is to confuse the instrument with the product which is brought in being with the help of that instrument. It is through the World Council or at least to a large extent through the World Council that many have come to realize dimensions of the life of the Church of which they had beforehand mainly theoretical knowledge. But that does not change the nature of the WCC as an instrument at the service of the churches.[4]

This text shows that Dr Visser 't Hooft considers it necessary to explain that the "ecumenical reality" (which he seems to regard as a sort of embryo of a true *Una Sancta*) is not born within the World Council, which is only an instrument for the churches. But this ecumenical reality does appear in the member churches themselves, and in their association called a Council of Churches.

Orthodox doctrine is unchangeable in its essence, which may be described as the sacred, living Tradition of the Church. The Church faithfully guards and explains (without marring it) the Apostolic and revealed heritage of the faith entrusted to it. As for Orthodox theology as a scientific discipline, it is natural that it should develop and perfect itself. From this point of view ecclesiology can also pass through phases of progressive development and renewal. However, this process cannot be bound by any external norms or formal obligations. It takes place naturally, freely expressing the new facts and conditions in which the life of Christ's Church goes on.

At the time the Russian Orthodox Church "appreciated the report entitled *The Church, the Churches and the World Council of Churches* adopted at Toronto in 1950 by the Central Committee of the WCC, which helped to clarify the interconfessional nature of the WCC."[5] In that report (known as the *Toronto Statement*) the following points are the most important:

> The World Council cannot and should not be based on any one particular conception of the Church. It does not prejudge the ecclesiological problem.
> There is room and space in the World Council for the ecclesiology of every Church which is ready to participate in the ecumenical conversation and which takes its stand on the Basis of the Council...
> No Church is obliged to change its ecclesiology as a consequence of membership in the World Council.
> Membership in the World Council does not imply the acceptance of a specific doctrine concerning the nature of Church unity. (Paras 3 & 5)

It is precisely these theses which have enabled the Russian Orthodox Church (through its hierarchs) to give its consent to its entry into the World Council, in the sense indicated above. With regard to Part IV of the *Toronto Statement* ("The Assumptions underlying the World Council of Churches"), in spite of a series of ideas contained therein which are perfectly acceptable for the Orthodox, the Russian Orthodox Church considers it as a special opinion which is not in any way binding upon the Churches belonging to the WCC. All the more so because it implicitly contains ideas about the Church which seem to be perfectly acceptable to Protestants but which are incompatible with the ecclesiological principles of Orthodoxy. Within the scope of this brief address I cannot go into that question: it would necessitate a careful analysis of Part IV of the *Toronto Statement*, and would undoubtedly arouse a long discussion. But in order to show why we consider this text merely as a personal and arbitrary opinion, it suffices to recall that it is concerned with "the ecclesiological implications of membership in the WCC" (see introductory sentences to Part IV), whereas Part III clearly affirms that "the World Council does not prejudge the ecclesiological problem" (III, para. 3).

Many of the World Council documents express the idea that the task of its member Churches is to reveal the unity which already exists between them. I have already quoted these words from the decision taken at the Amsterdam Assembly "on the authority of the World Council" where it is said that the Churches which constitute the World Council have no need to create their unity; that is a gift of God; but their duty is to seek together to manifest this unity in life and action.[6]

> "They know, that it is their duty to make common cause in the search for the expression of that unity in work and in life." The same idea recurs in the Statement on "The Purpose and Function of the Basis" adopted at the Evanston Assembly, which says: "The churches enter into relation with each other, because there is a unity given once for all in the person and work of their common Lord, and because the Living Lord gathers His people together."[7]

These views were often expressed, and still are. They show that Christians are aware of the sin of their division. Admittedly an initial unity does exist, in the person of the one Lord and Saviour. There is also a certain degree of unity in thought, hopes, ethical norms, conduct, etc., in spite of the state of division. But how can one confine oneself to reassuring statements about the existing state of things and ignore what a great number of Christians miss: the real, essential unity which belongs to the integral body of the Church of Christ, which we Orthodox call "catholicity"?

On this subject I cannot avoid mentioning the well-known definition of unity first worked out at St Andrew's in 1960, and then included in the report of the Section on

Unity which was adopted by the whole Assembly at New Delhi in 1961. This definition reads as follows:

> We believe that the unity which is both God's will and his gift to his Church is being made visible as all in each place who are baptized into Jesus Christ and confess him as Lord and Saviour are brought by the Holy Spirit into one fully committed fellowship, holding the one apostolic faith, preaching the one Gospel, breaking the one bread, joining in common prayer, and having a corporate life reaching out in witness and service to all, and who (i.e. those who are baptized into Jesus Christ and confess him as Lord and Saviour) at the same time are united with the whole Christian fellowship in all places and all ages in such wise that ministry and members are accepted by all, and that all can act and speak together as occasion requires for the tasks to which God calls his people.[8]

Despite the affirmation in this same Report that this description of "unity does not presuppose any one particular doctrine of the Church"[9], it is perfectly evident that it contains a concept of unity which is completely Protestant. Unity is regarded as a gift from God belonging, despite the divisions, to the whole of Christendom. This unity is not always visibly manifest to the necessary extent. Christendom as such is thus considered as essentially the one, complete body of the Church of Christ. As for division, it is not understood as the destruction of inner unity and a painful crippling of certain parts of the body of the Church. It is merely regarded as an inadequate awareness (in the minds of divided Christians) of their inner health, and as a lack of courage to proclaim that health to the world through acts which manifest their unity.

The description of unity contained in this Report can refer only to the future when — after intercession, ecumenical collaboration and seeking have come to an end — that unity has been attained.

The sin of division consists not in insufficient awareness of allegedly existing unity, but in the destruction of that unity, thus injuring some of its parts and harming the whole body of the Church of Christ. It is true that the unity of the Church is a gift of God, but only in a well-defined sense. It is a fact that there exists now and will exist until the consummation of time a divine objective basis of ecclesial unity in Christ, i.e. the possibility of intimate communion with Him through faith and through participation in sacramental life, especially in the true Eucharist, on condition that full obedience is paid to the fullness of the divine revelation. In itself this objective aspect, outside our obedience or disobedience to the divine revelation, does not assure complete, essential unity in any part of the Christian brotherhood. Only the one, holy, catholic and apostolic Church, which is the full, healthy foundation of the Body of Christ, possesses the true and full unity, because it is obedient to the voice of the divine Truth. Outside its limits the essential unity can be lost to a greater or lesser extent. It can be incomplete, or may also disappear. Full and perfect unity can be appropriated by the whole Oekumene not through a simple "manifestation" or "visible expression", but solely by re-building the broken unity, by returning to complete obedience to the truth. This will enable the limits of the whole Christian brotherhood to become identified with those of the one, holy, catholic, apostolic Church.

I will not speak in detail about the progress of the ecumenical movement between the Assembly at New Delhi in 1961 and the Assembly at Uppsala in 1968. In my view progress has undoubtedly been made, and that gives one hope for the future. One has only to study the work done by the Faith and Order Commission to see how much wider and deeper the search has grown for the treasures of the one undivided Church, its doctrine and its experience. We warmly welcome the statement expressed in recent documents of the Faith and Order Commission "that patristic studies are a necessary part of ecumenical concerns and must be expanded", and "that common study of patristic texts should continue, and further recommend a study of 'The Fathers and the Bible'."[10]

We also appreciate many aspects of the practical work of the World Council of Churches. Compared with the past it has greatly increased in importance as the result of fresh contacts, especially with the Roman Catholic Church, the Christian Peace Movement, and other Christian groups and movements. However, we do not close our eyes to certain phenomena which we regard as negative, and which are still preventing the World Council of Churches from adopting a more decisive position that is more in harmony with its principles in face of the intolerable violations of international peace and infringements of the sovereign rights of peoples who are victims of aggression. In such cases we Christians must not seek a balance of forces which usually satisfies no one. We must call a spade a spade and oppose evil, so that well-being and peace may be man's heritage, as the child of God.

We sincerely hope that in the process of our future ecumenical cooperation Christians will become increasingly aware of the true nature of the divisions which still exist within Christendom. That will not only deepen their understanding of the sin underlying those divisions; it will also strengthen their sense of responsibility so that they put an end to any arbitrary stubbornness which injures the body of the Church and brings it into disrepute, besides causing deep inner suffering. Through close coopera-tion between Christians, mutual enrichment and the sharing of experience, we hope that Christians will become a great moral force that merits the respect of all who long for peace, justice and really human relationships. When confronted by problems, if the Churches belonging to the ecumenical movement share the same attitude based on their devotion to Christian Truth and inspired by the love of Christ, their unanimity will bear its perfect fruit and will act irresistibly, for "our appeal does not spring from error or uncleanness, nor is it made with guile" (1 Thess. 2:3, RSV).

I should like to add something about some of the ideas contained in Dr Blake's report at the meeting of the Central Committee of the World Council of Churches at Heraklion, Crete, in 1967. In this report, which was very informative and well-written, he says that in his view "the way for the World Council of Churches to serve the ecumenical movement in our time is to become as radical an influence for a revolutionary new obedience to Jesus Christ as we must be a conservative force to preserve for the world the ancient Gospel of the transcendent God who makes Himself known in Jesus Christ, His Son our Lord."[11]

We Orthodox strongly approve this prudent conservatism in the sphere of faith, as we are admonished by the Apostle in the Epistle to the Hebrews: "Do not be led away by diverse and strange teachings" (Heb. 13:9). For these are the gifts bestowed by God on His Church: "some apostles, some prophets, some evangelists, some pastors and teachers" so that we may "no longer be children, tossed to and fro and carried about with every wind of doctrine" (Eph. 4:11,14, RSV).

We welcome in Dr Blake's report those passages in which he stresses the importance of pan-Christian firmness in face of heretical modern trends in theology, which are endeavouring to situate on this earth the only Son of God who is in the bosom of the Father (John 1:18) and to humanize completely the Word which was with God in the beginning. It was only later that "the Word became flesh, and dwelt among us" (Gal. 4:4; John 1:14) and now sits at the right hand of the Father as God-Man. "Although I am sure that the posture and attitude of the ecumenical movement towards the proponents of 'new theological views' must be pastoral and attentive" (said Dr Blake) "I believe it to be highly important that we do not give reason to anyone to suppose that we as a World

Council of Churches are calling into question the being of the God and Father of the Lord Jesus Christ who is revealed in the Bible to the eye of faith."[12]

However, a pastoral attitude towards those who support modernist views must not on any account give the impression that we are prepared to accept any attitude whatsoever in the interpretation of the Christian faith. There is a limit, beyond which "free thinking" becomes destructive of Christian faith, and of Christian unity.

With regard to Dr Blake's ideas about "a revolutionary new obedience to Jesus Christ", and about the influence of the WCC in this direction, we Orthodox consider it our duty to show a certain prudence and reserve here. Undoubtedly "the renewal of mind" which enables one to discern "what is the will of God, what is good and acceptable and perfect" (Rom. 12:2) is an extremely important and constant law of the Christian life. If they are not to die spiritually, the People of God must, through a free manifestation of His will, collaborate constantly with the Spirit of God in the renewal of hearts (Ezech. 18:31) and of " a willing spirit" (Ps. 51:12). However, it is difficult to say what form this process ought to assume today — evolutionary or revolutionary. We are not infallible prophets. When we hear statements like the following: "It is quite clear that controversial revolutionary changes are required of us and our churches in our time"[13], we involuntarily feel that it is a somewhat risky generalization. Possibly it is natural for Protestant theologians not only to think, but also to speak, in terms of a stormy dynamism, which tends (like the prophet Elijah) to expect the Lord to manifest Himself in the earthquake and the fire rather than in the "still small voice" (1 Kings 19:11-12).

In any case the Orthodox Churches do not feel any such burning need for a "revolutionary" renewal of their ecclesial life. This is not due to any routine, nor to ignorance of the changes taking place in the world, nor to unawareness of the "spiritual ecumenism" that is so aptly stressed in the Decree on Ecumenism of the Second Vatican Council (Para. 8). It is due to the very nature of Orthodoxy which prefers quiet *aggiornamento* to violent reforms which often have sad and irreparable consequences. One example of this is the well-known "renewal" which took place within the Russian Church in the 1920's. It would be desirable for all the arguments concerning the need for renewal in church life to be subject to ecumenical discussion; they should be included in the official documents in an absolutely clear form, so as to avoid any suspicion, or misunderstanding, and too vague generalizations.

In his report on "The Transcendence of God" given in Crete, Dr Blake also said that the Churches belonging to the World Council of Churches must always be ready to transcend the influence of their environment, which might limit or alter their judgment. "The attempt to transcend all human limitations and the faith that God makes such transcendence possible is at the heart of the ecumenical movement."[14] Of course, everything must be spiritually discerned, especially the gifts of the Spirit of God (1 Cor. 2:14). However, such an extreme spiritualization of the Church's thought, which endeavours to transcend all human limitations and to rise above all national and state interests, is not always in accordance with the will of God and with the true spirit of the Gospel, which reminds us to "render to Caesar the things that are Caesar's, and to God the things that are God's" (Matt. 22:21). It is better to follow the plain but sound advice of the Apostle: "Test everything; hold fast what is good" (1 Thess. 5:21).

Lastly, Dr Blake said that "the World Council of Churches must find the way to speak in the faith that the guidance of the Holy Spirit will be available to us all together in a way that guidance is not so fully available to any of us separately."[15] This can only be regarded as a personal opinion. Although the possibility of illumination from on high cannot be completely excluded ("the Spirit blows where it wills", John 3:8), in the Orthodox view there is no adequate ground for such generalizations.

One of the constant temptations of the World Council of Churches is the desire of certain ecumenists to discover a "new ecclesiological reality" among the churches belonging to the WCC. Of course, it is possible in principle to transcend the Christian consciousness; this would mean the disposition to unite on the basis of the apostolic heritage, preserved in its integrity and expressed by the early undivided Church. I will go further; the faith that God will enable us to do so may really be called the heart of the ecumenical movement. If the association of Churches belonging to the WCC really manifested (with the necessary fullness) the characteristics of the Church of Christ such as holiness, catholicity and apostolicity, it would mean that with the aid of the Spirit of Truth the nature of that fellowship will really be transformed in the way desired by the God-Man, the Son of God, who prayed His heavenly Father "that they may all be one" (John 17:21).

For the moment, unfortunately, there is no sign of any transcendence of this kind!

The slowness with which confessional unity is growing is manifest not only in the divergences in the doctrinal documents adopted by the WCC but also in the fear recently shown when the question was raised of modifying the Basis of the WCC. Some ecumenists compared this attempt with the attempt "to open Pandora's box". At New Delhi no calamity occurred; although a new Basis was adopted, Pandora's box did not fly open. But no one is likely to propose any modification in the Basis, for instance by making membership in the World Council of Churches conditional on confession of the Nicene Creed.

In any case, it is impossible to speak of any essential change in the nature of the churches belonging to the WCC as long as ecumenical cooperation is centred exclusively on joint action between representatives of two main church-groups: the Orthodox and the Protestant, while the direct dialogue between these same Churches does not yet seem able to bear sufficient fruit. That is just why we Orthodox firmly insist on the inviolability of the principles laid down in the *Toronto Statement*, as expressed in its third part. We fully support the remark made by one of our ecumenical brethren and mentioned by Dr Visser 't Hooft in his report on "The Meaning of Membership in the World Council of Churches"[16]. "'Let us continue in fellowship, without too much self-consciousness which might become an occasion for pride.' It is better to live with a reality which transcends definition than to live with a definition which claims more substance than exists."

It is with optimism and hope that we perceive all the complications and difficulties of our common Christian path towards unity, inspired by love for the God-Man Jesus Christ our Lord, striving to increase faith and love for Him in the whole world, we will go forward. We will continue the ecumenical movement; for before us, like a Good Shepherd (John 10:4) goes the Saviour and Redeemer of the world, He who makes all things new (Rev. 21:5), He who is the way, and the truth and the life (John 14:6).

NOTES

[1] Published in French in *Messager*, No. 21, 1955, pp. 9-32.
[2] Amsterdam Report, p. 197.
[3] *Ibid.*, pp. 127-128.
[4] Minutes of the Central Committee, Rochester, 1963, p. 138.

[5] Address by Archbishop Nikodim at the Council of Bishops in 1961. See *Journal of the Moscow Patriarchate*, 1961, No. 8, p. 19.

[6] Amsterdam Report, p. 127.

[7] Evanston Report, p. 306.

[8] The New Delhi Report, p. 116.

[9] *Ibid.*, p. 117, para. 4.

[10] *New Directions in Faith and Order*, Bristol 1967, pp. 48, 153-154.

[11] Report of Central Committee, Crete, August 1967, p. 102.

[12] *Ibid.*, p. 101.

[13] *Ibid.*, p. 103, para. 7.

[14] *Ibid.*, p. 102, last sentence.

[15] *Ibid.*, p. 102, last paragraph.

[16] Report of Central Committee, Rochester, 1963, p. 138.

Declaration of the Ecumenical Patriarchate

On the Occasion of the 25th Anniversary
of the World Council of Churches, 1973

I

1. The Lord "who came to save us" accomplishes His redemptive work at "sundry times and in diverse manners". He constantly accompanies His people and through the grace of the Comforter, He builds and fosters the life of the Church, at every moment giving Her new vision, new ways of life and new activity, in order that His will may in all things be done and His kingdom be extended on earth.

2. The 20th century has offered to the Christian churches a possibility of seeing and experiencing this reality. The ecumenical movement which has long been a living reality, and the World Council of Churches which for twenty-five years has existed as a coherent expression and organized form of this movement, constitute one of the ways chosen by the Lord to make mankind more aware of His "new commandment" of love, and His Church more obedient to His teachings of reconciliation, peace and concord.

3. The Ecumenical Patriarchate is most happy to share in the celebration of the twenty-fifth anniversary of the foundation of the World Council of Churches, and attaches the highest significance to this occasion.

This period of a quarter of a century is an irrefutable witness of the churches' precious experience of their common march towards mutual acceptance and understanding, of their common activities in favour of reunion, and of their desire to walk in dialogue and in mutual love and fellowship so as "not to hinder the Gospel of Christ" (I Cor. 9:12), and in order "that the world may know the only true God and Jesus Christ" (John 17:3), as God and Saviour.

4. On this significant day the Apostolic Church of Constantinople ascribes praise and glory to God for everything achieved up to the present in the ecumenical field, and prays that the efforts for the coming together and final reunion of all that are jointly undertaken by the member churches of the World Council of Churches, may advance and be continually strengthened, "in one hope of our calling, one faith, one baptism, and in one Lord", that is to say in the one and eternal kingdom of God "who is above all, and through all and in us all" (Eph. 4:4-6), the Eternal Father.

5. This Ecumenical Throne also gratefully remembers those who have dedicated themselves to the ecumenical vision and who have now departed this life into eternity still hoping and looking for unity. It further remembers with warm appreciation all those who now untiringly work in obedience to the spirit of unity and all those whose valuable work, at all levels of responsibility in the ecumenical movement, contributes to the advance of the work of the World Council of Churches.

• Translated from the Greek original.

II

6. Now that twenty-five years of historical ecumenical striving have passed, we can naturally see more clearly the true dimensions of what has been achieved. As we start to review and evaluate what has happened we think first of those positive and fruitful initiatives within the ecumenical movement taken since the beginning of this century by the Ecumenical Patriarchate: the 1902 Encyclical by which the Ecumenical Throne called the whole Christian world to co-operation and common action; the second Encyclical of 1920, addressed "to the Christian churches wherever they may be", and which called them to "love one another whole-heartedly with all your strength" (I Peter 1:22); its particular contributions before, during and after the foundation of the World Council of Churches in 1948; and the 1952 Encyclical concerning relationships with the World Council of Churches and the various forms of participation in its debates and activities; these together constitute a humble sign and witness of the contribution of this Throne to the aims and work of the Council, which it has undertaken either on its own initiative or in close co-operation with its sister Orthodox churches.

7. Today it will be admitted by all that the Orthodox presence in the Council has borne fruit in many positive achievements and in the mutual enrichment of the Council and its member churches. The broadening of the Basis of the Constitution of the World Council of Churches, for example, in accordance with a proper trinitarian approach; the clarification of the theology of mission as basic to the aims of the One, Holy, Catholic and Apostolic Church; the recognition of the need to abandon former methods of proselytism and the unequivocal condemnation of these, along with the reaching of a common definition of the basic principles of religious liberty which allow for the respecting of the Christian witness of the other; the taking up into ecumenical theological studies of such traditional themes as an understanding of Holy Tradition, the witness of the Fathers and of the Ecumenical Councils, the Christology of Chalcedon, the doctrines of the Holy Spirit, of the nature and essential marks of the Church, of baptism, of the Eucharist, of the sacred ministry, and so forth; all these are signs of the enriching presence of Orthodoxy in the Council. There have also been several significant clarifications of tendencies that gave cause for concern within the Orthodox Church, in the early years of the Council in the discussions of the *Una Sancta* and of the famous statement "The Church, the Churches and the World Council of Churches", or more recently in the abandonment of the attempt to transform the Council into an "Ecumenical Council" or of the tendency to favour "inter-communion". These too point to the positive presence of Orthodoxy in the Council, in which today, on the initiative of the Ecumenical Patriarchate, all Orthodox Churches are participating as members.

8. On the other hand, it will also unanimously be admitted that these past 25 years have been equally enriching for Orthodoxy, whether in the fields of Church life and theological thinking or in that of generous, material expressions of Christian solidarity, help and love. These have all helped to build up Christ in the hearts of millions of distressed Christians and their fellow-sufferers. They have all contributed — and still do so — to the widening of human sympathies and the opening up to one another of Christian churches and traditions which all confess the same Lord.

III

9. The World Council of Churches has thus undoubtedly known twenty-five years of fruitful achievement. Yet as is inevitable in an institution characterized by movement and growth, it is today facing a time of self-criticism, even crisis. The Ecumenical Patriarchate, together with the whole of Orthodoxy, out of their profound trust in the Council, is following these critical developments with close attention.

10. As is well known, the World Council of Churches is constantly tending to move into new fields of activity. Its original calling to serve the churches in their witness and service to individuals, nations and to the world as a whole for the sake of their salvation has naturally led it to see its work as touching on many facets of the life of a world in travail. The problems of this world are inevitably the Council's problems, because they are the problems of the Christian churches themselves.

11. Contemporary social evils have many causes — secularization, rationalistic and materialistic teachings and tendencies, organized atheism, violence, corruption, unbridled licence, subversive movements, the hot-headedness of youth, racism, the arms race, war. These lead to the oppression of the masses, social inequality, economic misery, the uneven distribution and frequent scarcity of consumer goods, erosion and the despoiling of nature, the undernourishment and hunger of millions, the violent uprooting of men and families, to refugees, migration, illiteracy, to ecological irresponsibility, the problems of development in our unevenly industrialized and exploited world, the threatening crisis of population, over-ambitious ideas of conquering space and of a grandiose future. These all make up the untold sufferings of striving humanity in our time. The World Council of Churches knows itself called from within the family of mankind to make some effort to tackle the challenges of these many and ever-increasing demands.

12. That throws up, however, the question whether it is these issues and only these which properly constitute the objectives and orientation of the World Council of Churches. This is a fundamental question. The Council's member churches must apply themselves to finding the true answer, since it is here that the crisis threatening the ecumenical movement as a whole and the World Council of Churches in particular takes its root.

13. The divergent opinions on this point are already much discussed. Some consider the World Council of Churches as an organization pursuing certain social and political aims on behalf of the churches, which only looks into the theological considerations to do with those aims in so far as they can help to justify positions the Council and the Churches have already adopted. Others however see the Council in an exactly opposite way — as a forum for the theological discussion of the familiar patterns of doctrinal differences that lie behind the divisions of the churches and are still perpetuating these.

14. As faithful guardian of the unswerving position of Orthodoxy that honours the faith and doctrine entrusted to us, the Ecumenical Patriarchate considers that the impasse to which this polarization is leading can only be overcome if a proper balance is held between these equally extreme interpretations of the aims, hopes, indeed of the very *raison d'être* of the World Council of Churches.

15. To spell it out more fully, the Ecumenical Throne believes as follows:

a) The World Council of Churches is and must remain a "Council of Churches", as the Basis of its Constitution expressly declares. As such, it is to serve the churches in their wider efforts towards unity and co-operation among the family of mankind which, though divided, has within it the seeds of the fundamental unity of humanity. For as the human race is linked to the Creator by a single man — the first Adam — so also it is kept in unity with God the Father through a single man, the second Adam.

16. b) As an institution dedicated to the service of the churches, the World Council of Churches must at all times act as a specific organ of the churches in their common search for their proper unity, now damaged and elusive, whether in drawing out the common points of grace, truth and faith entrusted to them or in the investigation and resolution of the questions that divide them.

17. c) In this respect the World Council of Churches has to face a clearly defined challenge. On the one hand it is called to seek to include among its members certain churches who have not yet seen fit to join it — in particular the Roman Catholic Church — but with whom it is conducting extensive and prolonged negotiations. On the other, it seems to be interested in incorporating within itself a number of groups and movements which are neither churches nor linked with the churches. The Ecumenical Patriarchate expressly states that a constructive openness of heart on the part of all concerned is to be encouraged with respect to the eventual possible admission of these other churches, particularly that of the Roman Catholic Church, once the present difficulties and scruples have been resolved. This would truly enrich the World Council of Churches and give it still wider ecumenical standing. At the same time, the opposite tendency to incorporate non-church groupings must be restrained, since to follow it any further would not only put the World Council of Churches off its true course but would also gravely embarrass many of the present member churches.

18. d) As it works towards the fulfilment of its basic aims, the World Council of Churches must inevitably become involved in profound theological study, allowing each participating member to present its faith and doctrine openly, directly and with full theological integrity, and then bringing these various positions into dialogue so that from the apparent plurality of their teachings there may be distilled the unique revealed truth of Jesus Christ, as witnessed to us both by Holy Scripture and by Sacred Tradition. On this truth alone can any unity enabled within the World Council of Churches be founded and built up.

19. e) The World Council of Churches offers the churches a wide range of opportunities to make a common witness, whether in words or by deeds, in freedom and co-responsibility to the world. This can be done both by proclaiming the one and undivided Christ and by the mediation of His salvation to contemporary man.

20. f) As an organ which cannot take the place of the churches but is to act in their name and on their behalf towards the problems and sufferings of mankind today, the World Council must never forget the basic characteristic of human life; namely that whatever his longing to overcome the most pressing social and political problems, man knows himself as hungering for an answer to a still more profound question: What is the reason for human life on earth? What does it mean to be a person, a moral being, one who reaches out for something beyond this present life, for something ultimate and endlessly satisfying? The World Council of Churches must always have regard to the three dimensions of human life: that of his created nature, that of his moral obedience, and that of Christ's gracious calling.

21. g) The World Council of Churches must equally take seriously the reactions of our contemporaries to what the churches are offering, however justified or unjustified these reactions may be. It must weigh the reasons why so many object to the churches and their teachings, perhaps because of certain features of these. By doing so, the World Council of Churches may discover more appropriate ways of expressing

Christian doctrine. Its voice would then be neither that of one secular movement among many others, nor that of a sterile bureaucracy, but a living prophetic voice, the Word of Christ.

22. h) As an instrument of the churches which is engaged not only in theological studies but also in projects of love and mutual solidarity, and thus precisely by that mutual support making both witness and service to the men and nations of today, the World Council of Churches must persist in its efforts ever more widely and positively to meet the manifold sufferings of mankind. It is by doing this — whether by words or deeds, by visible or invisible actions, in all possible ways and at all possible times — that it will be proclaiming Christ and Christ alone. Any pursuit of aims foreign to its nature or which could move it away from its original and specifically churchly, spiritual goals, is on this account to be strictly avoided.

23. In formulating these views and requests concerning the future of the World Council of Churches, the Ecumenical Patriarchate is convinced that it is pursuing a straightforward and consistent course, as it always has done in its relationship with the Council. This is to take a proper share in the Council's work, with love and humility. This is also to share in the common desire and striving of the churches for yet greater effectiveness in our common search for the unity of all.

24. The Ecumenical Patriarchate wishes the World Council of Churches a long and blessed life of active service; of true witness amidst the suffering of mankind; and of heartfelt contributions to the upbuilding of the churches. May God bless all its efforts for unity. May the day be near when the Lord will fulfil the longing of the churches that there be "one flock, one shepherd" (John 10:14) in His one and no longer divided Church "which is His body and as such holds within it the fullness of Him who Himself receives the entire fullness of God" (Eph. 1:23).

At the Ecumenical Patriarchate
16 August 1973

Report of an Inter-Orthodox Consultation
"Confessing Christ through the Liturgical Life of the Church Today"
Etchmiadzine, Armenia, 16-21 September 1975

I. Witness and worship

1. Throughout history, the worship of the Church has been the expression and guardian of divine revelation. Not only did it express and represent the saving events of Christ's life, death, resurrection and ascension to heaven but it also was for the members of the Church, the living anticipation of the kingdom to come. In worship, the Church, being the Body of Christ enlivened by the Holy Spirit, unites the faithful, as the adopted sons and daughters of God, the Father.

2. Liturgical worship is an action of the Church and is centred around the Eucharist. Although the sacrament of the Eucharist, since the very origin of the Church, was a celebration closed to the outsiders, and full participation in the Eucharist remains reserved for the members of the Church, liturgical worship as a whole is an obvious form of witness and mission.

3. The human person, through membership in the worshipping community, in spiritual poetry, in church music, in iconography, with body and soul (I Cor. 6:20), actively participates in the gifts of grace. This involvement of the entire human nature — and not only of reason — in glorifying God, is an essential factor of Orthodox worship. It must be preserved and developed as a powerful means of Christian witness.

4. The involvement of the whole of man in the liturgical action presupposes that sanctification reaches not only man as an individual but his entire environment. The reverse is also true; one should take account of the fact that each Christian who actively participates in worship may bring into it his cultural heritage and personal creativity. This process presupposes a selection, based on Christian and moral values. Not everything in all cultural forms, known in the unredeemed world, is qualified to serve as meaningful liturgical expression. However, at all times, in the culture of the various nations, the Church has succeeded in finding and adopting cultural forms, which, through their richness and variety, were able to communicate the Gospel to these peoples in a manner akin to their mentality and their historical traditions.

5. The fact that Orthodoxy readily embraced the various national cultures and used them as powerful tools of mission does not mean that the unity of the Church — a God-established mark of the Body of Christ (Rom. 12:5) — can be sacrificed to values belonging to ethnic cultures (Col. 3:10-11; Gal. 3:28).

6. Worship is the centre of the life of the Church, but it should also determine the whole life of every Christian. "Every tree that does not bear good fruit is cut down and thrown into fire. Thus you will know them by their fruits. Not every one who says to me 'Lord, Lord' shall enter the Kingdom of heaven, but he who does the will of my Father who is in heaven" (Matt. 7:20-23). The realization of these words of Christ has a great significance for the success of the Christian mission.

7. Christ said: "Go ye therefore and make disciples of all nations, baptizing them in the name of the Father, and of the Son, and of the Holy Spirit" (Matt. 28:19). This means that together with worship other forms of Christian activity have great importance for mission, such as preaching, publications, personal contacts, welfare, religious education, youth movements, renewal of monastic life, etc. Each church should take advantage of these forms of mission if they are available to it.

8. In order to become a really powerful expression of the Church's mission in the world, worship must be meaningfully understood by its participants (I Cor. 14:6-15). We have discussed those aspects of the Orthodox Liturgy which may make it appear as frozen and thus irrelevant. We are convinced of the necessity of making the liturgical language used in some countries more accessible to the average faithful, and we have considered the desirability to take initiatives (with the blessing of ecclesiastical authorities) which would make our forms of worship more comprehensible to young people (for example, catechetical explanations could precede the services). We agreed that preaching, being an essential part of worship, should never be omitted, whatever the number of those present at every occasion.

9. Among the means of achieving the participation of a greater number of faithful in the liturgical life of the Church, we have considered particularly, wherever possible, a greater involvement of the laity, including women, in those forms of worship which are allowed to them by the Church, especially in congregational singing, and also, wherever that is possible, the establishment of new worshipping communities outside the existing parishes and temples.

II. Proclamation of the Gospel in worship

A clarification of the word "liturgy" is necessary. In the vocabulary of the Orthodox churches the word liturgy refers to the central action of the corporate worship, which is the Divine Liturgy, the Liturgy. Traditionally, the sacraments were linked with the Divine Liturgy. The practice is still the same with the ordination of the deacon, the priest, and the bishop. However, the sacraments of baptism and chrismation, as well as of matrimony, are occasionally linked with the Divine Liturgy.

1. Proclamation should not be taken only in the narrow sense of an informative preaching of the Truth but above all of incorporating man into the mystical union with God. At every step of the Liturgy we encounter the Word of God.

The saving events of the divine economy although chronologically belonging to the past, through the Holy Spirit's action transcend time's limitation, become really present, and the faithful in the here and now live that which historically belongs to the past, and to the eschaton. In the Liturgy we do not have simply a memorial, but a living reality. It is an epicletic contemplation and consecration. A continuous "parousia", a real presence of Christ emerges liturgically.

Holy Scriptures and Liturgy must not be isolated as self-contained autonomous entities. They are established to remain together, united forever.

To whom to proclaim?

2. The Incarnation was for the whole people of all ages and redemption of the whole cosmos. The Holy Eucharist was instituted, among other things, to proclaim the death and the resurrection of our Lord "until He comes again". Thus, the following categories of people should directly or indirectly hear the message of the Holy Eucharist:

a) the members of the Church who try sincerely to practice the faith should be made true evangelists by the Gospel proclaimed to them: St John Chrysostom said: "I do not believe in the salvation of any one who does not try to save others";

b) the nominal Christians who attend the Church just as a routine;

c) the mobile population, migrant workers, refugees, etc., some of whom have no permanent roots anywhere under the sun;

d) people of the diaspora of our modern age;

e) the non-Christians in the vicinity of our congregations and churches who are still to a large extent strangers to the healing and radiating power of the Gospel;

f) the fields where no one ever preached the Gospel.

How to proclaim the Gospel?

3. We have to state that during the Liturgy the readings from the Holy Scripture are done not as self-centred service and action, but in the service of the liturgical life of the Church. To accomplish the mission of the Church in proclaiming the Gospel, a variety of methods and approaches must be used, according to the possibilities and the needs of the local church:

a) the faithful should have continual education in understanding the meaning of the Liturgy and the message of the Gospel;

b) meaningful literature should be published, such as informative pamphlets, pictorial and illustrated publications, volumes of new homilies and sermons, etc.;

c) new forms of worship in the pattern of the old ones should be developed, having in mind the special needs of contemporary society (i.e. of travellers, youth, children, men in industry);

d) an effort must be made to bring into everyday life the liturgical rhythm of consecration of the time (matins, hours, vespers, saints days, feast days);

e) the mass media of television, radio, newspapers and others must be used;

f) a personal contact of the faithful should be established with the non-believers in order to transmit the personal spiritual experiences gained by a meaningful participation in the Liturgy;

g) as in the days following the Pentecost, a sharing "community" must be created to make the whole Church a practising "community of the saints and a holy nation";

h) a revision should be considered of the theological training of the priests, by emphasizing the importance of making them aware of the needs for pastoral care, missionary zeal and the proclamation of the Word;

i) the Orthodox Church should seriously study the renewing of the old tradition of having the order of the deaconess, as this is mentioned in the early Ecumenical Councils.

The Liturgy must not be limited to the celebration in the Church but has to be continued in the life of the faithful in all dimensions of life.

III. Witness and liturgical spirituality

1. It belongs to the very nature of the Church to bear witness to the Gospel in the world. This witness is rooted in the advent of the Spirit at Pentecost.

2. From Pentecost until the Parousia, the Risen Christ is made manifest and present by the Holy Spirit in the liturgical life, through word and sacraments. The whole life and prayer of the Church's members, whether meeting together for common worship

or celebrating each one "in the temple of the heart", centres on the Eucharist. Here all the prayers and liturgical acts of the people of God converge; here the Church discovers its true identity. In the whole field of Christian spirituality, eucharistic spirituality creates a dynamic piety, mystical bands with Christ, which overcome evil by living fully the mystery of incarnation and divinization in all its dimensions. Eucharistic man is in reality a human being who overcomes the conditioning of our fallen nature.

3. In the liturgical celebration, extending into the daily life of the Church's members, the Church announces and achieves the Advent of the Kingdom of the Holy Trinity. In all things, it commemorates the glorified Christ and gives thanks to God in Jesus Christ. The entire Tradition of the Church, its worship, its theology, and its preaching, is a doxology, a continual thanksgiving, a confession of faith in Christ's Easter triumph and man's liberation from all the forces which oppress and degrade him. Prayer and the Eucharist, whereby Christians overcome their selfish ways, impel them also to become involved in the social and political life of their respective countries.

4. The whole Church bears witness to the Good News of the renewal of the divine life in our fallen world. When the Church rediscovers its essence as a fellowship, we begin to live as the Church and not simply in the Church. The Church then ceases to be an oppressive structure and becomes again for its members the Father's House, providing them with shelter and with the heavenly bread. Here are developed the individual gifts in all their rich diversity — prayer, love, wisdom, testimony — all contributing to the upbuilding of the one Body of Christ.

What is the proper place of the individual members, and of women in particular, in this Church of Christ which is essentially a fellowship? In a time when equal rights are being affirmed, do we not have to remember that it is in the Body of Christ that woman finds both her true place and the forms of service which accord with her nature and her gifts?

5. The Church ensures the continuity and the authenticity of prayer by the variety and richness of its liturgical and sacramental life. The life of the Christian, renewed by the Holy Spirit, is founded on prayer. Through prayer, the Christian rediscovers his deepest roots, his bonds with life. In the spiritual life which it nourishes and which it prepares, the liturgical celebration finds its indispensable continuation.

6. A whole Orthodox spirituality is involved here: a spirituality which embraces the great variety of ways whereby human life is sanctified and which, through fasting and ascesis, makes it possible for man to participate in the divine life both physically and with the whole range of his faculties; a sanctification which also includes the human mind, in which its arrogant self-sufficiency is conquered and illumination granted to it in the confession of faith and in the act of praise. Orthodox spirituality is thus a tried and tested school in which human beings are initiated into the mystery of God, the mystery of His love and of His salvation accomplished and communicated. This tuition is given and received by various forms of spiritual and pastoral guidance, by confession, and it culminates in the authentic creation of a new life by the Holy Spirit, a life in which "it is no longer I that live but Christ lives in me".

The important educative role of the ikon, and of liturgical art in general, in this initiation into an understanding of the mysteries of the Church and of faith cannot be overstressed. The Church seeks to order the whole life of man by the sanctification of time, by the liturgical cycles, the celebration of the year's festivals, the observances of fasts, the practice of ascesis, and regular visitation. But it is in the ever-living communion of the saints that the Church's faith is experienced and passed on in the most intense and purest form.

7. We must not treat the common spirituality of the people of God and monastic spirituality as if these were mutually opposed. Nor must we restrict to just a few people the continual invocation of the blessed Name of Jesus. In Orthodoxy we attach great value to the plurality of forms and expressions of Christian devotion. At every stage in his spiritual journey, the Christian receives the gifts of the Holy Spirit in rich measure and can achieve the perfection to which he is called.

The most authentic experience of the monastic tradition provides the whole Church with an inner stimulus to liturgical and ecclesial renewal, to spiritual rebirth, and to an authentic testimony of the whole of man's life to Christ Jesus in the world. Reconciled in the very depths of his being, the Christian seeks not so much merely to speak of the Gospel as rather to proclaim the Risen Christ to his fellow human beings by his whole life. "Acquire a spirit of peace", St Seraphin of Sarov used to say, "and thousands will find salvation in your company".

Recommendations

I.   We recommend that a detailed study be made of the sanctifying role of Orthodox worship and spirituality within the whole range of human culture and in all the variety of man's creative activity in the earthly city.

II.   We have not gone deeply into the question of the contemporary liturgical renewal. We were mindful, however, of the rediscovery of ceaseless prayer, or again, of the contemporary revival of interest in and study of the teaching of the Church Fathers on the liturgy or on the practice of ascesis as a fundamental condition of spiritual progress and discernment. But we also believe that an effort should be made to recover the sense of the importance of the monastic life as a fundamental and indispensable dimension of the witness of the whole Church in the world.

Report of an Inter-Orthodox Consultation
"Orthodox Women: Their Role and Participation in the Orthodox Church"

Agapia, Romania, 11-17 September 1976

At the initiative of the World Council of Churches Unit on Education and Renewal, women from Orthodox Churches of both the Eastern and Oriental traditions met at the women's monastery of Agapia to discuss "The Role of Orthodox Women in the Church and in Society". The meeting, which took place from 11-17 September 1976, was held in the Moldavian region of Romania at the invitation of the Romanian Orthodox Church and under the patronage of Metropolitan Justin of Moldavia.

Meeting for the first time, the participants attempted to share their experiences and to articulate the problems they face in their commitment to the Church in its life and in society today. In the light of their different cultural and social situations, important questions were discussed concerning Education and Vocation of Women in the Church, Family in Church Life, Witness in Society, and Participation in the Ecumenical Movement. It was recommended that the question of the ordination of women be studied in the light of the Orthodox Tradition for a more effective articulation of the Orthodox position in the ecumenical dialogue.

Special concern was noted for the human problems confronting women in societies involved in political conflicts, and particularly for refugees, orphans and other victims of such conflicts. The Consultation also responded to the expressed needs of women to become more involved in theological education, church administration and decision-making in all levels of Church life, social service, religious and spiritual education in the Church, monasticism, and the strengthening of family life.

The members of the Consultation also experienced the liturgical and spiritual life of the Agapia Women's Monastery and the other monasteries in Moldavia, which served to deepen the experience of love and fellowship which developed in the Consultation.

OUR CONCERNS

Family

The biblical account of the creation affirms the fundamental unity and equality between man and woman (Gen. 1:27). The family is the response to a Divine call, a call to live in communion. It is through love that human fullness is realized in the couple; it is a love of becoming and which ought to be continually nourished. The man and the woman have been chosen and consecrated in the sacrament of marriage to the service of Him who calls and gathers, and who unites humanity in love. The work of the Church is the creation of communities of which the first cell, the building block, is the community established by marriage for the purpose of perpetuating in history the edification of the Body of Christ.

In the Church, the accent has always been placed on the priority of the family, as the image of communities and social groups. Each Orthodox Church should find resources for training the family for its missionary and liturgical role.

The family provides the environment where the experience of faith manifests itself in a communal way. In the Orthodox Church, the liturgical and sacramental life is the context in which the faith is lived and expressed. The role of parents is essential in helping children to discover the meaning of Christian life through the liturgy — by preparing them for the reading and proclamation of the Gospel, the celebration of feasts and fasts, and participation in the sacraments.

Though the education of the child rests upon the parents, nevertheless, one cannot overlook the influence that other family members might have on them, such as godparents, aunts, uncles and grandparents; the authority of parents is often questioned and godparents and relatives must help the parents in the task of educating their children.

The family must be liberated from the oppressions it has suffered in the past, so that women may be relieved of the many burdens which inhibit them from making their specific contribution.

The dignity of the woman, particularly that of the mother, is blessed in the Church by certain rituals and prayers inspired by the Old Testament and which refer to the uncleanliness of woman. Such rituals and prayers ought to be re-examined in the light of New Testament texts (Acts 10:15; John 2:1-11; 1 Tim. 2:15).

Monasticism

In Orthodox societies, the role of monasticism expresses a parallel life-style to that of family. Many comparisons can be drawn between the elements of the family community and the monastic community. The virtues inherent in monasticism — of obedience, humility and chastity — are also necessary in family life and find their particular expression in motherhood. Education in many monastic communities is communicated in a manner similar to the way it is given in a family — from mother to daughter or from father to son, in the spiritual relationship of spiritual mothers or fathers in monastic communities with their spiritual children. For this reason, monastic communities are also centers to which lay persons come for spiritual education and enlightenment.

In some countries, such as Romania, capable women in the monastic communities are given the opportunity of pursuing higher theological studies. Such a practice is commendable as it not only helps to deepen the theological understanding of the person who is dedicated to a contemplative life, but it also provides the monastic community with its own staff of teachers for the various levels of education required in the community.

Noting the lack of monastic centers and vocations in the Orthodox diaspora, it is necessary for Churches and Church or Sunday schools to give more attention to information about the monastic life.

Society

Orthodox women are aware of the fact that there are many obstacles preventing them from fulfilling their mission and duties, both in society and in the Church. However, the problems which need the attention of women are many: that of refugees, delinquents, prisoners, migrants and the unemployed, as well as the more general questions of the participation of Christian women in humanitarian and governmental bodies, mass media and artistic life which contribute to the shaping of the society.

Women are especially capable of organizing and providing special assistance and care for the poor, the aged, orphans, and those confined by illness in homes and hospitals. Women are also needed to staff special nurseries for children of working mothers. Specially trained women can assist the clergy in helping families to resolve conflicts, to meet the needs of broken families or those in the process of divorce, and especially to provide a special care and concern for the children in these families who face many difficulties and frustrations because of such circumstances.

Women must be encouraged to think out for themselves possible forms of cooperation and common action with other Christians in their particular societies. An example of a possible common concern is the care of migrant workers and particularly women migrants in a number of countries. Orthodox women might be in a position to set up some form of action of their own, or to associate themselves with existing programmes.

Many women are already serving their Church and community in the area of mission, social and welfare services, leadership training, youth work, etc. Churches should enable such women to increase their skills by assisting them to acquire additional education and training for this important work.

Education

Education is integrally related to the role of women in Church and society. Without proper religious training at all levels, including higher theological studies, the role of woman and her participation in all aspects of Church life is limited. Therefore, the concern for the education of Orthodox women is also the concern for their increased involvement in witness and service in the Church.

The family is the primary educational unit for the religious growth and development of the Orthodox Christian. In order to encourage and strengthen the educational role of the family, special training programmes for parents are needed to equip them for the task of preparing their children for participation in the life of the Church.

Lay persons, including women, should be given adequate training so that they may participate in the formal education of children in Church or Sunday schools. Parish councils, in which women can and should play a significant role, need to consider seriously their responsibilities in this educational task providing the necessary training, equipment, classrooms and materials for the education of all the members of the Church.

Special conferences and workshops in theological and psychological studies need to be organized in order to provide a sound foundation for such service. Higher theological studies should be encouraged for Sunday school directors and those responsible for the training of teachers.

In order to promote the increasing and widening role of women in service to the Church, opportunities need to be provided by parishes and dioceses for the higher theological training of Orthodox women. Such studies are important, not only for those who wish to be professionally engaged in the work of the Church, but for those who seek to be better informed lay persons, so that the life of the local parish may be enriched by the benefit of their educational experience.

Seminaries and Church councils at all levels are encouraged to examine the possibilities for new vocations, i.e. professional job opportunities or positions, for theologically trained women who can serve the emerging needs of the Church. Special courses for men (especially for future pastors) and women in theological schools or seminaries may be necessary for the examination of the role of women in the life of the Church, particularly in vocational opportunities for service. Special courses may also need to be added to the curriculum to make the training of women for Church service meaningful and relevant.

The selection of persons as teachers in theological and religious education should be based on competence and not on the person's sex.

Those Church bodies which are concerned with theological reflection and engagement should include theologically qualified women in their membership, and should promote the training of women for participation in such theological discussions.

Church Service

Traditionally, women have assumed a prominent role in the area of Church service in their parishes and local communities. These areas of service continue to be expanded through the higher education of women, especially in theological studies. The leadership and initiative of women is especially significant in the areas of education, social work, church administration and, in recent years, publications.

Women should be encouraged to take an active role in the decision-making bodies of the Church at all levels: in the parish, on the parish council and committees; in the diocese, in departments, committees and clergy-laity assemblies; in the national Church assemblies of clergy and laity, and in the departments and commissions of the Church administration which serve under the authority and direction of the bishops of the Church. They may also at times be called as consultants as these bodies engage in their work.

The inclusion of women in the decision-making bodies of the Church that include laymen is necessary for the following reasons:

a) Such decision-making bodies that laypeople are included in should represent "the whole body of Christ", i.e. all of its members.

b) As men and women bring different charismata, viewpoints and visions of the manner in which the Church can fulfil itself in its witness in society, it is important that all members be given the possibility to participate in this fulfilment. This will bring a mutual enrichment to the life of the Church and enable men and women together to realize and express the "image of God" in their mutual service.

c) As women in our churches are concerned most intimately with family education, youth and adult programmes, charitable and social work, prayer and the strengthening of the liturgical life, they have the ability to discern in a different light what plans and decisions need to be taken on behalf of the whole community at the local, diocesan and national levels.

Parish councils are asked to discern the needs of the Church and the training and skills required to fulfil those needs, e.g. readers, choir directors, cantors, teachers, church secretaries, etc. Women should be encouraged and assisted to receive the training necessary to assume some of these functions in church life.

Women are particularly conscious of the need for catechetical and liturgical materials for home and church use. In the light of the increasing demand for religious publications today, many competent women can provide the skills necessary for the production and promotion of education and news media in the Church. Women can contribute new creative elements to make church publications more accessible to the lay reader in the Church. There is also a need for special articles in existing publications where they may read about the role of women in the Bible and history, lives of women saints, and current news about the work of Orthodox women both at home and abroad.

The question of single women and especially those who have no monastic vocation, but wish to serve the Church, has never been discussed. The Church may consider a ministry for them, in the same sphere as the diaconate or by the creation of other structures.

In the early centuries of the Church and in Byzantine times, the deaconess played a significant role in fulfilling the service, i.e. the true "diakonia" of the Church. In some Churches — in Egypt, for example, where there are over 150 women, fulfilling a diaconal function — this important form of service has been restored to the life of the Church, and in others, a need is felt for providing women with a responsible and full-time vocation in the service of the Church. Although such a need is not universal at present, it is recommended that the office of deaconess be studied and considered for "reactivation" in Churches where the needs of society could be met more effectively by such a service.

a) The content of this diaconal service is similar to that mentioned above in the paragraphs dealing with Church service. The service of the deaconess, however, differs in that it is a service consecrated by the Church, with the blessing of the bishop, and is a life-time commitment to full vocational service in the Church, as presently dictated by the canons of the Church. Necessary adjustments or recommendations concerning the office of deaconess are subject to change by any future Councils of the Church, to meet present-day conditions and needs.

b) It must be noted that the role of the deaconess is that of a "diaconia" and is not a "priestly" function. Its form and content is that of serving and does not have the character of a liturgical-sacramental function, though the very nature of its service is an extension of the sacramental life of the Church into the life of society. The office of deaconess is distinct and is not now, nor can it be considered as a "first step" to the ordained priesthood.

In the light of the increasing debate on the ordination of women to the priesthood in churches of the Western tradition, it would be helpful to Orthodox women if special studies could be conducted on this subject in order to clarify and interpret the Orthodox position to other churches. This is an immediate need, especially for Orthodox women living in Western societies who are continually being engaged in dialogue on this question.

Witness and Ecumenism

Increased Orthodox participation in ecumenical life at the international level has made a great contribution towards the enrichment of the Church throughout the world. It is clear, however, that the participation of Orthodox women was growing very slowly and was often imperceptible. New forms of involvement, however, should continue to be sought.

Ecumenical participation takes place on at least two levels: that of international relations (e.g. World Council of Churches and other bodies) and at the local (parish) or national level, and both have to be taken into account. It is important that women should be included as official delegates of their church to national and international meetings.

There is a need to strengthen the ecumenical education and involvement of women in parishes and the importance of seeking — or forming — new leaders from among the parish membership. By building up this leadership, the churches would be able to draw upon appropriate people to participate in larger-scale, international or regional meetings. An important tool in this process of education is the encouragement of encounters between different Orthodox women's groups and between the Orthodox women's group and other women's organizations at the local level. A means to this end might be the establishment of a Pan-Orthodox Team of 5-6 people who would visit various countries to learn of the church life there, to share some of their life with sister Orthodox Churches, as well as with other confessions, and to foster greater ecumenical and inter-Orthodox awareness.

The members of the consultation expressed the hope that a further consultation, organized by the Orthodox, should be held in the near future, if possible in an Orthodox country or in a place where the participants can take part in the life of the local Orthodox Church.

In view of the recommendation that Orthodox Churches should have a larger representation on the staff of the World Council of Churches, it was hoped that at least one of the additional staff members appointed should be a woman. It was further recommended that the WCC be requested to seek funds for the employment of an Orthodox woman staff member to help in the work begun by the Consultation at Agapia (11-17 September 1976) and to further the concerns expressed by this Consultation.

Report of an Inter-Orthodox Consultation
"The Ecumenical Nature of Orthodox Witness"
New Valamo, Finland, 24-30 September 1977

A Consultation of Orthodox theologians on "The Ecumenical Nature of Orthodox Witness", organized by the Orthodox Task Force of the World Council of Churches, was held at the New Valamo Monastery from 24-30 September 1977, at the invitation of the Orthodox Church of Finland.

The purpose of the Consultation was to respond to certain ecumenical priorities which have emerged since the Fifth Assembly of the WCC in Nairobi, and to bring some Orthodox insights to bear on issues and programmes as these affect the life and activities both of the WCC and of the Churches themselves.

The Consultation dealt with three specific items on today's ecumenical agenda, namely "The Local Church", "The Proclamation and Articulation of our Faith", and "The Churches' Responsibility in the World Today".

The contents of the present report reflect a variety of opinions expressed throughout the meeting and they should be regarded as points calling for further reflection both within the various sub-units of the WCC and in the Orthodox Churches. In considering the main theme of the Consultation we felt it necessary to examine the ecclesiological basis of our ecumenical commitment, namely our eucharistic understanding of the Church.

The Orthodox understand the Church in the light of the Eucharist. The whole life of the Church, the Word and the Sacraments, stem from and find their fulfilment in the Holy Eucharist. Thus the Eucharist is not just a "sacrament", but the great mystery of our participation in the life of the Holy Trinity, the recapitulation of the entire history of salvation in Christ and the foretaste of the Kingdom to come. In the Eucharist, therefore, the Church is placed in the very centre of history, sanctifying and transforming the world, by being a new creation, creating a new mode of life. At the same time she is placed at the end of history as a sign of the Kingdom, judging the world (1 Cor. 5-6) in the light of the eschatological realities of which the Eucharist is a manifestation (cf. *Didache* 10).

The Church which has this eucharistic character is not an abstract or speculative idea, but a concrete reality. Whenever the people of God are gathered together in a certain place (*epi to auto*, see 1 Cor. 11:20) in order to form the eucharistic body of Christ, the Church becomes a reality. The Church, therefore, is primarily identified with the local eucharistic community in each place. It is by being incorporated into this concrete local community that we are saved and proclaim the salvation of the world in Christ "until He comes".

In order to be such a saving community the local Church must overcome and transcend the divisions which sin and death create in the world. The local community is a true and authentic manifestation of the Church of God only if it is catholic in its composition and structure. It cannot be based on divisions and discriminations either of a natural kind, such as race, nation, language, age, sex, physical handicap, etc. or of a social type, such as class, profession, etc.

Even the divisions created by time and space have to be overcome in this community. For this reason the eucharistic community includes in itself also the departed members of the Church, and although it is in fact a *local* community it offers the Eucharist on behalf of the entire "oikoumene", thus acquiring truly *ecumenical* dimensions in which the divisions of space are also overcome.

This catholic nature of the Church which is revealed in the Eucharist is safeguarded through the office of the bishop. The specific ministry of the bishop is to transcend in his person all the divisions that may exist within a particular area and also to relate a local Church to the rest of the local Churches both in space and in time. This link is sacramentally expressed in the synodal consecration of bishops. Because of the character of episcopacy it is essential that there should exist only one bishop in a given area and that all eucharistic communities should acquire their ecclesial authenticity through his ministry. The local Church, therefore, is not necessarily present in every eucharistic assembly but in the episcopal diocese through which each eucharistic gathering acquires its catholic nature.

This understanding of the local Church has always been essential to the Orthodox tradition. In the course of history circumstances often necessitated the creation of larger ecclesial units, such as the metropolis, the patriarchate, the autocephalous church, etc. However, in the function of these units, natural, social or cultural and racial divisions should not distort the original eucharistic understanding of the Church. The canonical structure of the Orthodox Church, as it was formed in the early centuries, has helped and can still help to protect Orthodoxy from succumbing to such dangers.

The community of the Church is united in confessing one faith. This faith is essentially identical with the apostolic teaching and with the "faith once delivered to the Saints". It found its articulation in the entire living tradition of the Church, especially in creeds accepted by the ecumenical Church and in the decisions of the Ecumenical Councils. The Orthodox Church regards the decisions of the Ecumenical Councils as faithful expressions of the one apostolic faith and therefore binding on all the members of the Church.

This faithfulness to past councils, however, must always be understood as a living continuity. This includes two essential aspects: fidelity and renewal, both of which are integral parts of Orthodox life and Orthodox witness. Fidelity is never merely a formal repetition of the things once given, but basically faithfulness to the original apostolic truth, in the spirit of creative obedience. Renewal thus comes to mean, in the first place, responding to new, changing situations on the basis of the truth once given. It may also be said, therefore, that renewal in this sense means the application of the apostolic tradition to contemporary questions and needs. This principle implies, first, that fidelity does not become a sterile, static attitude, without relation to the prevailing human and historical realities and, second, that renewal is not an end in itself nor something which can take just any direction whatsoever, but is always based on the original truth of the apostolic tradition.

This process of applying the apostolic faith to new historical situations explains the idea of the "reception" of a Council. Reception does not mean a "formal approval" of the Council. The faith which is pronounced by a Council establishes itself as Truth, by being received and re-received by the community of the Church in the Holy Spirit. Every form of confession of faith is shown to be in the end a matter of participation in the local eucharistic community. Faith becomes salvation only when it is life in the community of the Church.

This raises the issue of confessionalism. The Orthodox Church possesses its own "confessions" of faith in the forms of creeds and the decisions of the ancient Councils, especially the Ecumenical Councils. This makes it appear as a "confessional body" or "family" and it is often treated as such by the non-Orthodox. And yet such an understanding of Orthodoxy, sometimes encouraged by the Orthodox themselves, would contradict the fundamental character of its ecclesiology.

The Orthodox are actively involved in the ecumenical movement and have been members of the World Council of Churches since its foundation. How can their ecclesiology, as it was described above, fit into the context of this movement and in programmes and activities undertaken by the WCC?

In the first place it must be stressed that the participation of the Orthodox in the ecumenical movement of today is not, in principle, a revolution in the history of Orthodoxy, but it is a natural consequence of the constant prayer of the Church "for the union of all". It constitutes another attempt, like those made in the Patristic period, to apply the apostolic faith to new historical situations and existential demands. What is in a sense new today, is the fact that this attempt is being made together with other Christian bodies with whom there is no full unity. It is here that the difficulties arise, but it is precisely here that there also are many signs of real hope for growing fellowship, understanding and cooperation.

The World Council of Churches is made up mostly of Churches whose identity is basically confessional, in the sense in which we have just defined the word "confession". As a result, they normally see no reason why eucharistic communion should not be practised among the member churches.

The refusal of the Orthodox to practise "intercommunion" is thus seen as arrogance on their part precisely because it is assumed that they are another confessional body which regards itself as superior compared with the rest. In this situation it becomes difficult for the Orthodox to point to an ecclesiology so radically different from that assumed by the other members of the WCC. It is difficult to show in this context that to belong to a confessional body is not the ultimate thing in the Church and that the Orthodox Church regards itself as *the* Church not on a confessional basis but on the basis of the fact that it identifies itself with the eucharistic community in what it regards as its proper and saving form. Only when this is made clear can the frustration stemming from the issue of "intercommunion" be removed. It will be understood why it is more natural for the Orthodox to speak of "communion" rather than of "intercommunion" or "shared eucharist".

But this would lead to further consequences with regard to the Orthodox participation in the ecumenical movement. It will imply a re-orientation of the ecumenical problematic as a whole. This means basically that the unity which we seek in the ecumenical movement cannot be the product of theological agreements, such as a common signing of a *confessio fidei*. Theological work is certainly needed and should be of a serious kind and high quality. But its main aim should be directed towards the understanding of the existential significance of the community of the Church, particularly of her visible structure which provides man with the possibility of entering into new and saving relationships with God and the World.

The dynamics of the liturgical reality (eucharistic community) as expounded here is rooted in the experience of the Trinitarian life in Christ which continuously saves and illuminates man and history. The members of the Church living, practising and witnessing this eucharistic experience create a new life-style. This life-style was realized in the life of the Apostles, martyrs and all the saints who throughout history refused to change the "heavenly" for the "earthly". This mortal life is manifested today in the sins of our times, especially in a culture of individualism, rationalism, consumerism, racism, militarism, deprivation and exploitation in all forms. In each culture the eucharistic dynamics leads into a "liturgy after the liturgy", i.e. a liturgical use of the material world, a transformation of human association in society into *Koinonia*, of consumerism into an ascetic attitude towards the creation and the restoration of human dignity.

The dynamics of the concept of "liturgy after the liturgy" is to be found in several programmes and activities of the WCC which have emerged since Nairobi and to which the Orthodox Churches have given their support based on their ecumenical solidarity. The emphasis on helping "the poorest of the poor", on establishing peace and justice between nations and states, on eradicating hunger, destitution and sickness, on promoting human rights, on diminishing tensions, on searching for a just and responsible society and on directing science and technology along creative lines, on the peaceful and safe use of atomic and other sources of energy, should be given due attention by our Churches as the above issues are part of their Christian concern and an integral element in their social witness.

The reality of salvation is not a narrow religious experience, but it includes the dynamic which — through the synergy (cooperation) of God and man — transforms human individuals into persons according to that image of God which is revealed in the Incarnation, and societies into Koinonia, through history, into the image of Trinitarian life.

Thus the eucharistic communion is the Church with all its implications. As the Saints have said: "Save yourself and you will save those around you."

The Nairobi Assembly has defined that the WCC is constituted "... to call the churches to the goal of visible unity in one faith and in one eucharistic fellowship expressed in worship and in common life in Christ, and to advance towards that unity in order that the world may believe". The Consultation expressed its appreciation that the WCC has already launched the debate on the local Church and it expressed its hope that the WCC will do more to direct the attention of its members to the importance of the eucharistic understanding of the local Church and the eucharistic community within the continuity of the apostolic faith as the basis of the unity we seek and to disentangle its constitution from some elements and possibly some structures which make it so difficult for the Churches to find their way to unity. This would make it easier for the Orthodox to take a full and creative part in the ecumenical movement. In that respect the Consultation expressed its appreciation of the fact that the decision of the First Preconciliar Pan-Orthodox Conference to ask for a fuller and integrated participation of the Orthodox in the WCC has been taken into account by the WCC and that negotiations have been initiated in order to implement that decision.

"An Orthodox Approach to Diaconia"

Chania, Crete, 20-25 November 1978

Introduction

The Commission on Inter-Church Aid, Refugee and World Service (CICARWS) and the Orthodox Task Force of the World Council of Churches (WCC) responded to the New Valamo call for further Orthodox reflection on the Orthodox approach to diaconia by convening a consultation on "Church and Service" at the Orthodox Academy in Chania, Crete, from 20-25 November 1978. Participants represented the various Oriental and Eastern Orthodox Churches. The following report reflects the discussions in the two work groups. In none of the aspects developed is it to be regarded as exhaustive but only as a first step in the continuing endeavour to examine diaconia from the Orthodox standpoint.

Theological Background

Christian diaconia is rooted in the Gospel teaching according to which the love of God and the neighbour are a direct consequence of faith. The diaconal mission of the Church and the duty of each of its members to serve are intimately bound up with the very notion of the Church and stem from the example of the sacrifice of our Lord Himself, our High Priest, who, in accordance with the Father's will "did not come to be served but to serve and to give up his life as a ransom for many" (Mt. 20:28).

Christian diaconia also flows from the divine liturgy in which our offerings are sanctified by Christ's offering and requires our active cooperation (synergeia) with God in the exercise of our free will which is rooted in our common agreement (symphonia) (Mt. 18:19).

Diaconia is therefore an expression of the unity of the Church as the Body of Christ. Each local celebration of the Eucharist is complete and universal, involving the whole of creation, and is offered for the material and spiritual needs of the whole world.

Christian diaconia is not an optional action, duty or moral stance in relation to the needy, additional to our community in Christ, but an indispensable expression of that community, which has its source in the eucharistic and liturgical life of the Church. It is a "liturgy after the liturgy" and it is in this sense that diaconia is described as a judgment upon our history (Mt. 25:31-46).

The main emphasis in this eucharistic and loving diaconia is not on quantity, money or material aid, but on quality and intention. The widow's "tiny coins" (Lk. 21:2-3) are worth more than offerings from our "more than enough". To offer out of the little that we have is an expression of our need to engage in diaconia.

In church collections and *agapes* from the earliest days right down to the present, diaconia is understood by the Orthodox Church as an *offering* intended for the whole man, for his total spiritual and material needs.

The ultimate goal of diaconia is the salvation of man. But poverty, oppression and material penury often constitute an obstacle, jeopardizing man's salvation, as the teaching of the apostles and the Church fathers points out. Diaconia therefore embraces the need to liberate mankind from everything which oppresses, enslaves and distorts the image of God, and by doing so to open the way to salvation. In this sense, diaconia is liberation for salvation.

Christian diaconia today requires a renewed spirit of asceticism, i.e. of self-denial and concern for our neighbour leading to a simpler life-style. The witness borne by monastic communities in our midst through fasting, prayer, *metanoia*, the contemplative life and solidarity with the poor and the oppressed, as well as through active service, inspire us to grow in genuine Christian community.

Diaconia challenges us, therefore, to sacrifice, self-denial and sometimes even to martyrdom. It knows no limits. It is not something we do spasmodically to alleviate certain needs and sufferings as they arise but rather an integral part of a living Christian community's concern and pastoral care for all those within the community and for all those who come within range of its knowledge and loving care.

The object of Christian diaconia is to overcome evil. It offers deliverance from injustice and oppression. When the Church fails to offer its witness and to be prophetic, the reaction of the world will be indifference and apathy. Diaconia is therefore an essential element in the life and growth of the Church.

Because of the varied and adverse historical circumstances within which the Orthodox Church has had to struggle and continues to struggle in order to live, its diaconia has not always found visible expression in highly organized forms.

Confronted today with rapid social change, modernization, secularization, industrialization, etc., the Orthodox Church recognizes that it must remain open and flexible in order that it may offer various forms of diaconia in a variety of complex situations. Some forms of its diaconia will be directed to individuals, others to groups and institutions. Some forms of diaconia are needed in local situations, others are required to respond to regional or international needs. Some will be spiritual in character, assisting people who are lonely and in despair; others will be material in character, feeding the hungry and liberating the captives.

Clearly, therefore, money alone will not be enough for the diaconal ministries which the Church must seek to perform. It is also clear that preventive diaconia is just as essential as therapeutic diaconia.

Suggestions for the Orthodox Churches

In order that our Orthodox faith and spirituality may find practical expression in more effective diaconal work, the following suggestions are offered for consideration by the Orthodox Churches.

In order to strengthen their diaconal work, our Orthodox Churches should renew the role of deacons and deaconesses in the total life and witness of the Church and make it possible for both laywomen and laymen to participate more fully in diaconal service, this being understood as a *leiturgia* and as an extension of the Holy Eucharist.

Since the basis of our diaconia is the deaconship of our Lord Jesus Christ, whose sacrifice was made for the redemption of all humankind, our Churches should develop more vivid and compelling ways of communicating to their members the biblical imperative to serve the neighbour whoever that neighbour may be, in order that in our diaconia we may attain the ultimate goal of the ecumenical movement, namely, the unity of the Church, and indeed, according to our Lord's will, the unity of all humankind. Due attention should therefore be paid by our Churches to WCC concerns for a macrodiaconia in the field of peace as well as in the fields of disarmament, human rights, racism, development, ecology, etc.

Through their diaconia of prayer and their use of material and human resources, our Churches everywhere should contribute to local, regional, and worldwide efforts to restore human dignity and to serve humanity.

Suggestions for the WCC and CICARWS

As an integral part of the WCC, the Orthodox Churches have found in it an open platform for encounter and cooperation. We would nevertheless offer the following suggestions for promoting a more effective participation of the Orthodox Churches in the life and work of the WCC.

1. We endorse the request placed before the officers and staff of the WCC by the Orthodox members of the Central Committee that membership rules, staff patterns and unit membership should be reviewed in order to facilitate greater participation by the Orthodox in the life and work of the World Council of Churches.
2. We recommend a periodic review of WCC structures, style, publications and services with a view to a greater effort to present points of view in a more inclusive way, one which permits the expression of Orthodox perspectives and concerns.
3. In respect of CICARWS, we suggest:
   a) more attention to the Orthodox understanding of their priorities and the interpretation of diaconal needs in each situation;
   b) assistance to be given to Orthodox Churches in their efforts in the field of macrodiaconia;
   c) the development of better forms of communication with a view to the discovery of better and new forms of diaconia;
   d) the encouragement of relationships and exchanges between Orthodox Churches and other Christian communions;
   e) that CICARWS should be the instrument for the participation of Orthodox Churches in diaconal service in other Christian communions through its project list, country programmes and emergency appeals;
   f) that the attention of CICARWS be drawn to the fact that specialized agency mandates as applied in current procedures may hinder a response to the real needs of the Churches. Conscious of the need to foster direct relationships between donors and recipients and fully respecting the interests of the different Churches in specific situations, we believe that non-earmarked contributions will help the Churches to express their real needs instead of seeking to meet the requirements of the funding agencies;
   g) we look to CICARWS to give greater expression to the spiritual dimension of diaconia: prayer for one another; receptivity to guidance from the Holy Spirit; concern for non-physical suffering and distress; sensitivity to the expression of love in "I, thou, God" relationships.

* * *

Other matters discussed at the "Church and Service" Consultation, regarded as important and as requiring fuller development by the staff of the WCC and of regional councils or by other conferences, included:

1. The issue of Church/State relations in the area of service, as well as church relationships with other non-governmental agencies and with multi-national corporations.
2. The question of violence.
3. The need to develop new and better forms of communication between Orthodox Churches and the WCC, and between donors and recipients.
4. The need for historical and theological research and for a survey of contemporary efforts to evaluate Orthodox diaconia.
5. The need for a WCC delegation to visit the occupied areas of Cyprus to determine the situation of Christians living there.

Summary of the Conclusions of an Inter-Orthodox Consultation
"The Place of the Monastic Life within the Witness of the Church Today"

Amba Bishoy Monastery, Egypt, 30 April-5 May 1979

Identity of the Monastic Life

1. There is no definition of the monk that would be fundamentally different from that of a Christian. To be a true monk or true nun is also to be a true Christian. Monastic life, as also the Christian life in general, remains a mystery; it is a mode of existence in the communion of faith and the love of God. However, in Jesus Christ, many different ways and diverse charismata co-exist in the life of the Church itself (1 Cor. 12:4-31), a diversity which the Orthodox Church has always encouraged.

2. The presence of a monk in the world can only be a paradox. He is a pilgrim (1 Peter 1:1, 2:11), who does not belong to this world, but nevertheless finds himself within it (2 Cor. 5:6-7).

3. We have sought to define, as far as possible, the vocation of a monastic community in today's world as also in the life of our churches today. The monastic vocation has existed germinally in the life of the Church from its very beginning; its current forms, however, have a historical origin and are rooted in particular cultures and traditions. There have been periods in the history of several local churches when they have existed without an organized or powerful monastic group, even as the Church has existed for long periods without ecumenical councils. However, even a glance at the history of the Church is sufficient to convince us of one fact: at least in the Orthodox churches, the life and witness of the monastic communities have shaped the worship, the theology, the spirituality, and the pastoral and apostolic ministries of the Church through the centuries. In accordance with its needs and possibilities, each local church has developed diverse forms of monastic life, which she has integrated into her pastoral, missionary and spiritual work through the ages.

4. Each period of renewal in the spiritual life of our churches has been marked by a corresponding renewal in the life of the monastic communities. In the Orthodox churches, we are convinced that the renewal of spiritual life today should begin with a revitalization of our monastic communities, both of monks and of nuns.

5. The life of the monastic communities serves the life of the churches in many ways. It is from this source that the churches receive spiritual fathers and mothers, as well as disciplined and devoted labourers in the vineyard of the Lord. But the raison d'être of monastic life and monastic communities cannot be limited to the function of

---

• The consultation, which brought together some 40 delegates from Eastern and Oriental Orthodox Churches, was organized by the WCC's Commission on World Mission and Evangelism. This is a summary of the main conclusions on the specificity of the monastic vocation, and the recommendations regarding the role of the monastic communities in relation to the mission of the Church and the renewal of spiritual life in the Churches.

furnishing effective workers for the Church. To so limit the function of a monastic community would be to misunderstand its profound significance and to reduce it to a training centre.

6. Whatever definition one advances for the monastic vocation, it is bound to be criticized. Monastic life is called an askesis, but it is not an automatic mechanism for ensuring the salvation of souls. Of course the monk or nun practices asceticism, one of the natural dynamisms of human nature; monastic life cannot however be reduced to asceticism. On the contrary, that life is realized in a divine-human synergy, in a loving cooperation with the grace of the Holy Spirit.

The monastic vocation does not create another superior state within the Church. On the contrary, the monk is inclined to confess always and anew that "Jesus Christ came into the world to save sinners. And I am the foremost of sinners" (1 Tim. 1:15). The monk is a man of the Gospel; this means that he is a human being who thirsts for salvation in the resurrected Christ. The roots of the life of a monk are in repentance and faith, in a perpetual *metanoia* wherein he lives the reality of the fall of human nature, as also the new reality of the salvation in Christ, in which he participates as a living and active member. In faith and in humility, he lives this continuous *metanoia*, as a renewal of the baptismal gift, as a "growth in God" (Col. 2:1a), a growth towards one and only one goal — the union with God in Christ.

In fact, the whole Christian life is rooted in the grace of baptism. Even if its character as "responsible conversion" is not fully realized, the monk recovers the grace and the water of baptism in the tears of "sorrowful joy", as St John Climacus says. It is a truly evangelical life of children of God, the life in Christ, life in the Spirit, life in the community of faith, in the community which seeks the realization of the love of Christ.

7. But the monastic community has a particular vocation within the community of faith. First of all it is a sign, a paradigm, an anticipation and foretaste of the Kingdom. This is particularly true, since, throughout history, churches have been too easily tempted to make compromises with the world, to assure themselves a secure and comfortable place in society, guaranteed by the authorities, and thus to seek to escape the necessary tension between history and the Kingdom of God. It is in such situations that the monastic community has the task of proclaiming the Kingdom and of living as a sign of the coming Kingdom — a paradigm of the parousia.

8. The Apostle Paul exhorts all Christians not to be comforted to the spirit of the age (Rom. 12:1-2). The vocation of each Christian is to refuse to be shaped by the patterns of this world, but rather to take responsibility for it, in order to transcend it and transfigure it by the renewal of the mind. The monastic community responds to this appeal for liberation from conformism and for inner transformation in a more disciplined, more communitarian and more radical manner.

9. At the heart of the monastic discipline is the sanctification of time and the renewal of the inner man by unceasing prayer. It is in concentrating upon God in prayer and in seeking at the same time to embrace the creation in love and intercession, that the monastic community opens the channels for the Spirit of God to transform both the individual and the community from within. It also thus enables him to resist the pressures of the world which drive him to the pursuit of all sorts of vanities. Through his direct experience of the world, as also by his gift of discernment, the monk can also help to go beyond a superficial understanding of the

world, and help Christians to have a contemplative attitude to history and the created order.

The discipline of prayer — all the way from the eucharistic liturgy through the canonical daily offices to the perpetual prayer and invocation of the name of Jesus — can undoubtedly also be practised by a lay person. But, in general, monastic life makes better provision for practising the discipline. All vows and commitments — whether it be to chastity, poverty and obedience, to silence and solitude, or to fasting and self-denial — can only be ancillary to the principal task, the life of prayer, which is the foundation of all monastic life. As this central principle of prayer becomes rooted in faith and in love, all other things are added to it.

10. The phenomenon of monasticism takes up again in the Church the witness of the martyrs of the early centuries. By the principle of non-attachment and availability for God and one's fellow human beings, the monk or nun bears witness to the eschaton inside the Church, and thus exercises a truly prophetic ministry, in showing forth the Gospel's way of the Kingdom. It is the radical faithfulness of the martyrs which assures that the gates of hell shall not prevail against the Church.

On the other hand, by its insistence on renunciation of the world and on the eschatological dimension of history, the monastic community runs the risk of becoming an escapist movement which seeks to run away from the major problems which preoccupy the minds of other members of the Church who live in society. It is the duty of the monk, as part of his task of spiritual direction, to help the faithful to fulfil their responsibilities in society in full liberty and with discernment.

11. We are convinced that the discussion about the identity of the monastic life today raises also the question of identity both of the Christian and of contemporary man. One should not forget that the name of the man of the spirit is "beauty" (kalogeros), that beauty which saves the world, and that his science, his ardent longing to know virtue, is called "the love of beauty" (philokalia).

Monasticism, Mission and Renewal

The Christian in the World

Some Christians live in affluent and secular societies. They are unable to find in them spiritual values upon which they can regulate their lives. Sensing this secular vacuum, they look to the monasteries. Indeed, all the faithful can find spiritual good in the monastic life. Many young people, ignorant of Christian monasticism, have wandered away to follow various forms of Asian, non-Christian ascetic practices. These expressions of certain pseudo-mystical life-styles often have religious bases, but they are also often foreign to the Good News of Jesus Christ. Some who seek that "peace from above" confuse it with a quiet return to nature.

It is our belief that by re-affirming, clarifying and setting forth our ancient Christian monastic ideals, we are presenting an authentic Christian life-style to those seeking peace and integrity of life.

The Church under Stress

The Church, which is the Body of Christ in the world, existing and acting in the present social context, is itself in need of the contributions of a strong monasticism. She needs to remind herself of this great treasure of witnessing. It is also from monasticism that the Church will continue not only to live but also to grow, re-vitalize and perfect herself in the spirit of the Gospel.

Given this authentic, living example of the life of sacrifice and self-denial, as witnessed to by monastic communities, the Church has a real and valid touchstone by which to measure and re-align her actions.

In some areas of the world, the joy of living together in the Lord is absent from the community. The weight of individual effort is borne without the Christian expression of oneness in fellowship. This communal, unifying experience of sharing is well expressed in monastic communities as a sign for all.

Monasteries: A Christian Witness in the World

Monasteries have and can continue to offer their special and unique experiences to benefit the entire believing community. Retreats held under the care of the monasteries for both clergy and laity offer possibilities for profound renewal and rededication to Christ. In a spirit of monastic praise and calm, lay/clerical consultation would take on deeper meaning and be of far greater benefit to the Church.

Where beneficial, tracts dealing with and providing guidance on specific daily problems could be made available through the efforts of monastic publishing facilities.

Today, as throughout history, spiritual counsellors are available from within the monastic ranks. Confessions, discussion and solid scriptural guidance related to the personal needs of each individual is the particular gift of monastic communities to the churches.

We recommend that in private and corporate worship, monks ought to make mention of the specific needs of the Church and in this way to keep in touch with the everyday needs of the rest of the Christian community.

Specifically, we recommend that monastic communities ought to pray for the unity of the Church and for the spreading of the Kingdom of God.

Taking advantage of modern means of communication, monastic communities can and should exchange letters of spiritual experiences, spiritual direction and visits. Further, extended visits to other monasteries would be useful to all concerned.

To facilitate this, we recommend that a directory of Orthodox monastic communities be published and distributed through the offices of the World Council of Churches in cooperation with the Orthodox churches. We suggest that a committee be set up which would integrate, encourage and facilitate the execution of these suggestions.

While exhorting that the doors of the monasteries ought to be open wide to all, we would also draw attention to the real danger of possible negative influences from outside which could be detrimental to the spiritual integrity of the community. Among these we are concerned with the growing number of tourists who come to monasteries on sight-seeing tours. We recommend that such sight-seeing visits should always have a definite spiritual dimension. They should be conducted in such a way that they not only do not upset the life of the monastic community, but also become an expression of pastoral concern for the visitors. Monasteries should train guides to fulfil the task adequately. The monasteries should be aware that maintaining the integrity of their spirituality is the necessary condition for fulfilling this ministry.

Without altering past monastic forms, but in the hope of utilizing talents, we suggest that specific monasteries consider becoming definite centres of service to specific Orthodox needs. Such subjects as music, iconography, research and study of Scripture and Patristics would draw together like talents and would strengthen and broaden growth in these fields.

As monasteries have often been guardians of the Faith, so too they can become repositories for manuscripts, artifacts and treasures particular to each tradition. The presence of such articles would be an open invitation to the faithful and to all serious persons interested in taking advantage of Christian culture displayed in its original setting.

We recall, finally, that in other eras, some monasteries were centres from which missionary activities spread. Today other monasteries may be in a similar position to aid in the mission of the Church. We encourage those who are in such situations to act in love for the extension of the Kingdom of God.

Recommendations

Our Churches are certainly aware of the important place which monasticism occupies in their life and witness. We can only recommend that they take to heart this grand theme of monasticism and of its role, that they plan research on this subject, giving special importance to the writings of the Fathers, and of the monastic texts of the Church, and to their translation into modern languages, as also for their publication and diffusion.

It is desirable that CWME, in collaboration with other concerned sub-units in the World Council of Churches, plan the formation of a pan-Orthodox group for study and reflection on the relation between the monastic community and the parish community, inviting all the Orthodox member churches of the WCC to name their delegates to this working group.

The consultation recommends that CWME take the necessary steps to produce a preparatory study on *The Monk as Witness to the Kingdom* in view of the World Missionary Conference in Melbourne in 1980. The Consultation regards this theme as very important; but, due to lack of time, it was not possible to study the subject in sufficient detail at the St Bishoy Monastery meeting.

"Your Kingdom Come!"

Orthodox Contribution to the Theme of the World Conference on Mission and Evangelism

Melbourne, 1980

Mission means the proclamation of the Good News, i.e. of the coming of the Kingdom: "The time has come; the Kingdom of God is upon you; repent, and believe the Gospel" (Mk. 1:15).

But Jesus only proclaimed this Good News to "the lost sheep of the house of Israel" (Mt. 15:24). Not until after his resurrection did he send his disciples beyond the frontiers of Israel: "Go forth, therefore, and make all nations my disciples; baptize men everywhere in the name of the Father and the Son and the Holy Spirit" (Mt. 28:19). But he commands them to wait in Jerusalem until he sends upon them the "Father's promised gift" and they are "armed with the power from above" (Lk. 24:29), and then he sends them "to bear witness... to the ends of the earth" (Acts 1:8).

The Church thus discovers the splendour of the Kingdom of God in the person of the Risen Christ, revealed to the disciples of all times by the coming of the Holy Spirit, and in this way it finds the power to proclaim the Kingdom to the ends of the earth.

Rejoicing, therefore, in the communion of the Holy Spirit and marvelling at the resurrection, the Church proclaims to the world the reign of "Jesus Christ crucified" (1 Cor. 2:2), the reign of "Him who is and who was and who is to come" (Rev. 1:4; 1:8; 4:8).

Proclaiming and Manifesting the Reign of God in the Power of the Spirit

The Church and the Coming of the Kingdom of God

The Reign of God which has come and is coming is presented to the world by this society of repentant and pardoned sinners, the Body of Christ, the Church. Despite the sins of its members and because the Word lives in it, the Church proclaims the Kingdom of God to the world. Because the Church is given the presence of the Holy Spirit as guarantee, the Kingdom is in our midst, the End — the eschaton — is already accessible to the world. The Kingdom is already at work in the world, a joyful hope.

Therefore the Church is an eschatological community, a pilgrim people, which lives in the ardent expectation of the return of its Lord and bears witness to him before the world.

• This working document was produced by an Orthodox reflection group meeting, organized by the Orthodox studies desk of the Commission on World Mission and Evangelism of the World Council of Churches. It was held in the Saint Serge Orthodox Institute of Theology in Paris from 25-28 September 1978. This report is an Orthodox contribution to the theme of the world missionary conference in Melbourne, 1980. It was published in the *International Review of Mission*, Vol. LXVIII, No. 270, April 1979.

The weaknesses and betrayals of which the members of the Church are guilty may all too easily obscure this reality but cannot cancel out the fundamental calling of the Church: "Heaven and earth will pass away; my words will never pass away" (Mt. 24:35). This summons remains even if some of us are deaf to it: the power of death, the gates of Hades will not prevail against the Church (cf. Mt. 16:18).

The Liturgy as Dynamic of the Reign of God

Defaulters that we are, therefore, how are we to experience the Kingdom so as to become what we are called to be, namely, the Church of the Lord? How are we to fulfil our mission and to appear before the world — not as a hypocritical and piously disguised copy of the society to which we belong but as the Bride of Christ "without spot or blemish", an image and an anticipation of the Kingdom?

It is the role of eucharistic liturgy to initiate us into the Kingdom, to enable us to "taste... and see that the Lord is good" (Ps. 34:8, quoted by 1 Pet. 2:3). It is the function of the liturgy to transform us as individuals into "living stones" of the Church and as a community into an authentic image of the Kingdom.

The Divine Liturgy — divine because, though celebrated by human beings, it is essentially the work of God — therefore with a cry of joy and gratitude: "Blessed is the Kingdom of the Father, Son and Holy Ghost". The entire eucharistic liturgy unfolds within the horizon of the Kingdom which is its raison d'être and its goal.

This Kingdom is a dynamic reality: it has come and it is coming, because Christ has come and Christ is coming. The mission of the Church will therefore be to summon people of all nations and of all ages to become a pilgrim people. The liturgy is an invitation to enlist with the Lord and to travel with him. This appears at the beginning of the Orthodox liturgies in the Little Entrance with the Gospel and in the Great Entrance with the offering of bread and wine: "In thy Kingdom, remember us, O Lord, when thou comest in thy Kingdom... May the Lord God remember us all in his Kingdom...". This movement of the liturgy carries us along with Christ towards the Promised Land.

The Kingdom, prepared for us before the creation of the world (Mt. 25:34) and proclaimed to men in the whole of Christ's preaching, was given to the world by the Lamb of God offering himself on the cross and by his rising again from the dead. In its liturgy, the Church gives thanks, makes eucharist, for this gift, in the words: "Thou... hast left nought undone till thou hadst brought us unto heaven and bestowed upon us thy Kingdom for to come". By its thanksgiving, by its eucharist, the Church receives the gift of the Kingdom.

This gift donated by the Son in his self-offering on the cross is communicated to the people of all ages by the Holy Spirit who received what belongs to the Son and communicates it to us (cf. Jn. 16:14). When the Holy Spirit is invoked in the prayer of epiclesis, the celebrant prays: "that thy Holy Spirit may come upon us and these gifts... that they may be to them that partake thereof unto sobriety of soul, the remission of sins, the participation of thy Holy Spirit, the fulfilment of the Kingdom of heaven..." In the course of the liturgy, the radiance of the Holy Spirit projects onto the Church gathered together by Him the full image of the Kingdom. The liturgy is the continuation of Pentecost. When all the faithful come to communicate, they enter into the splendour of the Kingdom.

Immediately after they have in this way met with Him, who has come but whom they also expect to come again, they cry out: "Grant that we may partake of thee more truly, in that day of thy Kingdom which shall have no night". Everything is given to us in this communion yet everything is not yet accomplished. The efficacy of the Church's missionary witness depends on the authenticity of our communion. Our ability to present the Light of the Kingdom to the world is proportionate to the degree in which we receive it in the eucharistic mystery.

Holiness, Prophetic Sign of the Coming of the Kingdom

The liturgy does not end when the eucharistic assembly disperses. "Let us go forth in peace"; the dismissal is a sending off of every believer to mission in the world where he or she lives and works, and of the whole community into the world, to witness by what they are that the Kingdom is coming. Christians who have heard the Word and received the Bread of Life should henceforth believe in prophetic signs of the coming Kingdom. Having been sanctified, for they have been kindled by the fire descended from heaven, they hear the exhortation: "Heal the sick... and say, 'The Kingdom of God has come closer to you... And now you see that I have given you the power to tread underfoot... all the forces of the Enemy'" (Lk. 10:9-19). Every Christian is called to proclaim the Kingdom and to demonstrate its power. Hence a twofold function:

The exorcism of the demons: the struggle against the idols, racism, money, chauvinism, ideologies, the robotization and exploitation of man.

The healing of the sick: the Church exercises this function not only in the sacraments of penance and the anointing of the sick but also by tackling all the ills and disorders of man and society. It does this in the power of the cross: self-effacing service of the sick and prisoners, solidarity with the tortured and the oppressed, especially those who suffer for their opinions. As the voice of the voiceless, the Church will in the discharge of its calling, teach and practise respect for every human being, with the aim of restoring the divine image in each individual and communion among all. It will encourage respect for the whole of creation and everything in nature: a kingdom of priests, it will offer up the whole creation — obedient to Christ and renewed by his Spirit — to God the Father.

Those who practise a "Christian maximalism", renewal groups, religious orders, set us an example of mission. A joyful asceticism whereby the old man is crucified with Christ so that the new man may rise with him and live for God (Rom. 6:5-11) carries the cross and resurrection of Christ into daily life; it develops all the potentialities of baptism and constitutes an essential sign of the coming Kingdom.

Voluntarily accepted poverty in demonstration of solidarity with the Poor King (cf. Zech. 9:9), fasting with Him who said that "man does not live by bread alone", "for the Kingdom of God is not eating and drinking, but justice, peace and joy, inspired by the Holy Spirit" (Rom.14:17) and identification with all those who go hungry; chastity not only in monastic life but also in conjugal love and procreation; revaluation of the humility which makes it possible for the other person to be renewed; mutual submission (Eph. 5:21) in listening to the Spirit who speaks through the Church; a liberty which refuses to let itself be intimidated by threats or taken in by false promises; constant interior prayer throughout all the vicissitudes of daily life — all these are many aspects of a life based on an eschatological vision of existence, on an evangelical life worthy of the children of the Kingdom.

Bearing Witness to the Reign of God in the Struggle for God's Truth and Justice on Earth

Mission as Work of the Spirit and Gift of the Truth

The proclamation of the Kingdom of God lies at the very heart of the Church's vocation in the world. Without mission there is no Church, for the Church continues the work of mankind's salvation revealed and achieved by Jesus Christ our Saviour. Only by the Pentecostal outpouring of the Holy Spirit is the mission of the Church possible and the apostolic community endowed with the power of the Spirit for the announcement of the Gospel of the Christ who died and rose again for our salvation. The coming of the Holy Spirit in the Church is not an isolated historic event in the past but a permanent gift which gives life to the Church, ensuring its existence in the history of humanity, making possible its witness to the inaugurated Kingdom of God. The Holy Spirit is the divine power whereby the Church is able to obey the command of the Risen Lord: "Go forth then and make all nations my disciples" (Mt. 28:19); "Go forth to every part of the world and proclaim the Good News to the whole creation" (Mk. 16:15; cf. Lk. 24:47 and Acts 1:8). This permanent Pentecostal outpouring of the Spirit on the Church is a reality in the Church's worship, in its public prayer, in the Sunday celebration of the Eucharist, but it overflows the limits of ecclesial worship and constitutes the inner dynamic which gives character to all expressions of, and all activities in, the life of the Church.

Neither the Church nor its worship or mission can be defined exclusively as forms of the existence and activity of the human beings gathered together in the name of Jesus Christ. The Church is above all the true manifestation of the divine presence in the history of the world, the sign of the constant intervention of the Love of God in the existence of human society, in and through the most concrete everyday conditions of human life, in its most diverse and even profane activities. The coming of the Spirit of the Risen Christ into the world and His presence in the world moves inexorably in the direction of the abolition of the frontiers between a sacred spiritual world, reception to the divine grace, and a profane material world which is thought to exist only in accordance with its own internal laws. In face of the contemporary world it cannot be too strongly insisted that human existence in all its aspects is subject to the proclamation of the Gospel and that the fundamental principles of the spiritual life of the human person (pardon, mercy, justice) must permeate all aspects of the social and political life of human society.

If the missionary proclamation of the Gospel of the Kingdom is to reach human hearts, there must be a palpable and real correspondence between the Word preached in the power and joy of the Holy Spirit and the actual life of the preacher and of the Christian community. The gap between the message and the life of the historical Church and its members constitutes the most massive obstacle to the credibility of the Gospel for our contemporaries. "See how these Christians love one another" — declared an ancient Christian apologist. The love of Christians is the very substance as well as the radiance of the Gospel. In the apostolic community of Jerusalem as well as in the communities founded by St Paul, the sharing of material things and concern for the poor became the spontaneous and necessary expression of their experience of the Trinitarian love which is disclosed in the life of the Church. The sharing of material things and of life itself thus flows from eucharistic communion and constitutes one of its radical requirements. When the Church identifies itself with the prayer of its Saviour, "Your Kingdom Come!", it must above all ask itself in a spirit of penitence how far the unworthiness of Christians acts as a screen hindering the radiance of Christ Himself from shining through.

The dynamic of the Church's mission springs from a deep awareness of the suffering of a human race steeped in ignorance of God, torn apart by hatred and conflict of every sort, alienated by material and spiritual poverty in all its forms. Together with the whole of creation man experiences a profound nostalgia for a paradise lost, in which justice, well-being and peace would prevail. The Church's responsibility is to bring to this tormented and enslaved world the vigorous response of God to its questionings and rebellions. This response is the living Truth of Christ which reaches down into the very depths of man's being and liberates him. It is also the gift of the infinite love and compassion of God who ignores no human suffering and distress, and towards whom the blood and tears of the oppressed arise in mute appeal.

We are convinced that the sacred deposit of the Truth and Love of its divine Founder, of which the Church's faith is the expression and of which the Church has been the channel throughout the centuries, is the living response which is needed to the quest of man in all ages. The infinite love of the divine Trinity is communicated to us by Christ, true God and true man, in the power of the Holy Spirit. The doctrine and preaching of the Church should be nothing other than an education in this living love of God, a visible manifestation of the presence of Christ in our lives. "Dear children — for my children you are, and I am in travail with you over again until you take the shape of Christ" (Gal. 4:19). The only goal of the Church's mission, in the last analysis, is to manifest the presence of Christ and his love in the life of Christians both individually and in their love for one another, as well as in their witness in the world by their life, actions, and love.

The Life of the Christian as a Prophetic Witness of the Kingdom of God

Although the mission of the Church and the proclamation of the Kingdom are above all the work of the Holy Spirit who manifests in power and truth the intervention of God Himself in history, it is also important to remember that man is called to cooperate in the divine plan for the salvation of the world.

"We are God's fellow-workers", declares St Paul (1 Cor. 3:9). Through human voices and human lives, Christ's call to follow him reverberates throughout the centuries. For those who take it seriously and at cost, this "service" of the divine Word and the divine Love entails a deep and permanent surrender of their lives. The Christian who obeys the word of his Lord must resist the temptation to overrate his own importance and to come between God and His children. The service of God and His Word demands a radical exercise in self-renunciation and spiritual poverty, the better to be able to serve God and one's brothers and sisters. What St John the Baptist said of himself in relation to Christ must also be true of us: "He must increase, I must decrease" (Jn 3:30). This way of voluntary impoverishment following the pattern of the "Poor Man" thus helps us to "liberate" the inner man and to make him capable of receiving the diverse charisma of the Holy Spirit so that through his sanctification, community and communion is strengthened and developed among human beings. "Acquire a spirit of peace", St Seraphim of Sarov (early 19th century) used to say, "and thousands around you will find salvation".

That is the basis of the Orthodox theology of mission: to acquire the dynamic, the power of the Spirit of Christ. It is He who creates the languages, forms and methods of mission...

The efficacy of missionary witness will be directly proportionate to the Christian experience of the love of Christ. This love, says St Paul, "constrains us" (2 Cor. 5:14).

Once this flame of love sets a man's heart ablaze, it prevents him from isolating himself comfortably in his own personal existence or that of his community. The dismissal of the faithful at the end of the liturgy with the words "Go forth in peace!" does not mean that the liturgy is "over" but that it is transposed into another form in which it continues, in the inner worship of the heart, in a life immersed in the daily life of human society. It is high time we overcame the very real temptation to make an absolute distinction between a spiritual life and a secular life. All human existence is sacred and remains within God's sight. It is within that existence that Christ's sovereignty purposes to be installed, so that no realm or aspect of human life may be abandoned to the forces of evil.

The Christian thus experiences in his own flesh and blood the inevitable tension between existence in the world and not belonging to the world. It is precisely because of the Christian's heavenly citizenship (Heb. 13:14) that he is able to enter fully into the whole life of human society and to bring the light of Christ to bear on that life.

In every area of human activity there needs to be a constant reminder, in season and out of season, of the meaning of human dignity, of the unique and intrinsic value of the human person who cannot be reduced to a mere cog in the social machine.

The Church of Christ cannot shut its eyes to, or rest content with merely pious words about the deeply ingrained defects which disfigure modern society, nor ignore the inequalities in the distribution, use and management of the material riches of the earth of which man is meant to be the steward. Nor can it be indifferent to the hunger and destitution of a large proportion of humankind. Is real solidarity still possible within the vast community of Christ's disciples in face of the ocean of suffering and poverty, especially in the Third World, around us? We should not forget the social preaching of a St John Chrysostom who reminded the rich and powerful of his time (4th century) that compassion to the poor is also a sacred liturgy in which man is the priest and which in God's sight has an incomparable dignity.

In speaking of poverty the Church does not identify its message with the political and social programmes of our time. Yet the Church cannot turn a blind eye to the fact of human poverty by which a great part of humanity is burdened today. Poverty and its consequences are themselves only the fruit of a deep disorder from which humanity has suffered since the fall of Adam. None of the social programmes and efforts to achieve prosperity and justice are able to bring mankind healing for its deepest ills, its sin, its hatred, egotism, pride. It is when man becomes the slave of his spiritual and physical passions that he succumbs to poverty in its most real form, especially when he fails to realize it.

The Gospel of Christ is a message of life and healing addressed to all who are poor on this human earth. From all, the Gospel demands thorough conversion, the abandonment of human glory and the abjuring of the idols we have made of money, political and economic power, ideologies, racism... The Gospel alone brings to all men, whatever their racial, social or political origin, true liberation and life.

This radical conversion of the heart is the principal fruit of the invisible action of the Holy Spirit within us, fashioning us in the image and likeness of Him who though "he was rich, yet for your sake... became poor, so that through his poverty you might become rich" (2 Cor. 8:9). The disciples of Christ are called to a voluntary poverty which makes it possible for them, on the one hand, to become available for the inauguration of the Reign of Christ in our human life and, on the other hand, to serve their own apprenticeship to love and complete sharing, and to communicate it to others.

The Church in our time should resist the temptation to insure itself, and even to enter into partnership with the authorities and powers of this world, lest it betray the most precious gift of the Spirit, namely the liberty of the child of God. In all the struggles and conflicts which rend asunder the extended human family, the Church should seek to reflect the sufferings, injustices and forms of violence (open or concealed), to reverberate the cries and appeals of all those — Christians and non-Christians — who are persecuted for their faith, brutally treated in violation of human dignity and the basic principles of justice.

The Transfiguration of the World in Order that God's Justice May Be Fulfilled on Earth

The action of the Christian in the transfiguration of the world begins in the growth and development of each individual and in that of the ecclesial community. The impact of the Christian mission on the materialist society in all parts of the world depends on the spiritual renewal of the Christian world. The advance towards unity and the quest for unity are indispensable elements in this process. Our commitment to the service of men springs from a vision of man and the cosmos en route for the Kingdom of God.

It needs to be strongly emphasized that it is principally within the family cell that the Christian life becomes a reality and the health of all nations is thus renewed. In face of contemporary threats to the very existence of the family, it should be remembered that it is within its setting that the spiritual worship and the proclamation of the Word of God takes place day by day, that the priesthood of the father and mother, who offer their children to the divine light and who are thus the provisional representatives and mirrors of the divine paternity and compassion, is exercised.

Nor can the Church today ignore the question which presses on the universal human conscience concerning the place and role of the woman in human society, the special difficulties which she faces in an industrial society in which she participates as man's equal, in the development of society, but in which, in virtue of her special charisms, she helps to uphold and carry the Church and bears children both for life and for the Spirit. The Church cannot be content to leave to others the burden of solving these questions about the distinctive dignity of woman in keeping with her nature and about her liberation from all bondage by the Spirit of Christ.

The confusion and difficulties of young people cannot fail to concern the Church at the deepest levels of its pastoral mission. Because of the vulnerability of the young but also because of the dynamism and vigour which is naturally theirs, special care needs to be given to the training of young people as they face up to the immense problems of life, love, suffering, and the struggle for existence. It is well to recall here that the year 1979 is the Year of the Child and that efforts and resources will be devoted to this theme by the main international bodies, secular and ecclesiastical. The Orthodox Church has a vision and a profound experience of the problems of infancy which it should share with all men of goodwill.

The problems presented by marriage, by the growing incidence of divorce, by the difficulties of human love in a hedonistically oriented society, can only be solved in the spirit of the spirituality of a Transfiguration of human nature, by the path of asceticism and spiritual combat, the only way in which the demon to which our society is possessed can be exorcized.

* * *

"Your Kingdom Come!" — this is Christ's prayer: it constitutes in itself the prophetic message of the New Testament which the Church should announce forcibly to the world today. The Church itself lives in this tension towards the Kingdom and is really itself only as it moves towards its crucified and risen Lord.

We believe that the prayer "Your Kingdom Come!" should inspire the Church today with a greater enthusiasm and dynamism. We believe that it should bring a new breath of authenticity to the Christian witness which our human race looks for and hopes for in its agony.

The whole people of God is summoned to be a true sign of the Kingdom of God. It must confess courageously that the future of the Church will come only as a gift of Him who is the Lord of the future.

Once Christians pray sincerely: "Your Kingdom Come!" they hear the voice of Him who is saying to them: "Yes, I am coming soon!" "Amen, Come, Lord Jesus!" (Rev. 22:20).

Report of an Eastern Orthodox-WCC Consultation

"Orthodox Involvement in the World Council of Churches"

Sofia, Bulgaria, 23-31 May 1981

Introduction

In accordance with the wish of local Orthodox churches and the World Council of Churches, expressed in recent years, an agreement was reached between leaders of the WCC and Orthodox members of the Central Committee, meeting in Jamaica, 1979, to hold a consultation on ecumenical issues. It would focus on the Orthodox contribution to the WCC's activities.

Organized by the General Secretariat and the Orthodox Task Force at the WCC headquarters in Geneva, the consultation of official delegates of the Eastern Orthodox Churches and representatives of the World Council took place in Sofia on 23-31 May 1981. It was hosted by the Bulgarian Patriarchate. There were 30 participants.

The main topics on the Agenda were:
1) the Orthodox understanding of ecumenism and participation in the WCC;
2) Orthodox experiences and problems in the WCC;
3) perspectives of Orthodox contributions to the activities of the WCC;
4) "Jesus Christ — the Life of the World".

Various papers and statements on these issues were presented on behalf of the respective Churches, the General Secretariat of the WCC and the Orthodox Task Force. There was an extensive discussion regarding a constructive Orthodox partnership in the WCC, the search for better ways and means of cooperation within the ecumenical fellowship, the strengthening of the role of the Eastern Orthodox Church in WCC activities and ensuring their ever more effective presence within the WCC.

1. The Orthodox understanding of ecumenism and participation in the WCC

All the participants considered it symbolically important that the consultation met on the 1600th anniversary of the Second Ecumenical Council, Constantinople (May 381) — a council of a relatively small number of bishops from the East which nevertheless was acknowledged as "ecumenical" by all because "it gathered together the separated" and reflected the Orthodox consciousness of the whole Church. Even those who previously differed with each other in the formulation of the faith were reconciled because they discovered a common expression of the living divine Truth as expressed in the creative theological effort of the Fathers.

The participants of the Sofia consultation were inspired and guided by that example. Conscious of being members of the same One, Holy, Catholic and Apostolic Church, preserving the same Truth, the representatives were unanimous in recognizing the ecumenical movement as an important sign of our times, which places before the Orthodox Church a challenge which she must meet responsibly. In their discussion of problems related to Christian unity, they were aware of the fact that "ecumenism in space" (i.e. concern for unity today) is inseparable from "ecumenism in time" (i.e. faithfulness to the apostolic and patristic teaching). They acknowledged the tension which inevitably exists between the necessary faithfulness to holy tradition and the concern for ecumenical relations and eventual unity between separated Christians today. They rejected any idea of compromise in the faith and remembered with satisfaction that the Central Committee of the WCC, meeting in Toronto (1950), declared: "No church need fear that by entering into the World Council it is in danger of denying its heritage."

They also noted other important points made by the Toronto Declaration, e.g. that "membership in the Council does not in any sense mean that the Churches belong to a body which can make decisions for them", and, furthermore, that "membership does not imply that each Church must regard the other member Churches as Churches in the true and full sense of the word".

Although it was recognized that the Toronto Declaration would need development or correction, its text was seen as an essential factor in the continuation of Orthodox membership in the World Council of Churches.

The members of the consultation were unanimous in their understanding of ecumenism, as a necessary expression of Catholicity itself. The Orthodox Catholic Church is concerned to strive for unity among Christians, just as it cannot be indifferent to all other forms of division or hostility in humankind, or in creation. The Son of God, in his Incarnation, assumed the fulness of the human nature, and it is in God that humanity finds its true destiny and life. Consequently, the Christian faith cannot separate our human movement toward God from the concerns of human action in creation, and we do not accept the distinction between the so-called "vertical" and "horizontal" dimensions of the Gospel. Christ is indeed the life of the whole world, and the Holy Spirit descending upon the apostles "called all to unity" (Kontakion of Pentecost).

If ecumenism is understood in the light of the catholicity of the Church, it is clear that the World Council of Churches, an institution, cannot be seen as the only expression of the ecumenical movement. Indeed, the Council does not comprise all the Christian churches existing today, and other ecumenical organizations and initiatives are also performing an important function in the development of the ecumenical movement. However, the World Council of Churches today represents the most comprehensive ecumenical fellowship, which all Orthodox Churches have joined, and in which they have found:

— an opportunity to have living encounters with other Christians, praying for each other;

— a panel for a continuous theological dialogue on Christian unity;

— a possibility for inter-church aid and cooperation in the service of peace and justice in society, along with many other areas of Christian action and mission in the world;

— an occasion for enjoying fellowship not only with non-Orthodox Christian churches, but also among themselves.

In the opinion of the participants, WCC has been able to produce these fruits because, as it defined itself in Toronto, it exists "to serve the Church... as an instrument, whereby they may witness together to their common allegiance to Jesus Christ, and cooperate in matters requiring united action". While the Council can neither "become the Church" nor assume the role of convening an ecumenical council, the fellowship among Churches which it has initiated and nourished will have served to realize the unity of all.

The membership of the Orthodox Churches in the WCC is therefore an expression of the concern which the Church had since Apostolic times for the life, salvation and unity of all. Thus, the consultation of Orthodox theologians, held in New Valamo, Finland (24-30 September 1977) said:

> The participation of the Orthodox in the ecumenical movement of today is not, in principle, a revolution in the history of Orthodoxy, but it is a natural consequence of the constant prayer of the Church "for the union of all". It constitutes another attempt, like those made in the Patristic period, to apply the Apostolic faith to new historical situations and existential demands. What is in a sense new today is the fact that this attempt is being made together with other Christian bodies with whom there is no full unity. It is here that the difficulties arise, but it is precisely here that there are many signs of real hope for growing fellowship, understanding and cooperation.

The Orthodox Churches, members of the WCC, have committed themselves to this understanding of ecumenism and intend to remain faithful to that commitment. But they also consider that the future of a fruitful Orthodox membership in the WCC can only be secured if some basic facts of past experience are taken into consideration.

2. Orthodox experiences and problems in the WCC

The present evaluation of these issues stems out of the following convictions:

1. Orthodox Churches were active in founding the ecumenical movement and are full members and partners in the WCC.
2. The Orthodox Churches, here represented, acknowledge the promising, challenging and enriching role of the WCC since its foundation in 1948, for the cause of Christian unity and common Christian witness.
3. Participation in the WCC is a growing process wherein all member churches are bound to seek a fuller and more effective participation on their own proper terms, not at the expense of other member churches, but with them in mutual understanding.
4. The Orthodox Churches here represented feel that in order to render a genuine contribution and a witness to the cause of the One, Holy, Catholic and Apostolic Church, they should always be able to act on the basis of their ecclesiology and according to their own rationale.

a) Positive aspects of Orthodox participation in the WCC

It is an undeniable fact that the Orthodox Churches have benefitted tangibly from their presence in the WCC and have had serious impact on its thought, aspiration and work along the lines of mutual understanding, serious discussion of doctrinal issues, exchange of views and experiences and common witness. Progress towards Christian unity has been made, though we still have a long way to go.

Among the positive aspects of this ecumenical endeavour, we would like to point out the following by way of selection, hoping to stimulate a keener interest, a deeper involvement and a more genuine thrust in the ecumenical undertakings.

1. WCC was instrumental in promoting ecumenical consciousness at various international, regional and national levels, in countries of many Orthodox Churches. It was in this spirit during meetings of the WCC that Eastern Orthodox Churches and Oriental Orthodox Churches have entered into an informal theological dialogue. The getting together of the Orthodox during meetings of the WCC has also contributed to further strengthening of the existing bonds of brotherhood between Orthodox Churches. The WCC has also brought the Orthodox together in a series

of consultations, seminars and workshops on various issues, to clarify their stands
and bring their thinking into the life and action of the WCC.

2. WCC has also rendered great services to the cause of Christian unity and unity
    of humankind through its various units, sub-units, commissions and working
    groups. We specially mention the work of the Commission on Faith and Order
    to find points of convergence between differing confessions on fundamental
    doctrinal issues such as Baptism, Eucharist and Ministry, or the endeavours of
    the Commissions on World Mission and Evangelism (CWME) and on the
    Churches' Participation in Development (CCPD) to bring the Orthodox
    theological thinking in the field of mission and evangelism, and of social ethics
    and development, respectively. We also mention the solidarity and the material
    and moral assistance of such Commissions and working groups, as the
    Commission on Interchurch Aid, Refugee and World Service (CICARWS),
    Church and Society, Programme to Combat Racism, the Commission of the
    Churches on International Affairs (CCIA), to respond to human and social
    needs.

3. On the other hand, the Orthodox presence has influenced considerably the life
    and work of the World Council of Churches, by promoting trinitarian theology,
    the primacy and urgency of unity of doctrine, the ecclesiology of the local
    Church, spirituality and sacramental life and the centrality of the Liturgy.

b) Problems emerging from the Orthodox participation in the WCC

It should be recognized that from the very beginning the participation of the
Orthodox in the WCC has not been an easy task. This is especially due to the
peculiar structural framework of the Council in which Orthodox theology could not
always find its way. The affiliation of the local Orthodox Churches in the WCC at
different times (1948, 1961, 1965, 1972, etc.) and for reasons proper to each
Church, as well as the absence of an integrated Orthodox approach vis-à-vis the
Council and the ecumenical movement did not ease the situation.

While committed to the Council and to its activities and while giving a
common witness and service in it, the Orthodox Churches nevertheless have
encountered some specific difficulties, which in substance could be summarized as
follows:

1. Because of the working style of the Council, from time to time the Orthodox
    feel uneasy in it. They have not always the opportunity to promote their
    priorities in the programmatic undertakings of the Council. On the contrary,
    issues alien to the Orthodox tradition and ethos are adopted on the Council's
    agenda as priority issues, such as the question of ordination of women to
    priesthood. Therefore, efforts should be made in order to bring Orthodox
    priorities and concerns before the Council, as listed in various documents of
    Orthodox member churches.

2. The Orthodox believe that they are ecumenical because of the very nature of
    the Church. Therefore, they are called to make a specific theological contribu-
    tion to the ecumenical debate. However, the language used and the methodol-
    ogy of elaborating theological statements have not always been sufficiently
    transparent to allow Orthodox positions to emerge and become an integral part
    of documents emanating from the WCC bodies. Because of this, the Orthodox
    do not exclude the possibility of re-introducing the practice of producing
    separate statements.

3. The opinion was emphasized that the Council being primarily a Council of Churches, member churches should have the right of appointing their representatives to the various bodies of the WCC.

3. Perspectives of Orthodox contributions to the activities of the WCC

In view of the light of their past experience in the WCC and in view of a better contribution to the work of the Council, the members of the consultation have expressed the following desiderata:

1. A reference to Baptism should be included in the basis of the Council or at least in the criteria for admission of new members.
2. An increased Orthodox representation should be secured in all Assemblies, Committees and other WCC bodies based on the following considerations:
   a) The Orthodox Church is the representative of one of the two basic traditions represented in the criteria for admission of new members.
   b) The number of Orthodox Christians as compared to the number of other Christians represented in the Council.
   c) The fact that, under the Constitution of the WCC and Orthodox canon law, it is difficult for more Orthodox Churches to become members of the Council while membership is constantly increasing by admission of Protestant groups, thus reducing the proportion of Orthodox votes to the total number of votes in the Council.

      Accordingly there should be a substantial increase in the number of Orthodox representatives in the General Assembly, the Central Committee, the Executive Committee, the Unit and Sub-unit Committees.
3. All Orthodox Churches should be represented on the Central Committee in proportion to their membership and historical importance.
4. Each Orthodox Church should be represented at least in one of the Sub-unit committees.
5. Nominations of Orthodox members to the Central Committee should only be received from the Orthodox Churches concerned and should be implemented.
6. Nominations of Orthodox members to other committees and bodies of the WCC should be the result of an agreement between the Orthodox Church concerned and the relevant organ of the WCC.
7. Concerning the Orthodox presence on the staff of the WCC, there should be an increase in the number of the Orthodox staff and all Orthodox Churches should be represented on the staff to the extent possible.
8. Greek, as one of the languages used in Pan-Orthodox meetings and bilateral dialogues of the Orthodox Church, is commended to be used as a working language of the World Council of Churches, it being understood that the Churches concerned are prepared to take financial responsibility for such use.
9. The Orthodox members in the various WCC bodies and consultations should actively participate in the drafting of WCC documents from the early stages, through the discussions and in the preparation of the final text. The WCC should give attention that such participation is actually sought and made effective.
10. More Orthodox speakers, advisers and experts should be involved in various meetings of the WCC and in positions of leadership.
11. It was recognized that there is a need to change the procedure and methods of the final adoption of the emerging ecumenical consensus on doctrinal issues. This problem deserves serious attention from the constituency of the WCC. The consultation invites the General Secretary of the WCC to initiate an ecumenical

discussion on this issue. Concrete proposals have been made by the Russian Orthodox Church. Final solutions to this problem and procedural provisions should be the subject of study and proper formulation in consultation between the General Secretariat and the Units and Sub-units concerned.

12. The members of the consultation heard with gratitude reports from Orthodox members of the WCC staff about the efforts made until now to bring Orthodox thinking into the activities of the WCC and encourage them to persevere in their efforts. The members of the consultation pledge to report to their respective Churches about the activities of the various Units and Sub-units of the WCC and to request increased cooperation and responsible material support wherever necessary.

13. The consultation considers it essential that during the General Assemblies and meetings of the Central Committee contact should be maintained between the Orthodox representatives in order to make a better contribution of the Orthodox to these meetings. It would be desirable to have special consultations in preparation for the work of the Central Committee.

14. Special attention was given to the Orthodox preparation for the Sixth Assembly in 1983. The Orthodox Churches represented at the Consultation understand the Sixth Assembly of the WCC in Vancouver as a very privileged opportunity for them and are determined to bring on this occasion a full contribution to the ecumenical dialogue and community. They consider their consultation in Sofia with the leaders of the WCC as an integral part of the preparation for this ecumenical event. They expect that every effort will be made by the WCC leadership and the host churches in Canada to secure full participation of all Orthodox delegates in conditions excluding external interference and leading to a fruitful work. In the process of preparation leading up to the Assembly a particular importance should be given to:

a) Reflection on the meaning of the theme: "Jesus Christ — the Life of the World". Orthodox have the firm conviction that they can give a specific theological interpretation to the Assembly theme. For them "Jesus Christ — the Life of the World" should become the major concern for the whole ecumenical reflection and solidarity in the years after the Assembly. They are ready to contribute to this purpose with a theological study on the theme, on the basis of the Patristic Christology, Eastern iconography, hymnology and spirituality. They encourage the publication by the Orthodox Task Force of the WCC of a booklet including preparatory material on the Assembly and a comprehensive book on the Orthodox Church.

b) Local or regional consultations in which member churches from a particular country (or region) should have an opportunity to take part in preparatory work, in cooperation with local clergy and communities. The purpose of these consultations is to strengthen local ecumenism and to start a fresh evaluation of the meaning of the ecumenical fellowship in a given place.

It would be extremely helpful if the preparatory and background material for the next Assembly (including the Sofia Report) could be translated and circulated ahead of time to the local churches for the above-mentioned purpose.

c) The team visits represent an important element in this preparatory process. The purpose of the ecumenical visitations during this period should help to promote the ecumenical consciousness and especially to emphasize strongly that the WCC is a fellowship and a council of *churches*. The churches should feel free but responsible to prepare and to coordinate such visits indicating the form, the issues to be discussed and propose names for persons to be contacted.

The Orthodox Churches here represented strongly insist that before and during the Assembly they should have a structural possibility to bring their priorities on the agenda of the Assembly. They also should have a platform to evaluate the programmes of the WCC and to contribute to the shape of the WCC.

4. "Jesus Christ — the Life of the World"

The consultation heard several papers on the theme of the Sixth Assembly and proceeded to a discussion which, however, due to lack of time, could not be completed. The participants were pleased to learn of a forthcoming WCC symposium of Orthodox theologians to deal specifically with the theme of the Sixth Assembly. In view of this they thought it better to confine themselves to the following points:

1. They reaffirmed the readiness and the wish of the Orthodox to fully contribute to the development of the Assembly theme.
2. They indicated that one of the specific topics of the forthcoming symposium should be the question of how the theme of the Assembly will be reflected in the life and work of the WCC and our Churches after the Assembly.
3. They agreed that the Orthodox contributions should mainly concentrate around:
   a) the Patristic teaching on Jesus Christ as the Life of the World;
   b) their varied experiences in this century of Jesus Christ as the Life of the World.
4. They requested that consideration be given to the possibility of publishing in some appropriate form the insights of the papers presented at the consultation, as part of the total Orthodox contribution to the Assembly background materials.

With regard to the teaching of the Fathers, the members of the present consultation proposed that the forthcoming symposium should deal carefully with the following issues:

1) The methods employed by the Fathers for integrating faith and life, diagnosis and therapy, as a total human experience in praise of the Lord and life.
2) The exact meanings of the terms "life" and "world".
3) Grace in creation.
4) The Logos — "light of every man" (John).
5) The divine image in man before and after the fall and the appearance of death.
6) The Logos as educator and saviour in the Old Testament.
7) The Logos as Redeemer of the world in his incarnation, death and resurrection.
8) Jesus Christ as the giver of the Holy Spirit, "abundance of life" (John) for Christians.
9) The Church as the new life of the world (mission, unity and holiness).
10) Jesus as the Bread of Life eternal in the sacraments.
11) The mystery of the love of the neighbour, in whom we see Christ, and through whom we experience our new life in Christ (witness and service).
12) The reality of life through death in Christian existence (suffering and joy in self-sacrifice for the life of the world).
13) The life of the world to come — "God all in all" (1 Corinthians).

Conclusion

The consultation in Sofia provided a great opportunity for fraternal sharing of information, for enriching and strengthening of inter-Orthodox relations, for a more effective dialogue and coordinated Orthodox actions in the ecumenical field. It was a creative encounter of Orthodox representatives with leaders of the WCC and a new instrument of united endeavours towards Christian unity, common witness and service in the contemporary world.

The meeting was seen as a contribution to Orthodox commitment to the ecumenical movement, and a sign of renewed Orthodox sharing in the covenanted fellowship and activities of the WCC.

It brought satisfaction and hope to the participants, called to be obedient servants of the Holy Church, heralds of reconciliation, community, peace and justice.

"Jesus Christ — the Life of the World"
Orthodox Contribution to the Theme of the Sixth Assembly of the WCC

Vancouver, 1983

The following document was drawn up by an Orthodox Theological Symposium on the Sixth Assembly theme "Jesus Christ — the Life of the World" (Vancouver 1983). The Symposium took place from 5-10 February 1982 in Damascus, at the invitation of His Beatitude Ignatius IV, the Patriarch of Antioch and All the East. It was organized by the Orthodox Task Force of the World Council of Churches, and brought together participants from both Eastern and Oriental Orthodox Churches. This report is part of the preparatory material being sent to WCC member churches and to the delegates to Vancouver in order to stimulate reflection on the Assembly theme. The Orthodox Task Force envisages the publication of a book in the near future, which will express the Orthodox understanding of the theme, and will include hymnography and iconography. — Ion Bria

I. Who is Jesus Christ and what is the life of the world?

"God so loved the *world*..." (John 3:16). "The bread of God is that which comes down from heaven, and gives life to the world" (John 6:33). "The bread which I shall give for the life of the world is my very flesh" (John 6:51).

What did our Lord mean by the "life of the *world*"? Is it only another way of saying the life of human beings, or the life of Christians? As Christians we affirm that Jesus Christ came into the world to save sinners; but we also affirm that Jesus Christ is the first-born of all creation, since he is the one who was from the beginning, "before all things" in him all things hold together (Col. 1:17). The one who is the head of all creation — the Pantocrator. The one whom they crucified is none other than the Lord of glory (1 Cor. 2:8), the Angel of the Lord who appeared to Moses in the burning bush (Ex. 3:2) and who said to him: "I am God of your Father Abraham" (Ex. 3:6) — the same who had appeared to Noah, to Abraham, to Jacob and to Isaiah, the only-begotten Son of God. The Fathers of the Church have strongly affirmed that it was the only-begotten who manifested himself even before his incarnation (see e.g. St Basil in *Refut. of Eunomius' Apology* II:18; St Athanasius, *Contra Arianum* III:12-14, Gregory of Nyssa in *Contra Eunomium* XI:3).

These two affirmations go together: (a) that Jesus Christ who is proclaimed as the life of the world is none other than the one in whom all things were created and by whom all things subsist; and (b) that the Son of God incarnate is the Saviour of the whole world, and not just of a few human beings.

We are convinced that both points should be affirmed at the Sixth Assembly in Vancouver — that the Jesus Christ to whom we bear witness is not simply, as his unbelieving contemporaries thought, the man from Nazareth, the carpenter son of a carpenter, but the only-begotten Son of God; and that it is for the life of the world that he has come and taken our humanity — the whole of our humanity — unto himself.

In recent times, it is becoming more generally acknowledged that salvation in Christ is not just for individual human beings, but extends to the whole of human society. This is as it should be. But should we not go further? If the whole cosmos has been affected by human sin, should not the redemption in Christ bring salvation and healing to the whole world? Is this not why "the creation waits with eager longing for the revealing of the sons of God" (Rom. 8:19)? Is not the creation itself to be set free from its bondage to decay and obtain the glorious liberty of the "children of God" (Rom. 8:21)? The different levels at which salvation in Christ becomes operative should be specified — the level of the individual, the level of the Church, the level of the whole humanity, and the level of the cosmos or universe. It is also important to distinguish between the various kinds of life.

For our purpose, we can distinguish five different kinds of life:
a) God's life, self-existent, eternal, without beginning or end, not derived from others, and the source of the life of all;
b) angelic life — created, unmixed with evil;
c) human life — created, now pervaded by sin and mortality;
d) sub-human life — of animals and plants, created, mortal and affected by human sin in a fallen world; and
e) the life of the evil powers — created as good, but now by their own will and action, under the power of evil, opposed to God's purposes, and distorting life on our earth.

The drama of redemption involves all five levels and is of significance to all levels. But the incarnation of our Lord Jesus brings into existence a unique new life — that of the Word (type a), united with the flesh (type c). This is God's eternal life in bodily human form, the life of Jesus Christ.

The temptation must be resisted at the Assembly to idolize life as such, and to think of physical death as the main problem. What the Church proclaims is not just ordinary human or biological life, but the life of the Son of God who became a human being. This life is proclaimed in a world where death confronts us all, not life as mere survival, but life that overcomes death.

Another temptation to be resisted at the Assembly is to think of this life as flowing directly from the Cross, as if the incarnation of Jesus Christ began and ended with the Cross. It is important not only to keep the cross and resurrection together — but to keep the whole incarnate life of Christ as a single unit. There can be no Christian "theology of the Cross" divorced from the annunciation to the Blessed Virgin, the birth, the baptism, and the public ministry ending in the Resurrection, Ascension, Pentecost and second coming. It would be equally misleading to contrast a "theology of glory" and a "theology of the Cross". The cross is where Christ was glorified ("Now is the Son of Man glorified", John 13:31). The glory of Christ was manifested also in the washing of the disciples' feet as in the Cross and Resurrection and in all the acts of the economy of salvation.

A third temptation is to see the life of Jesus Christ as somehow unrelated to the life of the Holy Spirit.

II. The life of the world and the work of the Holy Spirit

Christians are often tempted to confine the activity of God the Holy Spirit to the Church, or to individual human hearts or to the inspiration and illumination of the Bible.

But the Spirit was with Christ from the beginning of creation, brooding upon it, giving life to it, bringing form and perfection to all things. Long before man appeared on the face of the earth, the Spirit has been at work in the world, proceeding eternally from the Father.

The Church glorifies the Holy Spirit along with the Father and the Son, for the Spirit is Creator, Life-giver and Perfector. He is with Christ always. It was the Spirit of the Lord who abode upon Jesus at baptism, and who anointed him to preach the good news (Luke 4:18-19). It is the Spirit who gives life (John 6:63), because it is the Spirit of him who raised Jesus from the dead (Rom. 8:11). To set the mind on the Spirit is life and peace (Rom. 8:6).

It is important to affirm these five elements about the work of the Spirit:

a) The whole saving activity of Christ is inseparable from the work of the Holy Spirit, and the christological and pneumatological affirmations should be kept integrally related to each other, in a fully trinitarian context.

b) The work of the Holy Spirit as Life-giver and Perfector should be seen in its wider cosmic sense and not just in a narrow ecclesiastical or individual sense. It is the Spirit who makes all things new — the Spirit of the new creation.

c) The bread of life, the body and blood of our Lord, becomes that by the invocation of the Holy Spirit. The Holy Spirit is not an impersonal force, but the living Spirit of God, who is also the Spirit of the community, the Spirit who perfects and completes all the sacramental mysteries of the Church.

d) The salvation of the world should be seen as a "programme" of the Holy Trinity for the whole of creation. The kingdom of God is the inner movement and the final goal of not only every human adventure, but of all the dynamic of the universe. True life is life in the Holy Trinity, in Christ by the Spirit coming from and oriented towards the Father.

e) The Son of God has assumed the fulness of our humanity into himself; in that process, he affirms, he heals and restores humanity by placing it in himself, and therefore in the Holy Trinity. It is the great mystery of the perfect divine-human unity that becomes the source-spring of the new life of the world. In making Christ central in our theological understanding, however, the trinitarian and incarnational aspects of the new life should always be held together, in a christocentric but not in a christomonistic manner.

III. The life of the world — as it is, was, and will be

The life of the world, just as the life of humanity, as we see it today, is a picture of groaning and sighing, of suffering and sin. We see distortion and disfigurement, despair and disunity, corruption and hatred, deceit and self-destruction. We experience a possessed world, maniac, malicious and full of self-hatred. It is a world over which the mushroom cloud of doom may rise any day. It is a world starving not only for food, but also for human dignity, for a ray of hope, for the knowledge of true love and deep joy. It is a world of oppression and exploitation, of torture and persecution, of loneliness and lovelessness, oppressed by the darkness of evil, haunted by the ghosts of hell. It is a world gripped by sin.

But that is not the whole truth. There is much here for which we can truly give thanks, both inside and outside the Church: the cup of cold water given to the thirsty, the love that suffers and sacrifices, the joy of the home, the peace of the forgiven sinner, the ability to enter deeply into the suffering and joy of others, the exhilaration of true worship, the consolations of a life of prayer, the sweetness of the inner liturgy of the heart, an earth that gives fruit in due season, technology (with all their ambiguities), health and holiness, hunger and thirst for righteousness, and myriad other gifts from the loving hands of God.

The world is not evil by nature. Human beings are not sinful by nature. Men and women, as well as the world in which they live, are intrinsically good, for they were so created. By the grace of creation human beings have within them all the potential for trust, sacrifice, freedom, peace, love and community. Physical nature in its beauty and grandeur can manifest the glory of God. Jesus Christ is the life of the world: he renews and recapitulates all things — humanity, history and the creation.

The world, because of the presence of sin and evil in it, has also people who take offence at the Good News of the death and resurrection of Christ. The word of the cross is a scandal and folly to those who are perishing (1 Cor. 1:18,23). Christians cannot thus assume that all men and women are always ready to receive life from the one who was crucified and risen for the life of the world. On the contrary, Christians, in seeking to mediate Christ's life to the world, often met with opposition, hostility, persecution, and sometimes death. This happened often despite the utmost sanctity and faithfulness in the Christian. Therefore we as Christians should always be prepared to give account of our faith and to make fearless confession of Christ before the world (Mt. 10:26-33).

Demonic forces are operative in the world. To identify these evil forces is a first step towards their exorcism. The Holy Scriptures and the whole Orthodox tradition remind us of the perennial conflict that pits the Light against the Darkness. The Cross and Resurrection is the high point of this conflict, and the victory of light over darkness.

The conflict, however, continues to our day. We cannot proclaim Jesus Christ as the life of the world without thinking about the millions who suffer — from poverty and want, from oppression and exploitation, from religious persecution, from ignorance and injustice, from torture and imprisonment without trial, from punishment by false trial, from the violation of human rights. We have to relate the proclamation of Christ to every manifestation of the struggle against these evils — movements for the liberation of the oppressed, for improving the health of millions, for removing ignorance and injustice.

That is the world as it is — a field in which the wheat and the tares grow together, where good and evil are intermingled. But that is not how it was in the beginning. When it was first made, God saw that it was good. Sin is an intrusion. Evil is not the true nature of the world. The destiny of the world is to be brought together into unity and be harmonized in Christ, without sin and death pervading it.

It is this eschatological world as it shall be (because Jesus Christ was incarnate in it and has redeemed it by his death and resurrection) that we have to affirm at the Assembly; not as an escape from the world, as it is, but as possibility for the world now, by the grace of God, as the standard by which it should not be judged, and as the goal towards which it should not strive to move.

Our understanding of Jesus Christ, of the Holy Spirit, of salvation, of the life of the Church and of its mission and ministry should be set firmly in the context of this eschatological understanding of the world at the Assembly.

The world as it shall be cannot of course be separated from the "manifestation of the sons of God" (Rom. 8:19), but then the eschatological fulfilment of the sons and daughters of God should not be separated from the salvation of the whole world either — of humanity, of the whole of life, of the whole of history, of the whole cosmos. The preparatory work for the Assembly should clarify how the work of Christ and of the Spirit affect the whole world, both through the life of the Church and otherwise.

The "life of the world" includes the whole creation, but at the centre of it is humanity. The salvation of humanity includes, however, the salvation of the world itself. Our salvation will be manifested in its fulness at the time of our resurrection. At that time the whole creation will also be reconstituted. As our mortal bodies are transformed into immortal resurrection bodies, the whole constitution of the material world will also be transformed, so that it is no longer subject to decay and disintegration. This participation of the world as such in the salvation wrought by Christ is an important aspect of proclaiming Jesus Christ as the life of the world.

IV. The life of the world and the life of the Church

The world is sick. The Lord came for its healing. The Church is planted in the world for the healing of the nations. The Church should not be seen simply as Noah's Ark to salvage a few specimens of the human race (species) about to perish. The Holy Spirit came upon that small Jerusalem community on the day of Pentecost in order that, through them and through others who were to believe in Christ through their word (John 17:20), the world may be healed and redeemed.

If we want to affirm at the Assembly that Jesus Christ is the life of the world, we will have to show the world how the life of the Church mediates that life to a world torn by strife and dissension, blackened by sin and evil, losing hope day by day, a world where love, joy and peace have become words without concrete and meaningful content, where poverty destroys millions of people, where man's inhumanity to man cries out for redress. This is a most important part of the preparatory work, to make clear how Jesus Christ is to be mediated and his life made available for the life of the world. It requires not only a deep knowledge of the sickness of the world, but also developing the skills necessary to set the healing forces in operation — a true diagnosis and therapy for the world's sickness.

The world seeks to escape suffering and to enjoy comfort; it wants security without faith; it seeks pleasure hoping it will bring joy; it does not know how to overcome the pain of loneliness or to make suffering creative. It strains and strives for money, power and property, thinking that these will bring wealth and happiness.

To say that the bread of life which came down from heaven is the body and blood of Christ means everything to the believer; but it may mean practically nothing to the world. How do we mediate the Eucharistic Bread of Life and make it nourish the life of the world? What are the distortions that have beset the body of Christ to prevent this new life from reaching the world for whose life Christ came into the world?

These are some questions about how the true life of eucharistic community and Christians' prayer of the heart can directly or indirectly contribute to the life of the world. Do we do it through a particular style of life? Are there some distortions in our understanding of God's purpose, of the life of the Church, and of the way the eucharist is to shape our lives which prevent the flow of life to the world? The Orthodox especially have a lot of room for self-criticism on this point, as well as for creative reflection on how the eucharistic life can really nourish the life of the world in our different societies.

It is obvious that throughout history Christians have failed to be faithful and have obstructed the work of God in the world. God in Christ has equipped the Church with all the gifts of the Spirit necessary for its upbuilding and its ministry; the eucharist and the other sacramental mysteries of the Church as well as the provision of bishops, presbyters, and deacons, are all for this purpose. The fasts and feasts, the liturgical calendar and offices, the churches (parishes) and monasteries, the various ways of sanctifying different times and places, the growth of saints in the Church, all these exist both for the healing of Christians, and for the mediation of the new life to the world. A rich tradition of iconography makes the unseen world of the holy events and persons physically present in the Church.

In the Church, the Spirit of God is at work despite our failures as Christians. Those who have the Spirit can discern the work of the Spirit in the Church and in the world, despite human belief and disobedience. The Spirit has not abandoned the Church or the world. Along with our confession of faith in God the Holy Spirit, we confess our belief also in the One, Holy, Catholic and Apostolic Church.

Yes, despite our failures — and they are many — God is at work. But that is no ground for complacency. Neither does that fact justify our failures. Our lack of love, however, hinders the Spirit. Our indiscipline makes the heart of God grieve. Because of our unbelief God does not do his great work of healing the sick, cleansing the leper, opening the eyes of the blind, as Christ did where there was faith.

So, the first step in effectively mediating the life of Christ to the world is to call ourselves to repentance and to a life of renewed faith and disciplined obedience to the will of God. The healing of the nations demands that Christians be disciplined healers. We have to put to death the old Adam in us, and be clothed with the new man in Christ. The deep spiritual *askesis*, or discipline, of daily dying to ourselves and being born anew in Christ by the Spirit, has to be practised by all Christians, whether living in a monastery or not. *Theosis* is a continuing state of adoration, prayer, thanksgiving, worship, and intercession, as well as mediation and contemplation of the Triune God and his infinite love. This life of participation in the life and worship of the Church and the "inner liturgy of the heart" constitute a foretaste of *theosis*, for every Christian, as he walks his pilgrim way through life. "Be still and know that I am God", says the Lord. We need to practice that deep silence of the Spirit, in order to receive the life of God and to mediate it to the world. We need also to "put on the whole armour of God, for our struggle is not against flesh and blood, but against the powers of darkness, against the spiritual hosts of evil" (Eph. 6:10-16).

The life of Christ can be made available to the world only through communities of disciplined Christians. True witness is *martyria*, the martyrdom of dying to self, living in Christ, and serving the world. It includes proclamation by word and deed, but demands also a life of *askesis* or spiritual training. Christ himself fasted forty days and prayed all night. Members of his body can do no less.

But is God not all powerful to accomplish everything without our aid? There are four aspects to the answer to that question:

a) *Incarnation:* God can always do everything. And God has willed that humanity should be assumed by the second person of the Holy Trinity. In Jesus Christ, God and humanity are so united that there is no question of two different agents or two different subjects. When Christ acts it is the Incarnate God who acts. The saving act is a divine-human act. Humanity has been chosen to be a full participant in God's actions in the world.

b) *The Holy Spirit:* The Holy Spirit, through whom God the Word became a human being, acts in such a way through human beings that while it is God who acts, the subjectivity of human beings is not abolished. God the Holy Spirit becomes so deeply united with the human spirit that a human being can so act in the unity of the Spirit; while it is the human being who acts, it can also be said equally truly that it is God who acts.

c) *The Body of Christ:* The Church has become the Body of Christ. Our bodies are thus members of Christ's body (1 Cor. 6:15). "He who is united to the Lord becomes one spirit with him" (1 Cor. 6:17). We are not our own. We are to glorify God in our bodies, which have now become the Body of Christ (1 Cor. 6:20). When we are united with Christ our actions become the actions of Christ, and thus divine-human acts. There is here no idea of cooperating with God as equals, or of salvation by works.

d) *Synergeia:* This is the deep foundation for the patristic teaching on salvation. It is not the case that we are equal partners with God or that God cannot act independently through us. God calls us to surrender ourselves to Christ in order that he may unite us to himself and work through us, enhancing our freedom and in no way abolishing our personal subjectivity.

Our flesh is weak, but we are not daunted by the weakness of the flesh, for the Word of God has become flesh. The life of Jesus Christ includes our bodies of flesh, our minds and wills and all our human faculties.

It is precisely in our weakness that the strength of God is manifested. The Spirit helps us in our weakness. When we acknowledge our natural limitations in humility and repentance, then God takes us and does his mighty acts through us. Where there is faith, God works through the feeble and the powerless. The apostles were not chosen because they were wise or learned, wealthy or powerful. The people of Israel were chosen when they were an enslaved people in Egypt. Not many of us Christians were chosen because we were wise and strong.

But weakness remains weakness where there is no repentance or faith. Our problem today is that we are so preoccupied with our past failures and present powerlessness that we do not set our minds on the Spirit of God, who is wise and powerful. So long as we put our trust in our own wisdom and resources, the Spirit of God does not do his mighty acts through us. "We have this treasure in earthen vessels, to show that the transcendent power belongs to God and not to us" (2 Cor. 4:7). That transcendent power is not limited by our limitations, but only waits for our repentance and faith to receive that power.

Theosis, that infinite process by which the Spirit of God transforms us and transfigures us into the glory of Christ, begins here, while we are in this mortal body, amidst all our weakness. That process is true life, and the necessary precondition for the Church's mediating the life of Christ to the world.

This is not a question of somehow just living, but living from God, in God, towards God. It is through such a life in God, united with Christ in the Spirit, that we can mediate the life of Christ to the world.

We have to spell out in greater detail the impact of the saving economy of Christ as the life of the Christ, and on human life in general. God the Holy Spirit constitutes our sinful and disordered lives into an orderly and holy life, in accordance with the "new man" in Christ, created in holiness and righteousness.

The Eucharist animates the dead and reconstitutes broken human beings into a life that grows in Christ by the Spirit. Orthodox hymnography describes the mystery of the Eucharist as life-giving ("zoopoion") and as living bread ("artos zoes"). In the Church, broken human lives are rescued and restored; physical life receives eternal life planted within it; human beings are rescued from the tyranny of sin, death and corruptibility.

In communion with God in Christ, the Spirit bestows life, nurtures and feeds life, and himself becomes the guarantee and foretaste of life without death.

This does not mean, however, that we must first become perfect, before we begin to mediate God's life to the world. It is in the process of mediating the life of Jesus Christ to the world that our own lives become transfigured and we are set in motion on the way of theosis or becoming Christ-like and therefore God-like. This is why true Christian witness is an integral and inseparable part of the new life in Christ.

V. The dialectic of openness and community

We have to be open both to the healing and saving power of God, and open to the world, so that Jesus Christ becomes the life of the world.

We have to be fully open to the world, experiencing its suffering and joy, in true Christian "com-passion" or co-experiencing. We take upon ourselves the pain and suffering of the world, as we identify ourselves with the world in true acts of self-giving love. As we live in this double openness to God and to the world, the powers of the Kingdom operate in us and transform us.

Such openness to the world cannot be achieved by giving some money while closing our hearts. Com-passion with the world means understanding and respecting people different from us — different in race or class, sex or status, belief or unbelief, religion or language, habits and manners.

The Eucharist is offered at all times and in all places, not just for the Church, but also for and on behalf of the whole of creation. Openness towards the whole of humanity and to the whole of creation is the hallmark of an authentic eucharistic spirituality.

And yet, our eucharistic openness to the whole world does not imply that the eucharistic community loses its identity as the chosen and elect body of Christ. While the eucharistic community itself cuts through all barriers of class and race, of Jew and Gentile, of bond and free, the community has its own integrity, and the unbaptized (including catechoumens) are not allowed to share in the Eucharist. The Eucharist is an act of the community incorporated into Christ by baptism and chrismation. The community opens its doors to the world when the Word of God is proclaimed, but closes its doors before it enters the presence of the Almighty where Christ is seated at the right hand of God and where the eucharistic sacrifice is offered eternally by Christ the High Priest.

This dialectic of alternate closing and opening of the doors (of the Church, but not of our hearts) is the central mystery of the Church's identity and cannot be compromised. Because the table is the Lord's, it does not follow that anyone can indiscriminately partake of the body and blood of the Lord. The eucharist is for the community; the fruit of the eucharist life is for the world. The eucharist is offered on behalf of the whole creation but only members of the body of Christ, incorporated into Christ by baptism and chrismation and living his or her life in Christ, can partake of the holy mysteries. None of us are worthy of such participation but God, in his infinite mercy, has made us partakers of the mystery of the eucharist.

The life of the eucharistic community has thus its eucharistic identity. This identity is an *anamnesis* or awareness of the fact that our lives come from God the Creator, and that we have been redeemed by the death and resurrection of Christ. The liturgical anamnesis perpetually renews our identity as the members of the body of Christ. Part of the sickness of the world comes from a refusal to remember and acknowledge the source and ground of our life.

This community which lives by the perennial liturgical *anamnesis* of creation and redemption bears witness to Jesus Christ through its daily liturgy of intercessory prayer for and loving service to the world. Orthodoxy, or the right glorification of God in eucharistic worship, results in orthopraxy or the life of prayer and service in the lives of individuals, groups, and congregations.

The therapy that the Church experiences in the Eucharist and in the other mysteries of the Church should result in a therapy for the sick world. This does not mean a system of social ethics which the Church prescribes for its members; it implies, rather, a healing ministry directed not only towards individuals in the world, but also towards its socio-economic and political life. The compassion of the Church for the whole creation works itself out in the struggle against the world rulers of darkness, against injustice and oppression, against the denial of freedom and dignity for all, against torture and confinement without trial, against the suppression of minorities, against the violation of human rights. It results also in positive services to humanity, for education and health, for sane and healthy human communities, for just and equitable economic development, for a stable and strong family, and for making a human life possible for all.

The actual form and content of this *philanthropia* and *diakonia* will vary from country to country, from age to age. But in all times and all places the Church has to be perceptive and sensitive as well as creative in suiting the *diakonia* to the needs of the people.

VI. The unity of the Church and the unity of the Churches

The Orthodox Church confesses its faith in the oneness of the Church. Therefore there can be no churches (in the plural) except as manifestations of the one true Church. The unity of the Church does not mean creating a worldwide organization, often called structural unity. The one Church cannot be created by putting all the local churches and individual denominations into one worldwide structure.

The unity of the Church is the unity in Christ, by the Spirit, with the Triune God. The Church is Christ's body, and there is only one body, as there is one Christ and one Spirit. The Church then is that great mystery in which Christ unites to himself all those whom God has chosen, by the Holy Spirit. This includes all those from Adam and Eve till our day, and we the Christians living today form but a segment of that whole reality which spans the ages and unites heaven and earth. Thus the unity of the Church means being united with this great, mysterious transcendent reality. It is this Church that manifests itself in its catholic fulness in each local church; the local church is not to be conceived of as part of some other reality called the universal Church, which is sometimes understood as composed of local churches.

The unity of the Church thus is not simply something we confess in the Creed, but also experience in the local church, as the eucharist community presided over by the bishop with his presbyters and deacons.

The promises and assurances in the discourse and prayer of Christ recorded in St John 13:31-17:26, including the promise that when the Spirit of Truth comes "He... will guide you into all the truth" (16:13), were fulfilled at Pentecost. Christ came in the Spirit and formed those who believed in him into his body, the Church. Thus Pentecost is both the birthday of the Church, and the continuing experience in history of those who have since joined the communion of those illumined and glorified in Christ. It is thus that the prayer of Christ for unity (John 17:11) was fulfilled and is being fulfilled, and all the Truth is being revealed.

It is also a unity which is to be consummated and manifested when Christ appears in glory, devoid of all spots and blemishes, freed from sin, perfectly united to the head of the body, Christ, sharing in the life of the Triune God. "That they all may be one, even as we are one" (John 17:11). This unity in the Triune God, with Christ in us and we in Christ, Christ in the Father and the Father in Christ by the Spirit, as an eschatological reality, is the standard and norm for the unity of the Church today. This Church which is the "fulness of Christ" cannot itself be judged by us, for Christ with his Church is the Judge of the world itself. A great deal of confusion is sure to be caused at the Assembly by the Orthodox as well as others using the word "Church" sometimes in this sense and sometimes in the sense of the institutional structures of various local churches.

The fact that this God-given unity of the Church is something assured by God himself does not, however, mean that the Orthodox need not be concerned about the unity of all churches, for which the World Council of Churches is a privileged instrument. The division of Christians is a scandal and an impediment to the united witness of the Church. A world hungering for life can be ministered to much more effectively if all churches were united; but that union of churches has to be based on their unity with the One Church, the Body of Christ. Our efforts for the unity of all churches should be based on the norm and standard of the God-given and eschatological unity of the One, Holy, Catholic and Apostolic Church of Jesus Christ in the Triune God, the Church which we confess in the Creed and experience in history.

It is also a warning to the Orthodox participants not to be pressured into any minimalist conceptions of Christian unity and therefore of "intercommunion". We all acknowledge the Lord Jesus Christ as our God and our Saviour, we are all committed to live for the Glory of the Triune God, Father, Son and Spirit. We all acknowledge the unique and primary authority of the Holy Scriptures as the Word of God. This is the recognized basis of our collaboration in the life of the World Council of Churches. But the Orthodox do believe that they bring something essential to the richness of the ecumenical fellowship. We live by a faith and tradition which has been handed down to us from Christ and the apostles. We wish to keep this tradition open to criticism from other Christian brothers and sisters; we are willing to learn where we are contrary to the authentic tradition. But we should not be asked or pressured to be unfaithful to that tradition on the basis of some argument which appears rational and Scripture-based. Our memories are long, and we have the experience of being led astray by arguments which looked rational and were based on Scripture.

We have a common need to widen the basis of our ecumenical fellowship. We need to understand afresh the fundamentals of the unbroken Tradition of the Church to which the Orthodox seek to bear witness.

We hope that the Assembly will open a new stage in mutual openness, respect and understanding between the Orthodox and other Churches. This document is part of an attempt to contribute to such openness and mutual understanding.

The Assembly will of course be an occasion for a torrential flow of words. Let us hope that it will also be an experience of genuine ecumenical openness to God and to the world, marred as we would be by our divisions.

Such openness is difficult, painful, for all of us. It is beyond our feeble powers. But the moment we confess that it is beyond our power, the transcendent power of the Spirit will take hold of us and lead us where He wills, i.e. nearer to our God-given unity in the Triune God, Father, Son and Holy Spirit.

Report of an Inter-Orthodox Symposium
"Baptism, Eucharist and Ministry"

Boston, USA, 11-18 June 1985

I. Introduction

1. We give thanks to the triune God that we, hierarchs and theologians representing the Eastern Orthodox and Oriental Orthodox Churches, members of the World Council of Churches, were able to gather together at the Holy Cross Greek Orthodox School of Theology in Brookline, Massachusetts, USA. Our task was to help clarify a number of questions which might arise for the Orthodox Churches when they consider their official response to the document on *Baptism, Eucharist and Ministry* (BEM) adopted in Lima (1982) by the Faith and Order Commission of the World Council of Churches.

2. We would like to express our gratitude to the hosts of the meeting, the Greek Orthodox Archdiocese of North and South America and the Holy Cross Greek Orthodox School of Theology, as well as to the Orthodox Task Force of the World Council of Churches and the Faith and Order Commission which made possible such a widely representative gathering. We are also grateful for the opportunity to meet with several Orthodox parishes in the Boston region.

His Eminence Archbishop Iakovos, Primate of the Greek Orthodox Archdiocese of North and South America, formally welcomed at the opening session the members of the Symposium together with other distinguished guests from the Orthodox and the other churches from the region.

3. The Moderator of the Symposium was His Eminence Prof Dr Metropolitan Chrysostomos of Myra (Ecumenical Patriarchate of Constantinople). Papers were presented on the following topics: "General Introduction on Baptism, Eucharist and Ministry in the Present Ecumenical Situation" (Rev Dr Günther Gassmann, Rev Dr Gennadios Limouris); "The Meaning of Reception in Relation to Results of Ecumenical Dialogue on the Basis of BEM" (Prof Dr Nikos Nissiotis, Response: Bishop Nerses Bozabalian); "The Significance and Status of Baptism, Eucharist and Ministry in the Ecumenical Movement" (Archbishop Kirill of Smolensk); "The BEM Document in Romanian Orthodox Theology — The Present Stage of Discussions" (Metropolitan Dr Anthony of Transylvania); "The Question of the Reception of Baptism, Eucharist and Ministry in the Orthodox Church in the Light of its Ecumenical Commitment" (Rev Prof Dr Theodore Stylianopoulos, Response by Rev Dr K.M. George); "Tasks Facing the Orthodox in the 'Reception Process' of Baptism, Eucharist and Ministry" (Rev Prof Dr Thomas Hopko, Response Metropolitan Prof Dr Chrysostomos of Myra).

4. On the basis of these papers, plenary discussion on them, and deliberations in four discussion groups, the participants in this Symposium respectfully submit the following considerations and recommendations.

II. The Significance of BEM and the Responsibility of the Orthodox

1. It appears to us that we, as Orthodox, should welcome the Lima document as an experience of a new stage in the history of the ecumenical movement. After centuries of estrangement, hostility and mutual ignorance, divided Christians are seeking to speak together on essential aspects of ecclesial life, namely baptism, eucharist and ministry. This process is unique in terms of the wide attention which the Lima document is receiving in all the churches. We rejoice in the fact that Orthodox theologians have played a significant part in the formulation of this document.

2. In general we see BEM as a remarkable ecumenical document of doctrinal convergence. It is, therefore, to be highly commended for its serious attempt to bring to light and express today "the faith of the Church through the ages" (Preface to BEM, p. x).

3. In many sections, this faith of the Church is clearly expressed, on the basis of traditional biblical and patristic theology. There are other sections in which the Orthodox find formulations which they cannot accept and where they would wish that the effort to adhere to the faith of the Church be expressed more accurately. As often stated in the document itself, in some areas the process needs to be continued with more thinking, further deepening, and clarification.

4. Finally, there are sections in which a terminology is used which is not that to which the Orthodox are accustomed. However, in some such cases, beneath the unfamiliar terminology, one can discover that the meaning is in fact close to the traditional faith. In other parts of BEM we notice a terminology which is familiar to the Orthodox but which can be understood in a different way.

5. We also think that the Orthodox Churches have the duty to answer responsibly the invitation of the Faith and Order Commission mainly for three reasons:

a) because here we are concerned with a matter of faith — and it has been the insistence of the Orthodox Churches for some time that the World Council of Churches should focus its attention especially on questions of faith and unity;

b) because the Orthodox have fully participated in the preparation of the text from the beginning and made a substantial contribution to it;

c) because it is important to have the response of all the Orthodox Churches, and not just some of them.

III. Response and Reception

1. Both at the Sixth Assembly of the World Council of Churches at Vancouver (1983) and at the last meeting of the Central Committee (1984) of the WCC, the Orthodox undertook to respond to BEM as a matter of obligation and commitment with a view to furthering the ecumenical movement.

2. We would like to distinguish between the immediate response of the individual Orthodox member Churches of the World Council of Churches to the BEM document and the long-range form of the reception of the text in the Orthodox tradition. We hold that the notion of reception of the BEM document here is different from the classical Orthodox understanding of the reception of the decrees and decisions of the Holy Councils.

3. Reception of the BEM document means that we recognize in this text some of the common and constitutive elements of our faith in the matter of baptism, eucharist and ministry so that we may stand together as far as possible to bear witness to Jesus Christ in our world and to move towards our common goal of unity. Thus reception at this stage is a step forward in the "process of our growing together in mutual trust..."

towards doctrinal convergence and ultimately towards "communion with one another in continuity with the apostles and the teachings of the universal Church" (Preface to BEM, p. ix).

4. Reception of the BEM document as such does not necessarily imply an ecclesiological or practical recognition of the ministry and sacraments of non-Orthodox churches. Such a recognition would require a special action of the Orthodox Churches.

5. As an initial step towards this kind of reception we would wish to see official action on the part of the Orthodox Churches to facilitate the use of the BEM document for study and discussion on different levels of the Church's life so that the Church evaluates the document with a view to the ultimate unity of all churches.

6. In this process of discernment the Orthodox Churches should be sensitive to the similar process of evaluation of the text and of the process of bilateral dialogues in the member churches of the WCC and the Roman Catholic Church. Thus our evaluation will be fully informed of the ecumenical reflections and experiences stimulated by this text.

IV. Some Points for Further Clarification

1. We Orthodox recognize many positive elements in BEM which express significant aspects of the apostolic faith. Having affirmed this initial appreciation of BEM, we offer some examples among the issues which we believe need further clarification and elaboration. There are also issues which are not addressed in the text.

2. In the section on *Baptism*, we note:
   a) the relationship between the unity of the Church and baptismal unity (para. 6);
   b) the role of the Holy Spirit in baptism and consequently the relationship between baptism and chrismation (confirmation), linking water and the Spirit in incorporating members into the Body of Christ (para. 5, 14);
   c) the role of exorcism and renunciation of the Evil One in the baptismal rite (para. 20);
   d) the terms "sign", "sacramental sign", "symbol", "celebrant" (para. 22), "ethical life", and other terms throughout the text.

3. In the section on *Eucharist*, we note:
   a) the relationship of the eucharist to ecclesiology in the light of the eucharistic nature of the Church and the understanding of the eucharist as "the mystery of Christ" as well as "the mystery of the Church" (para. 1);
   b) the relationship between participation in the eucharist and unity of faith;
   c) the role of the Holy Spirit in the eucharist, with special reference to *anamnesis* in its relation to *epiklesis* (para. 10, 12);
   d) the relationship between the eucharist and repentance, confession, and reconciliation to the eucharistic congregation;
   e) the meaning of sacrifice (para. 8), real presence (para. 13), ambassador (para. 29), and the implications of "for the purpose of communion" in regard to the reservation of the eucharistic elements (para. 15);
   f) the participation of baptized children in the eucharist.

4. In the section on *Ministry*, we note:
   a) the link between ordained ministry today and the ministry of the apostles and apostolic succession (para. 10, 35);
   b) the distinction between the priesthood of the entire people of God and the ordained priesthood, especially in light of Pauline teaching on the different functions of the members of the one Body of Christ (para. 17 & commentary);

c) issues related to the ordination of women to the priesthood (para. 18), including the way in which the problem is formulated in the text of BEM;
d) the relationship between bishop, presbyter and deacon;
e) the relationship between *episcopé*, the bishop and the eucharist.

V. Tasks Facing the Orthodox Churches

In view of future work in connection with BEM, we offer the following considerations and recommendations.

1. Steps should be taken to enable translation and distribution of the BEM document in the languages of all Orthodox Churches.

2. Orthodox Churches should see to it that the BEM document is studied and discussed in clergy and laity groups, theological faculties and seminaries, clergy associations, as well as in interconfessional groups.

3. Orthodox Churches should be open to reading BEM and to responding to it in a spirit of critical self-examination, particularly in the area of current practices in churches and parishes. They should also use this process as a stimulus and encouragement for the renewal of their life.

4. In studying and evaluating BEM, the Orthodox should move beyond the theological scholasticism of recent centuries by reappropriating the creativity and dynamics of biblical and patristic theology. This will enable them to move towards broader perspectives and to think more deeply about certain issues.

5. In their ongoing bilateral conversation, Orthodox Churches should take BEM into account.

VI. Perspectives for Future Faith and Order Work

In view of the future work of the Faith and Order Commission and the WCC as a whole, we recommend the following perspectives for a proper inter-relationship between BEM and the Faith and Order study projects "Towards the Common Expression of the Apostolic Faith Today" and "The Unity of the Church and the Renewal of Human Community".

1. The process of an ecumenical reappropriation of the apostolic faith and tradition as it was begun in the BEM document should be consciously continued in the two other study projects.

2. There should be a clear understanding that baptism, eucharist and ministry are essential elements of the apostolic faith and tradition. At the same time, they are fundamental expressions of the witness and service of the Church for today's world and its needs, its concerns and its renewal. Renewal of both the life of the Church and of the world cannot be separated from the liturgical and the sacramental life of the Church nor from its pastoral responsibility.

3. These two other projects should also be open to insights and suggestions expressed in the responses of the churches to BEM and profit from them.

4. The Lima document highlights the important relationship between the "rule of faith" and the "rule of prayer", to which the Orthodox are so deeply committed. Therefore, we hope that in the two other study projects of Faith and Order this significant insight is seriously taken into account as well.

5. We further recommend that one important point in future work of the Faith and Order Commission in relationship to BEM should be the clarification of theological terminology and of linguistic problems in translation. This seems to be necessary in

view of the heading "Ministry" of the third section of BEM and terms such as "sign", "reception", and "believer's/adult baptism".

6. Starting from a clarification of the vision of the Church which undergirds BEM, the future work of Faith and Order should concentrate on ecclesiology by bringing together the ecclesiological perspectives in BEM, in the responses of the churches to BEM, and in other study projects of Faith and Order.

* * *

We, the participants in the Symposium, experienced this meeting as an occasion for exchanging our views and clarifying common perspectives. We saw in it also an important means for furthering contacts and cooperation among the Orthodox Churches and thereby promoting our conciliar spirit.

An Orthodox Statement
on the Prague Consultation

V. Rev. Dr G. Dragas, Dr (Ms) D. Koukoura
V. Rev. Dr G. Limouris

The inclusion of such a brief statement was requested by the small minority of the Eastern Orthodox participants in the above consultation. The final plenary approved the inclusion of such a statement, to be written at a later date. It represents some critical remarks about certain procedural and methodological aspects of the consultation.

On the whole we felt that the consultation was imbalanced and one-sided. There was a predominance of women participants who were concerned with women as such, in most cases from a feminist point of view. This is manifested in the choice of topics for presentation and discussion and especially in the daily lengthy feminist reflection on the Bible to which no response was allowed in spite of strong objections from several participants especially the Orthodox. In the opinion of the Orthodox such a reflection not only did not take seriously the traditional stance of the churches, but was openly offensive inasmuch as it distorted the historical teaching of the Bible, explicit and implicit, by imposing value judgments of feminist ideology on the biblical data.

The strong commitment to feminist ideology of many of the participants meant that critical theological discussion in a spirit of mutual respect was often replaced by an unprecedented emotionalism which opted for particular contexts, cases and concerns at the expense of common basic experience. Thus the women's plea for inclusiveness was made in such a way that it excluded the traditional Catholic and ecumenical Orthodox perspectives. Women's rights and concerns tended to determine most of the agenda and the discussion and thus the actual subject of communion of women and men in church and society was partially treated. The attempt of the Orthodox participants to direct attention to the central theme of the consultation was greatly resisted and unfairly criticized. As a result of this one-sided feminist approach, there was no discussion on such central topics like family, divorce, the children, the young people and the elderly. Such topics central to the theme of the consultation and of central concern for the churches today were replaced by partial modern and general ideological and sociological concerns including women's rights, the ordination of women and other related subjects. Though particular concerns and issues are important, the central concerns which bring out the mind of the participating churches should be given priority.

From the methodological point of view the consultation was yet another example of the trend that seems to be dominant in several contemporary secular/sociological

---

● This statement was drawn up at the consultation organized by the WCC's Faith and Order secretariat in Prague, 25 September-2 October 1985, on the Community of Women and Men and issues of unity and renewal.

and religious contents, which involves the promotion of positivist tactics, which push for this or that particular case or cause. The imbalance which results from such an approach leads to false pretences which neither enjoy any special value nor carry any authority among the Orthodox. Even more seriously such approaches undermine the significance of Faith and Order as such, and transform it into a source of independent challenges to the member churches of the WCC rather than proving it to be an effective instrument in promoting a profounder and more objective understanding of the common and uncommon stances of the member churches which might lead the churches to appropriate constructive ecumenical actions.

The Orthodox are very firm on the catholic Christian perspectives (apostolic and patristic) which constitute sine-qua-non's of Christian integrity. By structuring the agendas of consultations having in mind the concerns of all the member churches we can be more successful in achieving the true objectives of the Faith and Order movement. Exposure of difference is not easy either to do or accept. It is necessary, however, if more positive and long-lasting results are to be attained to, not only to expose but patiently to investigate the exact presuppositions which lie behind them, so that real advance in mutual understanding and mutual undertaking of responsible action might be taken.

The Prague consultation exhibited most of the possible problems which beset the modern approach to the dialogue — inadequate or one-sided or preliminary treatment of the subjects in question by emphasizing specific/limited cases and contexts and giving the impression of deliberately ignoring the total picture (including the histori-cal/traditional dimension of the case). Yet it ended with a sense of optimism. The unhappiness, frustration, disappointment and tension which were experienced at the beginning of the consultation, were transformed by clear indications of a willingness to understand, to appreciate and to integrate the particular and general concerns.

This statement may still retain something of the sharpness and tensions which emerged at Prague, but it can certainly conclude with a sign of optimism and hope. Whatever the inadequacies of us Christians are, the mystery of the Church is so great and adequate that we can be healed by it especially when we are exposed. Dialogue, serious dialogue, and faith and commitment will indeed lead us to the conquest of the truth, for Christian unity.

Decisions of the Third Preconciliar Pan-Orthodox Conference

The Orthodox Church
and the Ecumenical Movement

Chambésy, Switzerland, 28 October - 6 November 1986

1. The Orthodox Church, in her profound conviction and ecclesiastical consciousness of being the bearer of and witness to the faith and tradition of the One Holy Catholic and Apostolic Church, firmly believes that she occupies a central place in matters relating to the promotion of Christian unity within the contemporary world.

2. The Orthodox Church notes that in the course of history, for a variety of reasons and in diverse ways, there have been numerous and important deviations from the tradition of the undivided Church. Thus arose in the Christian world divergent conceptions about the unity and the very essence of the Church.

The Orthodox Church grounds the unity of the Church on the fact that she was founded by our Lord Jesus Christ, as well as on the communion in the Holy Trinity and in the Sacraments. This unity is manifested through the apostolic succession and the patristic tradition and to this day is lived within her. It is the mission and duty of the Orthodox Church to transmit, in all its fulness, the truth contained in the Holy Scripture and the Holy Tradition, the truth which gives to the Church her universal character.

The responsibility of the Orthodox Church, as well as her ecumenical mission regarding Church unity, were expressed by the Ecumenical Councils. These, in particular, stressed the indissoluble link existing between true faith and the sacramental communion. The Orthodox Church has always sought to draw the different Christian Churches and Confessions into a joint pilgrimage aiming at searching the lost unity of Christians, so that all might reach the unity of faith.

3. The Orthodox Church, which unceasingly prays "for the union of all", has taken part in the ecumenical movement since its inception and has contributed to its formation and further development. In fact, the Orthodox Church, due to the ecumenical spirit by which she is distinguished, has, through the history, fought for the restoration of Christian unity. Therefore, the Orthodox participation in the ecumenical movement does not run counter to the nature and history of the Orthodox Church. It constitutes the consistent expression of the apostolic faith within new historical conditions, in order to respond to new existential demands.

4. It is in this spirit that all the Local Holy Orthodox Churches actively participate today in the work of the various national, regional and international bodies of the ecumenical movement and take part in different bilateral and multilateral dialogues,

---

● The agenda of the forthcoming Great and Holy Council of the Orthodox Church includes an item concerning the ecumenical movement and the role and place of the Orthodox Church in it. This is the working paper which the Council will use as a basis to elaborate further its presence on and commitment to the ecumenical movement, with particular emphasis on the WCC and other ecumenical organizations.

despite the difficulties and crises arising occasionally in the normal course of this movement. This many-faceted ecumenical activity derives from the sense of responsibility and from the conviction that coexistence, mutual understanding, cooperation and common efforts towards Christian unity are essential, so as "not to hinder the Gospel of Christ" (1 Cor. 9:12).

5. One of the principal bodies of the contemporary ecumenical movement is the World Council of Churches (WCC). Despite the fact that it does not include all Christian Churches and Confessions and that other ecumenical organizations are also playing an important role in the promotion of the ecumenical movement at large, the WCC represents today a structured ecumenical body. Some of the Orthodox Churches were among the Council's founding members, and later on all the local Orthodox Churches became its members. As has already been stated on a pan-Orthodox level (4th Pan-Orthodox Conference, 1968), the Orthodox Church is a full-fledged and equal member of the World Council of Churches and with all the means at her disposal, contributes to the progress and success of all WCC activities.

6. The Orthodox Church, however, faithful to her ecclesiology, to the identity of her internal structure and to the teaching of the undivided Church, while participating in the WCC, does not accept the idea of the "equality of confessions" and cannot consider Church unity as an interconfessional adjustment. In this spirit, the unity which is sought within the WCC cannot simply be the product of theological agreements alone. God calls every Christian to the unity of faith which is lived in the sacraments and the tradition, as experienced in the Orthodox Church.

7. The Orthodox member churches of the WCC accept its Constitutional Basis as well as its aims and goals. They firmly believe that the ecclesiological presuppositions of the Toronto Statement (1950) on "The Church, the Churches and the World Council of Churches" are of paramount importance for the Orthodox participation in the Council. It is therefore self-understood that the WCC is not and must never become a "super-Church". "The purpose of the WCC is not to negotiate unions between Churches, which can only be done by the Churches themselves, acting on their own initiative, but to bring the Churches into living contact with each other and to promote the study and discussion of the issues of Church unity" (Toronto Statement, para. 2).

8. Theological studies and other programmatic activities of the WCC are instrumental in bringing Churches together. Particular mention should be made of the Commission on Faith and Order, which carries the work of the "World Movement for Faith and Order". It is underlined that the document on "Baptism, Eucharist and Ministry", elaborated by the Commission with the participation of Orthodox theologians, does not express the faith of the Orthodox Church on many points of capital importance. It constitutes, nevertheless, a significant step in the history of the ecumenical movement.

9. The WCC, however, as an instrument of its member churches, does not confine itself to maintaining a multilateral dialogue within the framework of the Faith and Order Commission. Its manifold activities in the fields of Evangelism, Diakonia, Health, Theological Education, Interfaith Dialogue, combating racism and promoting peace and justice, respond to particular needs of the Churches and of the world today and provide an opportunity for common witness and action. The Orthodox Church appreciates this multidimensional activity of the WCC and fully cooperates in the above-mentioned fields, within the limits of her possibilities.

10. Following the Sixth Assembly of the WCC in Vancouver, there are new perspectives for a more meaningful Orthodox participation in the Council.

The balancing of the vertical and horizontal dimension of the Council's work attempted at Vancouver opens new ways for bringing the Orthodox theological thought in the life and activities of the WCC.

11. It is a fact, however, that an essential Orthodox witness and its specific theological contribution will be weakened, if we cannot find within the WCC the necessary conditions which will enable the Orthodox Churches to act on an equal footing with the other WCC members, on the basis of their own ecclesiological identity and in accordance with their own ways of thinking. Something which often does not occur because of the very structure of the WCC and the procedural principles, applied in the running of the Council.

The same applies with reference to the Local Orthodox Churches' participation in and cooperation with other inter-Christian organizations, such as the Conference of European Churches (CEC) or any other local or regional council, in which the Orthodox Church is called upon to co-operate and bear her witness.

In this connection, concern is expressed about the ongoing enlargement of the WCC, resulting from the admission of different Christian communities as new members. Such a development will reduce in the long term the Orthodox participation in the various governing and consultative bodies of the WCC and will be detrimental to a healthy ecumenical dialogue within the Council. Consequently it is necessary to make new adjustments within the Council, in order to enable the Orthodox to give their witness and theological input, as the WCC expects them to do, according to the mutual understanding between the WCC and its Orthodox member churches (the Sofia desiderata).

12. The Orthodox Church is conscious of the fact that the ecumenical movement takes new forms in order to meet the new conditions and face the new challenges of today's world. In view of this development, the creative contribution and witness of the Orthodox Church, on the basis of the Apostolic tradition and her faith, is indispensable. We pray that all Christian Churches work in common in order to bring nearer the day when the Lord will fulfil the hope of the Churches that there will be "one folk, and one shepherd" (Jn 10:16).

* * *

Points requiring immediate action

1. It is essential to create within the World Council of Churches, the Conference of European Churches and other inter-Christian organizations the necessary conditions which will enable the Orthodox Churches to act on an equal footing with the other members of the above-mentioned organizations, on the basis of their own ecclesiological identity and in accordance with their own way of thinking, which often is not the case, because of the structure and the procedural principles governing the work of the above-mentioned inter-Church organizations.

It is therefore necessary to work out in the WCC and the other ecumenical organizations new regulations in order to enable the Orthodox Church to bear her witness and give her theological contribution, as expected by her partners in the ecumenical movement.

More particularly, concerning the relations of the Orthodox with the WCC, it is necessary to deal with those of the "Sofia desiderata", on which so far there was no decision.

2. The Orthodox Church, while participating in the multilateral theological dialogue within the framework of the Faith and Order Commission, should find ways of coordinating her efforts, especially as regards the ecclesiological criteria of her participation in this multilateral dialogue.

Report of an Inter-Orthodox Consultation
"Orthodox Perspectives on Creation"

Sofia, Bulgaria, 24 October–2 November 1987

A group of Orthodox theologians representing twelve Eastern Orthodox and Oriental Orthodox member churches of the World Council of Churches throughout the world met in Sofia, Bulgaria, from 24 October to 2 November 1987. The consultation was sponsored by the Programme on Justice, Peace and the Integrity of Creation of the World Council of Churches and enjoyed under the gracious hospitality of the Bulgarian Orthodox Church. At the end of the consultation a report on "Orthodox Perspectives on Creation" was made available with a special request that it be taken into consideration for the preparation of the WCC Conference on the Integrity of Creation to be held in Oslo (Norway), 24 February-4 March 1988. The report is specially commended to the Orthodox member churches of the WCC for study, prayer and action.

1. The creation

Creation and Holy Trinity

1. We believe that the created world itself is a "mystery" originating in the sovereign will of God accomplished by the action *(energeia)* of the Holy Trinity. We confess in the Nicene-Constantinopolitan creed (325/381) that the Father is the "Creator of heaven and earth and of all things visible and invisible", the Son "He through whom all things were made", and the Holy Spirit, the "Creator of life" *(zoopoion)*. Thus, the three persons created together the world, which is the fruit of the common action of the Holy Trinity issuing out of the one essence.

2. As St. Basil the Great said, "We should understand in the creation the original cause of the Father as a founding cause, the cause of the Son as a creative one, and the cause of the Spirit as an implementing one" (St. Basil, *De Spiritu Sancto*, P.G. 32, 136B). Thus, the Father is the "Creator of all things" *(Ta panta:* 1 Cor. 8:6; Rom. 11:36), the Son is the one "through whom all things were made" (John 1:3; 1 Cor. 8:6; Col. 1:16; Heb. 1:2), and the Holy Spirit is the one "in whom are all things" *(en o ta panta:* Gen. 1:2). "Everything that he (God the Creator) had made... was very good" (Gen. 1:31), because "first He conceived, and His conception was a work carried out by His Word, and perfected by His Spirit" (St. Gregory the Theologian, *Homily* 38,9, P.G. 36,320; cf. also St. John of Damascus, *De Fide Orth.* 11, 2, P.G. 94, 865).

3. Thus, the action of the Holy Trinity, rooted in the Father, is presented as the "economy" of the Son and the Spirit; the former bringing God's desire into existence and the latter perfecting it in goodness and beauty; the one calling the creation and leading it to the Father, and the other helping the creation to respond to His call and communicating perfection to it. Thus, the creation is the result of the communion

(koinonia), close relationship and cooperation of the Holy Trinity. The community of three Persons participates actively in the execution of the whole of God's plan.

Creation "out of nothing"

4. "In the beginning" the Holy Trinity created the world (heaven and earth) "out of nothing" *(ex nihilo)* and not out of pre-existent matter. The world is a production of God's free will, goodness, wisdom, love and omnipotence. God did not create the world in order to satisfy some need of His. Rather he created it without compulsion and without force in order that it might enjoy His blessings and share in His goodness. God then brought all things into being out of nothing, creating both the visible *(oratôs)* and the invisible *(aôratos)*.

5. "Out of nothing" (ex nihilo) finds its first expression in the Bible (cf. Gen. 1; John 1:3; Isa. 42:5, Ps. 33:6). "Beholding the heavens and the earth, and seeing all that is there, you will understand that God has created it all from nothing" (2 Macc. 7:28). Thus, the creation springs into being or passes into being out of non-being. As St. Gregory of Nyssa affirms, "It begins to be, and the very substance of the creation owes its beginning to change" (St. Gregory of Nyssa, *Homily* 29, P.G. 31, 89-91). This transition from non-existence to existence is a change brought about by God's creative Word "who has established the world so that it shall not be moved" (Ps. 93:1).

Creation of the cosmos — integrity of the world

6. God is the Creator of the world. The world as cosmos, i.e. a created order with its own integrity, is a positive reality. It is the good work of the good God (Gen. 1), made by God for the blessed existence of humanity. The Cappadocian Fathers teach that God first creates the world and beautifies it like a palace, and then leads humanity into it. The genesis of the cosmos, being in becoming, is a mystery *(mysterion)* for the human mind, a genesis produced by the Word of God. As such, the world is a revelation of God (Rom. 1:19-20). Thus, when its intelligent inhabitants see it as cosmos, they come to learn about the Divine wisdom and the Divine energies. The cosmos is a coherent whole, a created synthesis, because all its elements are united and interrelated in time and space. A serious study of the mystery of creation, through faith, prayer, meditation and science, will make a positive contribution to the recognition of the integrity of the creation. The daily office of the Church (vespers) begins with a psalm which exalts the beauty of this mystery (Ps. 104, LXX 103), while the Fathers of the Church often comment on the various biblical passages which describe the integrity of the creation.

Value of the creation

7. The value of the creation is seen not only in the fact that it is intrinsically good, but also in the fact that it is appointed by God to be the home for living beings. The value of the natural creation is revealed in the fact that it was made for God (something which is beautifully expressed in Orthodox iconography), i.e. to be the context for God's Incarnation and humankind's deification, and as such, the beginning of the actualization of the Kingdom of God. We may say that the cosmos provides the stage upon which humankind moves from creation to deification. Ultimately, however, the whole of the creation is destined to become a transfigured world, since the salvation of humankind necessarily involves the salvation of its natural home, the cosmos.

Human being as a microcosm

8. The fact that Adam and Eve were created by God last of all the other created beings and in a different way — not just by the utterance of a Divine Word but by the direct involvement and action of God — indicates not only the outstanding position of the human race in the whole of the creation but also its special relation to God. According to the Church Fathers, Genesis 1:26ff "... Let us make man..." *(poiesomen anthropon)* shows that the creation of the human being was the result of a Trinitarian act. Particularly significant in this connection is the statement that "man was made according to the image and the likeness of God". The reference to "the image of God" is to be understood in terms of Jesus Christ, since he is explicitly identified with it (2 Cor. 4:4; Col. 1:15; Heb. 1:3ff). Thus for mankind to be in the image of God means to be in, or assimilated to, Christ. This is a matter of grace and act and not a matter of nature, because only Christ is by nature God's image as God's eternal and natural offspring, his only begotten Son. The "likeness of God" is often connected with the grace of the Spirit who assimilates us to Christ.

9. In the created world only the human being combines material and spiritual elements. Human existence is thus differentiated from non-human creation in a qualitative way. In light of this fact, the Church Fathers often speak of the human being as a "little world", a "microcosm" of the whole of the creation. Using this notion, the Church Fathers teach that the human body contains in it all levels of existence of the natural world which preceded it in the order of the creation, and considered the physical elements which make up the human body as in no way different from those which constitute the physical world. This means that the natural world is fully integrated with the human being and the whole of the creation.

10. At the same time, the Fathers' use of the notion of microcosm means that humanity, created in God's image and likeness, transcends the material world because it participates in God spiritually and consciously, unlike the rest of the creation. Humankind then stands on the boundary *(methorion)* between the material and the spiritual worlds as a connecting link. It is directly related to the earthly aspect of created existence as well as to the uncreated existence of the Creator. As such, on the one hand, it directly influences our thinking about the integrity of creation, and on the other hand it gives to human nature a dynamic spiritual dimension.

11. St. Gregory the Theologian *(Homily* 45,8) says that we are fully involved with the material creation by virtue of our physical existence, and that the material created reality is deeply involved with us. If we move to the direction of deification, our human nature, progressing towards God, will somehow carry the created material world with it. If, however, we move to the opposite direction, the created material world will suffer with us as well (cf. Rom. 8:19-22). This means that we are called to exercise dominion over all creatures on earth (cf. Gen. 1:28), i.e. to be stewards *(oikonomoi)* of God's material world, caring for it, maintaining it in its integrity and perfecting it by opening it up to God through our own deification.

The Incarnation as the renewal of the creation

12. God's will, wisdom and love for the creation in general and for humankind in particular are revealed in the Incarnation in an inexpressible way. The Son of God, as the one through whom the process of creation was fulfilled, came down from heaven into the world and became fully man, i.e. assumed human nature in its integrity and led it to the fulfilment of its God-given destiny, deification. The Orthodox Church

teaches that the Virgin Mother of God, the Theotokos, is the model of the renewal of humankind and the creation in Christ. In her receiving of the Son of God, the whole humankind and the whole of the creation participate. In the Incarnate God the Father "made known... his will... as a plan for the fulness of time, to unite all things in him (Christ), things in heaven and things on earth" (Eph. 1:10). In other words, Jesus Christ, the Son of God became man, restored and renewed humanity and the whole of the creation, uniting both of them with the Creator in and through Himself. One of the Trinity, thus, became Incarnate, became man, revealing his Lordship over the whole of the creation, and showing humanity a Lordship in stewardship and service.

II. Disintegrated creation

The human fall and the disintegration of the creation
    13. Before their fall the first human beings experienced the creation as one harmonious whole. It was like a beautiful garden (*paradeisos*, Gen. 2:8) which they tended with care and love. The human fall, however, which was essentially a sinful exercising of human freedom, introduced forces of disintegration into the body of creation. Humanity experienced a two-fold alienation. On the one hand, it was estranged from the Creator, since Adam and Eve tended to hide themselves away from the sight of God (cf. Gen. 3:8) as their communion with the source of life and light was broken. On the other hand, humanity lost its capacity to enter into a proper relation with nature and with the body of the creation. Enmity between the natural world and human beings replaced the relationship of harmony and care. Domination and exploitation of the creation for selfish ends by greedy human beings became the order of history. Thus, manifold forms of disintegration set in which converged in the fact of death and corruption. Fear of death instilled anxiety, acquisitiveness, greed, hatred and despair in human beings. Modern forms of economic exploitation, racial oppression, social inequalities, war, genocide, etc. are all consequences of the fear of death and collective signs of death.
    14. Creation was given to humanity as a gift that they may share it in a eucharistic sense, so that the sustenance and fulfilment of life might be achieved. The divine plan assumes that there is a material give-and-take relationship between human beings and the natural world.
    15. Sin obscured the glorious image of God in the human person, but it did not efface it completely, as St. Athanasius and the whole of the patristic tradition affirmed. St. Gregory the Theologian teaches that through the fall humanity lost only its condition of wellbeing, but not its possibility of being. Through the Incarnation of the Word of God the door of salvation was opened to humanity, through which human beings can enter again into a relation with their Creator which restores them in the divine image and enables them both to secure the being and to regain the lost condition of their well-being. It is in this context of the salvation which is offered by God in Christ not only for human beings but also for the whole of the creation that human beings have a special responsibility to exercise their freedom in a way which serves God's gracious activity for the reintegration and transfiguration of all reality.

Human sin and forms of injustice
    16. Several issues, which bear the stamp of human sin, should be identified and underlined because they exemplify some of the glaring forms of injustice and disintegration which we experience today (cf. Habakkuk 1:3; James 5:4). They should

be given serious and immediate attention by the Church and all people of goodwill. They call for the urgent exercise of Christian responsibility towards the creation and for the practical manifestation of the Christian concern for the human person and the humane community; recognizing their shortcomings in the past in this respect, Christians have now also to show their solidarity with all people of goodwill in fostering the forces of justice for manifestation of the kingdom of God in humankind and in the whole Creation.

Poverty and economic injustice

17. The poverty of millions of people in some parts of the world and the accumulation of unmerited wealth in some other parts reveal the demonic face of injustice created by human beings in God's creation. It has become clear today that political, economic and technological forces, operating at transnational levels, can arbitrarily inflict poverty and socio-economic crises wherever they want, as well as inordinate and unjust affluence. Two thirds of humanity suffer from the loss of the dignity, which is one of the chief marks of the divine image in the human person. Consumerism, profligate styles of life, exaltations of money and material values, catering to illegitimate pleasures of the senses, greedy competition for material success, etc. are other prominent elements of the syndrome of injustice which results in the increasing impoverishment of our world.

The environmental crisis

18. Environmental issues like air and water pollution, depletion of non-renewable resources, destruction of the ozone layer, increasing nuclear radiation, deforestation and desertification of vast areas, etc. threaten the life itself on this planet. The gifts of science and technology are being misused by human beings to the extent of abusing nature and turning today's life on earth into a hell, not only for the many millions of existing people but also for the generation to come. The voice of those who call for a just development, equal distribution of resources and ecological life-styles is being systematically suppressed. Advances in bio-technology and genetic engineering need to be seen in the light of the Holy Spirit because without adequate knowledge of the transcendent (divine) vocation and spiritual nature of humanity, these new techniques run the risk of initiating biological disruption leading to disastrous mutations that are extremely dangerous for the true life on earth. While human creativity and freedom can be affirmed as supreme gifts of God, it should also be emphasized that they should be rooted in divine wisdom and in human spiritual maturity.

Racism and discrimination

19. It is a great insult to the God-given dignity of human beings that various forms of discrimination on the basis of race, colour, creed and culture are practised in our world today. Very often an alliance between dominant economic forces and powerful political forces supports and helps to maintain racial, political, cultural and religious discrimination. The cry of millions of people who are oppressed because of their race or their cultural identity is a serious concern of all Christians and of all other people of goodwill. Racial discrimination with all its violent and inhuman manifestations is one of the tragic consequences of colonial and imperialist domination. Christian faith affirms that diversity of race and culture reflects the beauty of God's creation. To deny the inherent right of people to affirm their identity with self-respect, dignity and openness to others is a sin against God's creation.

Injustice to women

20. Injustice to women all over the world is another sign of the human fall and the disintegration of the creation. In many parts of the world, women's dignity as human beings is trampled upon through sexism, inequality in wages and discrimination. The conditions of life in many parts of the world are such that women are subject to physical and mental harassment, insults and insecurity. There is a genuine issue of injustice towards women and the churches need to be seriously concerned with this.

21. Orthodox Church calendars have a long list of women martyrs and saints. Orthodox women participate responsibly in the teaching of the Christian faith, diakonia, church choirs and other vital activities in the life of the Church.

22. But one has to admit that, due to certain socio-historical factors, women have not always been provided with opportunities for active participation in the church's life at parish and diocesan levels.

The arms race

23. Production and sale of arms and the accumulation of nuclear weapons by nations constitute a grave affront to human dignity and to the cause of justice in the creation (cf. Isa. 2:4; Ezek. 39:10). Much of the misery and suffering of many human beings today can be traced to the demonic world of arms race and arms production. Nations plunder the bread-bowls of humanity to create weapons of death in the name of national security or defence against enemies. So many of the human sources are today dedicated to the arms race that all other efforts for the improvement and betterment of the human condition suffer from lack of adequate resources. Not only is butter traded away for guns, but also much-needed social reforms, or constructive economic development programmes, or the commitment of funds for medical research, for the healing of all kinds of illnesses, for increased educational opportunities, and for a host of humanity-benefiting projects are set aside. The arms race forces humanity to trade away its birthright for a full and god-like existence in exchange for a militaristic bowl of pottage (Gen. 25:27-34). This is the distinctive sin of the 20th century, for not only do this attitude and pursuit destroy many potentialities and opportunities for human growth and development, but they threaten humanity itself with the ultimate sin of nuclear destruction.

III. The transfigured creation

Jesus Christ Saviour and Redeemer

24. The terrible consequences of sin in all of its manifestations in humanity, in society and in the environment make it imperative for all human beings to search for ways and means to do away with the evil which has accumulated in the world at the present time.

25. Christians confess that, "left to itself", humanity is unable to rid itself of the power of sin and its consequences of corruption and death. Humanity is incapable of saving itself (Rom. 3:10-20). Salvation can only come from Almighty God, the Holy Trinity. Sin was perpetrated by humanity through its exercising of free will. On the other hand, the redemption of sin is a perfect act of God's will "who is love" (1 John 4:8). Thus, salvation is a divine answer to the evil which "exists" parasitically in the whole of the creation. The essence of salvation is expressed in the sacrifice of the God-man, our Lord Jesus Christ on the Cross and His victory over death, sin

evil, through His Resurrection: "… so that as Christ was raised from the dead by and the glory of the Father, we (human beings) too may walk in newness of life" (Rom. 6:4).

26. Thanks to Christ's sacrifice on the Cross, every human being and the whole of the creation receive the gift of victory over sin, evil and corruption (Col. 1:14-17). Death did not triumph on Calvary. Christ is risen. Christ's resurrection is a solid and fundamental hope for every believing human being in the struggle against evil in all of its manifestations. It is already a guarantee of the ultimate triumph of life and therefore a hope for the salvation of every person and of the entire creation.

27. The New Testament reveals the eschatological reality of the new, renewed and perfected world — the New Jerusalem (cf. Gal. 4:26; Rev. 21:10). In the Eucharist one is given to live and experience the world which is in unity with God, and to enter into communion with the eschatological world (John 6:26ff.). This new reality, granted by the Holy Spirit, is present in the Church, its sacraments, diakonia, witness and thought. Having thus received spiritual vigour and hope as with Christ through this vision, Christians see their responsibility to transfigure — always with God's grace — creation in both a spiritual and a material way. The eschatological vision thus creates prerequisites for this effort on the part of Christians to work for justice and peace and the integrity of creation (cf. Rom. 8:18-24).

28. Furthermore, the views about an inevitable and necessary nuclear destruction of God's creation (the so-called "Armageddon concept" found in sectarian fundamentalism) are, according to Orthodox teaching, completely unfounded and provoke new sins. According to God's promise and Testament, after the flood, such a destruction will never recur (cf. Gen. 8:21-22).

Human freedom and response

29. Humanity receives everything from God as a gift (cf. Rom. 3:23-24; 1 Cor. 12:4-7), but it receives salvation by active participation in it (cf. Thess. 5:23). The redemptive sacrifice on the Cross and the Resurrection of Jesus Christ form a blessed and dynamic reality involving the free response of humanity. Already, at its creation humanity was imbued with the dynamics of creative development through the grace of God's image which was given to it.

30. Consequently, human beings have been able to become co-workers with God responding to his calling them to be creatively masters to tend and transform the world in harmony with the divine will and purposes. Inasmuch as humanity was created in the likeness of God, it was entrusted with the task of perfecting not only human nature, but also the created nature which forms its natural habitats. Conversely, in perfecting the created world humanity contributes to its own perfection. Thus salvation goes beyond the framework of the individual human being and moves into the wider sphere of social diakonia in the Church, the society within which the Church finds itself and the wider sphere of the entire created world.

31. The understanding of salvation as a gift from God rests on the free response of human beings both in the way they think and in the way they act. By participating in the divine grace humanity experiences both the good works and the good will of the Creator. Human beings became "partakers of the divine nature" (cf. 2 Pet. 1:4) and for this reason they are instructed to respond through a certain way of life (cf. 2 Pet. 1:2-11), which implies sharing the image and likeness of God both on the personal and the social planes (cf. Rom. 12). The fact that God has endowed humanity with freedom (cf. Gal. 5:1) creates the opportunity for a positive or a negative involvement in the

God-established order and harmony in the world *(sedeq)* and for the restoration of this order *(sedeqa)* (cf. Amos 5:21; Gen. 30:33).

32. Hence, humanity has been given the responsibility to work together with the grace of God in the process of salvation for personal transformation of all humanity and for renewal of the earth which is our home.

33. In the course of appropriating salvation to itself, humanity brings about the transfiguration of the material world as well, which is also God's creation, since both the spiritual and the material forms are the one reality of God's creation. Thus, Transfiguration is granted to both the human being and the material creation. The creation exists for humanity, while humanity exists as a microcosm which is designed to bring the whole of the creation to sanctification and to fulness of life, by bringing it into communion with its Maker.

How shall Christians respond?

34. It is by the grace of God, which comes from the Father through the Son in the Holy Spirit that human beings are given to follow their Lord Jesus Christ, by existing for each other in self-sacrificing love, in affirming peace and justice and in collaborating for the restoration of the integrity of creation.

35. There is always the need for the faithful to draw on the sacramental treasures of the Church in order to live a life of prayer and ascetic discipline for personal growth in God-likeness, so as to make themselves ready to follow their Lord in the service of their fellow human-beings. This includes taking care of social structures of their bodily and spiritual needs in Christian service (diakonia). This life of selfless dedication ministers to the needs of the integral human being (soul and body) as well as that being's social milieu. It is the expression of true discipleship. "I was hungry and you gave me food. I was thirsty and you gave me drink, I was a stranger and you welcomed me" (cf. Matt. 25:35-37). Christians are called to respond to the problems created by human sin against justice, peace, and the integrity of creation, by taking appropriate action. "For God is at work in (us), both to will and to work for his good pleasure" (Phil. 2:13). Thus the churches need to be vigilant against evil forces that operate in subtle and in overt ways against the forces of life and truth in our world.

Economic injustice

36. As churches of Jesus Christ we must challenge the sins of imposed poverty and all forms of economic injustice. We have a special responsibility to struggle for an economic order which is based on genuinely spiritual and moral values. This means we must become knowledgeable regarding the powers and forces which perpetuate economic injustice. Our pulpits cannot ignore the just needs of the economically abused. Christians in places of power need to exercise it in the spirit of Christ and against those institutional structures which perpetuate the conditions which keep poor nations and peoples subservient to the economic super-powers (cf. Deut. 15:9). Positively we need to encourage efforts at international interdependence, co-operative economic enterprise and economic support of the developing peoples and nations, always with due respect for their human dignity and integrity.

A reintegrated environment

37. The environmental crisis is a sin and a judgment upon humanity. We need to find ways, as churches, to support sound programmes which seek to preserve from pollution air, water and land. To speak of the reintegration of creation today is first to

speak words of repentance and to make commitments towards the formation of a new way of living for the whole of humanity. The contemporary world must repent for the abuses which we have imposed upon the natural world, seeing it in the same kind of relationship to us as we see the unity of our human nature in both body and soul. We must begin to undo the pollution we have caused, which brings death and destruction to the mineral, vegetable and animal dimensions of the world environment. We must work and lobby in every way possible to us in our different situations to encourage the scientific community to dedicate the good potentials of science and technology to the restoration of the earth's integrity. For ourselves, this means a recommitment to the simple life which is content with necessities and — with the Church Fathers — sees unnecessary luxuriousness as the deprivation of necessities owed to the poor. In all of its aspects, concern for the reintegration of the creation calls Christians to a new affirmation of self-discipline, a renewal of the spirit of asceticism appropriate to Christians, regardless of their status, position or condition. In short, we must see the created world as our own home, and every person in it as our brother and sister whom Christ loves.

38. Words, however — even changed attitudes — will no longer suffice. Wherever we find ourselves, as Christians we need to act in order to restore the integrity of creation. A creative, cooperative, active and determined plan of action is required for implementation.

Respect for human dignity

39. We must deplore the sins which repeatedly tear apart the fabric of our common and shared humanity: racism, prejudice, discrimination. Our Lord's deep and compassionate concern for "the least of His brethren" cannot but provoke every Christian who takes seriously the call of discipleship to repent of our own abuses of justice and to raise our voices on behalf of the oppressed. One aspect of the Christian mission to the world today is to be truly apostolic in restoring fallen humanity to its divine-human dignity, as manifested in Christ. For this the Church has to express its deep-rooted commitment to justice in concrete and relevant ways in our time. We must affirm, loudly and clearly, the truth that God's image is present in every human being. We need to seek out and actively cooperate with all forces of good working for the eradication from God's creation of all forms of prejudice and discrimination. We ourselves must teach our people to respect the integrity and dignity of all peoples of every nation, economic condition, race, sex, political affiliation, so that reconciliation and tolerance may replace coercion and violence in our relationships. Our goal is nothing less than the reign of God's love among all peoples.

Women in the world and the Church

40. Both in personal attitudes and in institutional life the world has a long history during which women have been unjustly treated, and their essential humanity as God's image and likeness has not been fully respected. Such sinful divisiveness is not acceptable from an Orthodox Christian perspective (cf. 1 Cor. 11:11). In the world recreated by Christ, both male and female dimensions are integrally related to each other (cf. Gal. 3:28). The genuine harmony between these two dimensions is a symbol of the integrity of creation in its diversity. We Orthodox must recommit ourselves to the truth of our faith according to which women's true dignity is as "joint heirs to the grace of life" (cf. 1 Pet. 3:7) existing together with men. We must raise in our consciousness the important affirmation of our faith that, as members of the Body of

Christ, women share in the "royal priesthood" (cf. 1 Pet. 2:9) of all believers. It is of fundamental importance in the Orthodox Church that a woman became the mother of our Incarnate Saviour and that she remains the model *par excellence* of the integral humanity to which all Christians, men and women, aspire. Historically, we have always recognized in the Church the diaconal (cf. Rom. 16:1; Tim. 5:9-10) witnessing (cf. Matt. 28:10) and nurturing roles of women (cf. 2 Tim. 5:9-10). In particular, Orthodox men must acknowledge that, as full members of the Church, women share in the intercessory vocation of the Church to stand in the presence of the Lord on behalf of all creation. In concrete terms we must find means to allow the considerable talents of women in the Church to be devoted as fully as possible in the Lord's service for the building up of the Kingdom. This means more opportunities for theological education for women and the opening of career opportunities in the Church for women. Serious consideration must be given to the re-introduction of the ancient order of Deaconess by the hierarchies of the local churches.

Towards a peaceful world

41. In the messianic prophecies one of the specific actions of humanity in building the new world is disarmament. The people of the messianic age are presented as hammering their swords into ploughshares and their spears into pruning hooks (cf. Isa. 2:4). The prophet Ezekiel speaks about making fires of the abandoned weapons. The people — says this prophet — "will not need to take wood out of the field or cut down any out of the forest, for they will make their fires of the weapons" (cf. Ez. 39:10).

42. Orthodoxy condemns war, which it considers to be the result of evil and sin in the world. The arms race has reached such proportions that its consequences go far beyond legitimate needs for defence. As Orthodox we must continuously affirm the strong bias of our Church for peace so evident in our liturgical life and in the writings of the Church fathers. St. Nicholas Cabasilas says that "Christians, as disciples of Christ who made all things for peace, are to be 'craftsmen of peace'" — *(technitais eirenes)* (*Life in Christ*, P.G. 150, 676). One of the foremost responsibilities which we have today is to engage in a concerted struggle against the arms race as an evil force in our day. We must clearly declare our position on behalf of a reduction of armaments affecting all kinds of arms; both the conventional and the nuclear, on land, at sea, in the air and in the outer space, especially in view of the fact that nuclear war can destroy all life on our planet.

43. Because we live in a new age of potential total destruction, our ongoing concern for peace takes on a greater intensity. We must join others of good will to work for peace in the world, and people must be pressured to give up the arms race and seek alternative ways of security and development for all peoples. Above all, Christians should continue to pray constantly for peace and to support all initiatives for peace based on justice.

Other concerns

44. Many other tasks relating to the integrity of creation and the world in which we live face us. Among these we mention two without developing them. Orthodox Christians and churches need to enter more fully and more responsibly into intellectual discussion of the major problems related to the integrity of creation; the considerable resources of the Orthodox faith must be brought to bear on these problems together with the insight of other faiths. This makes it imperative for the churches to use all means at their disposal, including communications/mass media to witness to the faith,

especially to youth. We need a deeper and more studied approach to the contemporary issues which face us. Among those are the problems of the modern family and the stress it faces, including powerful forces seeking its disintegration.

Conclusion

45. We confess that God is the creator of all that exists, beautifully and wonderfully made, a fitting manifestation of his glory (cf. Ps. 103). But we stand today before a wounded creation which suffers under distorted conditions which are the result of the sin of humanity. In our selfishness and greed we have used our otherwise good technological abilities to exploit God's creation, to destroy the balance of nature and to deform what God originally made to be in wholesome communion with us and with Him. Creation is no longer integrated with humanity nor is it in harmony with God. In fact it stands in danger of conflagration, in the face of nuclear war.

46. The creation needs to be reintegrated, but this can happen only as it is brought once again into communion with the Lord, so that it may find its fullness of purpose and its transfiguration. Humanity can no longer ignore its responsibility to protect it and preserve it. In order to do this, however, humanity must learn to treat the creation as a sacred offering to God, an oblation, a vehicle of grace, an incarnation of our most noble aspirations and prayers.

47. Just as bread and wine are lifted up as an offering for the sanctification of the world and all people in the Eucharist, a sacramental approach to the creation is needed for its reintegration.

48. We specifically recommend to all Orthodox churches and all Orthodox Christians that special support be given to the work of the WCC programme for "Justice, Peace and the Integrity of Creation" as it prepares for the forthcoming convocation on JPIC in 1990.

49. The Lord God created His universe and all that is in it as an integrated whole. Today, we have brought about disintegration in what God intended to be integrated. We call upon individuals, nations and churches to give effect to a vision of the rightful harmony between the human dimension and the mineral, plant and animal dimensions of the creation. In spirit and in body, we are called to offer the whole of God's creation back to Him as a sacrament and as an offering cleansed, purified, restored for His sanctification of it.

50. O God, "the things that are Yours, we offer them of You according to all things and for all things. Amen." May this be our prayer for the "integrity of God's creation".

Address by His All Holiness Dimitrios I, Ecumenical Patriarch

On the Occasion of His Visit
to the World Council of Churches, 11 December 1987

Reverend General Secretary of the World Council of Churches, honourable staff and members of this select gathering:

We are very happy to be visiting today this House, House in the service of the Church, and our own House. And we are most grateful, Sir, for the honour you are paying us in your capacity as principal spokesman of this august institution.

We thank you for all of this, and likewise hasten right away to thank this inter-Church organization for all that it is doing, in the course of its activities in so many fields, for the Church and the whole of the Christian world, for the sister Orthodox Churches, and for our Patriarchate, towards which its sentiments are well-known and proven.

The Ecumenical Patriarchate has been keen on the ecumenical idea right from the start, and has always considered it — like all related activities inspired by it — the most positive beginning and most helpful means for bringing the Churches together, for achieving their coexistence, collaboration and common development, and for their common progress towards the accomplishment of their final, visible Christian union under the lordship of the one Christ, their Saviour, the one shepherd of the one flock (cf. John 10:16).

The World Council of Churches was founded some forty years ago as a "koinonia of Churches", in accordance with the original vision of the Ecumenical Patriarchate in 1920. Since then, and up to the present day, it has placed itself at the disposal of all the Churches and denominations which confess Jesus Christ as God and Saviour, and which have responded to the call to visible unity in the world, to the glory of the Triune God.

We are delighted that our visit coincides with the eve of the Council's fortieth anniversary. At this solemn moment, we can unreservedly say that the World Council of Churches enjoys due recognition and deep respect from us. Consequently we reiterate our conviction right from the start that the Orthodox presence in the Council should be seen as a normal phenomenon, both indispensable and useful in many ways. The ecclesiological self-awareness of the Orthodox Church means that it sees the longed-for unity of the Churches as a gift in Christ, really present in Orthodoxy as it lives the reality of the One, Holy, Catholic and Apostolic Church.

For us, there is no doubt that this is the model to be used in the search for unity.

We know that there have been genuine instances in the Council where, repeatedly and from the very start, this point has been stressed. We also know, Mr General Secretary, that you yourself, since taking up your responsible post in the Council, have repeatedly spoken and worked closely for the increase of this Orthodox presence and witness in the Council. We greatly appreciate your attitude and express our pleasure at it. At the same time we hope that, in the near future, as a result of your efforts and of appropriate decisions by the various instruments concerned, this Orthodox presence may, in helping to achieve the Council's aims, grow ever stronger and more representative in its personnel, in its potential and in the contributions it makes both theologically and in spirituality.

In seeing the relationship and cooperation between you as Council and us as Orthodox Churches in such a context, we recall with emotion the figures of the great leaders and enthusiastic pioneers of ecumenism, whether belonging to our Orthodox Churches or to the other sister Churches in the Movement — those figures who have exchanged this present life for heavenly abodes. May their memory be eternal and their example remain luminous for those now working under this roof, those continuing the good fight.

Needless to say, the Ecumenical Patriarchate, as a member Church of the World Council of Churches, follows with great interest the initiatives taken at all times by the Council. The latter's study programmes, theological and otherwise, and its various activities in very many fields of joint Christian witness and service, are truly most positive elements. In this, if in no other way, the hopeful reality is affirmed whereby, even if the desired full unity of the Churches on a purely ecclesiological and theological level is not assured, it is nevertheless possible to act together in the service of modern man in the most pressing and urgent issues of his life. We feel that this in itself is an important victory for the ecumenism, which we, as a Church, are cultivating.

Now, may we be permitted to go into some details concerning issues, most of which are already being dealt with in the Council's programmes under way.

We would, first of all, like to draw attention to two main current issues, those of "Justice, Peace and the Integrity of Creation" and "The Churches' Witness in the World Today". The former, aiming at the mobilization of the Churches into a "conciliar process" that will be mutually binding on questions of justice, peace and integrity of creation, has the Orthodox Church's approval, though it is not always happy with the wording. Such agreement is possible because, as you know, the Third Pre-Conciliar Pan-Orthodox Conference, in dealing with these particular issues, expressed a unanimous opinion and drew up a most important document, the fourth of that Conference, on "The contribution of the Orthodox Church to the triumph of peace, justice, freedom, brotherhood and love between peoples and the elimination of racial and other forms of discrimination".

As for the second issue, concerning the witness of the Churches in the modern world, we would state that we consider this effort to be praiseworthy. For, both as the proclamation of the joyful message of redemption today in Christ and as the preaching of the one undivided Christ, the joint witness of all Christians is an urgent, a most urgent, need in the deeply divided, secularized, suffering and largely alienated world of today, which certainly wants to know the meaning and application of that petition of the Lord's, "Thy will be done on earth as it is in heaven".

Let us remember what John Chrysostom says on the matter: "He commanded each one of us who are praying to undertake providential action on behalf of the oikoumene. He did not say: Thy will be done in me or in us, but everywhere in the world, so that error may be wiped out and truth be planted, so that all evil may be cast out and virtue return" (PG 57, 279/280).

We could say the same about the other initiatives being undertaken by the Council in response to the demands of the member Churches in relation to the mad upheavals in today's world.

We repeat the principle, often declared by the Ecumenical Patriarchate, and to which it faithfully adheres, that, being preeminently an ecclesiastical institution, it does not dabble in politics. But this does not mean that it turns a blind eye to the immediate effects that events of all kinds have on the life of Churches and their flocks. So our own Church of Constantinople follows with interest the initiatives of the World Council in such fields.

The Ecumenical Patriarchate shows an equal interest in the Council's dialogues with other ideologies, and also those with the other religious systems in the world, especially the monotheistic ones, for basic convergence with these in recognizing one God and Father of all constitutes a capital element of relationship in faith.

In fact, all the other activities of the Council to eliminate the ills besetting humanity — from the pollution of the environment to all sorts of "aberrations"; from the other plagues and disasters affecting contemporary humanity, such as hunger, want, epidemics and suchlike, to the various upheavals which create the problems of refugees, migrants, the homeless and so on — all the efforts being made to combat these ills are interesting and praiseworthy, provided they do not run counter to the main concern of the Council, but constitute acts bringing the Churches closer together in the field of unity.

Hence we particularly wish to highlight, together with the above, the important theological work being done in the Council, notably in Unit I and especially in the Commission on Faith and Order. We believe this to be in line with the main aim of the Council, as an organization in the service of Church unity.

First, let us refer to the text on "Baptism, Eucharist and Ministry" (BEM), produced by the Commission on Faith and Order, in which the Orthodox Churches and most definitely the Ecumenical Patriarchate expressed uniform interest. We are pleased that, in the work of the Commission, the sister Roman Catholic Church participated fully, as a Church not standing aloof from the Council's activities; indeed, we hope that its complete inclusion in the Council will be speedy, and that negotiations in this direction will have a happy end.

Following that, we would like to mention the subject currently being studied, "Confessing One Faith". Right away we can say that this subject also interests us immensely. The effort being made to interpret the apostolic faith, as expressed in the Nicene-Constantinopolitan Creed, is of positive importance; for it will, we hope, lead to a positive explanation of many basic tenets of the one prevailing faith in the Church for centuries, and will on the other hand give a definite answer to the question: How can the faith, handed down by the Apostles to the undivided Church, be interpreted today amid the problems and anxieties of people of our times? We greet with joy and satisfaction the announcement that the aim of this programme on the Apostolic Faith is not the elaboration — even less the imposition — of a new "ecumenical creed" to oust the Creed affirmed under divine inspiration, in the fourth century in the undivided Church, but is to be a means of helping the Churches to confess the same faith in their mission and service to the world, a sort of international consistency in the weighty matters of faith, expressed in the modern vernacular.

After all this, it is already time to conclude.

We have confidence in Christ our Lord and Head of the Church and in the paths which He, in His inscrutable will, is opening up before those who believe in Him and invoke His name.

One such path, we consider the Lord is opening up before us, is the opportunity given to the Churches to meet and progress together towards the common goal of their existence, which is their unity in the one Lord. We rejoice in the coexistence of this Council's member Churches under the same roof, as they search for the direct ways to unity granted by the Lord to the One, Holy, Catholic and Apostolic Church. We also rejoice because, as Orthodox, we find beneath this roof the possibility of witnessing to the faith and teaching we have received — a witness we consider and carry out as a humble service to the Lord's will.

We declare that we, the Ecumenical Patriarchate, will cling to the ecumenical idea and to this Council, which is today its chief voice. We strongly hope that the original aims of the Council will not only not be perverted, but will be reinforced, and that we were not wrong in saying, at the beginning of our speech, that we consider this House as a House in the service of the Churches and our own House.

We stand in this House not as strangers and guests, but as if coming home and talking to our familiars. So, on our own behalf and on that of our Church, we extend warmly to you our loving embrace, our kiss of peace and reconciliation to all the member Churches of the Council, to you, Mr General Secretary, and to all your valued colleagues; and we pray that the Lord will grant the rosy dawn of the day of the union of all in the one, undivided Church, which "he obtained with his own blood" (Acts 20:28) and which he handed down to the centuries "without spot or wrinkle or any such thing, that she might be holy and without blemish" (Eph. 5:27) and also one and undivided unto the end of time.

So be it!

Message of the Ecumenical Patriarchate

On the Occasion of the Fortieth Anniversary
of the World Council of Churches, Phanar, 1988

1. We glorify and praise the Triune God for enabling us joyfully to celebrate this year the fortieth anniversary of the foundation of the World Council of Churches. The Apostolic and Patriarchal Ecumenical Throne of Constantinople jubilantly rejoices over this occasion; it considers the foundation, forty years ago in Amsterdam, of the WCC — the institutional expression of the contemporary ecumenical movement — to be a fulfilment of its vision and realization of its proposal, through the Synodical Encyclical of 1920, to form a "League of Churches", the aim of which was the rapprochement of the churches and confessions around the world through contacts collaboration and mutual solidarity, with the ultimate goal of realizing their unity, under one shepherd, Jesus Christ.

2. Our Ecumenical throne has always taken a lead in whatever concerned Christian unity and it has repeatedly emphasized that the churches of Christ in the world are called to walk on the path leading to unity — a path prepared by the WCC, which thus facilitates mutual acquaintance and rapprochement, helps the multilateral dialogue of churches and so becomes a vehicle in the common pilgrimage of the churches in the fields of theology, of diakonia and of Christian witness in the world.

3. As the Third Pan-Orthodox Pre-Conciliar Conference declared: "The Orthodox Church by her inner conviction and ecclesial consciousness that she is the bearer of and the witness to the Faith and Tradition of the One, Holy, Catholic and Apostolic Church, deeply believes that she has a central and unique position in the Christian world today in order to further the unity of the Church." Therefore, the presence in the WCC of the Ecumenical Patriarchate and of the Orthodox Church as a whole should be considered as natural and seen as both indispensable and useful in many ways. Natural, because of the very nature of the Orthodox Church, with its mission and duty of transmitting the truth contained in Holy Scripture and the Holy Tradition, the truth which gives the Church its universal character. Indispensable, because without the Orthodox participation, the WCC would be an ecclesiastical instrument representing only a fraction of Western Christendom. And finally, useful, because the presence of the Orthodox Church in the WCC enriches the Council's theological thought and brings it closer to the theological thinking of the undivided church.

4. As we already stated in our Declaration made on the occasion of the 25th anniversary of the WCC, many of the Council's positive achievements in the fields of theology, mission, diakonia and Christian witness in the world "are also the result and fruit of the Orthodox presence in the Council". It is our wish that in the near future, through the actions of the various decision-making bodies of the WCC, the Orthodox presence in it will become substantial and more representative, both qualitatively and quantitatively, so that programmes undertaken by the Council and documents prepared in it, may have a really ecumenical character and may constitute the fruit of the

collaboration of all the churches participating and acting within the WCC. To achieve this, however, all local Orthodox churches should also be activated by supporting, so far as they are able, the programmes of the Council, and by proposing new persons, who could offer the Orthodox witness in the Council responsibly and efficiently.

5. As the Ecumenical Patriarchate, we always follow with particular interest the initiatives undertaken by the WCC and participate in them. The theological and social activities of the Council implemented throughout these forty years have undoubtedly represented a response to the urgent needs of the world. At the same time they have justified what was said in the Encyclical mentioned above, that even if on purely ecclesiological and theological grounds the unity of the churches cannot so far be ensured, joint diakonia to contemporary men and women, in the vital and urgent problems of their life, can be made possible.

6. As we contemplate the future of the WCC, we look forward with particular attention and more expectation to the initiative undertaken by the Commission on Faith and Order to interpret the Apostolic Faith as it is expressed in the Nicene-Constantinopolitan Creed. As the natural follow-up of the long-term study on baptism, eucharist and ministry, this effort takes on a special meaning for the future of the ecumenical movement and of the Council itself, for as the Orthodox delegates already stated at the First Faith and Order World Conference in Lausanne (1927) any "reunion can take place only on the basis of the common faith and confession of the ancient, undivided Church of the Seven Ecumenical Councils and of the first eight centuries". This is so, because the very existence of all Christian churches and confessions springs from the Apostolic Tradition and from their common history. The above study, while on the one hand explicating the basic tenets of the one faith prevailing in the church for centuries, will, on the other hand, give an answer to the question: How can the faith handed down by the Apostles to the undivided church be interpreted today amid the problems and anxieties of people of our time?

7. As in the past, so too in the future, the WCC will be called to respond to the multiple needs of contemporary men and women and to give answers to the problems faced by today's world. These are the refugee problem, the combating of racial discrimination, the bringing of peace and justice to the world, the struggle against hunger and poverty in many parts of the globe, the protection of the environment, the good stewardship of which has been placed by God in our hands. The related programmes of the Council however should not constitute an end in themselves nor be isolated actions, but should be part and parcel of a coherent and well harmonized multidimensional activity, within the framework of a common witness to Christ in the world.

8. In congratulating the WCC on this happy anniversary, we declare that the Ecumenical Patriarchate, which from the beginning has been committed to supporting the ecumenical ideal and interchurch cooperation to promote Christian unity, will in the future continue its consistent and responsible collaboration in any beneficial and useful work of the Council, until our Lord shall "deliver us from this present evil age, according to the will of our God and Father" (Gal. 1:4) and lead us all "to the unity of the faith" (Eph. 4:13).

> The grace of the Lord Jesus Christ, the love of God, and the fellowship of the Holy Spirit be with you all. Amen. (2 Cor. 13:13)

Phanar, 28 July 1988   In fervent prayer to God
                                                               Dimitrios of Constantinople

"The Place of the Woman in the Orthodox Church and the Question of the Ordination of Women"

Rhodes, Greece, 30 October-7 November 1988

A. Theological Approaches

I. The Mystery of the Incarnation and the Church

1. The Church, as the great mystery of the work of salvation by Christ, has as her centre the Incarnation of the Son and Word of God. The recapitulation and renewal of all things was realized by the shared energy of the Holy Trinity, for which reason it is in God's Church that the whole mystery of the divine Economy is fulfilled and the Kingdom of God realized in the world.

2. The manifestation of the Kingdom of God is inaugurated in the Church and through the Church, as the historic Body of Christ, into which all of the faithful are incorporated as members, and as such are constituted the People of God.

3. As members of the one and the same body, the faithful are united with each other and with the divine Head of the Body through divine grace in the new life in Christ. Through this they live the new reality as a continuous communion (koinonia) with the Triune God, thus becoming "a chosen race, a royal priesthood, a holy nation" (1 Pet 2:9). All of the members of the Church share in the prophetic, high priestly and royal office of Christ. They become through divine grace communicants of all of the blessings of divine glory by their adoption. They live the fullness of the divinely revealed truth in the Church and obtain the experience of the variety of the gifts of the Holy Spirit in the mystical (sacramental) life of the Church.

4. The Holy Spirit was given to the Church "so that it could unite those who are divided by different races (genei) and conditions (tropoi). For the aged and the young, the poverty-stricken and the wealthy, the infant and the adolescent, the woman and the man, every soul becomes one thing" (St John Chrysostom, *Homily on Ephesians* 9,3, *PG* 62, 72) in the body of the Church. Thus, in the mystery of the Church, the faithful are interconnected and, as an unbroken unity, they celebrate (leitourgoun) the Paschal and Pentecostal Mystery of Christ. This they do by means of the grace of the sacraments through which "in Christ, we live and move and have our being" (Acts 17:28).

II. The Priesthood of Christ

5. As the head of the Church, Christ is forever the only Mediator and great High Priest. For the means of His whole work of salvation and His sacrifice, He reconciled humanity to God (2 Cor 5:18-20). Through the grace of the Sacraments in the Church, the Holy Spirit testifies to the continuity of the presence and mediation of Christ, through which the faithful are constituted "children of God", "heirs of God and co-heirs with Christ". "All have received the Spirit of adoption" (Rom 8:15-17) and all have been made members of the body of Christ (1 Cor 12:17, Eph 4:25, 5:30),

"conformed to the likeness of the Son" (Rom 8:29), and have become the "people of God" (1 Pet 2:10). All the faithful then, are able to participate "in accordance to the measure of the faith" which they have (Rom 12:3-8) in the gifts (charismata) of the Holy Spirit and in the varied ministries (diakoniai) in the body of the Church (Acts 1:17, 24; Rom 12:2; 1 Cor 12:5; 2 Cor 4:1; Eph 4:12; Col 4:17; 1 Tim 1:12; 2 Tim 4:5). The sacramental Priesthood is a distinctive gift (charisma) of the Holy Spirit. It unifies all of the gifts (charismata) and all of the ministries (diakoniai) in the Church. The Lord Jesus Christ remains forever the great High Priest and the sole celebrant of Sacraments.

6. Among the many gifts (charismata) of the Spirit in the life of the Church is the "sacerdotal" or "special" Priesthood. Granted by the Lord Himself, the sacramental Priesthood leads, nurtures and builds up the body of believers. It was given by the Lord to the Apostles and to their successors in the apostolic ministry of *episkopé* for the people of God. This sacramental Priesthood, iconically presenting Christ, as the head of the body, is granted to the Church through the grace of the Holy Spirit at the sacrament of Ordination (Cheirotonia) by which those being ordained are made "servants of Christ and stewards of the mysteries of God" (1 Cor 4:1).

7. Jesus Christ gives this special Priesthood to the Apostles and to their successors. The consciousness of the Church from the very beginning excluded women from participation in this special priesthood, on the basis of the example of the Lord and the Apostolic Tradition and practice, in the light of the Pauline teaching concerning the relationship of the male and female in the new reality in Christ (1 Cor 11:3).

III. The Typology of "Adam-Christ" and "Eve-Mary"

8. This distinction in the relationship of man and woman, in regard to the sacramental Priesthood according to the "order of nature", flows from the deeper understanding of the relation of men and women in the plan of salvation in Christ, yet it was never, in any case, understood in the Orthodox Tradition as a diminution of the role of women in the Church. In the mystery of the whole divine Economy of salvation, women are understood as equally sharing with men in the *image of God*, and as being of equal honour with men. As such, women in the Church assume their own roles for the restoration of the distorted image of God, which are a consequence of sin.

9. The distinct role of women is expressed by means of the typological analogy "Eve-Mary" and by means of the special relationship of women to the distinct work of the Holy Spirit in the whole plan of salvation in Christ. The typological relationship "Adam-Christ", by means of which Adam is the prefiguration of Christ on the one hand, while Christ — being the New Adam — is the model (typos) of the old Adam who recapitulates the human race, is foundational to the whole patristic theology and life of the Church. Consistent with this, the typology determines the special content of the ministry of women in the work of the realization of the recapitulation of the New Adam and the salvation of the whole human race.

10. The central person in the special ministry of women in the divine plan of salvation is the Mother of God, the Theotokos. In her is fulfilled the special work of the Holy Spirit for the Incarnation of the Son and Word of God. The typological relationship "moving from Mary to Eve" was necessary for the release of the bonds of Eve and the Incarnation of the Son and Word of God, through the Holy Spirit and Mary. Thus, while on the one hand Eve "being disobedient, became the cause of death, for herself and all of humanity", on the other hand, the Virgin Mary, "being

obedient, became the cause of salvation for herself and for all of humanity" (St Irenaeus, *Adver. Haer.* III, 22, 4. *Sources Chrétiennes*, vol. 211 (1974), pp. 441). So in this manner, Eve represents the fallen ancient humanity, while the Theotokos represents the renewal of that ancient fallen humanity, through the birth in Christ of the new humanity.

11. This ministry of woman was fulfilled through the creative descent of the Holy Spirit upon the Virgin Mary, which became a "new locus" (topos) for the "power of the Most High which descended upon her". The Holy Spirit cleansed her and granted to her the necessary "creative ability" (gennetiken dynamin) through the wondrous Incarnation of the Son and Word of God which took place through her. Thus, the Virgin Mary, the Theotokos, at the Annunciation, became the receptor of the epiphany of the Holy Spirit for the fulfilment of the typological reclamation by Mary of Eve (tes apo tes Marias eis tén Evan anakykléseos), and for the Incarnation of the New Adam who recapitulates in Himself all things. This relationship between the special work of the Holy Spirit and the Virgin Mary, and the typological relationship of the Old and New Adam in history, thus provides us with important insights into the Church's approach to the issue of men and women in regard to ordination to the sacramental Priesthood.

IV. The Male Character of the "Sacramental" Priesthood

12. The Theotokos has been presented to us as the model (typos) of the Church. The Church, like the Theotokos, receives the Holy Spirit, through whose energy Christ is born and, also, the children of the new humanity in Christ are brought into the world. Thus, in the patristic tradition, there is presented the typological relationship of the *motherhood* of the Theotokos and the *motherhood* of the Church. The special functional relationship of the role of the Theotokos with the work of the Holy Spirit in the Incarnation is extended to and lived in the age of the Church.

13. This typological relationship provides the foundation — through the example of the Theotokos — of the general content of the consciousness of the Church concerning the impossibility of ordaining women to the Christocentric sacramental Priesthood (*Apostolic Constitutions* III, 6,1-2, 9,1-4. *Sources Chrétiennes*, vol. 329 (1986), pp.132-140; see also Tertullian, *De Virginibus Velandis*, 9,1, *PL* 1, 902; St Epiphanius, *Adver. Haer.*, 59, 2-3; *PG* 42, 741-744). Whenever this ecclesiological consciousness is changed, it creates serious ecclesiological problems. These have appeared in the past, and today they are clear in the ecclesiology of those who support the ordination of women to the special priesthood. This is so precisely because this change in ecclesiology weakens the patristic teaching regarding the balance in the Church of Christology in relation to Pneumatology.

14. Thus, the impossibility of the ordination of women to the special priesthood as founded in the Tradition of the Church has been expressed in these ecclesiastically rooted positions:

a) on the example of our Lord Jesus Christ, who did not select any woman as one of His Apostles;

b) on the example of the Theotokos, who did not exercise the sacramental priestly function in the Church, even though she was made worthy to become the Mother of the Incarnate Son and Word of God;

c) on the Apostolic Tradition, according to which the Apostles, following the example of the Lord, never ordained any women to this special priesthood in the Church;

d) on some Pauline teachings concerning the place of women in the Church, and

e) on the criterion of analogy, according to which, if the exercise of the sacramental priesthood by women were permitted, then it should have been exercised by the Theotokos.

V. Christ and the Theotokos in the Recapitulation of Humanity

15. Jesus Christ is the saviour of all persons, both men and women. Yet, in the typological and iconic experience of worship and the pastoral life of the Church, Christ as the High Priest is presented to us appropriately and fittingly only by a male in the High Priestly image. Conversely, the Theotokos, the Mother of God, represents all of humanity, both female and male in the divine act of the Incarnation, giving to the eternal Son of God his human nature. She is the Mother of all, especially the members of the Body of the Church. As such, the Theotokos, in the typological and iconic experience of worship and the whole experience of the Christian life, presents us before the Lord's throne in a way which uniquely speaks for us as creatures of God.

16. All Christians, women and men, must come into personal communion (koinonia) with Christ, who shows no discrimination toward us, for He is the Saviour of each and all in total disregard of any humanly based discriminations. Just as Orthodox Christians, men and women, we find in the first of all Saints, the Theotokos, the person who gave the flesh and soul of humanity to the Son and Word (Logos) of God for His Incarnation, a "ready help", an "intercessor" and a "true mother of all Christians".

17. However, in the typology of worship the unbroken Tradition of the Church, with no exception at all, has called upon only certain men to serve at the Altar as Priests who iconically present to the Body of Christ her head and Lord, the High Priest Jesus Christ. In like fashion, the female figure of the Theotokos is the typological representation of all the People of God. The representative and intercessory place of the Theotokos is made manifest in the iconographic cycle in Orthodox architecture, according to which the icon of the Theotokos, holding the Christ in her lap (Platytera), dominates the liturgical space over the Altar Table. Thus, in the iconic and typological framework of worship, the male figure is appropriate to the High Priestly role, and the female figure of the Virgin appropriately models the Church for all of the members of the Body.

18. We are here not simply dealing with theological concepts and ideas. We are in a sphere of profound, almost indescribable experience of the inner ethos of the world-saving and cosmic dimensions of Christian truth. The iconic and typological mode of dealing with the issue tells us that rational constructs will not be adequate alone to describe and express it fully. Like all of the mysteries of the Faith as lived in Orthodoxy, this one too is articulated with the fear of God and with a sense of reverence. Yet, deep in the inner workings of the ethos and Tradition of the Church, we sense that our words are words of truth and not mere apologetics, and that ignoring the reality of which they speak will not only deny the past reality of the Church, but will deprive all who do so of foundational and essential dimensions of the full Christian experience of life in Christ.

B. Special Concerns

VI. The Equality and the Distinctiveness of Women and Men

19. As was noted above, the Orthodox understanding both of God and the human person is rooted in the fact of Divine Revelation. The manner in which we approach

God, and the way we understand women and men is not left solely to our limited reason, valuable that it is. Rather, God has acted to provide us with insight into who he is and to who we are (Ps 118:27).

20. Because of the Divine Revelation, which is centred upon the Incarnation of our Lord, the Orthodox would affirm the following features as central to our understanding of men and women. Firstly, God is the creator of both men and women. Each has his or her origin with God. This conviction is further strengthened by our acknowledgement that Christ has come to save men and women equally and to restore both men and women to communion (koinonia) with God (Col 1:20).

21. Of equal significance is the Orthodox conviction expressed throughout the Holy Scriptures and Tradition of the Church that there is a distinction between the male and the female which is rooted in the very act of creation (Gen 1:27). This distinction does not imply any form of inferiority or superiority before God. On the contrary, it is a distinction established by God Himself as part of His divine plan. Salvation does not involve, therefore, the denial of our identity as women and men — but rather the transfiguration of this identity.

22. Witnessing the tragic dehumanization which we often encounter in our contemporary society, the Orthodox are bound to affirm in the strongest possible way the dignity of the human person, both the female and the male. Any act which denies the dignity of the human person and any act which discriminates against women and men on the basis of gender is a sin. It is therefore the task of the Church to affirm before the world the dignity of the human person, created in the image and likeness of God (Gen 1:26).

VII. Fuller Participation of Women in the Life of the Church

23. With spiritual discernment throughout the centuries, the Church has encouraged the Christian woman to practice, together with man and in accordance with her nature and her personal inclinations and vocations, a whole variety of ministries. These have been in the area of liturgical, pastoral, catechetical, didactic, missionary, and social work. Special attention should be paid to female Monasticism for the manner in which it has contributed to the advancement of the position of women in the Church in particularly difficult circumstances.

24. While recognizing these facts, which witness to the promotion through the Church of the equality of honour between men and women, it is necessary to confess in honesty and with humility, that, owing to human weakness and sinfulness, the Christian communities have not always and in all places been able to suppress effectively ideas, manners and customs, historical developments and social conditions which have resulted in practical discrimination against women. Human sinfulness has thus led to practices which do not reflect the true nature of the Church of Jesus Christ.

25. Therefore, it is necessary that the fullness of truth should be constantly preserved through intense and unceasing prayer, calling upon the Divine assistance for "discernment of spirits" (1 John 4:1) and interpreting the true meaning of "the signs of the times" (Mt 16:3). Only thus the Church will be able to re-order her ability to walk according to the will of God and to declare His Kingdom in each particular time and in each particular place.

26. The Church should re-examine potential data, views and actions, which do not agree with her unshakable theological and ecclesiological principles, but have intruded from outside and, being in fact perpetuated, may be interpreted as demeaning towards women.

27. Moreover, the necessity for a specific delimitation of roles in the Church should be emphasized, especially in matters pertaining to ecclesiastical organisation. The Orthodox underline spiritual authority rather than temporal power. When we speak about authority in the Church, we are in no way advocating a sort of bureaucratic organisational clericalism but rather we are emphasizing a special charism in the Church.

28. It follows that when we speak of roles in the Church, we speak of special gifts (charismata) of the Holy Spirit to be received with gratitude rather than of what may be interpreted as administrative "ranks" to be enforced by a hierarchical structure. We would here note the importance of highlighting the pastoral dimension that is ours to address issues raised by Orthodox women. These fall within the therapeutic function of the community manifested in different tasks entrusted to its members. We would also underline the importance of the actual work which women are undertaking at the parish level today, but often without sufficient support and encouragement from the leadership of the Church.

29. Among such tasks we would note the following:

a) Education and Christian nurture at all levels ranging from Church schools to higher theological education in seminaries;

b) Pastoral counselling of married couples, families, preparation for marriage, preparation for baptism, and care of people in situations of distress;

c) Church administration, the participation in decision-making bodies at the level of the parish, the diocese and the national church;

d) Social service including working with the elderly, hospital work, working with the deprived and the neglected;

e) Choir directors, readers, singers;

f) Iconography;

g) Youth work;

h) Representation in the various aspects and areas of the ecumenical movement, and

i) Publications/communication.

All these tasks are to be seen as supportive diaconia, a complementary pastoral dimension in harmony with the specific sacerdotal ministry of the clergy.

30. We would also make special reference to the fact that the increasing number of women who are graduates of theology and other fields of advanced study in certain Churches creates a new reality which the Church is called to consider constructively. The zeal, the faith and the dedication of many of these women could effectively contribute to the renewal of parish life and church life as a whole, especially if greater attention were paid to them and if the undertaking on their part of their charismatic and theological ability in their work of teaching in their ministry and pastoral care for the people were blessed through a special ecclesiastical act. The same applies to a greater degree for able and charismatic nuns, who, alongside the practice of asceticism in the monastery, could be present in the parish and care for special needs of the Church militant. Similarly, the wife of the priest exercises a distinctive ministry. Special attention should be given to her vocation as it exists within the contemporary society.

31. All the above, and all other related matters, connected with the place of the woman and more generally of the laity in the Church, regarding their active participation in the various church services and ministries, should become the object of

further study by Theological Schools and specialized researchers. To this end would contribute positively the more regular convocation of theological meetings and consultations, such as the present one, and would promote our spiritual cooperation and participation in the trials and hope of the Church.

VIII. The Diaconate and "Minor Orders"

32. The apostolic order of deaconesses should be revived. It was never altogether abandoned in the Orthodox Church though it has tended to fall into disuse. There is ample evidence, from apostolic times, from the patristic, canonical and liturgical tradition, well into the Byzantine period (and even in our own day) that this order was held in high honour. The deaconess was ordained within the sanctuary during the Divine Liturgy with two prayers, she received the Orarion (the deacon's stole) and received Holy Communion at the Altar.

33. The revival of this ancient order should be envisaged on the basis of the ancient prototypes testified to in many sources (cf. the reference quoted in the works on this subject of modern Orthodox scholars) and with the prayers found in the *Apostolic Constitutions* and the ancient Byzantine liturgical books.

34. Such a revival would represent a positive response to many of the needs and demands of the contemporary world in many spheres. This would be all the more true if the Diaconate in general (male as well as female) were restored in all places in its original, manifold services (diakoniai), with extension in the social sphere, in the spirit of ancient tradition and in response to the increasing specific needs of our time. It should not be solely restricted to a purely liturgical role or considered to be a mere step on the way to higher "ranks" of clergy.

35. The revival of women deacons in the Orthodox Church would emphasize in a special way the dignity of woman and give recognition to her contribution to the work of the Church as a whole.

36. Furthermore, would it not be possible and desirable to allow women to enter into the "lower orders" through a blessing of the Church (Cheirothesia): sub-deacon, reader, cantor, teacher… without excluding new orders that the Church might consider to be necessary? This matter deserves further study since there is no definite tradition of this sort.

IX. The Challenges Posed by Feminist Theology in Non-Orthodox Churches

37. The urgency of speaking about the place of women in the Church in the overall context of clearly addressing real life issues confronting Christians is to be acknowledged. In this respect the importance of specific societal contexts in which our various churches live should be noted. Ours is a call to witness, and the expression of our witness should use a "language" that would clearly communicate our thinking as Orthodox Christians to our non-Orthodox partners in dialogue, be they other Christians within the ecumenical environment, non-Christians, atheists or advocates of specific ideologies and trends of thought.

The challenge of the feminist movement should be particularly addressed as one of the manifestations of real life issues raised within society today.

38. From the perspective of the Gospel, the Church is called by feminist theology to speak about her understanding of the equality of men and of women while respecting their distinctiveness in the perspective of faith. However the requirements or demands of the feminist movement should not be confused with vague theological uneasiness. Not all the issues raised by the feminist movement

are theological issues. Some of them are social issues clothed in seemingly "theological" formulations.

39. The issues raised by the feminist movement should be considered by us Orthodox with all reservations and vigilance in their totality as well as in the particular aspects stated by great feminist initiatives such as the following:

a) The use of inclusive language which should not be taken lightly by us within concrete limits.

b) The emphasis placed by feminists on the exegesis of specific biblical texts especially in the Pauline writings.

c) Their challenge to the idea of the submission of women as it relates to bodily uncleanliness reintroduced into our ethos from the Jewish tradition.

X. The Call to Holiness

40. Every believer has been called by the Lord to a life of discipleship which is characterized by love of God and of neighbour (Mt 22:36-40). The process of sanctification begins in this life through Baptism and Chrismation, it is celebrated in the Eucharist, it is nurtured through the Holy Scriptures and Tradition, it is strengthened through prayer. The activity of discipleship is manifested by each both in the liturgical assembly and in the liturgy of daily life in the world. Every faithful is called by the Lord to follow Him within the daily responsibilities, relationships and obligations of life.

41. The Orthodox believe that the lives of both the male and the female Saints have much to teach us. The Saints show us that they followed the Lord within the context of the circumstances of life. They remind us, therefore, that we too are called in this life to avoid sin and to live a life of virtue to the glory of God.

42. In our reflections during this meeting about the contemporary role of women in the Church, we have been constantly reminded especially of the Theotokos and of the many women Saints whose lives revealed the presence of the Lord Jesus Christ. Among these Saints we remember especially St Phoebe and St Olympia the Deaconesses, St Catherine the Philosopher, St Macrina the Nun, and St Nina the Missionary, St Monica the Mother, and St Olga the Princess. When we consider the example of these and other women Saints, we truly rejoice in the Lord because of their witness, their courage and their piety.

43. Indeed, we are surrounded by a treasured "cloud of witnesses" (Heb 12:1) and we constantly seek their prayer that we too might be worthy of our calling. As sons and daughters of the Father, as followers of the Lord and as persons blessed with the gift of the Holy Spirit, our ultimate goal is to be Saints in order to glorify God, Father, Son, and Holy Spirit — now and forever and unto ages of ages.

Report of an Inter-Orthodox Consultation

"Your Will Be Done: Orthodoxy in Mission"

Neapolis, Greece, 16-24 April 1988

I. Witnessing in the oikoumene today

The apostolic witness

God offers salvation to all human beings of all eras without limitation or exception because God wants all to be saved and to come to the knowledge of truth (I Tim. 2:4). As a result of his unlimited love for humankind, which submitted to evil, distortion and death by abusing the free will, God sent his only begotten Son "that whoever believes in him should not perish but have eternal life" (John 3:16).

Christ conquered sin and death, reconciled and granted peace to all things on earth and in heaven (cf. Col. 1:20), and granted the joy and the hope of the resurrection, which is the heart of the Christian message. "If Christ be not raised, our faith is in vain; you are yet in your sins" (I Cor. 15:17).

Christ ordered his disciples and apostles to proclaim the good news of salvation to all nations (Matt. 28:19), to the whole world and to all of creation (Mark 16:15) so that the salvific grace of Christ should be revealed to all who "sit in the darkness and the shadow of death" (Luke 1:79). The apostles had to be and to become witnesses of all salvific events of Christ's life (cf. Luke 24:48; Acts 10:39). The apostles considered this very witness to be their main mission. In replacing Judas they elected someone who, like they, was a witness to Christ's resurrection (Acts 1:22). Preaching the resurrection, they assured all that they were its witnesses (Acts 3:16). They could not avoid the obligation to proclaim all that they had seen and all that they had heard (Acts 4:20) because the joy of such an experience is only "fulfilled" when it is shared and transmitted to others so that they also might become communicants and participants (I John 1:4).

Throughout the centuries, the Orthodox Church had offered its apostolic witness to the crucified, buried and resurrected Christ. This same witness is continued by Christian mission today in the midst of such challenging conditions as secularization, pluralism, dialogue with other faiths and ideologies.

Witness in a secular world

The mission of the church has cosmic dimensions. Its aim is to embrace and to renew the whole world, to transfigure it into God's kingdom. Mission is to approach and draw near, to sanctify and to renew the world, to give new content to old ways of life, to accept local cultures and their ways of expression that do not contradict the Christian faith, transforming them into means of salvation.

• This consultation was organized by the WCC's Commission on World Mission and Evangelism.

During the first centuries of its existence, the church managed to transfigure the face of the oikoumene in spite of resistance by the world, which attempted to make the church conform to the world. The church responded to these tendencies towards secularization by entering into dialogue with Greek philosophy and pagan culture, which resulted in the production of creative theological patristic literature, the intensification of the ascetic elements of the Christian life of its communities and monasteries as a new means of martyria, and the expanding and enriching of its worship. Within the boundaries of liturgical life the church sanctified the activities and creative talents of human beings in all forms of art (literature, architecture, painting, music).

In Orthodox worship the Christian message is proclaimed through all the senses. The entire human being participates with soul and body, mind and heart; hearing, smelling and touching. The icons, incense, the embrace of peace, the partaking of the eucharistic bread and wine enrich and fulfil the teaching and the preaching.

Education is more successful when influenced by the good news of salvation and a life in Christ in which the principle components are asceticism and eschatological expectation. Ascesis, as a voluntary withdrawal from a consumerist enjoyment of material goods, together with the desire to offer these goods to the poor and the needy, makes the passion and the cross of Christ more conscious in the life of Christians.

Mission is closely related to ascesis. For example, the Thessalonian Saints, Cyril and Methodius, before departing for Moravia, planned their missionary programme and prepared themselves in a monastery of Olympos in Bithinia. Their missionary team was composed of priests, deacons, monks and lay persons. From the Saints of the Oriental Orthodox Non-Chalcedonian family, seven monks left the monastery of St Minas in Egypt, formed a mission and evangelized Ireland. Their relics are still to be found in Belimina (near Belfast). Christian mission in Switzerland has been greatly affected by St Verena, from Egypt. In all Orthodox countries, monasteries assisted in the proclamation and witness of the Christian message.

Unfortunately, in recent centuries, especially following the Enlightenment and the French Revolution, the Christian message was gradually marginalized and humanism became an autonomous anthropology leading to atheism. In such a context, links with the church are severed and the principles of state ideologies and education, as well as consumerism, dominate, satisfying industrial ambitions both in the east and the west. Secularization torments Christian communities in the whole world because the task of different ideologies is to separate human beings from the influence of the church. This separation is caused by destructive forces against the church, thus diminishing the church's diakonia in the world.

Some, who are not satisfied with secularized society, turn not to Christianity but to eastern cults. Islam, in confronting secularization, often turns to a more conservative lifestyle; the reaction to western humanism sometimes leads to an extreme theocracy, which demeans the human being.

The abundance of material goods and economic conformism, dechristianized state power and education, the lack of Christian perspective in the mass-media, the weakness of the family in exercising Christian pedagogical work and the diminishing of the spiritual and apostolic role of motherhood leads to secularism. The contradiction between words and deeds in the life of Christians further contributes to the development of a secular way of life.

Nevertheless, many human beings continue to be attracted to Orthodox Christianity through its asceticism and mysticism, the joy of the resurrection in its worship, the presence of ascetics and saints, and the proof through holiness that Christians are not conformed to the world (cf. Rom. 12:2; I Pet. 1:14).

Witness within a pluralistic society and among believers of other faiths

Today, Christianity is in a situation similar to that of the apostolic era when it faced syncretism and different philosophies or religions. A pluralistic world brings Christianity into confrontation and dialogue with other teachings and faiths. Despite intolerance and fanaticism, Christians can use the immense potential offered by contemporary technology to witness to and evangelize others, to lead them in Christ's way. Christianity sees in a positive way the creative work of human beings when it leads to the uplifting of humanity and to the glory of God. To understand the cultural particularities of the evangelized, we must speak their language, respond with love to both spiritual and material deprivation and bring life and brilliance to each eucharistic community. The love we owe to those of other faiths makes more imperative our duty to confirm, as did the early Christian Apologists, whatever truth may be found in them while affirming the fullness and authenticity of the salvific truth of Christianity, even under pressure of persecution. The Orthodox churches, continuing the apostolic witness, have given tangible proof of endurance through the cloud of witnesses and new martyrs.

The awareness of the real needs of other people in this world helps us in the fulfilment of our missionary work and diakonia. Here, the basic missionary principle does not lose its eternal significance for a consistent and holy Christian life, which impresses and is beneficial to the awakening of those outside the church. In the midst of peoples and cultures where Christians live with all other persons, mission in Christ's way ought to lead towards sanctity of life, as an early Christian text of the second century states:

> Christians are not distinguished from others because of their homelands, their languages and their customs. Moreover, they do not live in separate towns, neither do they use a different dialect.... However, while living in Greek and barbarian (non-Greek) cities, following the indigenous customs pertaining to clothing, food, and lifestyle, they provide an admirable and extraordinary way of life (Epistle to Diognetos, 5).

II. Mission and unity

Ecclesiological perspectives

The apostolic community was gathered into one body by the Holy Spirit in the power and joy of the resurrection (cf. John 20:22). Members of this community were called to be witnesses to the risen Christ "to the ends of the earth" (Acts 1:8). The ground of unity of the church, the body of Christ, is the love and unity eternally manifested in the life of the Holy Trinity. The church, as the presence of the kingdom of God, is called to manifest this trinitarian communion and love within its fold and towards the world. The church's mission is the expression of this unity and love.

God's love for the world is manifested in the incarnation of the Word of God (John 1:1), in the supreme sacrifice on the cross and in the power of the resurrection. It was his mission from the Father, the accomplishment of his will (cf. Luke 22:42; John 5:30). The church, as the body of Christ, is called to this missionary act of self-giving sacrifice and to proclaim the good news of salvation to the world.

In the eucharistic celebration every local church experiences the fullness of the church catholic and prepares itself to address the world through words and deeds of love. The church gathers into one body the whole creation and the joy and the sufferings of all people as it stands in the presence of God in the eucharistic act of praise, thanksgiving and intercession. This inward movement of gathering into one body is accompanied by the outward movement of going forth in mission and service to God's creation. Together, these movements constitute the church's witness to the crucified and risen Christ in whom the unity and the love of the Triune God is manifested in a unique way.

Common witness

In the church's "ecclesial" *(ek-kalo)* movement of calling out, incorporating and building up process, the following major aspects are necessary for its realization today:

1. As Eastern Orthodox and Oriental Orthodox Non-Chalcedonian churches, we need to fully restore the unity in communion of our two families of churches. While we gratefully acknowledge the steps recently taken by our churches towards coming together in mutual love and communion in the one apostolic faith, we wish to emphasize the urgency of the matter for our common witness today. We need to reaffirm our unity in faith above all historic, ethnic, racial, linguistic, national or political loyalties.

2. As active members of the wide ecumenical family of churches, we pray and work for the unity of all in accordance with the will of God expressed in the high-priestly prayer of our Lord. It is our special mission to witness to the apostolic faith of the one undivided church as all churches seek to grow more and more in "one Lord, one faith and one baptism."

3. It is God's *oikoumene* that is the wider context of our unity. Our theological and spiritual heritage is filled with the cosmic dimension of God's salvation. Nothing in the created realm is excluded from this sanctifying and transfiguring power of the Spirit of God. As the liturgical experience shows, the one eucharistic bread stands at the same time for the one church and the totality of creation that we offer to God in thanksgiving. While joyfully celebrating the marvellous gift of creation, we have to commit ourselves to humanity's struggles for human dignity, justice and peace. As Orthodox churches we can witness to the integrity of creation by dedicating ourselves to acts of healing, reconciling, enlightening and saving.

The outgoing ("processional") movement of the church's witness is what we usually call mission. This mission of the church has several points of reference, such as the eternal unity in the Triune God, unity between the divine and human in the incarnate Word of God and the unity between Christ, the head of the church and the church his body. All these dimensions of unity are constitutively qualified by love. The same divine love is the motivating power behind the sending of the Son by the Father and the mission of the comforter Spirit to the church. Thus, the mission of the church is in fact an outreaching processional movement of unity and love.

Therefore, the church, the people of God in the communion of the Holy Spirit, is missionary in its very being, ever proceeding and ever gathering, pulsating with God's all-embracing love and unity. The church, as the presence of the kingdom of God in the world, illuminates in one single reality the glory of God and the eschatological destiny of creation.

The missionary character of the church is expressed in diverse ways and forms: liturgical witness to the transcendent dimension of reality, direct evangelistic witness, witness in secular and pluralistic situations, witness through prayer and asceticism, witnessing the life-giving gospel to the poor and oppressed, witness through committed sharing of the struggle for justice and peace, etc. These are some of the expressions of the outreaching movement of the church's mission.

The constitutive character of mission as the expression of unity calls for a common witness. The situation of our world makes it imperative that what the churches can do together they should not do separately. The search for a common witness helps the churches to come out of their parochial loyalties and encourages them to seek together God's will for our contemporary world.

The Orthodox churches, living in diverse cultures, challenged by their socio-political, economic and linguistic situations, are called upon to engage in a common witness to the one apostolic faith in Christ in new missionary situations. By responding to these challenges creatively and in the unity of the Spirit, without catering to the narrow interests of each individual church, the churches are responding to the will of God.

A serious effort towards creating Orthodox missionary centres and a global missionary strategy will inspire and enable our local Orthodox churches not only to witness along with other Orthodox churches, but also to contribute substantially, from the Orthodox perspective, to other Christian churches engaged in similar forms of witness.

Proselytism

Proselytism, along with the actual disunity among the churches, creates major obstacles for our common witness. Some Christian churches and evangelical bodies are actively engaged in proselytizing Christians already belonging to Orthodox churches. All proselytism by any church should be condemned, and all antagonism and unhealthy competition in mission work should be avoided, as constituting a distorted form of mission.

Unfortunately, well-financed resources and the power of the media in western Europe and America, often play a key role in maintaining the unchristian missionary zeal of those involved in proselytizing efforts. The Orthodox churches have to continue efforts to persuade those churches and agencies involved in proselytism not to engage in dubious missionary activities detrimental to God's will for unity, and to seek the path of true Christian charity and unity.

At the same time, our Orthodox churches have to pay closer attention to the pastoral, educational and spiritual needs of our people and foster in every possible way a continual spiritual renewal in our parishes and monastic communities. It is especially important to develop ways of strengthening family life and caring for the special needs of youth that they might realize the communal love and concern of the church for their well-being and salvation.

The ecumenical vision

One impetus for the modern ecumenical vision was originally inspired by the committed search for a common witness to the good news of salvation. It still remains the primary objective of our ecumenical involvement — to offer common witness in love to the power of Christ, crucified and risen, so that those who are caught up in this world of division, conflict and death may believe and be transfigured.

III. Social implications of sacramental life

The sacramental dimension of life

In the sacrament — *mysterion* — of the church, human beings are restored to their proper relationship to God: to communion in Christ with God in the Holy Trinity. Through baptism, chrismation and eucharist, persons receive a new birth in Christ, are anointed in the Spirit and are fully incorporated into the body of Christ — the church. The gift of this new life in Christ implies a commitment to the renewal of all of life, a conversion of mind and heart, so that God's will may be done, so that the world itself may be transformed and raised up by the witness and work of his children.

In Christ's life, death and resurrection, all creation is restored and sanctified (cf. Eph. 1:10). Our life in Christ, therefore, must become a sacramental life, a life that continues the process of sanctifying all life and all time given to us as God's gift. The church, in the fullness of this sacramental and diaconal life, is and manifests dynamically Christ's presence to the world. Thus, as we participate in the church's life, through fasting, prayer, the celebration of feasts and sacraments, and active service to the poor, we renew ourselves and the entire cosmos, to the extent that our life conforms to Christ in the Holy Spirit.

The struggle to renew all things in God is a daily effort. It involves not merely individuals working for their own salvation, but the corporate work of persons seeking to unite all creation in communion with the living God. Such a life requires humility and sacrifice, self-emptiness, the giving of ourselves to others in love and service, as the Lord gave himself up for us "for the life of the world" (John 6:51). It is life lived in community with others and for others. This is the ecclesial, sacramental reality of life in Christ.

The eucharist and renewal of life

How is this sacramental life developed and nurtured today in the midst of a secular, broken and suffering world? How can all things be united once again in the love and sovereignty of God's kingdom?

For Orthodox Christians, the centre and vivifying force of renewal is the eucharist, where all persons and all creation are gathered together, lifted up, and united in the once-and-for-all offering of Christ himself. The eucharist gives us not only the bread of life necessary for our spiritual sustenance and growth, but lifts up our hearts and minds, enabling us to see with a new vision the life that God has prepared for us from all eternity.

It is in the eucharist that we come to know one another as members of one body, united in the love of Christ in the image of the Holy Trinity. It is in and through this communion in the Spirit that we are given the strength and the power to fulfil Christ's mission in the world.

But this same eucharist is also a judgement for Christians, for we may also partake of it "unto our judgement or condemnation" if this gift of communion is not personally appropriated and realized in our daily lives. We know that through our own weakness and sin, we continue to deny God's love and power in the world. When we ignore the sufferings of our brothers and sisters, when we misuse the gifts of creation through pollution, destruction and waste of natural resources, we create new idols of and for ourselves. Isolated in egocentric self-will and self-indulgence, we cause our own spiritual death and that of our neighbours by indifference, conflict, division and lack of love. We also realize that amidst the joyful unity revealed and given to us within our own church, the awareness of the continuing division of Christians saddens and challenges us.

Prayer and repentance

Consequently, the eucharist and the whole liturgical life of the church calls us to prayer and repentance. Through our common prayer in the church, we learn to pray personally, to offer glory and thanksgiving to God, to pray for ourselves and others, to consider the needs of the whole world, to keep one another alive in Christ through our remembrance of the sick and suffering, those in captivity and persecution, those who have departed this life before us, and especially the martyrs, saints and spiritual fathers and mothers whose witness provides an example for our lives, teaching us the true meaning of the words "Your will be done."

This prayer of Christ to the Father is a continual reminder of the need for repentance and forgiveness of sins. It is a call to re-examine our lives in the light of Christ's life. It is a call addressed personally to each of us for *metanoia* and conversion, a call to literally "turn around" our lives and recommit ourselves to Christ.

Witness and the sacramental life

Finally, for those who have strayed from the communion of the church, as well as for those who have never experienced the newness of her life and joy, the sacraments and the entire life of the church offer opportunities for witness to the truth about God and his relationship to us. Baptisms, marriages, visitations to the sick and dying, ordinations, funerals and rites of blessing, as well as the actual diakonia of the church in social concern and justice, provide unique occasions to proclaim God's message of hope, peace and joy in the crucified and resurrected Lord. It is at these moments, when lives are touched by joy or sorrow, suffering and compassion, that the truths about the ultimate questions of life can awaken minds and hearts to the love of God. It is at these times also that the best witness is the personal witness and presence of the church, through the love and care of her members as a supportive community renewed in faith, love and freedom.

Only in this way, through a sacramental awareness and commitment to the world and a personal offering of ourselves to God, all his children, can we carry on Christ's mission in the world: that all may know "what is the breadth and length and height and depth of the love of Christ... so (that we) may attain to fullness of being, the fullness of God himself" (Eph. 3:18-19).

IV. The missionary imperative and responsibility in the local church

The mission of the local church

The mission of everyone is to know Christ, to live in him and witness to him by word and deed. When our eucharistic assembly experiences this truth, the necessity to share the joy of the resurrection with all people is a natural consequence. This mission includes even those who are baptized, yet ignorant of the calling and election they have received through baptism. It is essential that contemporary means be developed to help them return to the fellowship of the church. The church's mission also calls us to the task of peacemaking, reconciling and defending justice for everyone, especially in contexts where the people of God suffer from injustice, violence, oppression and war. When the eucharistic assembly does not engage in such outreaches it fails to realize its missionary responsibility.

Catholicity of the local church

According to Orthodox ecclesiology, the building up *(oikodome)* of the body of Christ is an essential part of evangelization. Although there are normative forms of local communities, new forms of Christian communities may be necessary due to many social and cultural factors. In the process of building up new communities, the church, through its bishops, must be flexible in their creation.

The mission of the local church suffers when its "catholic" dimension, its ecumenical openness, is not sufficiently underlined and expressed. The local community must not only pray for the *oikoumene*, but must be aware of the necessity to preach the gospel to the whole world. It is the task of each local church to educate missionaries for this work wherever needed.

Some churches have already organized missionary departments to undertake the responsibility of sending missionaries. But the sending of missionaries is an ecclesiological act of establishing a concrete Christian presence in a given nation and culture. The indigenous church must be assisted to develop its own identity and local structure as part of a global fellowship. Every mission outreach should aim to create self-sufficient churches in fellowship with the whole church.

Encouraging various ministries

The church has always recognized the vocation of great missionaries and evangelists. It has also recognized the missionary vocation of the whole people of God, each member of the body of Christ being called in and by the Holy Spirit to mission.

The local bishop has the duty to identify, encourage, help and actualize various forms of lay ministry. The church needs for its evangelistic work catechists, readers, preachers, chanters and all those who participate in the service of the church. In this regard, it is necessary to renew the tradition of the deaconesses. In lay movements and associations, the church possesses an extraordinary missionary network for encouraging the participation of the people of God in mission: men, women, youth, scholars, workers and children.

In addition, monks and nuns may also find a special place in this great task, through prayer and ascetic witness.

Other mission challenges

1. The rise of various extremist Christian sects.
2. The dominating attitude of wealthy and powerful churches towards minority local churches.
3. The resurgence of other religions and various secular ideologies.
4. The disintegration of the family as the basic unit of church and society and problems resulting from broken families and single-parent situations.
5. The emergence of new cultures, which influence — positively or negatively — the spirituality of today's youth.
6. The search for a contemporary code of communication to transmit the message of eternal truth.

Recommendations to Orthodox churches

The participants in this consultation acknowledge the missionary involvement of their respective churches and the work already done in the mission field. With the following recommendations they aim to encourage the churches to continue, to enlarge and to enrich their missionary efforts all around the world for the sake of a most efficient evangelistic witness today.

1. That the missionary vocation must become a major concern and responsibility in the life of the church and that special programs for mission awareness be organized for men, women and children in various walks of life to help them fulfil their missionary obligation.
2. That Christian education and catechetical material must incorporate the missionary imperative.
3. That theological schools and other educational institutions incorporate missiological studies in their programs, and the training and skills needed for mission.
4. That Orthodox institutes and training centres for mission be established to accept and prepare candidates for work in the mission field. That experienced and qualified Orthodox missionaries be utilized as teachers.
5. That the church institute diaconal ministries, along with liturgical petitions and intercessions with emphasis on mission, for use in local parishes.
6. That special collections in every parish be offered for mission and that a special place be established for mission information and promotion.
7. That Associations or Friends of Missionaries be organized for moral and material support of those engaged in mission.
8. That regional forums be established for coordination, cooperation and sharing of the Orthodox mission resources of the various churches.
9. That Orthodox publications — especially translations — be utilized for the support of mission work.
10. That the church renew the vocations of the deaconesses, catechists, readers, musicians and preachers for particular service in the mission field.
11. That the churches call monks and nuns to establish a monastic witness, in places where missions are being established, as spiritual centers.
12. That all churches set aside a special time each year for the promotion and support of missions.
13. That Orthodox churches join with other Christian churches in increasing their moral and financial support for the work of the World Council of Churches in general and the Commission on World Mission and Evangelism (CWME) in particular.

Recommendations to the ecumenical community

1. That the Commission on World Mission and Evangelism of the World Council of Churches encourage and support young people in the study of missiology.
2. That all churches review and reflect upon their missionary programs in the light of their impact on the faithful of other churches to avoid mistakes or grievances that have occurred in the past and to prevent antagonism and competition in future mission work.
3. That through the CWME and related organizations educational programs be promoted to better inform members of all churches about the role of historic and present mission work of the Orthodox churches.
4. That prior to, during and after the World Conference in San Antonio, Texas, 22 May-1 June 1989, delegates be encouraged to become informed about Orthodox mission activity in North America and elsewhere through study and visits.

Report of an Inter-Orthodox Consultation
Orthodox Perspectives on Justice and Peace
Minsk, USSR, 1989

Participants from various Eastern Orthodox and Oriental Orthodox churches, members of the World Council of Churches from around the world, gathered in the beautiful city of Minsk, capital of the Byelorussian Republic of the USSR, just at the very moment when the people of this great land remembered, in May 1989, the 44th anniversary of the end of the involvement of the USSR in the second world war, which is referred to here as "the Great Patriotic War". Our meeting also took place at a time of significant renewal in the political, social, civic, economic and religious structuring of the USSR. These observances and the confident spirit of anticipation for a better future served as an appropriate background for our reflection and deliberation on the inseparable issues of justice and peace in the world. We came here to consciously reflect as Orthodox Christians on these burning issues from out of the long heritage of faith and Tradition of our Church. We anticipated contributing not only to the World Council of Churches' world convocation... but also to speak to our fellow Christians and our Orthodox churches throughout the world and to encourage their own responsible spiritual and practical involvement in the issues of justice and peace in our day and for the future of all of humankind. We reflected on these matters, having before us the results of the Third Pre-conciliar Pan-Orthodox Conference which took place in Chambésy, Switzerland, 28 October-6 November 1986.

I. The world searching for justice and peace
1. In each age and time of our troubled human history, the issues of justice and peace have been experienced by people in their own concrete situations. In our time this pattern is repeated, with the added dimension that all people of the earth now face these questions together. We have consciously come to understand that we are all part of one world in which all people, nations, cultures and traditions are inextricably interconnected. As we survey our world, we are conscious of the wide-ranging expressions of injustice and the threat to peace among us.

2. At every step in our lives today we are faced with manifestations of injustice. Some of these signs blatantly and directly threaten humanity and others lead gradually to the potential destruction of God's creation. Among the many concerns we have as we survey our condition on the threshold of the twenty-first century, we note some specific anxieties for the future of our planet and the people who live upon it, brought about by injustices perpetrated today and the consequent threat to genuine peace.

The unjust treatment of the planet earth
3. The irresponsible and thoughtless misuse of natural resources creates a condition we have come to identify as the "hot-house effect" upon the earth. This consists in

part of the warming up of the earth's atmosphere, the thinning of the ozone layer and an increase in radiation. Connected with this are other irresponsible and unjust activities which have led to deforestation and desertification of huge areas caused by the depletion of the rain forests and many non-renewable resources. All of this and other consequences arise from the unjust treatment of the planet by human beings. It is the result of the misuse of the wisdom gained through scientific research and technological advancement. In many areas these human accomplishments bring mixed blessings. For example, while genetic engineering and advances in biotechnology may be considered a blessing in therapeutic practices in medicine, they are also potential manifestations of injustice because of the threat posed in the field of mutation.

Injustice in military over-emphasis

4. While we see some encouraging steps being taken by all nations in the area of limitations of armaments, we also note that nations continue to allocate a major percentage of their national budgets to arms production in the name of national security or defence. The phenomenon of the arms race and the exaggerated sale of arms continue to be imposed upon third-world nations. An illustration of this is the reported information that in some developing countries per capita public expenditure for military purposes is US$42, while per capita public expenditure for health services amounts to only US$11.[1]

5. Another problem, specific to the church, is the dilemma presented by the phenomenon of Christian participation in war. The Orthodox Church unreservedly condemns war as evil. Yet it also recognizes that in the defence of the innocent and the protection of one's people from unjust attack, criminal activity and the overthrowing of oppression, it is sometimes necessary, with reluctance, to resort to arms. In every case, such a decision must be taken with full consciousness of its tragic dimensions. Consequently, the Greek fathers of the Church have never developed a "just war theory", preferring rather to speak of the blessings of and the preference for peace.

Economic injustice

6. Injustices tend to be interconnected. The two preceding examples show that many of the nations of the world and their people have been led into new forms of economic injustice. Today's international debt crisis is the result of the mismanagement of resources both in developing and developed countries. Misdirected enthusiasm and misguided efforts in development planning in the 70s have left the world today with the following reality. In 1985, the poorest fifth of the world's population had access to 1.6% of the total world Gross National Product (GNP), and the richest fifth accounted for 74.2% of the world GNP.[2] The world is marked by an unjust distribution of goods and, more importantly, by an unjust distribution of power.

7. Similarly, evidence indicates that in many nations, both poor and rich, the concentration of wealth in the hands of fewer and fewer persons results in an increase of poverty for more and more persons. The widening of the gap between the rich and the poor is highlighted by the demographic trends of higher infant mortality and shorter life expectancy. Many people in the third-world countries are deprived of basic human needs such as adequate health services, proper housing, clothing, sufficient food, and educational opportunities. In short, they lack the bare minimum for survival. While indebtedness was not the choice made by the common citizen in any country, in all these countries it is these people who suffer to enable the respective government to repay its debts.

Injustice and the institutions of social life

8. These threats raise human and social problems which further increase the burden of injustice on society. A critical example is the family. This important social institution and basis of social stability and human well-being is weakening. In many industrialized societies broken families have become a common phenomenon and in the third-world societies the extended family is gradually being replaced by the nuclear family. Alienation, alcoholism, drugs, street children, child abuse, and widespread abortion are blatant manifestations of this brokenness in our society, due to economic and systemic causes. Together with these problems, new patterns have arisen in society with consequent new roles for men and women. In particular, women are now participating in social, economic, political and educational spheres of life, and yet certain traditions still continue to discriminate against them and their full participation in the life of church and society.

9. Injustice against people is also manifested within and among nations and societies because of their race, colour, creed, ethnic identity and culture. Great numbers of people continue to suffer displacement and to live as refugees, some even within their own homelands, such as the Palestinian people. Economic and political injustices as well as various kinds of prejudice have led to the mass uprooting of people, causing migrations with all the negative consequences for personal, family and social life of these fellow human beings. We note as well that the communications media in one aspect of their expansion, through the quick dissemination of information and images, brings people together, thus pointing to our shared destiny as one world. But at the same time much is disseminated which threatens our basic human values.

10. In all this, human rights are repeatedly being disregarded in many places throughout the world. As believers we are especially concerned with religious rights. Religious persecution and intolerance have not disappeared among us in spite of decades of ecumenical activity and concern, and in some places it has been virulently oppressive. In some situations elementary religious education is made difficult or impossible.

11. In conjunction with this, the phenomenon of proselytism among Christians is a sad witness to the world, which in practice betrays our words of brotherhood and peace. Particularly as Orthodox, we have, in the past, suffered much from proselytism in its many forms, including the Uniate question. Today we see that the plague of proselytism continues in such places as the Middle East and Ethiopia, especially in the midst of crisis situations. An example of this behaviour was how relief efforts after the recent Armenian earthquake were used by some to persuade the Armenian Orthodox Christians to abandon their Church.

12. Above and beyond all of this there is the threat of nuclear war and destruction. Demonic forces pervade and often seem to control the destiny of our earth and all the people seeking to live their lives upon it. Injustice and the ongoing threats to peace provoke cries for healing and restoration from all of humanity and from the earth itself. In response, we turn to our faith as believing Orthodox Christians for wisdom, guidance and salvation.

II. The response of faith in the face of injustice and threats to peace

13. As Orthodox Christian believers our most precious resource in the face of such terrible problems is the awareness of God's active love and presence in history for the salvation of the world. This is communicated to us in the revelation of God as it is experienced in the life of the church. Space does not permit us to plumb the vast resources of the Holy Tradition in order to explicate all of its potential relevance to the

issues of injustice, and the demand for peace in the hearts of all right-thinking persons and nations. The experience of the saving presence of God's love for us, his creatures, has provided us with understandings which have been theologically articulated in the teaching, creeds and affirmations of faith in the church. From these many resources for insight in the face of injustice and the threats to peace we lift up these few affirmations for the attention of all.

14. In the Orthodox perspective the created world is the work of the Triune God. The original status of the creation expressed a communion and harmony (the biblical peace, shalom) in process of fulfilment, which finds its ground in the perfect personal relationship between Father, Son and Holy Spirit.

15. The Old and the New Testaments are records of the revelation that humankind is sick in the centre of its personal existence. Through sin, which is the loss of illumination or glorification, which is alienation from God, the "heart" has been "darkened" (Rom. 1:21). Believing that this state is normal for their lives, human beings have come to make God in their own fallen or sick image. The heart is the primary organ of communion with God, which makes human beings both free of the environment and yet active participants in it. The disruption of this communion with God causes the heart to become dominated by and enslaved to the environment through confusion of its own intellectual reasoning which gives rise to self-centred love, injustice and aggression in relation to others. Herein is the root cause of idolatry, injustice, exploitation and belligerence in humanity and the lack of peace among human beings.

16. For the Orthodox Church, the restoration of justice and peace cannot be measured merely by human standards, but by the divine-human standard of Jesus Christ, who is at the heart of the "good news" to the fallen world. The Christological standard rests upon the union of the divine and the human in the one person of Jesus Christ and upon his victory over death, sin and evil through his resurrection which followed upon his own unjust suffering and crucifixion. This unique event of the just God becoming a just man in the midst of an unjust humanity, and his willingness to suffer unjustly at the hands of the unjust for their salvation is for us the profound basis not only for the understanding of justice, but also for our solidarity with all those who suffer injustice.

17. Through his death, Christ has destroyed in principle the power of sin and death, which are the primary causes of injustice, and through his resurrection, Christ has made eternal peace between God and humanity, among human beings as well as with the created world itself. This is the "new creation".

18. For the Christian, this restoration of justice and peace brings liberation of the human heart through its purification from all thoughts, both good and bad, so that it may be filled with the prayer of the Holy Spirit. This process allows it to regain full communion with God. This communion of the human with the divine is the beginning of the restoration of justice and peace, which are gifts of God to us, leading to the transformation of selfish love into selfless love. This is our participation in the mystery of the cross and the resurrection of Christ.

19. Participation in the mystery of the cross is perfected by glorification, which is to see Christ resurrected in glory, together with the bestowal of perfect justice, peace and reconciliation with the Father and the gift of selfless love.

20. The fullness of justice and the establishment of peace in human relations can thus only come with this renewal in Christ and the communion with the Holy Spirit in the lives of men and women. Social justice and social peace can approximate it only

inasmuch as God's peace and God's justice are realized in the illumination and glorification of those who share in the common life of society. To this the life of the church is witness.

21. The church is the true Body of Christ. In this new ecclesial reality everything is recapitulated in Christ and the common spiritual experience of the ecclesial community removes the estrangement of individuals from each other, because it is based on an ontological unity expressed in the historical reality of the Body of Christ. The church, as the Body of Christ, projects in space and time the historical embodiment of the gospel and the realization of the living experience of the Christian faith.

22. But the Christian message of peace and justice goes further, to address all dimensions of human existence, thus becoming a judgment upon the world as a whole. The concern is not only with theologizing about earthly realities, but also in seeing earthly realities as God's continuing work in history through his church and with the illumination of the Holy Spirit.

23. It is true that Christian life has not always manifested the profound reality of the prophetic and sacramental message of peace and justice in its fullness, but there is always a conscious and positive declaration of peace and justice in the ecclesial experience. In this perspective it is clear that the spiritual process of human participation in the peace and justice of Christ is a continuous spiritual struggle, in which characteristics of both the weakness of human nature and its forward movement towards God-likeness continue to rise and fall. Nevertheless Christians are mandated to work synergetically with God in his oikonomia of the eschatological restoration and transfiguration of his creation.

24. In our age, the severing of the world from the living ecclesial experience and the ongoing profanation of society in modern times has challenged fundamental Christian affirmations on the relationship of God, humanity and the world. The era of ideological secularization has proclaimed a radical apostasy from these Christian affirmations. The church is not any more the only teaching authority, because in greater or lesser measure, various ideologies declare messages antithetical to the Christian message. This spiritual dichotomy of modern society is the challenge of the age for the church as it seeks to provide a vision of the genuine source of justice and peace for the world today. It is a vision which the world desperately needs to hear, adopt and realize in practice. The church does this not to project upon the world its own "ideology" in the place of others, but because without the saving and redeeming participation in the justice and peace of God, all our efforts are destined to fail. It is for this reason that the vision of the church concerns itself with the whole human being, with the whole of social life, with the whole of the physical and spiritual environment of our planet. Ours is, finally, an eschatological vision, in which we humbly recognize that justice and peace are of God: it is he who brings it into reality. Our task is to work with God's purpose so that justice and peace may reign on earth and among all people.

III. Orthodox Christians responding to the demands of justice and peace

25. It is not enough for us simply to theologize, to describe and to prescribe regarding the Orthodox vision of justice and peace. We must also mobilize and work together for God's purpose to defeat injustices and to establish justice wherever possible, as well as to overcome the forces which threaten peace on earth. In order to realize God's peace and justice on earth, we are called as Christians always and everywhere to be "servants of God" (Rom. 6:22) and "co-workers with God" (1 Cor.

3:9) by being obedient to his will and by imitating the example of our Lord and the saints of his church. We see this task as a clarion call to ourselves as Orthodox, first in our existence on the personal, the ecclesial and outreach levels.

The personal dimension

26. In our personal Christian lives, we are expected to acknowledge experientially that each Christian is called to be a peace-maker and a worker for justice in his or her personal life. Every Orthodox Christian has received the holy calling to realize and promote justice in the concrete and specific social environment in which he or she lives. This calling has been concretely received through the sacraments of baptism and chrismation by which we have each one of us been incorporated into the Body of Christ and have begun our growth in illumination and glorification, as members of God's royal priesthood and holy nation (cf. 1 Pet. 2:9). Having thus received the Holy Spirit and having become children of God, we are endowed with both responsibility and power to be peace-makers and advocates of justice.

27. This calling of all Christians presupposes that we constantly stay at the source of divine peace which is possible only in the constant sacramental communion of the church and the personal life of prayer. The prayers of the church together with the Holy Scriptures and Holy Tradition give to each of us the right orientation and the concrete guidelines and ideals for our lives.

28. It is not always possible, however, to live up to these ideals due to our human weakness and our lack of progress in growing in illumination and towards glorification and God-likeness, which is our sin. Therefore, repentance must be a permanent attitude and stance in life for us, a reality which also belongs to the sacramental life of the church as a normal element in its life.

29. This attitude leads Christian men and women not only to humility, but also to an ascetic approach to life, which prevents them from submission to such things as excessive consumerism, materialistic attitudes, and the greedy exploitation of others and the natural resources of earth. This perspective, as well, constantly reminds Christians of the needs of other persons who are also created in the likeness of God. According to the principles of the Christian faith, every human being should be considered by fellow human beings as a person created in God's image, and not simply as a statistical unit, or as a unit of material labour or a unit of consumption. We must relate with our fellow human beings in imitation of God's philanthropic love for all of his creatures. Consequently, Christians are called always to be aware of the needs not only of fellow Christians, but of all people who are in need of the necessities of life.

30. As a result, in their personal lives, Christian men and women have to be constantly vigilant and alert to the personal and social injustices in their surroundings, injustices which are at the heart of the disturbances of peace and harmony among persons and in the social environment. We must, with the grace of God, seek the gift of seeing the sin and evil present in the world. Christian men and women must also have the courage to spell out the injustices which they see, even though this might require them to make personal sacrifices. These sacrifices will include costly involvement and action. After all, every Christian is called to identify his or her life with that of Christ, not only in the glory of the Resurrection, but also in his suffering.

In ecclesial life

31. We are Christians not only in the context of secular life, but there must also be an imperative for justice and peace in our ecclesial life. Peace and justice are the

essence of the gift given to us by Christ, but they are also essential aspects for the programme entrusted to us by the Lord for fulfilment as part of our contribution to the world and the society in which we live, beginning with the very life of the church itself.

32. Certainly our ecclesial concern with peace and justice begins with our commonly shared prayer for justice and peace. Orthodox Christian men and women are called to offer constant and fervent prayers for peace, reconciliation and justice in mutual relations among people, in the church, between nations and in all the world. Prayers for justice and peace must be made in all of our daily and Sunday services, but not only generally. We must offer to God fervent prayers for peace in specific conflict areas, for a just distribution of the material goods of life among all peoples, for the protection and comfort of those who are suffering and for the final triumph of justice and peace.

33. But there is also a need for both guidance and encouragement for the bishops and priests and laity of the church to teach the people, preach to the congregations and inspire the youth of the church to be sensitive to the issues of justice and peace and to address them in practical ways. We must lift up in the consciousness of the church, the peace-making character of Christianity and the Christian duty to serve the cause of peace and justice.

34. But in addition, we must learn to use the expertise of the church's members who are specialized in the areas of sociology, economics, politics, ecology, medicine, etc., in order to help raise the consciousness and understanding of the faithful in the practical spheres of justice and peace work. It would be useful to designate one week each year throughout the world, dedicated to the issues of justice and peace. During this week, prayers, gatherings, presentations, seminars and discussions could be held with the intention of enhancing the awareness of Christians towards these issues.

35. Other corporate programmes are also needed. We can try to accomplish this through meetings held at times other than those of public worship; through the Church's periodical press in which peace and justice concerns should take a permanent place; through theological studies and the development of social ethical disciplines in all of our seminaries and theological schools; through regional, diocesan, national and international gatherings devoted to peace and justice issues in cooperation with fellow Christians of other church bodies, with non-Christian religious peoples and groups and with non-believers of good will everywhere.

36. As a church we are called to develop sensitivity to the way we function and live out our ecclesial existence at all levels of church life. As such, it is important that we not only speak about justice and peace, but also develop projects and contribute practically in programmes and sustained organized activity on behalf of the concrete realization of the values of justice and peace in our ecclesial life. In this regard the church must learn to dialogue especially with non-church bodies to find the most suitable common ways for the implementation of justice and peace.

Outreach

37. The church lives not only for itself, but also for the life of the world. There is an outreach dimension to the Christian faith which seeks to bring the saving message of the Gospel to all men and women, which in Christ's compassion seeks to meet the suffering and injustices experienced by our fellow human beings in their immediate needs for care, sustenance and protection. There is the Christian concern for the very orders and structures of the societies in which we live which oppress people, or contribute to the danger of war, or institutionalize injustice.

38. On the international level, the Orthodox commitment to justice and peace can be most effective and influential, and could give good results through our active and close cooperation with all other Christian churches within the framework of the ecumenical movement. Our membership in the World Council of Churches and participation in similar international and regional ecumenical bodies and organizations helps to mobilize and unite all spiritual and social forces in the common struggle for justice and peace. Indeed, Christians must consider every injustice done to anyone else as a demand for their own response.

39. Justice and peace are equally necessary for all people, and because of this, under the auspices of agencies such as the United Nations, we welcome cooperation on these issues with all people of good will, irrespective of their religious and political convictions. The main and most urgent task in this sphere of activity is to reduce the danger of nuclear holocaust, which would mean, in practice, the end of life on our planet. For this, we must reverse the arms race and help the nations move from confrontation to serious and practical negotiations about disarmament and cooperation in building a world free of nuclear weapons. For this to happen, Christians can help to increase the confidence of nations regarding each other and so lead towards increased understanding and trust.

40. We welcome the positive changes in the climate of international relations in recent times and express our hope and prayers that we and all of humanity may see the end of the second millennium of the Christian era, as a victory of justice and peace for all of God's people.

41. But for this to occur, it is quite obvious that it is necessary to make profound changes in the contemporary system of social mechanisms which not only produce great misery based upon injustice and exploitation, but also, for the same reason are fraught with permanent dangers of militarism and wars, which can destroy the whole of humanity and the very life on earth.

42. In all things we put our trust for our future and that of the world in the hands of the God of justice and peace. Clement of Rome spoke of peace whose meaning, as we have seen, includes the idea of justice. We conclude with his words: "... Let us run on to the goal of peace, which was handed down to us from the beginning. Let us fix our eyes on the Father and Creator of the universe and cling to his magnificent and excellent gift of peace and kindness to us..." (I Clement, 19:2).

NOTES

[1] Ruth Leger Sivard, *World Military and Social Expenditures 1987-88,* 12th ed., pp.46-47.
[2] *Ibid.*, p.21.

Orthodox Letter

To the WCC Conference on Mission and Evangelism

San Antonio, USA, 31 May 1989

Dear Brothers and Sisters,

We, the Orthodox participants in this Conference, men and women from Orthodox churches throughout the world, unanimously express to you the joy and happiness we have experienced during our participation in this gathering, which allowed us all the opportunity to deepen our understanding of evangelism and mission in Christ's way.

We wholeheartedly thank all those who have laboured to make this Conference a significant ecumenical event.

We wish, however, to draw your attention to some major concerns:

a) We have noticed that in some conference documents and in worship services there has been a distortion of the constitutional basis of the World Council of Churches and of some fundamental tenets of our common faith.

b) Faith in the Triune God constitutes *the basis* of the World Council of Churches. The confession of the holy name of the Father, the divinity of the Son and the existence of the Holy Spirit as an hypostasis (person) and their unity in the divine essence of God is the fundamental presupposition of the participation of the Orthodox churches to the World Council of Churches.

c) We, unequivocally, affirm that Jesus Christ is our God and Saviour. "He is the way, the truth and the life" (John 14:6). He is the one who saves us and leads us to unity.

d) We cannot accept any tampering with the language of the Bible or any attempts to re-write it, or make it conform to the beliefs or ideology of any particular culture, denomination or movement.

e) While the issue of the fuller participation of women in the life of the Church should be a subject of study in the World Council of Churches, their ordination to priesthood is not, for us, subject to debate, since it is contrary to the Christology, Ecclesiology, Tradition and practice of the Church throughout the centuries.

We submit this consideration in a spirit of love, for the sake of the integrity of our Christian fellowship and of our unhindered ecumenical involvement in the World Council of Churches.

The Orthodox participants

Report of an Inter-Orthodox Consultation
"Come, Holy Spirit — Renew the Whole Creation: An Orthodox Approach"
Crete, Greece, 25 November-4 December 1989

Preface

1. The following pages constitute the report coming up from the Eastern Orthodox and Oriental Orthodox Consultation held at the Orthodox Academy of Crete, Greece, from 25 November-4 December 1989. This consultation was sponsored by the World Council of Churches in order to reflect and carefully examine the main theme "Come, Holy Spirit — Renew the Whole Creation" and sub-themes of the Seventh Assembly of the World Council of Churches to be held from 6-21 February 1991 in Canberra, Australia, and to offer an Orthodox approach and insights to the Assembly. Therefore, more than thirty Orthodox participants from various Eastern Orthodox and Oriental Orthodox WCC member churches and WCC staff contributed to this consultation by presenting essential papers on the main theme and sub-themes for plenary discussion as well as group reflections.

The Consultation was moderated by Metropolitan Prof. John of Pergamon (Zizioulas) and organized and prepared by the WCC Orthodox Task Force under the responsibility of its Moderator, Rev. Dr Gennadios Limouris.

Introduction

2. It has become customary in the ecumenical movement of our time to regard the Orthodox as those who would always insist on stressing the importance of the Holy Spirit for all aspects of theology and Church life. This insistence, which has often, though not always, been connected with the *Filioque* issue, has helped the ecumenical movement to correct certain "Christomonistic" tendencies that appear in Western theology. It has also contributed, among other factors, to the decision taken by the World Council of Churches to devote the theme of its next Assembly to the subject of the Holy Spirit. Given the fact that all previous Assemblies of the World Council of Churches had taken their themes from Christology, this decision was hailed, not only by the Orthodox, as striking a right and necessary balance and as offering at the same time to the churches the opportunity to say something relevant to the problems and concerns of the world today. All this has naturally raised the expectations of many people concerning the contribution of Orthodox theology to the study of the next Assembly theme.

3. The present report represents a modest attempt to respond to such expectations. Its authors have been faced not only with the difficulty of reconciling and bringing in one voice a variety of approaches naturally existing within Orthodoxy itself, but also with the difficult task of producing a document, the structure and the questions of which were already determined and given by the organizers of the Assembly. What this report contains, therefore, is not an Orthodox Pneumatology in all its aspects and depth, but an Orthodox contribution to the four sub-themes into which the Assembly theme *Come, Holy Spirit — Renew the Whole Creation* was divided: (a) *Giver of Life*

— *Sustain Your Creation!*, (b) *Spirit of Truth — Set Us Free!*, (c) *Spirit of Unity — Reconcile Your People!*, and (d) *Holy Spirit — Transform and Sanctify Us!*.

4. In dealing with these subjects, this report has tried to apply throughout some of the fundamental principles which characterize the Orthodox approach to the doctrine of the Holy Spirit. Such principles, which the reader of the report will easily recognize in each section, include the following.

a) In the first place, all theology of the Holy Spirit must be placed within the context of Trinitarian theology. It is a well-known and fundamental claim of Patristic thought that in all actions of God in creation and redemption all three Persons of the Holy Trinity are involved and operate always in unity, although in a different manner each. What the Holy Spirit does, therefore, must be seen always in relation to what the Father and the Son are doing.

b) Secondly, following this principle Pneumatology cannot be separated from Christology. One has often the feeling that in the West many attempts to stress the importance of the Holy Spirit, such as Pentecostalism in our time, tend to overlook the principle that the Holy Spirit works with Christ and finally points to him as the Saviour. The right synthesis between Christology and Pneumatology is of paramount importance in today's theology.

c) One of the characteristic aspects of the work of the Holy Spirit is that it points to Christ's *transcending* power in existence. The fact that the Holy Spirit is God, one Person of the Holy Trinity, shows that God in being involved in the world through Christ remains free from the limitations of creaturehood. It also implies that the purpose of God's involvement in creation and history is to offer the human being and through it creation as a whole the possibility to transcend its creaturely limitations and enter into the glory and life of God (Rom 8:20-21). The work of the Holy Spirit in creation and redemption aims at liberating us, and creation in general, from all forms of self-sufficiency and "autonomy" vis-à-vis God. Creation and history cannot be enclosed in themselves without being led into disintegration and finally into an existential impasse. The Spirit of God opens up the boundaries of whatever He touches, and brings it to relation with the transcendent God. The Orthodox Tradition insists on the "epiclesis", the invocation of the Holy Spirit, because it believes that the world was created by God in order to overcome and transcend its limitations and enter into communion with the life of the Holy Trinity and share God's glory. The idea of *theosis*, which marks Orthodox soteriology, is based on such an assumption concerning the final destiny of creation.

d) This transcending and liberating aspect of the work of the Holy Spirit shows God to be the Spirit of *communion* (2 Cor 13:13). The Orthodox doctrine of the Holy Spirit involves a strong emphasis on the idea of communion. This is not only true with reference to the relation between God and the world mentioned above, but also with regard to interhuman relations, and indeed to the relation of the human being with the whole of creation. Wherever the Holy Spirit blows, the boundaries of individualism are transcended, and love and communion emerge. Liberation from individualism in the Holy Spirit results in freedom for others, in a community.

e) It is for this reason that another principle of Orthodox theology becomes also important, namely *ecclesiology*. The Holy Spirit is inconceivable without the community of the people of God which He assembles and creates. Being the Spirit of Christ (Rom 8:9-11) He naturally creates a Christocentric community, the Body of Christ. He endows it with charisms but also with a certain structure, Spirit and structure being not mutually exclusive or contradictory in the Spirit. Without limiting the Spirit to the institutional Church, we have always to remember that the destiny of the whole creation somehow passes through the Church, where the world finds its true meaning and salvation.

All this makes the community of the Church the place where creation is liberated from self-sufficiency and is offered to its Creator as being "His own". Having been purified through man's repentance and Baptism, creation passes through the hands of the ecclesial community to become *Holy Eucharist*. It is offered to God by the High Priest, our Lord Jesus Christ, through a properly ordained ministry which is His "typos" and "eikon", under the elements of bread and wine, and is returned to us as eternal life in the Body and Blood of our Lord. This whole movement takes place through the invocation of the Spirit *(epiclesis)*, and is significantly called *communion*.

f) The anthropological consequences of the work of the Holy Spirit become evident. Sanctification and holiness transform the human being into a person who sees God and shares his glory. A window is thus opened to the Kingdom of God for the world, and the Church becomes a sign of the Kingdom. The Spirit brings *the last days* (eschata) into history, albeit not permanently until the second coming of Christ. The Spirit offers us in this way a real foretaste of the eschatological state of things, and the world — and the Church — acquire a guidance, a criterion, to discern the spirits. All this is realized in "earthly vessels" (2 Cor 4:7) through the ambiguity of history and in a constant struggle with the powers of evil.

5. Transcendence, communion, Church, sacramental and particularly eucharistic life, transformation and glorification through holiness, foretaste of the Kingdom within history through a constant *metanoia* and struggle against the powers of sin and evil — these are some of the fundamental principles which Orthodox theology attaches to the doctrine of the Holy Spirit. In the pages of this report these principles will play a central role in dealing with the sub-themes of the assembly theme. It is hoped that they can be of some significance and use to the Orthodox themselves as well as to those who are interested in what the Orthodox would have to say to the Seventh Assembly of the World Council of Churches.

Sub-theme I: Giver of Life — Sustain Your Creation!

6. Creation is the work of God the Father accomplished through His Word and His Spirit (Gen 1:1-5), these "two hands of God", as they are called by one of the earliest Church Fathers, St Irenaeus of Lyons. Therefore, the mystery of created life and existence as a whole is rooted in the divine will of the Holy Trinity. The world exists because God, the Holy Trinity, willed and wills it to exist. Creation is a free gift, not a necessity. It has not always been there and does not possess any natural capacity for eternal life and self-existence. It is only by being constantly related to God that it can enjoy life and survive.

7. This dependence of the whole creation on God makes it a reality of communion. The Holy Spirit as the Spirit of communion (2 Cor 13:13) is the "giver of life" (cf. 2 Cor 3:6; Jn 6:63) precisely because the Spirit opens up the world to communion with God, and in this way allows it to transcend its limitations and share the life of the eternal God, the life of the Holy Trinity. In acknowledging, therefore, that the world is not self-existent and self-sufficient, we confess that any breach of its communion with God brings creation back to its natural limitations and threatens it with death.

8. Creation, although created by God as "very good", exists now in a state of disintegration and under the yoke of death. All parts of nature experience this as if it

were inevitable and "natural" reality. Life is so intermingled with death that creatures enter the process of disintegration and decay as soon as they are brought into being.

9. Related with this physical disintegration is a moral and spiritual disintegration brought about by human sin. Natural evil and moral evil are two aspects of the same reality which has to do with the creation's relationship with God. The world "groans in travail in all its parts" (cf. Rom 8:22) because "the prince of creation", the human being, refuses to relate it to God and regards it as its own possession. Sin is essentially a revolt against God, the self-proclamation of the human being as the ultimate point of reference in creation and its self-divinization. As this was the suggestion submitted to Adam by the Devil, all tendencies in human existence towards regarding creation as centred on the human being and as existing only for its sake amount to the demonic dimension in existence. The Devil constantly tempts man to regard every one and everything else outside himself as existing for his own pleasure and satisfaction. Life is thus constantly confronted with the demonic forces in existence, and the Christian is called to be aware of his life as a confrontation and fight with the Devil. The Holy Spirit is thus a "spirit of power" (Rom 15:19) involving humankind in a constant struggle for life and against all forms of disintegration and death.

10. These powers of disintegration and death operate in many cases of our actual life and culture. Although one could make a long list of such cases, the following will suffice to make us aware of certain acute problems facing us today in our civilization:
a) The misuse of nuclear power to create weapons that can annihilate all life on earth and to consolidate structures of exploitative power and dominion.
b) The criminal testing of nuclear weapons in the lands of the poor and and powerless people, especially in the Pacific, depriving these people of the dignity and right for life.
c) Production and sale of arms that deliberately maintain conflicts and political instability in many parts of the world for the benefit of rich and powerful nations.
d) Exploitative imbalances in international trade and the demonic presence of transnational corporations that suck the blood of the poor and kill the economic growth of poor nations.
e) The fatal disfiguring of the face of the earth by a consumerist style of life that devastates the biosphere and kills the gift of life.
f) Complicity of the economic and political powers that sustain apartheid regimes and encourages discrimination on the basis of colour, race and sex.
g) Denial of the land rights of indigenous peoples and violent encroachments on the self-respect and God-given dignity as human beings.
h) Unscrupulous and selfish manipulation of life in genetic engineering and biotechnology without any sense of the mystery of life as a gift of God.

11. In the face of these problems we call upon the Holy Spirit to intervene and sustain God's creation. We acknowledge and confess that salvation can only come from God, and that the Holy Spirit as the "giver of life" can help us find a way out of this vicious circle of life and death, of light and darkness, in which creation is caught up.

12. In invoking the Holy Spirit we do not shake off our shoulders our own responsibility as human beings. The first thing, therefore, that we ask of the Holy Spirit is to create in us a state of true and genuine repentance, a *metanoia*, which means a reversal of our ways and attitudes so that they may be turned from self-interest and egocentricism to true love, concern and care for the others and for all of God's

creation. Without this repentance God cannot intervene, for He respects human freedom and wishes to co-operate with the human being (in *synergy*).

13. This turning of ourselves away from self-centredness towards communion with others, this deep and true *metanoia*, involves the denouncing of all demonic powers that keep us in the realm of self-interested individualism and makes us members of the Body of Christ which was given and broken for the life of others, indeed for the whole creation. By so doing the Holy Spirit brings about the Church as the Body of Christ, the community which constitutes in the midst of a disintegrated creation the sign of life and the proclamation of a world liberated from all powers of disintegration and death. It is, therefore, in and through this Body of Christ, the Church, that the Spirit sustains creation. Baptism as the sacrament of entrance into this body through *metanoia* and renunciation of all demonic powers, through the death of self-centred individualism and the rising in the *communion of saints*, is the door that the Spirit opens for the world to enjoy true life. Chrismation (Confirmation) as the sacrament of personal receiving of the Holy Spirit heals us from sin and enables us to combat with the powers of darkness. Above all, the Holy Eucharist makes us partakers of the life of the Holy Trinity in the Body of Christ and allows us to offer with Him as the head of the new humanity the whole creation to its Creator: "Thine own of thine own we offer Thee in all and for all" (Divine Liturgy of St John Chrysostom). It is this sacramental and eucharistic experience that allows us to bring back, in the Holy Spirit, creation to God, acknowledging that we are not the possessors but the stewards of creation. All this is done through the invocation of the Holy Spirit *(epiclesis)*, who alone through Christ's Body can sustain creation by reuniting it to God, the source of life.

Sub-theme II: Spirit of Truth — Set Us Free!

14. It is of fundamental significance for our understanding that Christ called the Holy Spirit the spirit of Truth (Jn 16:13). It shows the person and work of the Holy Spirit. The Spirit constantly unveils truth and guides us to the fulness of truth. In praying to the Holy Spirit to set us free, we acknowledge the vital relationship between the work of the Holy Spirit in creation and our ultimate calling to the glorious freedom of the children of God. The Holy Spirit manifested the creative relationship between truth and freedom in the incarnate Christ in a unique way. Thus we confess that Christ is "the way, the truth and the life". Therefore, the whole creation now eagerly longs for the experience of truth and freedom in Christ through the Holy Spirit.

15. For the early Christian communities the relationship between Christ and the Holy Spirit was so close that one could almost interchange the Spirit's indwelling and Christ's indwelling in the Christian (Rom 8:9-10). Similarly one speaks either of being "in Christ" (Rom 6:1, 8:10) or "in the Spirit" (Gal 5:22ff) to describe our new life in God. The Spirit is given to the faithful and baptized members of the Church not just for their own justification, but for the enrichment of their common life in Christ and the actualization of the ministry of Christ in his Church.

16. In the New Testament this freedom in Christ means "having been set free from sin" (Rom 6:10,22; Jn 8:31-36), from the bondage of evil (Mt 12:22; Lk 13:16; Eph 6:12), from the law (Rom 7:3-6), from sin and death (Rom 6:20-23; cf. 8:2-21). This liberation has also cosmic dimensions since sin alienates human beings from their true nature or rather conditions social, political and economic structures and the life of the whole of God's creation. In the world today, we discern a great anxiety about the

survival of life on this planet. In this concern for new social relationships that advance peace, justice and equality for all, we discern the need for liberation of the whole of creation. Christians should be involved in all these efforts for the creation of a better world by struggling for the removal of all causes of injustice and oppression. This involvement should be guided and inspired by the love of God for all his creation and the principles of his Kingdom.

17. Although the Spirit constitutes the Church and acts in her life, the Spirit of God is not limited or contained exclusively by it. The Holy Spirit is everywhere present since it "blows where it wills, and you have the sound of it, but you do not know whence it comes or whither it goes" (Jn 3:8). The mysterious character of the Holy Spirit constantly helps us to transcend all narrow perspectives with regard to the work of the Spirit. The Spirit is at work in the whole of God's creation though not all are aware of it. It is the task of all faithful to recognize the presence of the Holy Spirit wherever the fruits of the Spirit are seen and to call upon the power of the Spirit in all situations when truth is disfigured and freedom misused.

18. Given the intrinsic ambiguity of history and the awareness that spirits other than the Holy Spirit may act in the world, we must be very careful not to identify in an absolute manner the Holy Spirit with human progress, actions, social movements and ideologies. Sometimes what we call human progress or liberation may be a passing from one slavery to another, more subtle and oppressive. Since the reign of God is an unconditional gift of the Triune God, we must concur that all human actions in themselves are essentially imperfect and thus contain hidden elements of evil. This awareness shapes the critical task of the Church in the life of the world as the power that unmasks and resists all new and old forms of idolatry and false messianic expectations.

19. Following the prophetic tradition and the example of Jesus' identification with the poor and the persecuted, Christians must actively care for the healing of those who suffer as a result of human brokenness. This healing involvement in the suffering of the world must not be one-dimensional. The people of God through the divine gifts of the Spirit are actively, and in diverse manners, involved in history to reduce the suffering of the poor, the weak, and the voiceless. The Church, by being faithful to its inner life of Spirit and the Gospel, becomes the power of healing and liberation for God's creation.

20. Humanity which constantly struggles to liberate itself from all structures of power paradoxically seeks also genuine forms of authority. Authentic authority is a gift of the Spirit. This gift of true authority fosters participation and creativity, self-discipline and compassion. All traditional forms of authority are crumbling and millions of people are yearning for a genuine form of spiritual authority. We as members of the Body of Christ are called to exercize a new authority, an authority not of law and oppressive power, but of the liberating and reconciling power of the Spirit.

21. Our civilization has narrowed down the scope of human freedom to the human possibility to consume more and more and indulge in all kinds of selfish enjoyment. This dangerous twisting of freedom is at the root of all unjust economic orders and exploitative structures in our world today. In spite of all the benefits of modern technological-industrial civilization, it has fundamentally enhanced human greed, acquisitiveness and selfishness. A fundamental questioning of the value system created by this civilization is urgently needed. Only individuals and communities that truly live in the freedom and power of the Spirit can challenge our life-styles and value systems. Our prayer to the Holy Spirit to set us free is also a prayer to grant us the prophetic power to do this.

Sub-theme III: Spirit of Unity — Reconcile Your People!

22. As Christians we see the source of the divisions which plague our human conditions to be the consequence of sin. While distinctions in the human family and among the various dimensions of creation are God-given enrichments in the created order, the sins of pride, greed, self-centeredness and hatred are manifested in disunity.

23. Since Pentecost the Church proclaims that, while the root cause of disunity among peoples of the earth is sin, it is the will of God that disunity be overcome and the unity in our many-faceted relationships be realized. It is in this perspective that the hymn of Pentecost:

> Coming down and confusing the tongues, the Most High divided the nations; but distributing the tongues of fire, the Most High called all to unity. Therefore, with one voice, we glorify the all-holy Spirit!

proceeds and highlights the role of the Holy Spirit as the embodiment and perfector of that unity among us.

24. If we are responsive to the promptings of the Holy Spirit, it will mean that we will also allow ourselves to be guided by the Holy Spirit and that we will respond wholeheartedly to the concrete and specific opportunities given to us to move towards unity in and among us in every sphere of our existence in this life. The Holy Spirit is a Spirit of Unity! Therefore, the Holy Spirit who is the Spirit of our Redeemer Christ comes to restore our personal and intimate relationship with God, which we have in the divine image given to us. We believe that God has sent His Son, the second person of the Holy Trinity, into the work for our redemption, reconciling us to the Father through Jesus Christ's saving work of teaching and direction and example, but particularly through His death and resurrection. "God was in Christ reconciling the world to himself, not counting their trespasses against them, and entrusting to us the message of reconciliation" (2 Cor 5:19).

25. As Christians we recognize that any unity among us primarily needs to overcome our disunity as fallen persons who as yet have not grown enough in the Holy Spirit, to overcome the spirit of divisiveness. We are called to experience "the grace of the Lord Jesus Christ and the love of God and the fellowship of the Holy Spirit" (2 Cor 13:14) being in communion with the Church by participating in its ecclesial life and practice. It is to the Spirit of Unity that we call in hope that Christ might be in our midst now and forever.

26. We lament also the divisions among those who bear the name Orthodox, calling for the formal proclamation of the sacramental and ecclesial unity of Eastern Orthodox and Oriental Orthodox Christians and churches. We continue to call upon the Holy Spirit to lead all Christians toward the blessed day when all who follow Christ and call Him Lord may be guided to ecclesial unity by the Spirit of Unity.

27. In many bilateral and multilateral dialogues the Lima document on "Baptism, Eucharist and Ministry" (BEM), elaborated by the Faith and Order Commission, and the ongoing promptings of the Holy Spirit lead toward a hoped for day of Christian unity. Our prayer is that one day, the unity of the Church, which is fully experienced in the eucharistic communion, will be shared by everyone who calls upon the holy name of the blessed Trinity, Father, Son and Spirit of Unity, and the Lord's prayer "that all may be one" (Jn 17:21).

28. The more we reflect on our disunity, the more convinced we become of our need for the reconciling power of the saving work of the Lord and Saviour Jesus Christ on the Cross, whose work of redemption has made possible our reconciliation and

communion with God, with our brothers and sisters of Christian conviction, with all the peoples of the world. In the Church we have access to his reconciling power through the grace of the Holy Spirit.

29. To assume one's role in the search for unity certainly means that the Orthodox must become more actively involved in those efforts among peoples of genuine good will who seek to promote unity and overcome divisions and hostilities of the past. Surely, there is a calling for us to support well-conceived plans for international peace, for the lessening of racial tensions, for the overcoming of economic injustices, for the promotion of the equality of women and men, for the protection of the unborn and the aged, for the restoration of the ecological integrity of creation, and so many other spheres of our broken life which cry out for reconciliation and unity.

30. The natural and God-given distinctions of gender, family, race, age, and national identity abused and turned by means of our sin into divisions, we turn to the Spirit of Unity to renew these relationships. In the sphere of the relations of men and women, the Spirit which came upon the Mother of God, the Theotokos, points all to the place of women in the plan of salvation. Our honour for the Mother of God leads us to work for the re-establishment of the proper relationship of men and women before God. Therefore, we appeal to the Spirit of Unity to overcome our brokenness and separatedness in families, among races, age groups and nations.

31. Special note must be taken of the terrible divisions in every nation and among the nations between the rich and the poor. It would seem that only the grace of the Spirit of God is capable of converting our hearts so that the grave economic injustices of persons and systems which divide us can be overcome.

32. The Christian life calls us to actualize the potentials to unity given us at our baptism. In it we have been reconciled with the Father, through Christ in the Spirit of Unity. To be baptized means we appropriate the gifts (charismata) of Holy Spirit in order to struggle against sin through repentance (metanoia) and purification that we might be illumined to confirm our communion with God, with our neighbours in every aspect of our relationships, and with the creation as a whole. Christian tradition affirms that we must be co-workers with the Spirit of God in overcoming disunity, building among us a life of unity and restoring the integrity of the world.

33. In a special way, Orthodox people throughout the centuries, and over long periods of time, have suffered and continue to suffer repression from political and other forces. The witness we have sought to give in such circumstances is one of Christ-like patient suffering. We have learned to pray for our oppressors, with the expectation that our prayer may touch their hearts. Often we have been led to a reconciliation with our enemies which transcends the forms and structures of this world. The grace of the Spirit alone makes such an effort possible for us.

34. The saving and redeeming work of the Triune God is most often articulated in worship and ascetic life as a victory over the demonic principalities, forces and powers which, among other ways, express themselves in our human existence as disunity. In the struggle against these evil forces, we know that alone we can do nothing. Only the Spirit of Unity can strengthen us in the struggle against them. Our strongest weapon is a continuing invocation (epiclesis) of the Holy Spirit that we may establish unity wherever God intends it.

35. Thus we have a foretaste of Christ's victory and of the coming Kingdom of God in our lives. But the unity of the life of the Kingdom is not now nor will it ever be completed and fulfilled in the times before the consummation when the Lord will return. In this period of our existence, the demonic forces of division continue to

challenge us, so we also pray for "knowledge and all discernment" (Phil 1:9) because the "gifts of the Spirit of God... are spiritually discerned" (1 Cor 12:10). By this faith we are sustained as we experience the foretaste of the unity of the Kingdom in the life of the Church. But we look forward to the eschatological completion of all things when our unity in all things good will be realized.

Sub-theme IV: Holy Spirit — Transform and Sanctify Us!

36. The Spirit of God is holy because the Spirit transcends all creation and is not of this world or part of it: "Now we have received not the Spirit of this world, but the Spirit which is from God, that we might understand the gifts bestowed on us by God" (1 Cor 2:12). The Spirit proceeds from the Father, therefore the Spirit of God brings into the life of all creation the holiness of the Triune God, the transcendence of the divine reality communicated to the world through God's energies. The Spirit is holy: "The Holy Spirit was, is, and ever shall be, without a beginning and without an end... together with the Father and the Son" (Pentecost hymn).

37. The Spirit of God is holy because it is the Spirit of Christ, who was anointed and received the fulness of the divinity in his humanity: "One is Holy, one is Lord, Jesus Christ, to the glory of the Father." Therefore Jesus "will baptize you with Holy Spirit and with fire" (Mt 3:11), and indeed he breathed on the Apostles and said to them: "Receive the Holy Spirit" (Jn 20:22). The Spirit is *the* witness and *the* revealer of Christ (cf. Jn 14:26; Acts 5:32; 1 Cor 12:3), the Spirit of sonship (Rom 8:15).

38. The Spirit of God is holy because the Spirit shares here and now the gifts of the eschatological kingdom of God (Rom 14:17). God poured out upon us the Holy Spirit, plentifully, through Jesus Christ, our Saviour (cf. Tit 3:5). The Spirit is the kingdom of God in us and among us, the eternal communion (koinonia) with God. "God's love has been poured into our hearts through the Holy Spirit which has been given to us" (Rom 5:5).

39. The Spirit is the sustainer and the life of creation (Gen 1:2). The Spirit dwells in every creature, and all existence depends on the power of the Spirit. Humanity is called to be the "temple of the Holy Spirit" (1 Cor 6:19).

The Spirit is the deifying God, light and life, purifying, acting, and distributing gifts. It is in and through the Holy Spirit that human persons, and indeed the whole creation, can renew their communion with God, so that God "will dwell with them, and they shall be his people, and God himself will be with them" (Rev 21:3).

40. The confession of the Holy Spirit as distinctive person of the Trinity and as the principle of the regeneration (rebirth) and renewal constitutes an essential point of the Christian Faith from the beginning of the Church. Paul insists on the words: "When the goodness and loving kindness of God our Saviour appeared, he saved us, not because of deeds done by us in righteousness, but in virtue of his own mercy, by the washing of regeneration and renewal in the Holy Spirit, which he poured out upon us richly through Jesus Christ our Saviour, so that we might be justified by his grace and become heirs in hope of eternal life" (Tit 3:4-7).

41. The transformation and sanctification of creation begins with our own personal transformation in baptism, which is a new birth through water and the spirit (Jn 3:5). It is through the waters of baptism that we are transformed, that we put away the old nature and put on the new, renewed in the image of God who created us, becoming children of the light and heirs of eternal life. The cosmos itself participates in this transformation as the Church prays to God — at the blessing of the water — to "come

down and sanctify this water, by the indwelling of the Holy Spirit", and to show this water to be the "water of redemption, the water of sanctification, the purification of flesh and spirit, the remission of sins, the illumination of the soul, the laver of regeneration, the renewal of the Spirit, the gift of adoption to sonship, the garment of incorruption, the fountain of life."

42. Similarly, the anointment with oil in Chrismation/Confirmation, the communion in Christ's body and blood in the bread and the wine, and other material means used to bestow the gifts of the Spirit through the sacraments and other services of blessing reveal the diverse manners in which the entire creation participates in the Spirit's work of sanctification.

43. The coming of the Spirit at Pentecost announces the inauguration of a renewed humanity. The condition for reception of the Holy Spirit, however, is repentance: "Repent and be baptized every one of you in the name of Jesus Christ for the forgiveness of your sins; and you shall receive the gift of the Holy Spirit" (Acts 2:38). Although they have received the Holy Spirit, Christians often ignore its presence and thus repentance is constantly necessary for the life-long process of sanctification and growth in the Spirit. This repentance (metanoia) signifies a real change, literally a "turning around" of mind, intention, behaviour and vision — a commitment to turn away from sin and to turn towards Christ. This commitment to a Christian way of life means a living out of our faith in all dimensions of our life.

44. Christian life is a spiritual life. It is life under God lived with Christ in the Spirit. The spiritual life is our continuing effort to acquire the gifts of the Spirit and to manifest their fruits in our lives: love, joy, peace, patience, kindness, goodness, faithfulness, gentleness and self-control (Gal 5:22-23). This effort involves asceticism (askesis), active spiritual combat against the temptations of evil and the satisfaction of self-indulgent desires. Fasting, prayer, self-discipline, reflection upon the teachings of Christ, charity and service to others are engaged to turn our thoughts and actions to positive values and habits, to the realization that life in Christ and the Spirit is a personal life lived in relation with others. The spiritual life is not "for myself alone" as an individual; life in the Spirit is life lived in freedom in the Spirit as a reflection of the life of the Holy Trinity. Thus, even the life of the Christian hermit or the saint who lives in the Spirit is one that is integrally related to other persons, to the human community and to the entire creation.

45. The spiritual life can become exclusive, enslaved to the individualism and self-satisfaction. Then the focal point of this discipline (of the life in Christ) is the transformation of the persons within the communion, the regulation of the personal life with the ecclesial life. It is the persons created in the image and likeness of God who are called to participation in divine life as "a chosen race, a royal priesthood, a holy nation, God's own people" (1 Pet 2:9). We are called to transform, to sanctify, and to offer our own lives as the integral part of the edification of the body of Christ in the Holy Spirit. The Holy Spirit is the creator of communion, therefore the Spirit sustains our growth and inner transformation as members of Christ's body. Continuing sanctification in the Spirit means continuous involvement in the life of a visible community, by overcoming the stumbling blocks to full unity. The saint (Christian) is the most vivid and strong building block of the visible community.

46. The extension (and prolongation) of the communion of the Spirit into the life of the society is an essential dimension of the life in Christ. In this sense, the person and presence of the saint is a great force for the transformation of society. The saint is one whose very life reflects the light and life of Christ. Saints are men and women who

have become transparent to the divine life. Thus saints are living signs of the kingdom, reflecting the glory of the only-begotten Son of the Father, through the power and divine energies of the Spirit. These persons of holiness, through whom God's light shines out upon the world, are able to see in others the image of God and restore to those around them a sense of their own absolute value and worth as human beings.

47. Saints restore integrity and harmony to the whole of creation; through them the world is transformed, animals are tamed, springs appear in the desert, the terrifying forces of nature are calmed, and people are reconciled. They show us that divine strength can give new power to the world, and their very way of living is a model for us to regulate the level of our consumption, comfort, and convenience for the love of the neighbour and for the sustenance and integrity of creation.

48. "He saw the Spirit of God coming down like a dove and resting upon him" (Mt 3:16). The dove is the symbol of peace, of integrity of creation. At Pentecost, the Holy Spirit came to seal a covenant of peace between heaven and earth, inaugurating the kingdom of peace.

The life of Christians and communities can be dislocated, disintegrated by all forms of divisions and discriminations. Conformity to the world, to the sociology of society, can become a form of slavery. The Church of the Spirit should serve the solidarity of the people. In the liturgy, the parish must bring all the aspects of society, naming also the social sins, the evils and injustices, the wars and divisions, making reconciliation.

49. We are called to be saints (1 Cor 1:2). We are called to "live by the Spirit" and also to "walk by the Spirit" (Gal 5:25). The transforming and sanctifying power of the Holy Spirit calls us to become part of the communion of saints, to live out our faith in the world through a life of holiness, witness and service.

50. As we look towards the WCC Assembly in Canberra, we affirm the following foundations of our faith and pose certain questions regarding our praxis:

a) We confess our faith in the Holy Trinity and affirm the image of the Trinity as the model for our relations with one another in community. The ideal spiritual community is manifested sacramentally in the Eucharist, as the Church gathers together with Christ in the Spirit to offer herself to the Father. How does this model speak to persons in terms of relationships in marriage and the family, the Church, monastic life, and the life of society in general? How, as persons, are we called to reflect the image of God in our communal life? Do new forms of community in certain renewal movements reflect the relationships expressed in the trinitarian model?

b) We affirm the diversity of gifts and ministries distributed by the one gift of the Holy Spirit. How do we hold together the diversity expressed within parish and monastic life, with their different relationships to society? What is the place or role of women and men, clergy and lay, youth and aged, and particularly of those who have been marginalized for reasons of race, disability, or other types of discrimination? What are we doing to transform and renew our communities and other social structures? How can we work with others towards renewal of social and international structures for the benefit of humanity?

c) We recognize the power and presence of evil in this world and affirm the need for cooperation with Christ and the Holy Spirit to combat and exorcize these spiritual forces, manifested in various forms and structures of human behaviour and anomalies present both locally and internationally. Building upon basic human values, the Spirit prepares human persons for the reception of the Gospel and salvation in Christ through baptism. As the water of the baptism is exorcized of evil and becomes a vehicle for the sanctification of creation, so those baptized in the sanctified waters and sealed with the Spirit receive the power of the Spirit to confront evil and the problems facing the world today, e.g. human rights, ecological problems, justice and peace concerns, drugs and other forms of chemical dependency, consumerism, human relations, community-building, etc.

d) We affirm the Church, the ark of salvation, as a worshipping, teaching and practising community in which spiritual formation is nurtured in a variety of ways: through prayer and the sacraments, monastic life, reflection and action in the world, elder/disciple relationships (parent/child, coach/athlete, etc.), and the presence of saintly models. We emphasize marriage and the family within the Church as inspired by trinitarian relationships, in which human beings receive their value as persons in the image of God. What are we doing to encourage the development or awareness of such educational opportunities in our local situations? How can we share with one another, personally and in our communities, the particular gifts, programmes or strengths that each possesses?

e) We affirm the sacramental character of ecclesial life which leads persons into a life of sharing and mutual commitment through baptism and the Eucharist, as well as through all sacraments and rites of blessing that serve to build up the Church and strengthen our relationship with God. As members of the new creation, the community of the Church is called to manifest the self-emptying love of Christ as it works with the Holy Spirit to transform the human community. How is this sharing extended first throughout the Church community, and then into the wider community?

Message of His All Holiness Dimitrios I, Ecumenical Patriarch

On the Day of the Protection of the Environment, 1989

This Ecumenical Throne of Orthodoxy, keeper and proclaimer of the centuries-long spirit of the patristic tradition, and faithful interpreter of the eucharist and liturgical experience of the Orthodox Church, watches with great anxiety the merciless trampling down and destruction of the natural environment which is caused by human beings, with extremely dangerous consequences for the very survival of the natural world created by God.

The abuse by contemporary man of his privileged position in creation and of the Creator's order to him "to have dominion over the earth" (Gen. 1:28), has already led the world to the edge of apocalyptic self-destruction, either in the form of natural pollution which is dangerous for all living beings, or in the form of the extinction of many species of the animal and plant world, or in various other forms. Scientists and other men of learning, warn us now of the danger, and speak of phenomena which are threatening the life of our planet, such as the so-called "phenomenon of the greenhouse" whose first indications have already been noted.

In view of this situation the Church of Christ cannot remain unmoved. It constitutes a fundamental dogma of her faith that the world was created by God the Father, who is confessed in the Creed to be "maker of heaven and earth and of all things visible and invisible". According to the great Fathers of the Church, Man is the prince of creation, endowed with the privilege of freedom. Being partaker simultaneously of the material and the spiritual world, he was created in order to refer back creation to the Creator, in order that the world may be saved from decay and death.

This great destiny of man was realized, after the failure and fall of the "first Adam", by "the last Adam", the Son and Logos of God incarnate, our Lord Jesus Christ, who united in His person the created world with the uncreated God, and who unceasingly refers creation to the Father as an eternal eucharistic Anaphora and offering. The Church in each divine Liturgy continues this reference and offering (of creation to God) in the form of the Bread and the Wine, which are elements taken from the material universe. In this way the Church continuously declares that Man is destined not to exercise power over creation, as if he were the owner of it, but to act as its steward, cultivating it in love and referring it in thankfulness, with respect and reverence, to its Creator.

Unfortunately, in our days under the influence of an extreme rationalism and self-centredness, man has lost the sense of sacredness of creation and acts as its arbitrary ruler and rude violator. Instead of the eucharistic and ascetic spirit with which the Orthodox Church brought up her children for centuries, we observe today a violation of nature for the satisfaction not of basic human needs, but of man's endless and constantly increasing desires and lust, encouraged by the prevailing of the consumer society.

But creation "groans and travails in all its parts" (Rom. 8:22), and is now beginning to protest at its treatment by the human being. Man cannot infinitely and at his pleasure exploit the natural sources of energy. The price of his arrogance will be his self-destruction, if the present situation continues.

In full consciousness of our duty and our paternal spiritual responsibility, having taken all the above into consideration and having listened to the anguish of modern man, we have come to the decision, in common with the Sacred and Holy Synod surrounding us, to declare the first day of September of each year a day on which on the occasion of the feast of Indiction, which is the first day of the ecclesiastical year, prayers and supplications are offered in this holy centre of Orthodoxy for all creation — to be the day of the protection of the environment.

Therefore, we invite through this our Patriarchal Message the entire Christian world, to offer together with the Mother Great Church of Christ (the Ecumenical Patriarchate) every year on this day prayers and supplications to the maker of all, both as thanksgiving for the great gift of Creation and as petitions for its protection and salvation. At the same time we paternally urge on the one hand all the faithful in the world to admonish themselves and their children to respect and protect the natural environment, and on the other hand all those who are entrusted with the responsibility of governing the nations to act without delay taking all necessary measures for the protection and preservation of natural creation.

Finally, wishing all good things for the world from our Lord we bestow upon all our Patriarchal blessing.

In Phanar, on 1 September 1989   Patriarch Dimitrios

Eastern and Oriental Orthodox Contribution

World Convocation on Justice, Peace and the Integrity of Creation

Seoul, Korea, March 1990

The representatives and the participants of the Eastern Orthodox and Oriental Orthodox Churches, participating in the JPIC Convocation on Justice, Peace and the Integrity of Creation, Seoul, Korea, 5-13 March 1990, have agreed to make the following contribution which concerns the ideas of "covenant", "covenanting" and "renewing our covenant with God" which are presented in the draft document as one of the main themes for the Convocation.

1. The evaluation of the second draft text of the JPIC is, without doubt, a major obligation of the representatives of the various local Orthodox Churches. This obligation flows not only from self-understanding and consciousness, but from the expressed will of the WCC to encourage and promote as much as possible a more representative contribution of all of the member churches toward the formulation of a commonly acceptable, or at least shared, theological foundation of its documents. Motivated by this spirit, there is an official need for some form of "synodical or conciliar process" which could especially be applied to this specific document of the JPIC. This observation of the Orthodox representatives is based on their absolute agreement, both with the analysis of the contemporary tragic reality which we face and with the need for the immediate mobilization of the churches and their faithful members in order to forestall the fearsome consequences which even threaten the continuation of life on our planet.

Nevertheless and in spite of this extensive agreement with the clear descriptive analysis of the problem and the discussion of the moral requirements for its resolution, serious reservations regarding the representative fullness of the theological presuppositions of the text were expressed by all of the Orthodox representatives. These reservations were formulated by the Orthodox representatives in the work groups, were recorded in summary form in the present document with the intent that they be taken into serious consideration by the appropriate drafting committee for inclusion in the final draft of the text.

2. Of course, these observations refer primarily to the theological structure of the text, but they would not have been necessary, at least in major dimensions,

a) if the texts, prepared at the Orthodox theological consultations sponsored by the WCC at Sofia in 1987 and Minsk in 1989, had been taken into consideration and more fully used in the preparation of the Convocation text I by the JPIC drafters. The proposals of these Orthodox meetings, even though they reported the Orthodox theological presuppositions to the JPIC, these topics were completely ignored or at least were not included in the text by the drafters of the document; and

b) if use had been made of the spirit and the theological presuppositions of the Pan-Orthodox statement which was unanimously accepted by the representatives of all of the Autocephalous and Autonomous Orthodox Churches at the Third Pre-Synodical Pan-Orthodox Conference concerning the "Contribution of the Orthodox Church toward the establishment of peace, justice, freedom, brotherhood and love among peoples and for the elimination of racial and other prejudices", is the official position of the Orthodox Church on the topic of JPIC, and it could have contributed positively to the expansion of the theological base of the document under discussion.

3. The foundational theological base of the text under discussion is announced by its authors and is, in reality, the idea of the "covenanting God" and the covenant, which underlays consistently the whole organization and structure of the text: "The informing metaphor throughout the document is that of covenant. This is, of course, more than a mere metaphor for Christians... Through it, however, we wish to focus our thought so that this might be a work of true theological praxis... To reflect on such a theme, rightly, is to renew our covenant with the One to whom the world 'belongs'... In renewing our covenant with God, we also join hands with the many concerned scientists ..." (para. 7, 110ff).

There is no question, then, that the choice of this theological basis by the drafters has taken place on the basis of the subjective criteria of a particular theological mentality which however is not that of the official basis of the church-members of the WCC, or at least that which is embodied in the various programmes of the Commission on Faith and Order, that is "Baptism, Eucharist, Ministry", "The Unity of the Church and the Renewal of Human Community" and "Towards a Common Expression of the Apostolic Faith Today".

This subjective choice of the document's theological basis by the drafters explains the clear theological one-sidedness of the text which could be characterized as a successful analysis of the Old Testament teaching regarding covenant and the covenanting God, but it is not adequate to express the broad theological vision of the developing programmes of "Faith and Order", and even more so, the theological and ecclesiological pre-suppositions of the Orthodox Church.

The idea of covenant is based on the acceptance of a particular meaning of "ownership" by God of the world (para. 80) which however "differs radically from the usual perceptions of possession and power" (para. 81). This is understood as God's pathos of love toward the whole creation, the Incarnation of Jesus Christ (para. 82). But it is proclaimed most clearly on the basis of Old Testament criteria, as is seen from the biblical references from which it is noted that "for the biblical faith none is more significant than the belief that God is a covenanting God" (para. 84), that "at the heart of the covenant is the promise and challenge", "I will be your God and you should be my people" (para. 85), and that "God elects human beings as God's covenant partners" (para. 86; see also paras 113, 119, 120, etc.).

This one-sided focus, however, leads to the clear relativization of the significance of the content of the new covenant in Christ which is interpreted by the Old Covenant perspectives concerning covenant and leads to a marginalizing of the value of the whole redemptive work of Christ. Thus, the incarnation of the Son and Word of God is presented as a simple expression "of God's pathos of love" for the world (para. 104) and the New Testament itself as a simple successive stage and natural continuation of the Covenants of the "covenanting God with Noah and Abraham". Within this context "God's covenant with Israel was focused finally in the New Covenant in Jesus Christ, crucified and risen".

The only difference which is presented refers to the fact that in Christ "the covenant is made open to all" (paras 88-89). The objective content consequently of the whole redemptive work of Jesus Christ is interpreted within this framework, since only through the outpouring of the Holy Spirit on the world and by means of this outpouring upon Jesus Christ at His baptism, the Kingdom of God, i.e. shalom, is established in Christ and through Christ it is made "real in history" (para. 91). This was revealed through the whole teaching ministry of Christ, for "through Christ's parables and the miracles of healing, the Kingdom of God becomes manifest as a dynamic, growing reality, transforming political, social, economic and ecological relationships" (paras 92, 102).

4. This exclusive theological foundation of the draft document serves to indicate its weak points because the one-sided projection of the idea of Covenant and the covenanting God

a) weakens the relation and the reference of the Covenants of God to the whole plan of the divine economy between the Old Testament promise and the fulfilment of the promise of the redemption of humanity and the world. A consequence of this weakening of the whole plan of salvation was not only the depriving of the concept of covenant of its objective redemptive content, but the weakening of the trinitarian character of the whole divine plan of salvation which is realized always by the Father, through the Son and in the Holy Spirit;

b) it introduces both explicitly and covertly a division between the New Covenant of God and the redemptive work of Christ, between Christ and the Church, between the Church and the Kingdom of God, etc. which represent certain partial theological trends within the wider ecumenical movement, but which further are not necessary for the JPIC document.

5. Further, based on these comments, we believe that God's covenant with humanity, that was established in the body and blood of Jesus Christ, our Saviour and Redeemer (Lk. 22:20; Mt. 26:28; 1 Cor. 11:25), is unbreakable and eternal. Therefore, we reject any possibility for human beings to break and then to renew or re-establish the Covenant with God. Thus

a) we acknowledge that the people of God may be faithful to God's Covenant or unfaithful and sinful against it. If we are sinful and unfaithful, we need sincere repentance and conversion of our hearts to God. But repentance never means renewal of the Covenant which can be neither broken nor renewed by us;

b) that is why we can accept the notion of "covenanting" only in a sense of "pronouncing mutual commitments", without applying to it any special theological and ecclesiological meaning. We cannot agree with the concept of "renewing our covenant with God" as proposed by the second Draft Document of the Convocation (paras 131-137) and explained by Dr Niles in his speech "Covenanting for justice, peace and the integrity of creation" (Document S. 1.4).

Our refusal to accept this theological idea of "covenanting" and "renewing our covenant with God" does not mean that by doing this, we deny the positive content of the Convocation as a whole. In all those who have gathered for this Convocation we see our brothers and sisters in Christ. We express our solidarity with the oppressed and the poor, with those who struggle for justice, peace and the integrity of creation in their societies. We are ready to commit ourselves to justice, peace and the integrity of creation. We are eager to bring our own concerns into the JPIC process and make our contributions to it.

c) However, we would like to participate in this process in a way, agreeable to our convictions and acceptable for our believers. It is our great hope that the JPIC process will develop further in a way acceptable to the various church traditions represented in the ecumenical community.

The positive and successful ecumenical experience which we have had persuades us that there exists a practical and real possibility of joint ecumenical gathering, prayer and action, marked both by mutual respect for differing theological systems and traditions, as well as by true Christian commitment to JPIC. We hope and pray that the spirit of mutual respect and brotherly love prevail in our joint work for justice, peace and the integrity of creation.

It is our hope that these views will be used to significantly modify the text in regard to its treatment of the "covenant idea" contained in it. Failing that, we feel strongly that the present statement should be published together with the documents of the Convocation.

Seoul, 10 March 1990   Metropolitan Damaskinos of Switzerland
                                        Metropolitan G. Yohanna Ibrahim

Reflections of Orthodox Participants
Addressed to the Seventh Assembly
of the World Council of Churches

Canberra, Australia, 7-20 February 1991

I. Introduction

The Eastern Orthodox and Oriental Orthodox delegates and participants at the Seventh Assembly of the World Council of Churches, meeting in Canberra, Australia, want to communicate with all in attendance through this statement in order to express to them some concerns. We preface our comments with an expression of appreciation to the World Council of Churches for its many contributions to the development of dialogue among churches, and to assisting all members in making efforts to overcome disunity. As Orthodox, we appreciate the assistance given over decades in the process of dialogue leading toward the full communion of Eastern and Oriental Orthodox Churches.

We also recognize the contribution of the WCC in the work it has done in its Commissions on Faith and Order and on Mission and Evangelism (CWME), its contribution to the Renewal of Congregational Life (RCL), its relief work through Inter-Church Aid, Refugee and World Service (CICARWS), and in the Justice, Peace and the Integrity of Creation Programme (JPIC).

Yet, our experience at this Assembly has heightened a number of concerns that have been developing among the Orthodox since the last Assembly. We want to share these with the Canberra Assembly and to tell you where these are now leading us.

The Orthodox concern about these issues should not be understood as implying a reluctance to continue dialogue. The present statement is motivated not by disinterest or indifference toward our sisters and brothers in other churches and Christian communities, but by our sincere concern about the future of the ecumenical movement, and about the fate of its goals and ideals, as they were formulated by its founders.

II. Orthodox Concerns

1. The Orthodox Churches want to emphasize that for them, the main aim of the WCC must be *the restoration of the unity of the Church*. This aim does not exclude relating Church unity with the wider unity of humanity and creation. On the contrary, the unity of Christians will contribute more effectively to the unity of humanity and the world. Yet the latter must not happen at the expense of solving issues of faith and order, which divide Christians. *Visible unity*, in both the faith and the structure of the Church, constitutes a specific goal and must not be taken for granted.

2. The Orthodox note that there has been an *increasing departure from the Basis* of the WCC. The latter has provided the framework for Orthodox participation in the World Council of Churches. Its text is: "The World Council of Churches is a fellowship of churches which confess the Lord Jesus Christ as God and Saviour according to the scriptures and therefore seek to fulfil together their common calling to

the glory of the one God, Father, Son and Holy Spirit" (Constitution). Should the WCC not direct its future work along these lines, it would be in danger of ceasing to be an instrument aiming at the restoration of Christian unity, and in that case it would tend to become a forum for an exchange of opinions without any specific Christian theological basis. In such a forum, common prayer will be increasingly difficult, and eventually will become impossible, since even a basic common theological vision will be lacking.

3. The tendency to marginalize the Basis in WCC work has created some dangerous trends in the WCC. We miss from many WCC documents the affirmation that Jesus Christ is the world's Saviour. We perceive a growing *departure from biblically-based Christian understanding* of (a) the Trinitarian God, (b) salvation, (c) the "Good News" of the Gospel itself, (d) human beings as created in the image and likeness of God, and (e) the Church, among others.

Our hope is that the results of Faith and Order work will find a more prominent place in the various expressions of the WCC, and that tendencies in the opposite direction will not be encouraged. The Orthodox, consequently, attribute special significance to the work of the Faith and Order Commission of the WCC, and view with concern each tendency to undermine its place in the structure of the Council.

4. The Orthodox follow with interest, but also with a certain disquiet, the developments of the WCC toward the broadening of its aims in the direction of *relations with other religions*. The Orthodox support dialogue initiatives, particularly those aiming at the promotion of relations of openness, mutual respect and human cooperation with neighbours of other faiths. When dialogue takes place, Christians are called to bear witness to the integrity of their faith. A genuine dialogue involves greater theological efforts to express the Christian message in ways that speak to the various cultures of our world. All this, however, must occur on the basis of theological criteria which will define the limits of diversity. The biblical faith in God must not be changed. The definition of these criteria is a matter of theological study, and must constitute the first priority of the WCC in view of its desired broadening of aims.

5. Thus, it is with alarm that the Orthodox have heard some presentations on the theme of this Assembly. With reference to the theme of the Assembly, the Orthodox still await the final texts. However, they observe that some people tend to affirm with very great ease the presence of the Holy Spirit in many movements and developments without discernment. The Orthodox wish to stress the factor of sin and error, which exists in every human action, and separate the Holy Spirit from these. We must guard against a tendency *to substitute a "private" spirit, the spirit of the world or other spirits for the Holy Spirit* who proceeds from the Father and rests in the Son. Our tradition is rich in respect for local and national cultures, but we find it impossible to invoke the spirits of "earth, air, water and sea creatures". Pneumatology is inseparable from Christology or from the doctrine of the Holy Trinity confessed by the Church on the basis of Divine Revelation.

6. The Orthodox are sorry that their position with regard to eucharistic communion has not been understood by many members of the WCC, who regard the Orthodox as unjustifiably insisting upon *abstinence from eucharistic communion*. The Orthodox once more invite their brothers and sisters in the WCC to understand that it is a matter of *unity in Faith and fundamental Orthodox ecclesiology*, and not a question of a triumphalistic stance.

For the Orthodox, the Eucharist is the supreme expression of unity and not a means toward unity. The present situation in the ecumenical movement is for us an experience of the cross of Christian division. In this regard, the question of the ordination of women to the priestly and episcopal offices must also be understood within a theological and ecclesiological context.

7. Finally, our concern is also directed to the *changing process of decision-making* in the WCC. While the system of quotas has benefits, it may also be creating problems. As Orthodox we see changes that seem to increasingly weaken the possibility of an Orthodox witness in an otherwise Protestant international organization. We believe that this tendency is to the harm of the ecumenical effort.

8. For the Orthodox gathered at this Assembly, these and other tendencies and developments question *the very nature and identity of the Council*, as described in the Toronto Statement. In this sense the present Assembly in Canberra appears to be a crucial point in the history of the ecumenical movement.

We must, therefore, ask ourselves "Has the time come for the Orthodox churches and other member churches to review their relations with the World Council of Churches?"

We pray the Holy Spirit to help all Christians to renew their commitment to visible unity.

Canberra, 19 February 1992

Report of an Inter-Orthodox Consultation

"Renewal in Orthodox Worship"

Bucharest, Romania, 21-27 October 1991

Introduction

The Sub-unit on Renewal and Congregational Life, of the World Council of Churches, organized a seminar on "Renewal in Orthodox Worship", held in Bucharest, Romania, 21-27 October 1991. Twenty people from both Eastern and Oriental Churches met together to reflect on preliminary elements of an Orthodox debate about liturgical renewal in our time. Such a debate is necessary because of new missionary and cultural situations in which most of the Orthodox Churches are living, especially in Eastern and Central Europe. We give thanks to the Triune God for his blessing of redeeming these nations from oppression and captivity. In this atmosphere of freedom after the 1989 revolution it became possible to organize such a meeting in Romania.

The Centrality of Worship

The entire life of the Orthodox Church is inspired and organized by the Liturgy, the concelebration of the Eucharist by the whole people of God. Its value lies not only in its beauty and solemnity, but even more in its ability in the midst of history to open the horizon of the Kingdom of God for all humanity. Here history meets eschatology, church meets cosmos, sacred meets secular, redeemed meets unredeemed. The Liturgy invites both Christians and non-Christians to this encounter between God and God's people in the name of Jesus Christ.

We need to make a clear distinction between the Eucharistic Liturgy, the sacraments, and other church services and prayers which do not have sacramental nature. The form and language of the Liturgy, as it is known today, have a permanent character, because they express the essentials of the sacrament of Eucharist as it was transmitted in the New Testament and the Tradition. The form and rituals of the other church services have varied according to the time, place and needs of the people. Yet the texts of services are not a matter of historical accident. They carry a profound doctrinal and theological content which constitute the *lex credendi* of all Orthodox Churches. They take on a certain uniformity and universality. In order to respond to the pastoral needs of the faithful and their communities, it is important that each local church take the responsibility to modify, expand or propose new texts for such services.

The Meaning of Renewal

After decades of systematic atheistic education, ignorance of Orthodox Liturgy in East European countries has become pronounced.

People today live in a state of anxiety. The upheavals of this century have had an effect on their very existence. There was a time when life conformed to the rhythm of nature which represented the order and unity of the cosmos and was mirrored in the social order. But now they have lost their internal equilibrium.

The tragic experience of totalitarian regimes, like that of the consumer society, places the Orthodox in a particularly dangerous position, but at the same time has thrust upon them greater responsibilities.

It is here that one must overcome the ruptures and dualisms by an appropriate Orthodox interpretation of Incarnation and Resurrection.

Tradition is one of the essential elements of Orthodox church life. It has kept the church alive in spite of oppression. It has also been forgotten and even lost among many of the post-war generation, especially in the cities. Tradition should be kept alive by all means. It is important because it represents a continuation of the centuries-old transmission of the teachings of the Fathers of the Church. This does not exclude local church practices which do not contradict doctrinal teaching.

Spiritual renewal as a means of renewing worship. Within many areas of discussion, there appeared one basic question for all aspects of renewal: the need for spiritually experienced persons, for spiritual fathers and mothers. Society is developing scientifically and technically — but only a few people can discern between pure emotion and specific spiritual experience. We need persons who follow a spiritual path, who have a profound experience of prayer and deep knowledge of mystery. Monasticism is the appropriate field for developing this quality since it is committed to this special dimension. Monastic centres need to communicate well both to the teachers of theology, the clergy, and all the faithful.

Some clergy exhibit a lack of spiritual quality by simply demanding that people submit to their authority rather than showing a loving attitude. To build up the spiritual life of the parish, priests should visit families to express pastoral care and to convey the sense and sacred symbolism of worship.

Current Challenges

All participants at the seminar emphasized that the Liturgy implies the participation of the community. The priest is not the exclusive celebrant of the Eucharist. All the believers, together with the priest, offer themselves to God and at the same time receive from Him the gift of Christ's Body and Blood.

1. Increased involvement of all the faithful. The Liturgy is a concelebration between the priest and the faithful, Jesus Christ being the High Priest who celebrates the Eucharist. In the church services (Matins, Vespers, Hours, etc.) the role of the faithful is predominant in terms of singing and reading. One way to improve the active participation of the faithful is to increase the number of non-eucharistic services.

The priest should reinforce this element of concelebration in the Liturgy and encourage involvement of the laity in the church offices. This is an essential way to develop a sense of community.

2. Issues of communion, confession and fasting. In many churches very few people receive Holy Communion. This trend has to be studied carefully and instruction given on the need for receiving Holy Communion as an integral part of the Liturgy.

There are many churches where people go to confession just once or twice a year. Spiritual growth is possible only when persons receive the Eucharist after proper confession. However, in urban situations and in churches with many members, it is not easy for the priest to hear confession of everyone regularly. Sometimes the priest decides that a person, whom he knows well, can partake of the Eucharist after absolution without confession. It is the responsibility of the priest to encourage the people to come for confession. At the same time he can use his discretion in giving absolution without the need for confession. Likewise, in some locations fasting before the Liturgy may be promoted according to the pastoral needs of the people.

3. The language of the Liturgy. The traditional liturgical languages must be retained but room must also be given for the introduction of the vernacular. There is a need for good translations approved by church authorities. The faithful, especially the young, should be prepared by the priests to follow the services with understanding.

The "silent" prayers of the priest, especially those of the Anaphora, should be read aloud. Both the celebrants and the congregation should know that the Liturgy is at the same time reality and mystery.

4. Music. The celebrants (priests and deacons) should sing clearly without hurrying. Chanters and choir directors must understand the text to be able to explain its meaning to the singers; only then can they convey it clearly through the music to the faithful, thereby creating a prayerful atmosphere.

Gradually, but very carefully, unison chant might be introduced. However, this should not replace the normal repertoire. Congregational singing should be encouraged whenever possible, especially responses to litanies, Trisagion, Creed, Our Father. There was common concern that the singing of choirs or soloists in worship often becomes a performance. Liturgical singing should be sober and pure, but this should not be misunderstood as cold and joyless. The music must fit the words. The text should always be understandable and the melodies should follow the linguistic structure of the text. It should convey the inner sense of the holy word. Some music makes it impossible to understand the text.

The practice of various forms — traditional and, if the occasion arises, new forms of monodic chant are encouraged, although any ongoing practice in parishes must be respected.

Creativity is an organic part of human-divine reality. This affirmation of the free vocation of the human being reaches beyond the dualism between the Church and the world, faith and culture, the sacred and the secular. New music is part of this creativity.

A new generation of composers is becoming inspired by old melodies. They can offer a great contribution to the present day Orthodox Church.

Moreover, some well-known composers have written a number of symphonic works inspired by the beauty and power of the old chants. These religious melodies have an important impact on culture as a whole.

5. Other kinds of participation. It is very necessary that all the people in the church participate in the Eucharist service. The ways in which that can be done are many.

All the people should take part in the singing or chanting. The people should sing with the choir as much as possible. Again, some of the prayers, that are normally recited by the priest alone, can be recited by all the people, e.g. the prayer of confession. The Creed should also be recited or sung by all.

The sermon can be preached by any authorized member of the church, man or woman. The young people should particularly be encouraged to participate fully either by joining the choir, preaching the sermon, or reading the scriptures. Committed members of the church can considerably improve its life provided that they collaborate with the priests who in turn should receive such offers.

6. Need for prayers. Worship is a place where people bring before God their sorrows and joys, success and failure, tears and happiness. No human need or situation should remain outside the liturgical order. Among the most urgent are:

— Prayers for local or current social needs. The majority of Orthodox Churches minister to a society which is still torn by social and economic crises. The victims of these changes need the spiritual support of the worshipping congregation with special prayers.

— Prayers for other Christians. Theological dialogue and common witness with other Christians have become a practice. We need to rediscover the power of intercession and common prayer in the search for visible unity among Christians.

7. Uncharitable ideas within the Liturgy. It is unfortunate that some of the chants in the Good Friday Service of the Orthodox Church contain portions where hatred against the Jews is expressed. They are classified as sinners without any hope of redemption and curses are heaped on them. A close scrutiny is necessary to remove such portions from Orthodox services.

New Challenges

1. Youth and the need for renewal in the Liturgy. In our broken and divided society there is an urgent need to rebuild our Christian communities around the living church. We must try and recapture the spirit of the early Church which was a Eucharistic family with the Liturgy at the centre.

Many young people find it extremely boring to attend a Liturgy. How can we help them feel at home? We need to be sensitive to them and offer the opportunity of participating by singing, serving and receiving appropriate instruction. This may give them the feeling of belonging and identity.

The following efforts have had an impact in some places:

— Family liturgies one Sunday a month in a church centre where there are facilities, for families to bring their children after the Liturgy, share a meal, have time for discussions, and provide religious instruction for children and others.

— Youth camps at which a model of life in a community can be experienced, complete with various activities, but with the Liturgy as central to the programme. Religious instruction can be offered in a more natural context. The group leaders organizing the camp continue to meet throughout the whole year with the priest in charge in order to receive guidance on leadership and religious instruction.

2. Diaspora. The term "diaspora" describes the dispersion of the Orthodox peoples around the world, outside the boundaries of their traditional lands.

Many living in this situation develop a new awareness of the "treasure" of Orthodoxy, in particular the Liturgy and the church, where people meet others and find their true identity.

The urgent questions are: how to hand down the faith and the tradition to the young? How to live at the crossroads of several cultures while belonging to more than one? Which identity to retain?

These questions are reflected in the ecclesiastical and liturgical life. For example, how do Orthodox peoples with different origins find a common language and learn tolerance in life as well as in the Liturgy? The Liturgy can become a school of life — retaining fidelity to one's spiritual heritage as well as keeping a common language with one's children, especially in the context of religious life. Other issues include the recruiting and training of clergy, and chanters, and learning to be a minority in a pluralistic society in which the Church is completely separated from the state.

3. Proselytism and rite. One of the consequences of the collapse of atheistic Marxism has been the opportunities offered to all types of religious communities to proselytize openly. This liberty is sometimes used against the Orthodox in the framework of the "new evangelisation of Europe". One example of this is the use of the "Byzantine Rite" in order to proselytize. People are made to believe that since the liturgical rite remains the same, recognition of another ecclesial authority is merely secondary. People are tempted by the material advantages of links with the West to believe that the essence of the faith is preserved in the rite.

It must be reaffirmed that Orthodoxy does not identify with a rite — be it "Byzantine" or "Eastern". It existed long before such rites came into being, it survived in the catacombs without priests or rites, and could continue to exist after the disappearance of the Byzantine rite.

Orthodoxy is a much deeper and integral reality, from which one cannot simply detach the Liturgy while rejecting the life on which it is founded. The Orthodox must deepen the existential meaning of prayer and community, just as their ancestors were forced to do when, having been abandoned by the hierarchy following the Union of Brest-Litovsk, they formed Orthodox fraternities founded on the spirit of conciliarity.

4. Openness of Orthodox worship. Orthodox worship is a treasure which needs not only to be preserved but also transmitted. The tradition lives only in the process of transmission. This raises the difficult problem of language and communication. Many are attracted by the liturgical doxology and the mystical power of the prayers. With the migration of the Orthodox populations bringing about ecumenical contacts, many hymns and prayers have been accepted into the worship services of other Christian churches. Certain parts of the *Lima Liturgy* have been inspired by the Eastern Tradition.

An exchange of worship music and material is needed to enrich the Eastern and Oriental Traditions, without losing their integrity. One can discover the confessional and cultural identity of others through their hymns and come to a wider understanding of the diversity of Christianity.

Recommendations

There is currently a growing interest in liturgical renewal. *Education* and *worship* are seen as inseparable values. In this regard the following proposals were made:

— To strengthen the subject of Liturgy in the formation of priests and theologians at theological academies.
— To organize regularly advanced-training seminars on the subject of Liturgy: liturgical singing, liturgical symbolism, liturgical sense, etc. for priests and those taking other roles in the Liturgy or interested lay persons.
— Initiation of clergy and lay people into the meaning of sacred signs is needed today since many young people cannot understand the depth of liturgical language or the meaning of liturgical rites. It is urgent to continue this process of training for a deep understanding of the Liturgy by publishing relevant patristic or other contemporary texts. These need to be communicated to the congregation by competent, well trained catechists, clergy or laity.
— To find ways for more people to have personal contact with spiritual fathers or mothers.
— To establish special schools for church music, where the various forms of monodic chant, the more recent developments of church music and the main streams of general music can be taught.
— To use modern media for teaching since there is a shortage of trained teachers.
— To use monasteries as places of special liturgical training.

An Appeal to the Churches

We make a strong plea that all Orthodox Churches improve their efforts for more intensive seminars and studies towards a participatory liturgical life. Further, results should be collected for thorough evaluation. It is urgent to increase awareness about the centrality of renewing worship in all its forms. Each autocephalous church is called to institute liturgical renewal processes in the context of local conditions and possibilities.

The eventual restoration of an Old Testament reading during the Eucharist is encouraged. Orthodox Churches should give attention to this and bring the matter before the Conference of the Inter-Orthodox Great Synod. In fact, the knowledge of the Old Testament, its message and its close relationship with the redemptive events of the New Testament are little known. The great theme of God's economy in two stages and the teaching of the prophets risk being marginalized, thus damaging the whole saving action of God in his Son.

We praise God for the very positive results of the last bilateral theological dialogue between Eastern and Oriental Orthodox Churches. We hopefully await the day when Anathemas will be lifted and when these venerable ancient churches will finally have mutual recognition and reconciliation. Inasmuch as these holy churches have preserved intact extremely precious liturgical traditions, this wealth will certainly enrich the process of renewal and consequent liturgical life.

Conclusions and Recommendations
of an Inter-Orthodox Conference
Environmental Protection

Chania, Greece, 5-11 November 1991

I

1. In 1989 His All-Holiness, the Ecumenical Patriarch of Constantinople Dimitrios I, issued a Patriarchal message calling for thanksgiving and supplications for all creation to be offered on the first day of September each year, the first day of the ecclesiastical year in the Orthodox Church. He called for this day to be a day of special prayer for the salvation and protection of God's creation.

2. This Message of the Ecumenical Patriarch created considerable interest within the Orthodox Church and beyond. In response to this interest His All-Holiness the late Ecumenical Patriarch Dimitrios invited the Heads of all the autocephalous and autonomous Orthodox Churches to appoint official representatives, one of them a hierarch, who would meet to discuss the consensus of the Orthodox Church as a whole about the problem of the protection of the natural environment. This led to the convocation of an inter-Orthodox conference for that purpose.

3. This conference gathered at the Orthodox Academy of Crete from 5-11 November 1991 under the Chairmanship of the representative of the Ecumenical Patriarch, His Eminence Metropolitan John of Pergamon. It was blessed by the presence of His Beatitude the Patriarch of Alexandria Parthenios III. His Royal Highness Prince Philip, the Duke of Edinburgh and International President of the World Wide Fund for Nature (WWF), gave the opening address and spoke about the nature of ecological crisis facing the world. Representatives of eleven autocephalous and autonomous Orthodox Churches took part. Observers from other churches and international organizations also attended. Specialists in various areas of theology and the natural sciences participated.

4. The participants in the conference had the opportunity to share in common worship of the Triune God, the creator and preserver of all, and to take part in the liturgical life of the Church of Crete.

5. The papers read at the Conference and the discussion that followed centred on the following broad areas: (a) General introductory examination of the causes, nature and importance of the ecological crisis, (b) Environmental problems, (c) Theological approaches to humanity's relationship with their natural environment, (d) Spiritual aspects of the problem, with particular reference to the Orthodox monastic tradition, (e) Practical suggestions. In the context of the work of the conference, the participants heard with pleasure the announcement of the foundation by the Orthodox Academy of Crete of an Institute of Theology and Ecology.

II

The Conference reached the following main conclusions concerning the fundamental principles emerging from a consideration of the Orthodox position with regard to the ecological problem:

a) The Orthodox Church shares the sensitivity and the concern of those who are distressed about the increasing burden on the natural environment due to human abuse, which the Church names as sin, and for which it calls all human beings to repentance. There is a tendency to seek a renovation of ethics while the Orthodox Church believes the solution is to be found in the liturgical, eucharistic and ascetic ethos of the Orthodox tradition.

b) The Orthodox Church is not to be identified with any ecological *movement*, party or organization either from the point of view of ideology and philosophy or from that of method or programmes to be applied for the solution of the ecological problem. The Orthodox Church, being the *Church*, constitutes a *presence* and a *witness* to a new mode of existence following its specific theological outlook of human beings' relationship with God, with one another and with nature.

III

Once these general principles are borne in mind, the participants of the Inter-Orthodox Conference would like to call respectfully upon their Churches to consider the following proposals.

1. That the Church draw attention to the Orthodox eucharistic and ascetic ethos which is a hall mark of Orthodox Church's relationship with nature. The Churches should offer once more this simple, just, yet fulfilled way of life to its own believers as well as to the wider world. Humanity needs a simpler way of life, a renewed asceticism, for the sake of creation.

2. That each autocephalous and autonomous Church dedicate the first of September to be a day of special prayers and supplications for all creation — as a day for the protection of all God's creation.

3. That each Church undertake programmes of Christian environmental education. This should include all aspects of theological education, the construction of courses and resources for catechetical schools and the preparation of appropriate materials for use in religious education in secular schools. These materials could also be used in those countries where the Church runs primary or secondary schools. In particular, it is recommended that the 1st of September be seen as an appropriate time for special emphasis in both teaching and preaching, on our need to care for God's creation.

In those places where the Church has higher education establishments, the Church should foster and encourage research into areas beneficial to the environment — such as alternative energy sources.

4. That each Church should engage in projects or local initiatives which lead to the enhancement of all creation. Each Church is requested to undertake such projects and initiatives at the local, diocesan and Church levels. For example

— In parishes: To organize recycling programmes for paper, glass, metals and compostable organic waste.

— To conserve energy within Church buildings by proper insulation and control of lighting.

— To encourage water conservation.

— To encourage less use of the car.

— In dioceses: To consider opportunities for the production and use of alternative energy (solar, wind or biomass) as an immediate and practical action.

— To support the creation and to further extension of nature reservations.

5. That each Church should examine its use of land, buildings and investments which it controls or influences, to ensure that they are used in a way which will not cause environmental damage, but will improve the environment.

6. That each Church should hold gatherings of members of the Church, covering fields from theology to environmental sciences, in order to aid the Church in further practical involvement in environmental and bioethical issues. Such a gathering should also seek to reach out, with the insights of the Orthodox Church, to those involved in scientific and ecological work, who are not members of the Orthodox Church, asking, in return, for their knowledge and expertise in helping the Church.

7. That the autocephalous and autonomous Churches should engage in a regional collaboration on specific environmental issues which transcend individual Church boundaries.

8. That the Orthodox Church make a formal appeal to the United Nation's Conference on the Environment and Development (UNCED) to be held in Brazil in June 1992. The appeal would ask for instance:

a) That in conformity with our Lord's saying in Luke 6:31, "As you wish that men would do to you, do so to them", no product or industry should be exported and no waste product should be deposited in any country, which the country of origin would not accept on its own territory.

b) That in conformity with the Christian call for the proper stewardship of resources, all possible assistance be given to the efficient use of energy. This may require the removal of taxes on insulating materials and the removal of subsidies on the production and use of particularly environmentally damaging non-renewable sources of energy. It may also require the increase of taxes to restrict use of fuels in order to induce a more thoughtful use of such resources as coal and petrol.

9. That the Orthodox Church encourage and support young people to initiate projects and programmes of environmental action, such as workcamps related to environmental issues, and education programmes.

SYNDESMOS, the World Fellowship of Orthodox Youth, should encourage Orthodox youth organizations to act in these areas, and could serve as a coordinating body for the development of Orthodox youth projects around the world.

Report of an Inter-Orthodox Consultation
of Orthodox WCC Member Churches
"The Orthodox Churches and the World Council of Churches"

Chambésy, Switzerland, 12-16 September 1991

Representatives of Eastern and Oriental Orthodox Churches have met in the Centre of the Ecumenical Patriarchate, Chambésy, Switzerland, 12-16 September 1991. Their task was to reflect on their relations with the World Council of Churches. They have done this in response to their experience at the Seventh Assembly of the WCC, held in Canberra, Australia, in February 1991, and in accordance with the intention expressed in their "reflection paper" addressed to the participants of the Assembly. This document briefly addressed certain theological, ecclesiological and organizational aspects concerning the involvement of the Orthodox Churches in the ecumenical movement, and in the WCC in particular. The Report of the Consultation is presented under three headings: (1) presuppositions of involvement for the Orthodox in the ecumenical movement and the WCC, (2) some problems for the Orthodox in the WCC, and (3) towards an improved Orthodox participation in the ecumenical movement.

I. Presuppositions of Involvement for the Orthodox in the Ecumenical Movement and the World Council of Churches

1. For the Orthodox, Eastern and Oriental, the primary purpose of the World Council of Churches is its work for the restoration of unity among Christians. In the Orthodox understanding, this means full ecclesial unity, that is, unity in doctrinal teaching, sacramental life and polity. The Orthodox recognize other important dimensions of ecumenical work and activity. Cooperative ecumenical efforts that contribute toward growing unity, the establishment or restoration of justice and peace, toward coherence in theological expression, toward mission and common witness, toward deepening the churches' self-understanding and toward growth of community in confessing, learning and service are important in themselves and as means for divided Christians to move toward ultimate doctrinal and sacramental union. But for the Orthodox, the ultimate goal and justification of the ecumenical movement in general, and for their participation in the WCC in particular, is the full ecclesial unity of Christians. It is thus an urgent task for the meaning of church unity to be clearly articulated and frequently repeated in the deliberations and work of the WCC, while concurrently striving to clarify appropriate and legitimate aspects of diversity in expressing the apostolic faith in worship and discipline within that ecclesial unity.

2. Toward this purpose, the Orthodox call all Christians and member churches, all WCC programme units and administrative organs to "a re-commitment to the constitutional 'Basis'" of the existence and work of the Council. The Basis Statement of the WCC is: "The World Council of Churches is a fellowship of churches which confess the Lord Jesus Christ as God and Saviour according to the scriptures and therefore seek to fulfil together their common calling to the glory of the one God, Father, Son and

Holy Spirit." This fundamental statement highlights the Trinitarian, Incarnational and salvific understanding of Christian faith, worship and life in the response of Christians to the Lordship of Jesus Christ. The Orthodox affirm it and insist on its centrality for the Christian churches gathered in fellowship for the purpose of working toward uniting all Christians. The Basis should be repeatedly displayed and frequently re-affirmed in the undertakings of the WCC so that all involved in its work and activities are constantly reminded of its contents.

3. In particular, the Basis and the Christian teaching historically related to it, should provide the theological underpinning of ecumenical reflection within the WCC and the documents and statements issued in its name. These fundamental Christian truths have come to the Church from God through the scriptures as divine revelation. We refer to the central affirmations of the apostolic faith and the credal statements of the Early Church, such as the Trinitarian understanding of God, the divine-human personhood of Jesus Christ, the Gospel of redemption and salvation in the work of Jesus Christ, creation and calling of humankind as the image and likeness of God, sanctifying work of the Holy Spirit in Church, etc. These fundamental beliefs of revelation need to be repeatedly referred to as such and respected by the WCC and its participants, and kept at the centre of WCC thinking and activities. Violations of the Basis and the concomitant faith affirmations arising from divine revelation as under-stood and taught in the historical undivided Church should be corrected or not admitted in the official work of the WCC.

4. The Orthodox Churches participate in the WCC's life and activities only on the understanding that the WCC "is a council of churches" (koinonia/fellowship/conseil) and not a council of individuals, groups, movements or religious bodies which are involved in the Council's goal, tasks and vision.

5. They consider seriously that their membership and participation in the WCC is based upon an encounter, cooperation and a dialogue of churches. The WCC cannot become a forum for the exchange of individual ideas. We together with other churches seek "... a conciliar fellowship of local churches which are themselves truly united..." and aim "... at maintaining sustained and sustaining relationships with [our] sister churches, expressed in conciliar gatherings wherever required for fulfilment of their common calling" (Nairobi Assembly 1975).

6. Participating thus in a dialogue structure, the Orthodox Churches should be the only responsible agents for their representation. Each member church has the right to decide how to be represented, in accordance with the criteria that apply to a council of churches. These decisions are made on an equal basis with the other member churches in respect to quotas, voting procedures, church polity issues, etc.

7. The Orthodox Churches strongly re-affirm that doctrinal issues in the WCC structures should be considered as an essential element of each church's membership. Such doctrinal or ecclesiological issues cannot be decided through a voting or parliamentary procedure (cf. WCC Constitution and Rules, XV/6,b). For the Orthodox, issues such as ordination of women, eucharistic hospitality, inclusive language with reference to God, are doctrinal.

8. In the past the Orthodox felt obliged to make their own "separate statements" on matters debated in the WCC. In the last decades, growing together in ecumenical fellowship, they abandoned this practice and took part in the production of common statements. The present situation causes some uneasiness among the Orthodox. This has led them to issue some reminders about the basic criteria of their participation. Some suggest a resumption of "separate statements" because the Orthodox point of

view is insufficiently reflected. Most feel that separate statements would be unfortunate for the nature of ecumenical work. New ways have to be found to implement the Orthodox view in drafting committees, issue-related consultations and WCC governing bodies.

9. Another source of uneasiness is the fact that membership in the Council of non-Orthodox churches is constantly increasing, thus rendering the Orthodox witness more difficult. The process of receiving new member churches and their representation in the Central Committee and Assemblies of the WCC deserves serious consideration.

10. The WCC describes itself, its ecclesial nature and significance by means of its Basis and with the safeguard of the Toronto Statement of the Central Committee on "The Church, the Churches and the World Council of Churches" (1950). There it is clearly affirmed: "The member churches of the WCC consider the relationship of other churches to the Holy Catholic Church which the Creeds profess as a subject for mutual consideration. Nevertheless, membership does not imply that each church must regard the other member churches as churches in the true and full sense of the word."

11. Our understanding of this statement is that the member churches of the WCC, and the Orthodox Churches in particular, respect the sovereignty of each other's ecclesiological teachings. The Council has no ecclesiological position of its own.

12. The Orthodox perceive that the WCC is drifting away from the Toronto Statement through some of its programmes and methodologies. For us the Toronto Statement remains as an essential criterion for our participation and membership in the WCC. Any eventual re-assessment of the Toronto Statement in the light of the experience of the forty years in the ecumenical movement should not undermine or contradict this fundamental criterion.

13. The Orthodox have a common understanding in relation to their participation in the WCC. They follow the recommendations of the Third Preconciliar Pan-Orthodox Conference (1986): "The Orthodox Church .. faithful to her ecclesiology, to the identity of her internal structure and to the teaching of the undivided Church, while participating in the WCC, does not accept the idea of the 'equality of confessions' and cannot consider Church unity as an inter-confessional adjustment. In this spirit, the unity which is sought within the WCC cannot simply be the product of theological agreements. God alone calls every Christian to the unity of faith which is lived in the sacraments and the tradition, as experienced in the Orthodox Church." (para. 6)

14. The Orthodox Church believes its own teaching and hierarchical structure to be based on an unbroken Tradition, which has been transmitted from generation to generation since the Apostolic times through the centuries. It participates in bilateral and multilateral dialogues through the WCC and the ecumenical movement. It does this because it is committed to the search for Christian unity. Therefore its presence and active participation is not merely a matter of "courtesy".

15. "The Orthodox Church, which unceasingly prays 'for the union of all', has taken part in the ecumenical movement since its inception and has contributed to its formation and further development. In fact, the Orthodox Church, due to the ecumenical spirit by which she is distinguished, has, throughout history, fought for the restoration of Christian unity. Therefore, the Orthodox participation in the ecumenical movement does not run counter to the nature and history of the Orthodox Church. It constitutes the consistent expression of the apostolic faith within new historical conditions, in order to respond to new existential demands." (Third Preconciliar Pan-Orthodox Conference, 1986, para. 3)

16. The Orthodox Churches understand the WCC as churches gathered in faithfulness to the calling of the Holy Spirit that we are all invoking. The WCC in a unique way has become part of the life and experience of our churches.

II. Some Problems for the Orthodox in the WCC

17. It is in this spirit that the Orthodox consider the issue of the involvement of the WCC with other religions. Commitment to dialogue among Churches with the goal of the unity of all Christians can and should be extended to dialogue with other religious traditions. The Orthodox have a long and living experience with members of other religions. Respect for the humanity of others and their sincerely held convictions calls for increased efforts at understanding and peaceful relations, and, wherever possible and appropriate, cooperation in areas of mutual concern. But this cannot mean that Christian churches acting through WCC agencies should be compromised in their central Christian commitments. The Orthodox hold that any syncretistic accommodation in WCC activities is inappropriate and contradicts the central affirmations and goals of the ecumenical endeavour. In particular, the recent practice of having representatives of other faith traditions at Assemblies and other expressions of ecumenical endeavour is welcomed, so long as the representatives of other religions are not invited to serve on drafting committees for the preparation of WCC documents. The dialogue with other religions ought not to compromise the identity of the WCC as a council of Christian churches, as it serves to broaden the understanding of the member churches regarding the variety of religious and non-religious stances in the world today and in promoting dialogue between Christians and members of other religions.

18. The Orthodox welcome the efforts of the WCC to address the question of the relationship of the churches to the world and are grateful for the many opportunities given us to explore that relationship in programmes such as "Justice, Peace and the Integrity of Creation". However, the theme of the Seventh Assembly, "Come, Holy Spirit — Renew the Whole Creation", as it was developed in some expressions, provokes us to express convictions about the topic. The Orthodox understand the Kingdom of God as God's ruling power over the whole world. The saving work of Jesus Christ has broken the power of evil and the demonic in the world, and the work of the Holy Spirit is to manifest God's Kingdom and lordship as an active reality transforming and transfiguring the world to the full service of God and His purposes. Thus, the whole creation is sustained and renewed by the Holy Spirit. However, the Holy Spirit dwells uniquely and in fulness in the life of the Church enabling the fulness of communion between God and humanity together with the rest of creation. The Orthodox hold that extreme emphasis on either of these poles is a distortion of the Christian faith and would call upon the WCC to cultivate an awareness in its deliberations of the Holy Spirit's action both within the Church and in the whole of creation. Further, acknowledgment of the Holy Spirit's leading of the churches to new and fresh understandings and experiences ought not to be presented as invalidating or contradicting the guidance of the Holy Spirit given to the Church in the past as embodied in the Church's Tradition. God's Kingdom is a reality already present, but which must also be progressively fulfilled and revealed. We urge the WCC through its agencies not to allow itself to succumb to extremist tendencies in either direction when it considers the relationship of the churches to the world.

19. The Orthodox Tradition is full of examples of involvement in activities of a social character and in an active defense of the dignity of the human person. This is

recalled in the "Decisions of the Third Preconciliar Pan-Orthodox Conference" where it is stated that "The Orthodox Church appreciates this multidimensional activity of the WCC and fully cooperates in [these] fields, within the limits of her possibilities" (para. 9). However, on several occasions, the Orthodox have had to react against a tendency within the WCC towards a one-sided "horizontalism" which tends to disconnect social, political, environmental problems from our commitment to the Gospel of Jesus Christ. Such one-sided horizontalism suggests an acceptance of an autonomy of secular life. The Orthodox believe that no aspect of life is autonomous or disconnected from the Christians' confession of the Incarnation and its consequence: the gift of the divine life in the image of the Holy Trinity. It is because we believe in the Incarnation and the Trinity that we are committed to problems of justice, peace and the integrity of creation.

20. The Orthodox must once again reiterate their position on the meaning of the eucharistic communion as it regards the nature of the Church and the ecumenical endeavour. The Eucharist is the supreme expression of the unity of the Church and not a means towards Christian unity. Shared belief, shared ecclesial order, shared ecclesial identity are manifested and expressed in their fulness through the Eucharist. Given this understanding of the Eucharist there is only Eucharistic Communion, and there cannot be something called "Inter-communion" since that term together with the practice it designates is a contradiction. To share in the common cup while still maintaining fundamental differences in faith, order and ministry does not make sense to the Orthodox, because it violates a major element of the meaning and significance of the Eucharist. We genuinely suffer about the fact that sharing the chalice is not yet possible in our ecumenical striving and regret misunderstandings on this matter which may have occurred during our ecumenical pilgrimage in the WCC. Thus, in our presently still divided condition, the Orthodox may not in conscience extend or respond to invitations involving "eucharistic hospitality". We look forward to the day when our shared faith, order and fellowship will require and permit sharing the common cup as the highest manifestation of our unity.

III. Towards an Improved Orthodox Participation in the Ecumenical Movement

21. The Orthodox Church as a koinonia of local churches transmits the teaching of the Church to the people of God (pleroma) on the local and regional levels. Its contribution to the ecumenical vision can only be articulated and fulfilled when it is involved on the "ground" level sharing and exchanging relationships with other Christian churches and movements in a common action, witness, concerns, etc.

22. The Orthodox think that their participation in the ecumenical movement would be greatly improved if more attention were devoted to a preparation of clergy and lay men and women in ecumenical issues. Living as we do in pluralistic societies, all aspects of our Christian life have an ecumenical dimension which requires training and education at all levels. Ecumenical participation would also be helped if the Orthodox learned to know more about one another to make inter-Orthodox collaboration more fruitful.

23. In the last decades, there has been a new interest in the Orthodox faith on the part of many. It is the duty of the Orthodox to respond to this by taking very seriously their responsibility to witness to Orthodoxy in its purity. This implies a permanent distinction between the fundamental and the secondary, a continuous effort to live in accordance with the doctrines confessed in the concrete aspects of daily life. In other words, an improved Orthodox participation in the ecumenical search for the unity of

Christians so that our witness to the world may be credible implies a continuous conversion of the Orthodox to a permanently purified Orthodoxy.

24. The process of a continuous deepening of their own Orthodoxy should lead the Orthodox not simply to respond to the questioning of an ever renewed historical context but to take initiatives themselves in many areas of modern life. This would certainly contribute to improve Orthodox involvement in the WCC and prevent some of the misunderstandings that the Orthodox so often deplore.

25. It is our belief that the Orthodox have much to contribute in the ecumenical movement. It is therefore highly desirable that they develop more and more a witnessing, missionary mentality.

26. This is all the more necessary in a context where proselytism in various forms is rife. Many Orthodox churches, due to persecution, have been weakened and their weakness is a prey to these various forms of proselytism. The latter should be denounced with utmost vigour. In particular, the Orthodox should call their partners in ecumenical dialogue to denounce themselves the unfair action of some of their own "missionaries", thus avoiding a flagrant contradiction between official language among "sister churches" called to a "common witness" and actual practice which amounts to "unchurching" the Orthodox Christians.

27. However, apart from the indispensable protests, the most potent answer to these deplorable situations is a recovery of a purified, well-informed, responsible Orthodoxy on the part of the Orthodox concerned. In carrying out this work, they need the help of all, in particular the assurance of their partners in the WCC.

"May we, by the power of the Holy Spirit, be sustained to renew the commitment of all Christians towards the visible unity."

Geneva, 16 September 1991

Message of the Primates of the Most Holy Orthodox Churches

Phanar, 1992

In the name of the Father and of the Son and of the Holy Spirit. Amen.

1. *Gathered together* in the Holy Spirit in consultation at the Phanar, today, 15 March 1992, on the Sunday of Orthodoxy, by the initiative and invitation and under the presidency of the First among us, the Ecumenical Patriarch Bartholomaios, after the expressed will as well of other brother Primates, we, by the mercy and grace of God, the Primates of the local Most Holy Patriarchate and Autocephalous and Autonomous Churches:

1. Bartholomaios, Archbishop of Constantinople, New Rome and Ecumenical Patriarch
2. Parthenios, Pope and Patriarch of Alexandria and all Africa
3. Ignatius, Patriarch of Antioch and all the East
4. Diodoros, Patriarch of the Holy City of Jerusalem and all Palestine
5. Alexiy, Patriarch of Moscow and all Russia
6. Paul, Patriarch of Belgrade and all Serbia
7. Teoctist, Patriarch of Bucharest and all Romania
8. Maxim, Patriarch of Sofia and all Bulgaria
9. Elias, Archbishop of Metschetis and Tiflis and Catholicos-Patriarch of all Georgia (represented by the Ecumenical Patriarch)
10. Chrysostomos, Archbishop of Neas Justinianis and all Cyprus (represented by the Patriarch of Alexandria)
11. Seraphim, Archbishop of Athens and all Greece
12. Wasyli, Metropolitan of Warsaw and all Poland
13. Dorothej, Metropolitan of Prague and all Czechoslovakia
14. John, Archbishop of Karelia and all Finland

have conferred in brotherly love on matters preoccupying our One, Holy, Catholic and Apostolic Orthodox Church and have concelebrated the Holy Eucharist in the Patriarchal Church of the Ecumenical Patriarch on this Sunday which for centuries has been dedicated to Orthodoxy. On this occasion we wish to declare the following:

We offer from the depths of our hearts praise in doxology to the Triune God, who deigned us to see one another face to face, to exchange the kiss of peace and love, to partake of the Cup of Life, and to enjoy the divine gift of Pan-Orthodox unity. Conscious of the responsibility which the Lord's providence has placed upon our shoulders as shepherds of the Church and spiritual leaders, in humility and love we extend to everyone of good will, and especially to our brother bishops and the whole pious body of the Orthodox Church, God's blessing, a kiss of peace and a "word of exhortation" (Heb. 13:22).

Rejoice, our brethren, in the Lord always! (Phil. 3:1)

Be strong in the Lord and in the strength of his might (Eph. 6:10).

2. The most Holy Orthodox Church throughout the oikoumene, sojourning in the world being inevitably affected by the changes taking place in it, finds herself today confronted with particularly severe and urgent problems which she desires to face *as one body*, adhering to St Paul who said: "if one member suffers, all suffer together" (1 Cor. 12:28). Moreover, looking into the future of humankind and that of the whole of God's creation in light of our entrance into the third millennium A.D. of history, at a time of rapid spiritual and social changes, fulfilling her sacred duty, the Church wishes to bear her own witness, giving account "for the hope that is in us" (1 Pet. 3:15) in humility, love and boldness.

The twentieth century can be considered the century of great achievements in the field of knowledge concerning the universe and the attempt to subject creation to the human will. During this century the strength as well as the weakness of the human being have surfaced. After such achievements no one doubts any longer that the domination of man over his environment does not necessarily lead to happiness and the fulness of life. Thus, man must have learned that apart from God scientific and technological progress becomes an instrument of destruction of nature as well as of social life. This is particularly evident after the collapse of the communist system.

Alongside this collapse we must recognize *the failure of all anthropocentric ideologies* which have created in men of this century a spiritual void and an existential insecurity and have led many people to seek salvation in new religious and para-religious movements, sects, or nearly idolatrous attachments to the material values of this world. Every kind of proselytism practiced today is a manifestation rather than a solution of the existing deep crisis of the contemporary world. The youth of our times have the right to learn that the Gospel of Christ and the Orthodox faith offer love instead of hatred, cooperation instead of confrontation and communion instead of division among human beings and among nations.

3. All these call the Orthodox to a deeper spiritual as well as canonical unity. Unfortunately, this unity is often threatened by *schismatic groups* competing with the canonical structure of the Orthodox Church. Having conferred also on this matter, we realized the need that all the local Most Holy Orthodox Churches, being in full solidarity with one another, condemn these schismatic groups and abstain from any kind of communion with them wherever they may be "until they return", so that the body of the Orthodox Church might not appear divided on this subject, since "not even the blood of martyrdom can erase the sin of schism", and "to tear the Church asunder is no less an evil than to fall into heresy" (St John Chrysostom).

4. In this same spirit of concern for the unity of all those who believe in Christ, we have participated in the *Ecumenical Movement* of our times. This participation was based on the conviction that the Orthodox must contribute to the restoration of unity with all their strength, bearing witness to the one undivided Church of the Apostles, the Fathers and the Ecumenical Councils. It was our expectation that during the period of great difficulties the Orthodox Church would have had the right to count on the solidarity — which has constantly been declared as the cardinal ideal of this movement — of all those who believe in Christ.

With great affliction and anguish of heart we realize that certain circles inside the *Roman Catholic Church* proceed to activities absolutely contrary to the spirit of the dialogue of love and truth. We have sincerely participated in the ecumenical meetings and bilateral theological dialogues. After the collapse of the atheistic communist regime by which many of these Orthodox Churches were tremendously persecuted and tormented, we had expected brotherly support, or at least understanding of the difficult situation created after 50 and even 70 years of pitiless persecutions. This situation in many respects is tragic from the point of view of the economic and pastoral resources of the Orthodox Churches concerned.

Instead, to the detriment of the desired journey towards Christian unity, the traditional Orthodox countries have been considered "missionary territories" and, thus, missionary networks are set up in them and proselytism is practiced with all the methods which have been condemned and rejected for decades by all Christians. In particular, we make mention and condemn the activity of the *Uniates* under the Church of Rome in the Ukraine, Romania, East Slovakia, Middle East and elsewhere against our Church. This has created a situation incompatible with the spirit of the dialogue of love and truth, which was initiated and promoted by the Christian leaders, the late Pope John XXIII and the late Ecumenical Patriarch Athenagoras I. This has inflicted a most severe wound on this dialogue making it difficult to heal. In fact this dialogue has already been restricted to the discussion of the problem of Uniatism until agreement is reached on this matter.

The same can be said with regard to certain *Protestant fundamentalists*, who are eager "to preach" in Orthodox countries which were under communist regime. The consideration of these countries as "terra missionis" is unacceptable, since in these countries the Gospel has already been preached for many centuries. It is because of their faith in Christ that the faithful of these countries often sacrificed their very lives.

In reference to this subject, we remind all that every form of proselytism — to be distinguished clearly from *evangelization* and *mission* — is absolutely condemned by the Orthodox. Proselytism, practiced in nations already Christian, and in many cases even Orthodox, sometimes through material enticement and sometimes by various forms of violence, poisons the relations among Christians and destroys the road towards their unity. Mission, in contrast, carried out in non-Christian countries and among non-Christian peoples, constitutes a sacred duty of the Church, worthy of every assistance. Such Orthodox missionary work is carried out today in Asia and Africa and is worthy of every Pan-Orthodox and Pan-Christian support.

5. Moved by the spirit of reconciliation, the Orthodox Church has participated actively for many decades in the effort toward the restoration of *Christian unity*, which constitutes the express and inviolable command of the Lord (John 17:21). The participation of the Orthodox Church as a whole in the *World Council of Churches* aims precisely at this. It is for this reason that she does not approve of any tendency to undermine this initial aim for the sake of other interests and expediencies. For the same reason the Orthodox strongly disapprove of certain recent developments within the ecumenical context, such as the ordination of women to the priesthood and the use of inclusive language in reference to God, which creates serious obstacles to the restoration of unity.

In the same spirit of reconciliation we express the hope that the progress made in certain dialogues, such as the dialogue with the *Oriental Orthodox* (non-Chalcedonians) may lead to favourable result once the remaining obstacles have been overcome.

6. Now, at the end of the second millennium A.D., turning our thoughts more specifically to the general problems of the contemporary world and sharing in the hope, but also in the anxieties of humankind, we observe the following:

The rapid progress of technology and the sciences which provide the instruments for improving the quality of life and relief of pain, misfortune and illnesses, is unfortunately not always accompanied by the analogous spiritual and ethical foundations. As a result, the aforementioned progress is not without serious dangers.

Thus, in human social life, the accumulation of the privileges of this progress and the power proceeding from it to only a section of humanity, exacerbates the misfortune of other people and creates an impetus for agitation or even war. The co-existence of this progress with *justice, love and peace* is the only safe and sure road, so that this progress will not be transformed from a blessing into a curse in the millennium to come.

Tremendous are also the problems which come out of this progress for *man's survival as a free person* created in the "image and likeness" of God. The progress of genetics, although capable of making enormous contributions to combating many diseases, is also capable of transforming the human being from a free person into an object directed and controlled by those in power.

Similar are the dangers for the *survival of the natural environment*. The careless and self-indulgent use of material creation by man, with the help of scientific and technological progress, has already started to cause irreparable destruction to the natural environment. The Orthodox Church, not being able to remain passive in the face of such destruction, invites through us, all the Orthodox, to dedicate the first day of September of each year, the day of the beginning of the ecclesiastical year, to the offering of prayers and supplications for the preservation of God's creation and the adoption of the attitude to nature involved in the Eucharist and the ascetic tradition of the Church.

7. In view of such tremendous possibilities, as well as dangers, for contemporary humanity, the Orthodox Church hails every progress towards reconciliation and unity. In particular, she hails *Europe's journey towards unity* and reminds it of the fact that within it live a large number of Orthodox, and it is expected that the Orthodox there will increase in the future. It should not be forgotten that the regions of South and Eastern Europe are inhabited by a majority of Orthodox people, contributing decisively to the cultural moulding of European civilization and spirit. This even renders our Church a significant factor in the moulding of a united Europe and increases her responsibilities.

We are deeply saddened by the *fractricidal confrontations* between Serbs and Croats *in Yugoslavia* and for all its victims. We think that what is required from the ecclesiastical leaders of the Roman Catholic Church and from all of us is particular attention, pastoral responsibility, and wisdom from God, in order that the exploitation of religious sentiments for political and national reasons may be avoided.

Our hearts are also sensitive towards all those peoples in *other continents*, who struggle for their dignity, freedom and development within justice. We pray especially for peace and reconciliation in the area of Middle East where the Christian faith originated and where people of different faiths co-exist.

8. This, in the love of the Lord, we proclaim on the Great and Holy Sunday of Orthodoxy, urging the pious Orthodox Christians in the oikoumene to be united around their canonical pastors and calling all those who believe in Christ to *reconciliation and solidarity* in confronting the serious dangers threatening the world in our time.

May the Grace of our Lord Jesus Christ and the love of God the Father and the communion of the Holy Spirit be with you all. Amen.

In Phanar, on the Sunday of Orthodoxy
15 March 1992   The Primates of the Orthodox Churches

The Ecclesiastical Significance of the WCC: The Legacy and Promise of Toronto

Vitaly Borovoy

Clarifying terms

The statement received by the World Council of Churches (WCC) Central Committee in Toronto (1950) — "The Church, the Churches, and the World Council of Churches" — has the explanatory sub-title, "The Ecclesiological Significance of the World Council of Churches". But the terminology of the discussion is far from clear. The "Report on the Concern for a Vital and Coherent Theology" by José Miguez Bonino,[1] when dealing with the question of ecclesiology, speaks of the "ecclesial" meaning of the ecumenical movement and the WCC as its "privileged instrument". (Perhaps the term "ecclesial" is used here in distinction to "ecclesiastical".) Other parts of the report refer to the "ecclesiological aspect of the WCC", the "ecclesiological meaning of the WCC" and related to this, the "ecclesiological perspectives of different units, etc. of the WCC". And in the WCC the term used in the title of this paper — "ecclesiastical" — is also employed. The very difference in the terms used ("ecclesiological", "ecclesial", "ecclesiastical", not to mention "meaning" and "significance") shows how difficult and ambiguous this question is.

The famous encyclical of the Ecumenical (Constantinople) Patriarchate of 1920 also formulates this question in the same unclear and ambiguous manner. The encyclical suggests that all the churches should have "koinonia fellowship", using the term in its New Testament, sacred meaning (1 Pet. 1:22), not in the meaning of a "league" or "association". Further on in the text, however, the term "koinonia" can easily be interpreted as meaning the "league of churches" on the pattern of the "League of Nations".[2] The same confusion between the notions "koinonia as fellowship" and the "league of nations" is to be found in the English text of the appendix to W.A. Visser 't Hooft's book *The Genesis and Formation of the World Council of Churches*.[3]

The WCC describes itself in all its official documents as a "fellowship of churches". This definition does not solve the question whether "ecclesiological", "ecclesial" or "ecclesiastical", or whether "significance" or "meaning", is intended. The question remains open both for the WCC member churches and for the WCC as a whole. Rather the limits of the functions and authority of the WCC are very clearly defined indeed, thus defining what the WCC, in its very nature and calling, is *not*. The Amsterdam (1948) definition is as follows: "The WCC shall not legislate for the churches, nor shall it act for them in any manner except as indicated above or as may hereafter be specified by the constituent churches."[4]

● Protopresbyter Prof. Vitaly Borovoy is deputy director of the Department of External Church Relations of the Moscow Patriarchate. This paper appeared in *The Ecumenical Review*, Vol. 40, Nos 3-4, July-October 1988.

What the WCC is not: Toronto as safeguard

This brings us to the Toronto Statement, which most clearly expressed what the WCC is not. For example:

— "It is not and must never become a super-church. It is not the world church. It is not una sancta of which the creeds speak."
— "Each church retains the constitutional right to ratify or to reject utterances or actions of the Council."
— "The authority of the Council consists only in the weight it carries with the churches by its own wisdom."
— "The WCC cannot and should not be based on any particular conception of the church. It does not prejudge the ecclesiological problem."
— "No church is obliged to change its ecclesiology as a consequence of membership in the WCC."
— "Membership does not imply that each church must regard the other member churches as churches in the true and full sense of the word."[5]

This precision in framing the functions and authority of the WCC, and in defining both its inner character and "what it is *not*", can and must be understood in the historical context of its genesis and of the first years of its existence.

The historical background

At the beginning the WCC was Protestant and Western (i.e. Western Europe and North America) in its composition. The Orthodox were but a small minority; for the most part these were the Constantinople-oriented Greek-speaking churches. The Orthodox churches in Eastern, Central and South-Eastern Europe (including the churches in the USSR, Poland, Czechoslovakia, Romania, Bulgaria, Yugoslavia, and Albania, where the main part of the world's Orthodoxy are concentrated) rejected the invitation to the Amsterdam Assembly as a result of the Moscow conference of 1948. In Greece there was strong opposition, suspicion and fear lest Orthodoxy and the Orthodox ecclesiology lose its integrity through membership in the WCC.

At the same time it was important to consider the position of the Roman Catholic Church with respect to the ecumenical movement and to the WCC, especially after "Mortalium Animos" by Pius XI. The reaction of the Roman Catholic Church and of the Catholic press in many countries was generally negative. Only in France, Belgium and Holland were there a few Catholic theologians who showed interest and sympathy in the ecumenical movement and for the WCC. However they were somewhat reserved and hesitant — as was only natural in their situation — about the nature and self-understanding of the WCC. Like the hesitant and suspicious Orthodox who were criticizing the WCC, they also had to be comforted and convinced.

In September 1949 this question was discussed at a meeting with Catholic ecumenists in the Istina Centre in Paris. The discussion resulted in the first draft of what later, in 1950, was to become the Toronto Statement. The Executive Committee of the WCC in February 1950 revised the draft and then submitted it to the WCC Central Committee meeting in Toronto in 1950.

The draft carried not only the introduction and six paragraphs on "What the WCC is not" with explanatory notes, but also offered eight paragraphs in its positive part, describing "the assumptions underlying the WCC" and reflecting on the self-under-standing of the WCC and on "the ecclesiological implications of membership in it".

I have deliberately mentioned here all the most important paragraphs of the first part of the Toronto Statement, showing "what the WCC is not", to refresh the reader's memory about what the Statement actually says. The point is that this document of the WCC, though very frequently referred to by both the Orthodox and the Protestant and Evangelical ecumenists, is in fact very little known and very little read. For the Orthodox this is the great charter of the WCC, and the main guarantee of the immunity and integrity of their ecclesiology within the membership of the WCC. For the critical Protestants and Evangelicals, however, the Statement is a hindrance to the ecumenical movement: it is outdated, a passed-by stage in the life of the WCC and, as such, it needs revision and re-articulation to reflect the new spiritual experience of our living together within the ecumenical fellowship.

This difference in approaching and evaluating the Toronto Statement manifested itself already when it was being elaborated, discussed and adopted by the WCC Central Committee in 1950. Especially sharp criticism was called forth by the following formulation suggested by Visser 't Hooft: "The World Council exists in order to deal in a provisional way with an abnormal situation." This was bitterly criticized because it seemed to imply that the World Council had only a provisional existence, whereas there were quite a few who believed that it was permanently necessary for the life of the churches.

The discussion also became heated when it came to the question of mutual recognition — or possible non-recognition — by the churches of one another. The draft of Paragraph IV,4 which was put for discussion read as follows: "The member churches do not necessarily recognize each other as true, healthy or complete churches, but they consider the relationship of other churches to the una sancta as a question for mutual recognition." The opponents of this formulation asked: "How could the Council be considered as a fellowship of churches, when some churches regarded others as untrue, unhealthy and incomplete?" After a heated debate a more moderate formulation was proposed, namely:

> The member churches of the World Council consider the relationship of other churches to the holy catholic church which the creeds profess as a subject for mutual consideration. Nevertheless, membership does not imply that each church must regard the other member churches as churches in the true and full sense of the word.

This formulation was adopted by the Central Committee. The speech by Father George Florovsky was very helpful in this matter. Visser 't Hooft presents the gist of it in this way:

> At this point Father George Florovsky of the Russian Orthodox Church in Emigration spoke with deep feeling, making an impressive appeal to fellow committee members. The issue, he said, was not simply the formulation of some sentences in a document: much more was at stake. His church regarded the other churches as *essentially* incomplete. If, as was possible, this tradition represented a viewpoint too difficult for some, it might be time to part. In the World Council, representatives of a high doctrine of the church were in a minority, but it was better to satisfy such a minority.[6]

A note concerning the change of the document's title may also be of interest. Originally the text was entitled "The Ecclesiological Significance of the World Council of Churches". Finally it was changed to "The Church, the Churches, and the World Council of Churches", with the sub-title "The Ecclesiological Significance of the World Council of Churches". "This was clearly better", explains Visser 't Hooft, "for it was anomalous to emphasize the 'ecclesiological significance' when the statement argued that the Council had no specific ecclesiological position of its own."[7]

The question of "ecclesiastical neutrality"

There were also different stands on the so-called "ecclesiological neutrality" of the WCC. The Statement guarantees that "the World Council deals in a provisional way ..."; that "it cannot and should not be based on any one particular conception of the church. It does not prejudge the ecclesiological problem"; that "membership... does not imply that a church treats its own conception of the church as merely relative"; that the Council has "no ecclesiological position of its own".

This "ecclesiological neutrality" of the WCC, as well as the absolute sovereignty in their respective teachings and life guaranteed to its member churches, was taken by many Protestant members of the Central Committee as demeaning the WCC and turning it into a mere forum for meetings and discussions. This was considered as too great a concession to "Catholic" convictions, and gave rise to the question: "How long the unstable equilibrium described in the statement could last?" (C.T. Craig)

Bishop Newbigin insisted that "it should be made clear that this neutrality was provisional. The possibility had to be open that the Council might have to abandon its neutral position on some of the ecclesiological issues which divided Christians..." "To commit the Council to neutrality as a permanent principle would be to reduce it to the status of a debating society."[8]

Of course, Newbigin was right when he pointed out that in the life of the WCC and in its development there should be a certain element of dynamism and moving forward to unity, that the Statement was only the starting point and not the way or the goal. In fact the very term "ecclesiological neutrality" was an unhappy one, since the Toronto Statement pronounced the equality of all, and the WCC's objective treatment of the existing differences, rather than its indifference or neutrality with regard to the question of ecclesiology as such. For this is where the main roads leading to — or away from — unity cross, and the permanent involvement of the churches in the ecumenical efforts for an agreement in understanding and confession of the main principles of faith and ecclesiology was, and must be, the prime commitment of the WCC.

Visser 't Hooft said, in addressing the third world conference of Faith and Order in Lund (1952), that the significance of the Toronto Statement consists in confronting the divided churches with two major questions which urgently call for an ecumenical answer, and which concern both what the WCC does and what it means to its member churches. These two questions are:

1. "How can a church justify its membership in the World Council of Churches in terms of its traditional ecclesiological convictions?" A good answer to this key question is given by Part I of the Toronto Statement: "What the World Council of Churches is not".

2. The other question is now (after Toronto) still open for the WCC and its member churches: "How can we give adequate expression to the spiritual reality which exists in the ecumenical movement?" Toronto made an attempt to answer this question in Part II of the Statement: "The Assumptions Underlying the World Council of Churches: Eight Positive Assumptions which Underlie the Ecclesiological Implication of Membership in it."

What the WCC is: the positive side of Toronto

Everyone realized then, and it is even clearer now from the Council's post-Toronto life and spiritual experience, that although the Statement was but the beginning of the

WCC's life, it contained all that was necessary for its further development. Indeed the Toronto Statement included many dynamic elements which enabled the WCC to become increasingly important later on both in the opinion and in the life of its member churches. Among other things, it stressed the duty of each church to do its utmost for the manifestation of the church in its oneness.

The developing significance of Toronto

In the post-Toronto life of the WCC,

> That the Toronto Statement was in fact not considered as a final or complete interpretation of the Council's comprehension of its own identity and role became clear in the following years. The subject was discussed again and again, and attention was called to aspects of the Council's life, which had not been sufficiently defined in Toronto...
>
> In 1954, the preparatory commission for the Faith and Order section of the Second Assembly held that year at Evanston made the Toronto Statement the "keystone" of its survey... It was, in the opinion of the commission, merely a contribution to a continuing discussion, and by no means said the last word on the nature and function of the World Council and the inter-relationship of the member churches.[9]

The discussion on the WCC's nature and ecclesiological significance within the framework of the Toronto Statement continues to deal with these two points, together and in accordance with other developments, especially the growing spiritual experience within the WCC and its member churches. And this is only natural in the course of the WCC's organic development and growth.

The Toronto Statement has never been a hindrance to the progress of the ecumenical movement and of the WCC as a fellowship (koinonia) of churches. On the contrary, the Statement has played a very positive and constructive role in the dynamics of the past and future of the WCC. The Toronto Statement has prevented the WCC from falling into the temptation of becoming a permanent institution of the ecumenical movement, and has protected it against possible accusations and suspicions that, as such an institution, it would limit the sovereignty and integrity of the doctrines and ecclesiologies of its member churches. The Statement clearly stated what the WCC was not and never could be, thereby doing away once and for all with the false and tendentious "fears" which were spread in the past — and which are still being instigated by the opponents of the ecumenical movement among Orthodox and Roman Catholic people, and among the conservative evangelicals from the so-called "free churches".

At the same time Part II of the Statement, "The Assumptions Underlying the World Council of Churches", contains many presuppositions for the positive development, growth and self-realization of the nature of the WCC and its impact on the life of the churches as they seek together to clarify and articulate what is necessary for the "ecclesiological significance" of the WCC as a body and as a "spokesperson" of the koinonia (fellowship) of the churches.

The life of the WCC has become a witness to the positive role of Part I of the Statement, and to the dynamic potential contained in Part II for the development and the ecclesiological formation of the WCC. Precipitate and flimsy statements made about the ecclesiological significance of the WCC, statements which could serve only to harm its fundamental development and distort its original nature, were not important in this process. The whole future dynamics of the development of the WCC as dictated by the very logic and meaning of Part II of the Statement proved to be important, creative and decisive.

Visser 't Hooft made a telling remark on the inevitable and irresistible logic of this development in his book *The Pressure of Our Common Calling*. He stated:

> In the most controversial section of the Toronto Statement... which discusses the question of how far the churches in the Council recognize each other as churches... ("Nevertheless, membership does not imply that each church must regard the other member churches as churches in the true and full sense of the word"), we find these simple words: "They (the churches which are members of the World Council) recognize one another as serving the one Lord". This is a statement of tremendous significance if it is taken seriously. For everything else follows from that. Where there is a clear acknowledgment of the common calling, the forces of *koinonia* must begin to operate in spite of all obstacles.[10]

Further developments have proved this diagnosis correct.

A growing koinonia among the churches

After Toronto and in the period between Evanston (1954) and New Delhi (1961), the Amsterdam Basis was enriched by three amendments important from the ecclesiological perspective. They show the WCC as a "fellowship of churches", "according to the Scriptures", seeking "to fulfil together their common calling to the glory of one God, Father, Son and the Holy Spirit".

Here the WCC self-understanding as "the fellowship of churches" has developed to a higher level of comprehension and confession of "koinonia", having "the goal of visible unity in one faith and in one eucharistic fellowship expressed in worship and in common life in Christ and to advance towards that unity in order that the world may believe".[11]

Great success has also been achieved in work on the nature of this "visible unity in one faith and in one eucharistic fellowship". This gives a basis for the further development and self-affirmation of the WCC. Thus the New Delhi "Statement on Unity" (1961) as "a unity with the whole Christian fellowship in all places and all ages" was a substantial step in defining this common goal as a programme for the near future. Uppsala (1968) profoundly enriched the self-understanding of the WCC as a "fellowship of churches" striving to express and realize "catholicity" in its life as the main feature *(nota ecclesiae)* of the church. And as a result of the Faith and Order consultation on "Concepts of Unity and Models of Union" (Salamanca, 1973), the Nairobi Assembly (1975) has deepened the notion of the WCC as a "conciliar fellowship of local churches which are themselves truly united".

The Vancouver Assembly (1983) was a landmark in the constantly developing and growing self-understanding and self-expression of the WCC as koinonia of the churches. Here the WCC turned from *defining* its fundamental task of achieving "visible unity in one faith and one eucharistic fellowship of the local churches truly united in a conciliar fellowship" to the relevant *practical steps* in the churches' life and relations with one another.

The Assembly was quite clear on this in its discussion in issue group 2, "Taking Steps Towards Unity". These practical steps to unity are linked with *BEM* (1982). The process of theological discussions and agreements between theologians of the Faith and Order Commission has developed into the process of the reception of BEM by the WCC member churches. Although BEM in its present form is not sufficient for the restoration of "eucharistic fellowship" between them, it nevertheless marks substantial progress and, what is most important, progress in the right direction. There the

Toronto Statement has not prevented the success of Faith and Order and the WCC as a whole, but rather facilitated and promoted its achievement.

It was the first time in the history of the WCC that the churches responded not to a document which defined the difference and visions among them, but to a common document worked out by their theologians, showing practical steps towards unity and testifying to the achieved mutual understanding and agreement on many problems which were formerly stumbling-blocks on the way to unity.

BEM, of course, is not the unity we seek and is not sufficient for full visible unity; but we should not fall into despair and speak, as some do, about a "crisis" in the ecumenical movement or the inefficiency of the WCC in solving its problems and fulfilling its goal. Quite the reverse. There are all possible grounds to be optimistic as we note numerous evidences of "the growing unity in fulfilling the common calling — by martyria (witness), diakonia and koinonia".

> The only way in which they (churches) can express their awareness of the common calling is to go together with other churches. As they do so, they discover that, in spite of their discord, a real unity grows up between them. It is often difficult to express that unity in words for it does not fit in with our traditional theological categories. But the facts of this unity cannot be denied.[12]

What Visser 't Hooft called "the pressure of our common calling" pushed the churches to go ahead towards unity in spite of their existing disunity and their doctrinal differences:
1) to launch and hold regularly bilateral and multilateral interconfessional dialogues, and to strengthen and expand practical cooperation in face of common tasks and difficulties;
2) to form and join in different regional, national and local conferences and ecumenical councils of churches with common programmes, actions and witness in response to the challenges and demands of their common life.

The WCC member churches, in response to the urgent needs of life today, have moved in exactly this direction. The horrible tragedies which humanity experienced in the historical confrontations and world wars in the first half of our century made Christians and their churches unite their efforts to fulfil their common calling in a world full of divisions, conflicts, hatred, enmity and triumphant evil. The times compelled them to join efforts and act together as one Christian entity.

Already in 1920 the Lambeth Conference had stated: "We believe that there are no principles at stake which can rightly be held to hinder all denominations from beginning without delay to act as if they were wholly one body in the department of public, moral and social witness."[13] The words "as if" have proved to be most significant in the life and further development of the ecumenical movement. "Act *as if* — Go forward *as if* the church of Christ here on earth were actually a united front" (Wilfred Monod). "In fulfilling the Master's law of love all Christians should act together *as if* they were one body in one visible fellowship without any injury to theological principles" (Archbishop Söderblom).[14] The Toronto Statement in its second, positive, part on the assumptions underlying the World Council of Churches confirmed the correctness of this premise of the unity of the ecumenical movement, and the significance of the WCC in expressing and realizing it. Indeed the ecumenical imperatives "Act as if..." and "Go forward as if..." have found their best expression in the Toronto Statement.

"Unity in action" and "ecclesiological significance" are indeed difficult to express and define in a concise formulation, especially if they are considered not as theoretical abstractions but from within the dynamic realities of life. The founders and pioneers of the ecumenical movement showed wise discretion in their formulations, and they were right in their prophetic confidence in the future development of the WCC's dynamic life and creative significance. They noted:

— "It is better to live with a reality which transcends definition than to live with a definition which claims more substance than exists in reality" (Visser 't Hooft).
— "We can live beyond Toronto, but we cannot formulate beyond Toronto" (Berkhof).
— "We may not pretend that the existing unity among Christians is greater than in fact it is; but we should act upon it as far as it is already a reality" (William Temple).[15]

This honest and courageous recognition of "what the World Council of Churches is not" gave an opportunity to the Toronto Statement to put clear perspectives before the fellowship of churches as well as to give them grounds for action and future development guided by generally agreed and adopted imperatives of Part II of the Statement, with its eight positive points. History has shown and proved the effectiveness of these eight assumptions.

The growing koinonia: what does it mean?

The practical activities of the WCC based on these assumptions have revealed all the richness and diversity of the koinonia of churches in their relationships with the WCC and within the WCC itself. The forms and expressions of these relations have gone beyond Toronto and have become its development and expansion.

Thus the question has arisen whether it is high time to reflect on this new and rich experience of the growing koinonia of the churches as it has developed and improved beyond the Toronto Statement, and to ask what this means for the ecclesiological experience and self-understanding of the WCC member churches. What does this new experience mean for their relation to the WCC, and specifically for their membership within it?

This question is valid and timely for the present stage in the ecumenical movement. The direction or "trend" of this process is important. On the one hand it can tend towards the denial of the Toronto Statement, calling Part I ("What the World Council is not") "obsolete" and "outdated", and trying to replace it with new, so-called "modern" formulations. But on the other hand it can be presented through a positive exposition of the new experience and achievements of the WCC, that is, the growth of koinonia within it and — related to this fundamental development — the growth of the ecclesiological self-understanding of the churches as they assess both their koinonia and the significance of the WCC. This brings them to a new and higher stage in their search for the unity which is the goal of the WCC, that unity for the sake of which the WCC exists and for which the churches have joined its fellowship.

The question of "reviewing" Toronto

In this context I would like to quote an expert in the history and problems of the ecumenical movement, Ans van der Bent. In his book *Vital Ecumenical Concerns* he writes:

> During the last few years of his life W.A. Visser 't Hooft has repeatedly stressed that the Toronto Statement of 1950 needs to be newly analyzed and up-dated. The question is

how this can be done in a convincing manner. What is today the ecclesiological significance of the World Council of Churches? Although the Faith and Order Commission has
increasingly drawn attention to the unity experienced in the ecumenical movement, to the
unity we seek, what unity implies, and what unity requires, it has not been able to spell out
what exactly the nature and purpose of that unity is. At its meeting at Stavanger in 1985 it
engaged in a difficult debate on the Church as mystery and prophetic sign, a theme which
was already discussed at a consultation at Chantilly (France).[16]

The question of reviewing the Toronto Statement came up in connection with the adoption
by the Vancouver Assembly of the report of the Programme Guidelines Committee. The
theme of "Growing Towards a Vital and Coherent Theology" was one of the programme
guidelines. On the basis of the general secretary's memorandum on "Vital and Coherent
Theology" (29 August 1985) the question was studied by the WCC staff (in groups from all
units and sub-units) for two months. As mentioned at the beginning of this paper, the
results were summed up in the report to the WCC Central Committee by José Miguez
Bonino (Buenos Aires, 1985), and were discussed at the WCC Executive Committee
meetings in Kinshasa (1986), Reykjavik (1986) and Atlanta (1987). The Central Committee meeting in Geneva (1987) also paid attention to this question.

The report on "The Concern for a Vital and Coherent Theology" says the
following:

> There is a question of ecclesiology. The Toronto Statement continues to be a relevant
> and necessary "protective" statement. But it needs to be supplemented by a positive
> reflection on the "ecclesial" (perhaps in distinction to "ecclesiastical") meaning of the
> ecumenical movement and the WCC as its "privileged instrument".

Questions arise in two areas; first, "the ecclesial significance of the WCC and its
implications for its policy and programmes", and second, "the relations between the
ecclesiologies implicit in the different sub-units, etc."

Thomas F. Stransky, a well-known ecumenical leader and Roman Catholic
theologian, raised sharp questions about reviewing the Toronto Statement in his article
"A Basis Beyond the Basis".

> What is becoming more obvious... is that the WCC is keeping intact both the Basis
> and the Toronto Document, but is developing, perhaps unawares, an ecclesial under-
> standing which flows from the Basis...
> ...One need only compare the original 1948 list of the WCC "functions" with the
> present list of "functions and purposes". The present list implies far more ecclesiological
> understanding...
> ...The Toronto Document is out-of-date. True, many of its affirmations about what
> the WCC is *not*, about what membership in the WCC does *not* imply, are still valid and
> need reaffirmation. But a 1950 Statement cannot be expected to do justice to the
> collective experience of the churches in the ecumenical movement since 1950, whether
> they be member churches or not...
> The Toronto Document does not reflect what we today are perceiving our common
> calling is for, and to what we are called. What have thirty-five years taught us?... But we
> have no articulated synthesis.[17]

Ulrich Duchrow, a very sincere but sometimes too radical ecumenist, strongly
advocates a revision of the Toronto Statement and a positive review of the question of
the "ecclesiological significance of the WCC" in his book *Conflict over the Ecumenical Movement*.[18] The fifth chapter is also devoted to the question of Toronto and the
ecclesiological significance of the WCC, with references to Ernst Lange[19] and Roger
Mehl.[20] Duchrow tries to prove that the Toronto Statement is based on the institutional
interests of churches and their unwillingness to touch questions of their ecclesiology:

Then we noted that even the World Council of Churches had been forced into choosing between being a "Super Church", on the one hand, or a "mere instrument of autonomous churches" on the other... it was, as we saw, impossible to agree as to the ecclesiological character of the World Council of Churches. Indeed, the Toronto Statement of 1950 even ruled that the World Council was not to call in question the ecclesiology of its member churches, but simply to accept them.

The main instrument for universal fellowship among the churches is the WCC... It is vitally important, nevertheless, that the suppressed question of the ecclesial authority of the ecumenical movement be looked at again and clarified, otherwise the universal Church of Jesus Christ lacks visible concrete forms.

The international confessional organizations must all make this universal fellowship of locally united churches the goal of their life and activity. As a first step in this direction they should unambiguously declare their provisional character. This is not to present them with a predetermined alternative but to invite them to travel a road full of promise.[21]

In the study cited above by Bruno Chenu on *La signification ecclésiologique du Conseil oecuménique des Eglises*, chapter XII is devoted entirely to "the ecclesiological meaning of the WCC". Of special note is its third part, "the ecclesial quality of the WCC". In the "general conclusion" to his work, Chenu writes:

It seems to us that the hour has come to accord to the WCC a substantial ecclesiological identity — not from doctrinal relativism but from theological necessity. For a static ecclesiology which wishes to work only with firm evidence, our approach may appear less secure and more daring. We are clearly located within a developing ecclesial reality [un devenir ecclésial], the product of both a growing theological awareness and the magnetism of the Spirit which moves the churches. The certainties of yesterday have become very fragile, the "obscure clarities" of today claim to resolve neither the debate nor the whole story [of our search for unity]. There remains the demand of God upon us and God's insistent, challenging presence, which we either accept or not... if the WCC is an expression of the obedience of the churches, then its theological legitimation is, equally, an expression of the theologian's obedience.[22]

In summary, all these considerations about the Toronto Statement and the "ecclesiological significance of the WCC" are based on one and the same affirmation and one and the same question, call and challenge which is addressed to all WCC member churches. The essence of this was expressed by Konrad Raiser in *Faith and Faithfulness*, a book of essays on contemporary ecumenical themes dedicated to Philip A. Potter:

The reports of the [Vancouver] Assembly could provide strong evidence for the claim that during these years of struggle and crisis [after Toronto] a new vision of ecumenical wholeness and integrity has been maturing. Will the opportunities of the ecumenical movement be seized? Will the churches, congregations and ecumenical groups have the courage to live in the present, instead of escaping into defensive justifications of the past or the absolute and mutually exclusive claims about the future?[23]

Drawing the balance

Now it is time to ask what conclusions can be drawn from the discussion on the Toronto issue in general, and on the question of the "ecclesiological significance" of the WCC in particular. The following statements sum up the present situation:

1. The time is indeed ripe for a new discussion in the light of the achievements of the WCC since Toronto.

2. All agree that the Toronto Statement had a positive impact on the development and the self-understanding of the WCC.

3. All agree that "the Toronto Statement continues to be a relevant and necessary 'protective' statement" (Miguez Bonino). "True, many of its affirmations about what the WCC is *not*, about what membership in the WCC does *not* imply, are still valid" (Stransky).

4. The main concern is to revise Part II of the Toronto Statement ("The Assumptions Underlying the World Council of Churches").

5. The development and the inner maturity of the WCC, its present role and the spiritual experience acquired in the course of the relations of the member churches with the WCC and among themselves, not only provide the right to this kind of re-thinking of the past, appropriating and making it real in our actions today — they *demand* it for the good of the future of the ecumenical movement as a whole.

6. However, the revision of Toronto is difficult because of its possible implications for the "ecclesiological significance" of the WCC. Is there any connection between this urgently called-for revision of Part II of the Declaration and the question of the "ecclesiological significance" as such, and does such revision necessarily lead to a new formulation of the "ecclesiological significance" of the WCC?

These questions must be discussed by all member churches within their respective conciliar and canonical jurisdictions and then answered together at a meeting of the Central Committee, similar to that at Toronto but held after the Seventh WCC Assembly in Canberra (1991).

The path ahead

Here it is important not to hurry with controversial and "all-solving" formulations; what is important is hurrying to live, to work, to develop, and to move forward, proceeding from the realities which help strengthen, expand, and enrich the inner life-experience of the churches within the one and truly ecumenical fellowship, shaping it into a conciliar and eucharistic koinonia with all the *notae* of the "ecclesiality" which is possible only after the unity of all Christians has been reached in one, holy, catholic, and apostolic church. After that, having fulfilled its historical role and its sacred calling of serving faithfully the Lord and its member churches, the WCC will cease to exist.

We must act courageously and prophetically, following, as we said, the principle of "as if" which has already justified itself in the history of the World Council, as noted above: to act without delay as if they [the churches] were wholly one body (in public, moral, and social witness) (G.K.A. Bell); "Act as if — to go forward as if the church of Christ here on earth were actually a united front" (Wilfred Monod); "All Christians should act together as if they were one body in one visible fellowship without any injury to theological principles" (Söderblom); act, as Franklin Clark Fry rightfully said,[24] always in the vanguard of the churches and even ahead of its own development — "And from the very moment it [the WCC] was born it has been expected to be an adult, girded like a man *(sic)* to run a race."

The road from Amsterdam to Vancouver and further on to Canberra is straight and clear:

1. Faith and Order — BEM — one apostolic faith, reception of the Lima document — unity of the church and renewal of human community

2. Justice, peace, and the integrity of creation — process of mutual commitment (covenanting) for JPIC — world conference (or convocation) 1990

3. Mission in Christ's way — Christianity and culture — world conference on mission and evangelism, 1989 (theme: "Your Will Be Done")
4. Sharing resources, participation in development — sharing in community
5. The nuclear crisis and a just peace
6. Struggle for human rights and human dignity

All these problems and concerns are equally urgent and important for all Christians, and all churches can act and speak together in the ecumenical fellowship of the WCC. They can and *should* act and speak with one voice; the WCC already is such a voice, and can become more so. The Roman Catholic theologian Yves Congar described the church as "we, Christians".[25]

"Toronto beyond Toronto"

The ecumenical fellowship of the churches in the WCC is gradually coming to such a stage in its self-understanding and self-revelation as to be able and eligible — with regard to most of the afore-mentioned questions of practical and public importance — to speak of itself as "We, the Churches".[26] By no means does this imply our "going back on" Toronto; rather, it is Toronto's further development: *Toronto beyond Toronto*.[27]

Such a "Toronto beyond Toronto" will be a step forward without unnecessary and presently dangerous "ecclesiological conclusions and implications" concerning the nature, the very essence, and goal of the WCC. The Orthodox, who have always been watchful and suspicious of the talk about the "ecclesiological significance" of the WCC, would not mind accepting this "Toronto beyond Toronto". This is because such a step — while making progress in the development and self-understanding of the WCC due to its expanding and deepening impact on the ecumenical community — will not repeal the ecclesiological guarantees of the Toronto Statement.

If we consider carefully the attitude of the Orthodox theologians, described well by Bruno Chenu in *La signification ecclésiologique du Conseil oecuménique des Eglises*,[28] and look through the official statements of the Orthodox churches on this subject,[29] including the latest appraisal of the attitude of the Orthodox churches as referred to in the documents reflecting the preparations for the future Pan-Orthodox Council, we have every reason to believe that a position on the significance and nature of the WCC which both affirms Toronto and opens a way beyond it will be understood by the Orthodox. The same is true of our Roman Catholic brothers, for whom it is equally essential both to retain the guarantees of Toronto and to go beyond Toronto towards such a koinonia as could be described in ecclesiological categories.

There is nothing to be afraid of here, as long as we remember never to press for it artificially. There was a time, as far back as 1933, when Dietrich Bonhoeffer dreamed of creating a theology of the ecumenical movement: "If the ecumenical movement is based on a new understanding of the church of Christ it will produce a theology."[30]

There have been many attempts of this kind in the history of the ecumenical movement, one of the most recent being the above-mentioned book by Ulrich Duchrow. They all have brought no tangible results because they aimed to create a theology of the World Council of Churches as a whole ecclesial entity. But the WCC is not a church and therefore it cannot have a theology and ecclesiology of its own, independent of the churches. The WCC has only the ecclesiologies of its member churches. These ecclesiologies are in constant dialogue, interacting with each other and thereby influencing each other. This is the business and concern of the churches themselves, as guaranteed by Part I of the Toronto Statement ("What the World Council is not"), whereas Part II ("The Assumptions Underlying the World Council of Churches") calls for further theological reflection on these ecclesiologies and for their further development. The post-Toronto history as a whole, given the experience and achievements of the ecumenical community within the WCC, has already raised the question of a theological rationale for certain (or indeed all) spheres and aspects of the World Council's life and activity.

The decision of the WCC to elaborate a "vital and coherent theology" is the way for ecumenical theological thought to go. It will be a practical and effective approach to the ecclesiology underlying the programmes of all the WCC's units and sub-units, to reveal the dynamics of their development, their interaction within one whole, their vital and coherent theology and ecclesial identity, thereby bringing it home to everyone who questions and studies the nature of the WCC that the WCC is not a super-church, neither is it the "Protestant Vatican", nor the "ecclesiastical UN", or a "condominium"; and of course it is not just the Assembly, the Central Committee, or the Geneva staff, nor again a "theological debating society" of its commissions, committees and working groups.[31] This could lead to a new vision and reality of the WCC as "the churches in continuing but organically growing conciliar fellowship" on their historical pilgrimage to the full koinonia, where their unity in diversity and their diversity in unity will be a common sharing in one apostolic faith and in one sacramental fellowship.

The prominent Russian theologian Sergius Boulgakov, trying to explain the essence and nature of the church, stated in his famous book *The Orthodox Church*:

> The Church exists, it is "given". It exists in us, not as an institution or a society, but first of all as a spiritual certainty, a special experience, a new life. The preaching of primitive Christianity is the joyous and triumphant announcement of that new life. The life is indefinable, but it can be described and it can be lived.
>
> There can thus be no satisfactory and complete *definition* of the church. "Come and see" — one recognizes the church only by experience, by grace, by participation in its life. This is why before making any formal definition, the church must be conceived in its mystical being, underlying all the definitions, but larger than them all.[32]

The WCC, of course, is not a church. But when defining "Toronto beyond Toronto" and dealing with the question of the so-called "ecclesiological significance" of the WCC, it is essential to recall and to heed what Boulgakov said about the church. While preserving the very essence of Part I of Toronto, we must focus all our attention and energy on the development and implementation, in the life of the ecumenical community, of the *practical conclusions and imperatives* implied by the new reading and dynamic prospects of Part II. And this must be done in the light of an ever-growing and expanding common experience of the WCC member churches in their service and witness on the way to unity.

Such new constructive experience and its results are sure to find recognition in the ecumenical movement, along with the external expressions and forms necessary for it — the reception of which will become an organic process and a sacramental reality in the life of the churches.

The Romanian theologian Liviu Stan, referring to this process, was right to say: "Reception occurred sooner or later spontaneously, not in an organized way with juridical forms of directives and by no means through a sort of general plebiscite. What is involved is rather another sort of plebiscite, which has its origin in the action of the Holy Spirit."[33]

And what is the Spirit saying to the Church (Rev. 2:7,11)? We, the churches in the World Council of Churches, believe that the Spirit is now saying to us: "Go and see, and participate in common life" (Boulgakov); "Go forward as if... Act together, as if... And we should act upon it so far as it is already a reality" (Söderblom, Temple, Visser 't Hooft); "... in our transitory phase from disunity to unity".[34] And indeed in this "transitory phase" Toronto was not a stumbling-block but a very important milestone.

NOTES

[1] Executive Committee meetings in Kinshasa 1986, Reykjavik 1986, and Atlanta 1987.

[2] Constantin G. Patelos ed., *The Orthodox Church in the Ecumenical Movement*, Geneva, WCC, 1978, pp.40-43.

[3] Geneva, WCC, 1982, pp.94-97.

[4] W.A. Visser 't Hooft ed., *The First Assembly of the World Council of Churches*, New York, Harper & Bros, 1949, p.198.

[5] "The Church, the Churches and the WCC", in Lukas Vischer ed., *A Documentary History of the Faith and Order Movement 1927-1963*, St Louis, Missouri, Bethany Press, 1963, pp.169-171.

[6] *The Genesis, op. cit.*, p.78.

[7] *Ibid.*, pp.78-79.

[8] *Ibid.*, p.80.

[9] *Ibid.*, p.81.

[10] New York, Doubleday & Co., 1959, p.71.

[11] David Gill ed., *Gathered for Life*, official report of the Sixth Assembly of the WCC, Vancouver 1983, Geneva, WCC, and Grand Rapids, Wm B. Eerdmans, 1983, Constitution, p.324.

[12] *The Pressure, op. cit.*, p.88.

[13] Report, Lambeth Conference, 1920, pp.74-75. See also George Bell, *Christian Unity, the Anglican Position*, London, Hodder & Stoughton, 1948, p.156.

[14] *The Pressure, op. cit.*, p.17 (emphasis mine). This statement was proposed — but not finally adopted — at the first world conference on Faith and Order in 1927.

[15] Cf. W.A. Visser 't Hooft, "The Basis: its History and Significance", *The Ecumenical Review*, Vol. 37, No. 2, 1985, p.171.

[16] Geneva, WCC, 1986, p.93.

[17] *The Ecumenical Review*, Vol. 37, No. 2, 1985, pp.213-222. The quotations are from pp.221-222.

[18] Geneva, WCC, 1981, transl. from *Konflikt um die Ökumene*, p.443.

[19] *And Yet It Moves*, Geneva, WCC, 1979, p.122.

[20] Cited from Bruno Chenu, A.A., *La signification ecclésiologique du Conseil oecuménique des Eglises: 1945-1963*, University of Lyon, 1972, p.207.

[21] *Conflict, op. cit.*, pp.356 and 359.

[22] *Op. cit.*, pp.353-354, editors' translation.

[23] Geneva, WCC, 1984, p.96.

[24] *The New Delhi Report*, New York, Association Press, 1962, p.335.

[25] See the preface to K. Delebaye, *Ecclesia Mater*, Paris, 1964, p.10. Cf. Bruno Chenu, *op. cit.*, p.347.

[26] Cf. "The World Council is not something wholly other than the member churches. It is the churches in continuing council." *The New Delhi Report, op. cit.*, p.132.

[27] On this whole question see T. Stransky, *op. cit.*, pp.213-222.

[28] *Op. cit.*, pp.320-329, cf. pp.80-112.

[29] Patelos, *The Orthodox Church, op. cit.*, p.360.

[30] *The Pressure, op. cit.*, p.13. Cf. *Conflict, op. cit.*, pp.315-322.

[31] Cf. John S. Conway, "Images of the WCC", *The Ecumenical Review*, Vol. 36, No. 4, 1984, pp.391-403. Lesslie Newbigin, "A Fellowship of Churches", *The Ecumenical Review*, Vol. 37, No. 2, 1985, pp.175-181.

[32] English translation 1935.

[33] "Concerning the Church Acceptance of the Decisions of Ecumenical Synods in Council and the Ecumenical Movement", *WCC Studies*, No. 5, p.70, quoted in G. Limouris and N.M. Vaporis eds, *Orthodox Perspectives on Baptism, Eucharist and Ministry*, Faith and Order Paper No. 128, Brookline, Holy Cross Orthodox Press, 1985, p.53.

[34] Lesslie Newbigin, *The Household of God*, London, 1953, p.21.

A Fresh Breath of Spirituality

Ion Bria

Spiritual and liturgical depth

There are new signs in the ecumenical community that the search for the visible unity of the church is not limited to the acceptance of theological convergence texts, to sharing of material resources or even to common advocacy for social justice and peace. Various contributions to the search for and different manifestation of unity go beyond a description in terms of agreements or statements. Among these are common prayers and intercessions, meditation and contemplation, community and monastic life, concelebration, singing and worshipping together. All these have made specific changes in the life of the WCC, which has been enriched by this aspect of contemporary Christian experience.[1] Spiritual enthusiasm and orientation is an integral part of the ecumenical movement today. The theme of personal and collective spirituality, neglected in the past, has come onto the agenda of those who are convinced of the unity of all in Christ.

Such a breath of spirituality is always the work of the holy and life-creating Spirit, who through baptism dwells in the very depths of our being, renewing the capacity to attain divine likeness. Receiving the gift of the Holy Spirit in the heart implies a continuous spiritual combat. So long as the Holy Spirit is in us and we participate in the Spirit's gift and grace, we should not walk according to the flesh but according to the Spirit (cf. Rom. 8:1-2). The breath of the Holy Spirit not only arouses in our hearts the winds of peace, justice and reconciliation, but also leads us to strive to overcome personal and social sin, including the exploitation of the earth. It helps us to advance further in the experience of sanctification. Inner sanctification, the renewal of the church, the transformation of society here and now and the search for the new heavens and the new earth are inseparable. Those who piously desire a new spirit cannot be opposed to change in the life and structure of their ecclesial communities.

The cognitive value of spirituality

Historically, all churches are associated with confessional creeds, with different ways of teaching doctrine, different theologies and methodologies. In exercising the church's teaching ministry, theologians continue to promote different formulations and to elaborate different doctrinal conclusions. This work cannot be neglected, but the question must be asked: do we have a criterion for self-correction in our formulations and conceptions?

Let us keep in mind the sacred rule of the ancient theologians: practise defining — expressing a decisive opinion on something related to God — as rarely as possible. It is

● Prof. Ion Bria was until recently moderator of the WCC's Unit on Unity and Renewal. This paper appeared in *The Ecumenical Review*, Vol. 44, No. 4, October 1992.

better to protect the mystery of God, to refrain from speaking or forming any improvised conception, if the message is not revealed in the holy scriptures. The Spirit protects our intimacy and our deep conversation with God without the association of words and images. The Holy Spirit, who knows the hidden mystery of God, gives us the power to resist the opposite, namely the description, the verbalization, investigation, communication about God. The Spirit helps us to direct our attention to God, the subject of our reflection, rather than always to the vocabulary of our expressions. Personal immersion into the mystery of God's love is real "theology", contemplation of God.

Therefore, let us go deeper into the depth of our life with God and not remain at the level of our separate intellectual constructions and imaginations. Let us liberate our hearts to feel the love of God. After that we can regulate our theological vocabulary. We may discover that the didactic level does not reflect the spiritual level, that our Trinitarian theology is a weak symbol of what we have seen, that is, the glory of One God undivided as one divine light.

The theologies of the ecumenical movement have been associated with "Christological" and "Trinitarian" principles, as expressed in the Nicene Creed (381). But controversies about Christ crucified and risen and about the *oikonomia* of the Holy Trinity continue. The WCC's seventh assembly in Canberra (1991), with its theme "Come, Holy Spirit — Renew the Whole Creation", rediscovered the power of the Holy Spirit, a power for the sanctification of the heart, transformation of society, renewal of the world. The member churches, gathered at the assembly, prayed: "Holy Spirit, transform and sanctify us!"

Spirituality calls us to move beyond the creed and to see that Jesus Christ takes up the Old Testament prophetic tradition, which represents a treasury of spirituality. Gregory of Nyssa (335-394) emphasized the prophets' contribution to understanding the glory of God in Christ and recommended the life of Moses as a model for Christian spirituality. Every baptized Christian must see in his or her life the risen Christ in glory; everyone is able to reach that degree of perfection and glorification. Salvation is not limited to the forgiveness of sins, but requires a preparation for the vision of Christ in glory which everyone will have. The faithful should become a mirror reflecting the glory of God, which was received by the prophets in the Old Testament. Christian advancement to higher spiritual stages means clearly that all are supposed to become prophets, that is, to reach glorification. "I would like all of you to speak in tongues, but even more to prophesy" (1 Cor. 14:5). Spirituality brings the prophetic experience into the apostolic tradition.

Description of diversity

So long as ecumenism is seen as a matter of external church relations and interconfessional diplomacy, it falls far short of its original vocation. The search for a visible unity was embraced by all precisely because it held up a vision of communion; through the churches it touched the human community and through the WCC it touched concrete ecclesial life. Ecumenism is blocked when it is removed from the life of the churches, when historical traditions are not open for renewal, controversial doctrines not up for debate, improvised conceptions not ready for correction.

The Orthodox church will agree that unity and renewal belong together, but all renewal, reforms and revival movements succeeded in dividing the faithful and creating "new churches". Renewal which ends in schism is not credible!

In fact the search for visible unity has not been influenced very much by a theology of the Holy Spirit, the Spirit who freely distributes blessings, graces and responsibilities within the body of Christ. The concentration on unity in one place, or on the link between the local and universal church, has overshadowed the concern for the diversity of gifts and the plurality of graces and missions given by the Holy Spirit. Diversity was destroyed, its reality reduced. In some places, the search for unity became uniatism — unity with Rome at any cost. One must go beyond confessionalism, *ex cathedra* dogmatism and uniatism to discover the diversity inspired by the Holy Spirit. The search for a model of unity is inseparably linked with the description of diversities.

Symbolic acts: Easter and saints

A common Easter: Some of the churches and Christian groups who have followed the *Ecumenical Prayer Cycle* in their intercessory prayers have asked whether the liturgical calendar and celebration of feasts could not be used as an expression of unity. Is our calendar a trap keeping us captive to past history, or is it an open door to see each other face to face? The issue of celebrating Easter on a common Sunday and date is more than a chronological adjustment; it is a sign that all churches are faithful to the same Risen Christ when we glorify "according to the scriptures".

One communion of saints: There is nothing to prevent Christians from following in the steps of Christ who left us the example of his holy way of life. Everyone has the freedom and grace to become his disciple, to contribute to a community of saints. It is in this spiritual combat for holiness in their life that Christians can reach a deeper level of unity. There is already a communion among the saints. We should recognize among ourselves those who have become fully conscious of the light of God's grace shining upon his people.

> Should we not look for a transformation of ecclesial communities before we speak of sharing holiness and sanctification? Structure, ministry, etc. of the community, what we call *visible* unity, cannot be irrelevant to holiness. It is a tragic reality that Christian communities do not recognize each others' saints, because of division at the level of both or either faith and order. Holiness and ecclesiality cannot be separated. Praying for holiness must go together with working for unity. (John Zizioulas, Canberra assembly, 1991)

Light of many lamps

Whatever one's views on the subject of spirituality, one is obliged to describe what those who remain faithful to the mystical and prophetic tradition have preserved and transmitted to us. Indeed, there are traditions which do not encourage the exercise of singular contemplation, of supernatural illumination and prophetic vision. They are afraid of subjective mysticism, they neglect mystical knowledge and the practice of silent prayer and sanctification. They do not appreciate devotional themes. It is, I think, desirable and necessary to go beyond this hesitation and to discover anew the diversity of gifts inspired by the Holy Spirit. In a time of ambiguity, this sometimes forgotten or neglected tradition of spirituality offers a personal and ecclesial way forward in the search for visible unity.

We cannot avoid the appeal for new personal and ecclesial spiritualities. Our fellowship will then become like a temple in which there are many lamps, whose lights all unite in one light, in which the light of no one particular lamp can be distinguished from all the rest. Our various spiritual ways are similar to the lights from lamps, wholly interpenetrating one another, yet each one retaining its integrity and distinction.

NOTE

[1] Ion Bria, "Towards an Ecumenical Spirituality", *One World*, no. 169, 1991.

The Liturgy after the Liturgy

Ion Bria

In the discussion of the consultation organized by CWME Desk for Orthodox Studies and Relations in Etchmiadzine, Armenia, 16-21 September 1975,[1] on the topic "Confessing Christ through the Liturgical Life of the Church", the question was raised: What is the relationship between the "liturgical spirituality", the personal spiritual experience gained by a meaningful participation in the Liturgy, and the witness to the Gospel in the world, witness which belongs to the very nature of the Church and is rooted in the advent of the Spirit at Pentecost? The consultation spoke of "the indispensable continuation" of the liturgical celebration and stated very clearly that "the Liturgy must not be limited to the celebration in the Church but has to be continued in the life of the faithful in all dimensions of life".

The second part of the Etchmiadzine consultation dealt with several aspects of the organic unity between liturgical spirituality[2] and witness, indicating methods and approaches which could be used to accomplish that unity. However, that consultation did not go deeply into the question of the continuation of Liturgy in life; so the participants were asked to provide their comments based on the initial discussion. One comment which in fact summarized the original debate was sent by Bishop Anastasios Yannoulatos, professor at the University of Athens, which follows in a revised form:

> The Liturgy is not an escape from life, but a continuous transformation of life according to the prototype Jesus Christ, through the power of the Spirit. If it is true that in the Liturgy we not only hear a message but we participate in the great event of liberation from sin and of *koinonia* (communion) with Christ through the real presence of the Holy Spirit, then this event of our personal incorporation into the Body of Christ, this transfiguration of our little being into a member of Christ, must be evident and be proclaimed in actual life.
>
> The Liturgy has to be continued in personal, everyday situations. Each of the faithful is called upon to continue a personal "liturgy" on the secret altar of his own heart, to realize a living proclamation of the good news "for the sake of the whole world". Without this continuation the liturgy remains incomplete. Since the eucharistic event we are incorporated in Him who came to serve the world and to be sacrificed for it, we have to express in concrete diakonia, in community life, our new being in Christ, the Servant of all. The sacrifice of the Eucharist must be extended in personal sacrifices for the people in need, the brothers for whom Christ died. Since the Liturgy is the participation in the great event of liberation from the demonic powers, then the continuation of Liturgy

* At the time of writing this article, Prof. Ion Bria was secretary for research and relations with the Orthodox churches, in the WCC's Commission on World Mission and Evangelism. He later became moderator of the WCC's Unit on Unity and Renewal. This text was first published in *International Review of Mission*, vol. LXVII, no. 265, January 1978.

in life means a continuous liberation from the powers of the evil that are working inside us, a continual reorientation and openness to insights and efforts aimed at liberating human persons from all demonic structures of injustice, exploitation, agony, loneliness, and at creating real communion of persons in love.

This personal everyday attitude becomes "liturgical" in the sense that (a) it draws power from the participation in the sacrament of the Holy Eucharist through which we receive the grace of the liberating and unifying Spirit, (b) it constitutes the best preparation for a new, more conscious and existential participation in the Eucharist, and (c) it is a living expression — in terms clear to everybody — of the real transformation of men and women in Christ.

What is the meaning of "the liturgy after the Liturgy"?

In recent years, there has been a strong emphasis in Orthodox Ecclesiology on the eucharistic understanding of the Church.[3] Truly, the Eucharist Liturgy is the climax of the Church's life, the event in which the people of God are celebrating the incarnation, the death and the resurrection of Jesus Christ, sharing His glorified body and blood, tasting the Kingdom to come. The ecclesial *koinonia* is indeed constituted by the participation of the baptized in the eucharistic communion, the sacramental actualization of the economy of salvation, a living reality which belongs both to history and to eschatology. While this emphasis is deeply rooted in the biblical and patristic tradition and is of extreme importance today, it might easily lead to the conclusion that Orthodox limit the interpretation of the Church to an exclusive worshipping community, to protecting and to preserving the Good News for its members. Therefore a need was felt to affirm that the Liturgy is not a self-centred service and action, but is a service for the building of the one Body of Christ within the economy of salvation which is for all people of all ages. The liturgical assembly is the Father's House, where the invitation to the banquet of the heavenly bread is constantly voiced and addressed not only to the members of the Church, but also to the non-Christians and strangers.[4]

This liturgical concentration, "the liturgy within the Liturgy", is essential for the Church, but it has to be understood in all its dimensions. There is a double movement in the Liturgy: on the one hand, the assembling of the people of God to perform the memorial of the death and resurrection of our Lord "until He comes again". It also manifests and realizes the process by which "the *cosmos* is becoming *ecclesia*". Therefore the preparation for Liturgy takes place not only at the personal spiritual level, but also at the level of human historical and natural realities. In preparing for Liturgy, the Christian starts a spiritual journey which affects everything in his life: family, properties, authority, position, and social relations. It re-orientates the direction of his entire human existence towards its sanctification by the Holy Spirit.

On the other hand, renewed by the Holy Communion and the Holy Spirit, the members of the Church are sent to be authentic testimony to Jesus Christ in the world. The mission of the Church rests upon the radiating and transforming power of the Liturgy. It is a stimulus in sending out the people of God to the world to confess the Gospel and to be involved in man's liberation.

Liturgically, this continual double movement of thanksgiving is expressed in the ministry of the deacon. On the one hand he brings and offers to the altar the gifts of the people; on the other, he shares and distributes the Holy Sacraments which nourish the life of Christians. Everything is linked with the central action of the Church, which is the Eucharist, and everybody has a diaconal function in reconciling the separated realities.

The Etchmiadzine consultation states that "the Church seeks to order the whole life of man by the sanctification of the time, by the liturgical cycles, the celebration of the year's festival, the observance of fasts, the practices of ascesis, and regular visitation". It was therefore recommended that "an effort must be made to bring into everyday life the liturgical rhythm of consecration of the time (matins, hours, vespers, Saints' days, feast days)". The problem remains, however, for the Church today not only to keep its members in the traditional liturgical cycles, but to find ways to introduce new people into this rhythm.

How does the Church, through its liturgical life, invite the world into the Lord's House and seek the Kingdom to come? The actualization of this will be the great success of the Church's mission, not only because there is an urgent need for the Church to widen its vision of those outside its influence (Mt. 8:10), but also because the worshipping assembly cannot be a protected place any longer, a refuge for passivity and alienation.

In what sense does the worship constitute a permanent missionary impulse and determine the evangelistic witness of every Christian? How does the liturgical order pass into the order of human existence, personal and social, and shape the life style of Christians? In fact the witness of faith, which includes evangelism, mission and church life, has always taken place in the context of prayer, worship and communion. The missionary structures of the congregation were built upon the liturgy of the Word and Sacraments. There was a great variety of liturgies, confessions and creeds in the first centuries of Christianity, as there is today.

"The liturgy after the Liturgy" which is an essential part of the witnessing life of the Church, requires:

1. An ongoing re-affirming of the true Christian identity, fulness and integrity which have to be constantly renewed by the eucharistic communion. A condition for discipleship and church membership is the existential personal commitment made to Jesus Christ the Lord (Col. 2:6). A lot of members of the Church are becoming "nominal Christians who attend the Church just as a routine". As the Bucharest consultation report[5] states: There are many who have been baptized, and yet have put off Christ, either deliberately or through indifference. Often such people still find it possible sociologically or culturally or ethnically to relate in some manner to the Christian community. The re-Christianization of Christians is an important task of the Church's evangelistic witness.

2. To enlarge the space for witness by creating a new Christian milieu, each in his own environment: family, society, office, factory, etc., is not a simple matter of converting the non-Christians in the vicinity of the parishes, but also a concern for finding room where the Christians live and work and where they can publicly exercise their witness and worship. The personal contact of the faithful with the non-believers in the public arena is particularly relevant today. Seeking for a new witnessing space means, of course, to adopt new styles of mission, new ecclesiastical structures, and especially to be able to face the irritations of the principalities and powers of this age.

There the missionary zeal of the saints and the courage of the confessors who run risks every hour and face death every day (1 Cor. 15:31) has a vital role. Since they are those who take the kingdom of heaven by force (Mt. 11:12), the Church should identify and support the members who confess and defend the hope in Christ against persecutors (Mt. 5:10-12; John 15:20).

3. The liturgical life has to nourish the Christian life not only in its private sphere, but also in its public and political realm. One cannot separate the true Christian identity from the personal sanctification and love and service to man (1 Pet. 1:14-15). There is an increasing concern today about the ethical implications of the faith, in

terms of life style, social, ethic and human behaviour. What is the *ethos* of the Church which claims to be the sign of the kingdom? What is the "spirituality" which is proposed and determined in spreading the Gospel and celebrating the Liturgy today? How is the liturgical vision which is related to the Kingdom, as power of the age to come, as the beginning of the future life which is infused in the present life (John 3:5; 6:33), becoming a social reality? What does sanctification or *theosis* mean in terms of ecology and human rights?

Christian community can only proclaim the Gospel — and be heard — if it is a living icon of Christ. The equality of the brothers and freedom in the Spirit, experienced in the Liturgy, should be expressed and continued in economic sharing and liberation in the field of social oppression.[6] Therefore, the installation in history of a visible Christian fellowship which overcomes human barriers against justice, freedom and unity is a part of that liturgy after the Liturgy. The Church has to struggle for the fulfilment of that justice and freedom which was promised by God to all men and has constantly to give account of how the Kingdom of heaven is or is not within it. It has to ask itself if by the conservatism of its worship it may appear to support the violation of human rights inside and outside the Christian community.

4. Liturgy means public and collective action and therefore there is a sense in which the Christian is a creator of community; this particular charisma has crucial importance today with the increasing lack of human fellowship in the society. The Christian has to be a continual builder of a true koinonia of love and peace even if he is politically marginal and lives in a hostile surrounding. At the ideological and political level that koinonia may appear almost impossible.

However, there is an "open gate", namely the readiness of the human heart to hear the voice of the beloved (John 3:29) and to receive the power of God's Word (Mt. 8:8). Therefore more importance has to be given to the presentation of the Good News as a calling addressed to a person, as an invitation to the wedding house and feast (Luke 14:13). God himself is inviting people to his house and banquet. We should not forget the personal aspect of the invitation. In fact the Christian should exercise his personal witnessing as he practises his family life.

It is very interesting to mention in this respect that St John Chrysostom, who shaped the order of the eucharistic Liturgy ordinarily celebrated by Orthodox, strongly underlined "the sacrament of the brother", namely the spiritual sacrifice, the philanthropy and service which Christians have to offer outside the worship, in public places, on the altar of their neighbour's heart. For him there is a basic coincidence between faith, worship, life and service, therefore the offering on "the second altar" is complementary to the worship at the Holy Table.

There are many evidences that Orthodoxy is recapturing today that inner unity between the Liturgy, mission, witness and social diakonia, which gave it this popular character and historical vitality. The New Valamo Consultation (24-30 September 1977) confirmed once more the importance of the missionary concern for "liturgy after the Liturgy" within the total ecumenical witness of Orthodoxy. The consultation declared: "In each culture the eucharistic dynamics lead into a 'liturgy after the Liturgy', i.e. a liturgical use of the material world, a transformation of human association in society into koinonia, of consumerism into an ascetic attitude towards creation and the restoration of human dignity."[7]

Thus, through "liturgy after the Liturgy", the Church, witnessing to the cosmic dimension of the salvation event, puts into practice, daily and existentially, its missionary vocation.

NOTES

[1] The Etchmiadzine Report, *International Review of Mission*, vol. LXIV, no. 256, 1975, pp.417-421.

[2] Metropolitan Georges Khodr, "La spiritualité liturgique", *Contacts*, 23(93), 4-12.

[3] Stanley Harakas, "The Local Church: an Eastern Orthodox Perspective", *The Ecumenical Review*, vol. 29, no. 2, April 1977, pp.141-153.

[4] Ion Bria, "Concerns and Challenges in Orthodox Ecclesiology Today", *Lutheran World*, no. 3, 1976, pp.188-191.

[5] "The Bucharest Report", *International Review of Mission*, vol. 54, no. 253, 1975, pp.67-94.

[6] George Munuvel, "La mission, incarnation et proclamation liturgique", *Journal des missions évangéliques*, nos. 1-2-3, 1977, pp.30-38.

[7] Report of the New Valamo Consultation, WCC, Geneva, 1978, p.20.

The Date of Pascha:
The Need to Continue the Debate

Pascha, which celebrates the Resurrection of our Lord and Saviour Jesus Christ, is the fundamental event of the Christian faith and constitutes the centre of all liturgical celebrations. However, shrouded in a mist of ambiguities, confusion and inconsistencies, the date for the celebration of this main feast becomes problematic for those living in a pluralistic society such as our own. In order to sustain annual heightened interest in the "correct" date for the celebration of Pascha, which noticeably dissipates quickly after the Great and Holy Week, we must seek an adequate solution to this sensitive issue, for the sake of all Christian people, in the spirit of the Fathers of the First Ecumenical Council.

A brief survey of several historical events and data will help us to understand better why Christians of the Eastern and Western Churches celebrate Pascha at different times.

The Hebrew Passover and the Christian Pascha: Controversies in the Early Church

In light of evidence from documents of the second century there appears to be certainty about an annual celebration of Pascha by the Apostolic Community. Several suggestions in the New Testament and facts surrounding the paschal controversies of the second century clearly indicate that the Christian celebration of the Lord's death and resurrection were closely related to the Hebrew festival of the Passover.

At the outset, therefore, a primary question to resolve concerns the point in time when the Hebrew Passover ("Nomikon Phaska") was celebrated. According to Mosaic Law (Ex 12:1-20, 43-50), the Passover is to occur annually in the month of Aviv, or Spring season (i.e., Nissan, March-April) which was considered to be first of all the months of the year. The Jews, like other ancient peoples, made use of the lunar calendar, which falls short of the solar year by roughly eleven days. Since festivals would eventually wander into the wrong season if their occurrence followed the cycle of the lunar month, the lunar calendar was regularly adjusted to account for such periodic changes, with the addition or intercalation of a thirteenth month, known as the Second Abar, immediately after the month of Adar, which preceded Nissan. The Jewish calendar was definitively regularized and systematized around 360 A.D., some thirty-five years after the Council of Nicea. Elements constituting the Jewish calendar are those universal to all calendars and include the day, week, month, and year. In the

---

● The Very Rev. Dr Alkiviadis Calivas was formerly dean and professor of liturgics of the Holy Cross Greek Orthodox School of Theology, Boston, USA. This paper was first published in the *Greek Orthodox Theological Review*, vol. 35, no. 4, winter 1990.

Jewish understanding, each day begins in the evening after sunset, with each new month marked by the appearance of a new moon. Thus, Passover was a movable nocturnal festival, celebrated annually on the first full moon on a fixed night, 14/15 Nissan which, according to Philo, also coincides with the spring equinox.

In light of this dating of the Jewish Passover, the Church inherited a context from which to observe the paschal mystery of Christ's cross and empty tomb. Ironically, it was precisely the differing emphases given to these two aspects of the paschal mystery by certain Christian communities at that time, that caused the paschal controversies of the second century and breached the unity of the Church. On one side, the churches of Asia Minor laid greater stress on the redemptive death of the risen Lord and defended the right to observe Pascha on the fourteenth day of Nissan, no matter which day of the week this should occur; such observance, they argued, represented ancient tradition. For the churches of Asia Minor, Pascha was essentially related to the Crucifixion and was observed on the fourteenth day of Nissan, the day on which the Lord was crucified. All the other churches claiming to embody the Apostolic tradition placed greater emphasis on the empty tomb and insisted that the Paschal feast be properly observed only on the Sunday following the Jewish Passover; such observance, they argued, was appropriate since the Lord himself was resurrected on that "First day of the Week" and the Church, from the start, observed each Sunday with a eucharistic assembly in honour of the Resurrection. This early controversy, called Quartodeciman, literally Fourteenthism, was especially intensified during the second half of the second century. Although the observance of Pascha on Sunday finally prevailed, even among the churches of Asia Minor, the controversy remained an unpleasant memory in the life of the Church because the Quartodecimans survived as a sect through the fifth century. Thus, by the end of the second and in the early third century, the Church had positively established Sunday as the sole fitting day to observe the annual commemoration of the Lord's resurrection.

In thus reckoning the day for paschal celebration, the early Church continued to rely on Jewish practice. More specifically, early Christians understood as immensely valuable one elemental characteristic of the Passover celebration: that it necessarily occur on the full moon of the spring (vernal) equinox. By emphasizing this important detail in the calculation of the Paschal feast, the Church was assured that the annual observance of the Resurrection would never occur twice in a single year.

The Paschalia: Towards a Common Dating of Pascha

By the third century, however, Christians in Rome and especially in Alexandria, a renowned centre of commerce, culture, and science in the ancient world, began to cite imperfections in the Jewish calendar. It appears that after the destruction of Jerusalem, Jewish communities in Palestine and the diaspora began to depend on various local calendars to determine the paschal moon, the result being, among other things, an allowance for the Passover to occur sometimes before the spring equinox. Thus, the Christian world, during the course of the third century, began to free itself from its dependence on the Jewish calendar for fixing the date of the Paschal feast. Only a small group of Christians, namely those from Syria, Mesopotamia, and Cilicia, persisted in following the Jewish reckoning of the Passover. Because of their unreserved dependence on the Jewish Passover, the first or protopascha, these schismatics were known as the Protopaschites.

First to devise a mathematical table, called "the paschal cycle" or the "pasachalia", by which the date of Pascha was fixed for a sixteen-year cycle, was Hippolytos of Rome (+ 222). Later, in the same century, Augustales developed a more accurate eighty-four year cycle which was destined to be accepted by other Western Churches in the first decades of the fourth century. An even more accurate paschal cycle, however, was developed by the distinguished Alexandrian mathematician and later bishop of Laodiceia, Anatolios (c. 268). His paschal cycle of nineteen years, based on the lunar and solar computations of earlier Greek astronomers, was the cycle to be adopted by all the churches of the East.

Despite such progress, a solution for a common dating of Pascha still frustrated the Church. Adoption of two distinct paschal cycles in the East and the West, the fixing of different dates for the spring equinox, as well as indifference by the West to the time of the celebration of the Jewish Passover, caused these churches, more often than not, to celebrate the feast on different Sundays. Couple this with the confusion added by the Quartodeciman and the Protopaschite sects, and one can sense the urgency confronting the Church at the dawn of the fourth century on this matter.

The Decision of the First Ecumenical Council and the Subsequent Development

Deeply affected by the paschal controversies, the early Church sought to find a solution for the common celebration of the feast. As evidence of the universality of this concern, the First Ecumenical Council, which was convened at Nicea in 325 A.D. to address the heresy of Arius, placed this issue on its agenda. In its deliberations, the Council put an end (or did it?) to the seemingly endless debate over the date of Pascha. However, the text of the Council's decision on the dating of Pascha and the reasoning by which it was dictated have never been sufficiently transmitted to the present generation, and, as some suggest, may be "the main cause for confusion in opinions about the canonical norms for paschalia".

Two canons, the first from the Council of Antioch (c. 341 A.D.) and the seventh of the so-called Apostolic Canons, together with several other authoritative documents of the post-Nicean period, fill this void with valued testimonies reflecting the definition given at Nicea. The decision at Nicea, according to evidence provided by these documents, appears to have had two main thrusts: first, to detach the Christian community from all dependency on the Jewish calendar, and second, to define broadly the principal guiding rules for the computation of the date of Pascha. In the case of the former, this was a clear move to counter the Protopaschites and all other Judaizers as well as being the very first step towards establishing a common paschal cycle. The Council did not deal with details regulating the paschalia, but apparently left the task of their computation to the Patriarch of Alexandria; who, by way of further explanation, was commissioned to communicate annually with all local churches, informing them of the date of Pascha. In the case of the latter, these rules can be summarized in three key phrases: the spring equinox, the full moon, and Sunday. That is to say, therefore, that Pascha must always occur on a Sunday, following the full moon of the spring equinox.

According to this prescription, Pascha is to be celebrated on the first Sunday after the full moon which occurs between March 21 and April 19, since the Alexandrians had determined March 21 as the day of the spring equinox. Thus, according to the calendar, the earliest possible day for the celebration of Pascha is March 22, if the full moon occurs on March 21, and the latest is April 25, if the full moon occurs on April 18. Were the issue as simple as it appears! Some further historical facts will help us to understand why this issue is not clear for us today, nor was it clear for the Christians of the fourth century. More importantly, however, it will enable us to assess where we are today, how we got here and where we can realistically go.

In spite of the fact that the Council of Nicea set a clear course and pattern, because of the use of diverse paschalia, the common celebration of Pascha was to remain elusive for several more centuries. In 387 A.D., for example, we are told that the churches of Gaul observed Pascha on March 21, those in Italy on April 18 and those in the East on April 25. Although the Council of Nicea was clear in its intent and purpose, two decisive elements can be attributed to dating differences in the celebration of Pascha; the computation of the spring equinox and longer or shorter paschal cycles being used by local churches. Eastern tradition, following the lead of Alexandria, settled on the Anatolian nineteen year paschal cycle and thus observed March 21 as the spring equinox. Gaul and the Celtic churches on the other hand used alternative paschal tables. Eventually, however, these Western churches adopted the Roman practice, which, in turn, conformed to the Alexandrian computation.

In 437 A.D., Patriarch of Alexandria Cyril the Great, to assure continuity and accuracy, devised a paschal table based on the Anatolian cycle which stipulated the date of Pascha for the ensuing ninety-five year period. His course of action proved providential, giving the local churches a ready and stable reference in a period marked by turbulence and uncertainty due to heresies and the encroachment of barbaric tribes.

A century later, the Scythian monk Dionysios (Exiguus), living in Rome in 525 A.D., was called upon to construct a new paschal table. Translating into Latin the table of Cyril of Alexandria, he thus introduced the Eastern tradition to Rome. It should be noted that the same Dionysios is also responsible for introducing the Christian Era, i.e. counting of the years from the Incarnation which was, in due course, accepted by all of Christendom.

Thus, after an arduously long and painful journey, the one holy, catholic, apostolic and undivided Church of the East and West was able to rejoice in the much desired common celebration of the Paschal feast. But alas, the journey is not over.

It may be useful, at this point, to take note of another important development, canonical in nature, which has had a powerful influence on the Orthodox Church's dating of the Paschal feast. John Zonaras and Theodore Balsamon, two famous twelfth century canonists, in their interpretation of the canons on Pascha, emphasized that the feast must always be held after the Jewish Passover. Thus, they placed the dating of the Christian Pascha in direct and constant dependence on the dating of the Jewish Passover. This interpretation gradually became incontestable. Matthew Blastaris, in his interpretation, added that the Christian Pascha must also not coincide with the Passover. In fact, however, according to modern canonists, the canons do not stipulate any principle of dependence of the date of our Pascha on the time of the Jewish Passover. The Nicean decision, as we have seen, freed the Church from any dependence on the Jewish calendar. Its definition, however, was such that the Christian Pascha, although independent of any and all Jewish calendars, is in fact celebrated after the Mosaic Passover (the "Nomikon Pascha"), as described in Exodus and as determined by the Christian calculations of the spring equinox and its full moon.

The Establishment of the New Calendar: Additional Complications

In the year 1582 a new chapter in the paschal controversy began when Pope Gregory XIII introduced the new calendar, bearing his name, which replaced the older, and by then inaccurate, Julian calendar. For the purpose of clarification it should be noted that the Julian calendar was devised in 46 B.C. by Emperor Julius Caesar. The length of the year in the Julian calendar was almost, but not quite accurate. In fact, by 325 A.D., the error was enough to cause the spring equinox to fall on March 21. Thus, the churches of the East, as we have seen, which had fixed March 21 as the day of the vernal equinox and the earliest possible date for the paschal full moon, suffered a dilemma. Unreformed, the Julian calendar wandered further forward in the seasons. By 1582 it was calculated that the spring equinox, which was fixed on March 21, was now in reality occurring on March 11; a date determined by virtue of the fact that the Julian calendar jumped forward one day towards the summer every 128 years.

The new calendar, devised by the Calabrian astronomer Luis Lilio, however, was neither sufficient in fully correcting the calendar nor did it win immediate and universal approval by the Christian world. It was seen as a "papal calendar" and, thus, not judged on its scientific merit and accuracy. One must recall that, at the time of its establishment, Western Europe was fragmented by the Protestant Reformation and the Schism of 1054 (which divided the Latin West from the Orthodox East).

Ironically, digressing for a moment, it can be argued that the need for calendar reform was first proposed in the East. The philosopher-astronomer Nikephoros Gregoras, in a memorandum of 1325 to the Emperor Andronikos II Paleologos (1283-1328), suggested the changes necessary to align the calendar with the true spring equinox. The emperor, while sympathetic, chose not to follow the recommendation out of fear that such a change would cause confusion and division among the masses. Ten years later, in 1335, the famous canonist and monk Matthew Blastaris recognized the same need for calendar reform, but shared the fears of the deceased Emperor Andronikos II. Once again, in 1371, the monk astronomer Isaak Argyros proposed amendments to the paschalia in order that they would conform to the true spring equinox, from which the Julian calendar was steadily moving away, but no change was made.

At the end of the eighteenth century, however, the new calendar was finally adopted by all of Western Christendom. In 1924, and shortly thereafter, following the lead of the Ecumenical Patriarchate, the new calendar was also adopted by a majority of the Orthodox Churches. Today only the churches of Jerusalem, Russia, Serbia, some jurisdictions of the diaspora, and the monasteries of Mount Athos, continue to follow the Julian calendar.

Coping with the Two Calendars: A Temporary Compromise

If the Paschal feast is to be celebrated annually on the first Sunday after the full moon following the spring equinox (this means, therefore, that in any given year the date of Pascha could vary over a thirty-five day period commencing on March 22 and ending on April 25), one ought to justifiably question why this formula appears to be inconsistent when the Orthodox Church functions with two calendars, resulting in the ambiguities and inconsistencies which surround the paschal feast.

The churches which adopted the new Gregorian calendar, beginning with the Ecumenical Patriarchate in 1924, made a conscious decision: In order to protect and maintain the unity of the Church, they would compromise, reckon and observe the paschal feast by the old Julian calendar; which by then had a thirteen-day difference from the Gregorian. This meant that the paschal cycle of the Julian calendar had to be superimposed upon the Gregorian. To translate this adjustment in terms of the new calendar, the five week period within which Pascha could occur now became April 4 through May 8, thus corresponding to the Julian dates of March 22-April 25. Because the spring equinox is not fixed in accordance with the Gregorian calendar, with which we are familiar, but by the Julian calendar, the Julian March 21 is in reality our April 2 (new calendar). The paschal Sunday is determined accordingly in order that all Orthodox churches celebrate Pascha "on the same Sunday, although technically not on the same date".[1]

Future Course of Action: Recovering the Spirit of Nicea

Having said this much, we now need to consider what implications such a scenario offers the future.

The first step in overcoming the ambiguities surrounding the date of Pascha and correcting, in the process, the uncomfortable inconsistencies which they project upon the Typicon, is the adoption of the new calendar by the canonical Orthodox Churches. While it is perhaps difficult to comprehend, a solution to the Paschal question remains the decision of those canonical Orthodox Churches currently adhering to the Julian calendar to break with an honoured, but no longer viable and operative, tradition. Such becomes especially true when we consider the fact that the early Church never created her own calendar but chose to accept and adopt the prevailing civil calendar. As the inexactness of the Julian calendar remains, so too does the genuine attachment to it by a large block of canonical Orthodox Christians. Oftentimes attachment to externals of the faith rooted in long traditions is the hardest to break. This important first step leading to the adoption of a common calendar is essentially a pastoral task. This fact was highlighted and emphasized in a communique issued in 1977 by the members of the Consultation on the Date of Easter, called by the Secretariat for the Preparation on the Great and Holy Council upon the mandate of the First Pan-Orthodox Preconciliar Conference. This Consultation, composed of specialists in canon law, astronomy, history and sociology, was held at the Ecumenical Centre of the Ecumenical Patriarchate in Chambésy, Switzerland, from 28 June to 2 July 1977. The communique reads, in part, as follows :

> To fulfil its mandate, the meeting on the one hand ought to consider the desire existing in the Orthodox Church to see Easter celebrated by all Christians together, but on the other hand it ought also to take account of the pastoral difficulties which the Church must examine attentively from every angle. This Church has the burden of taking into account the present pastoral imperatives of Orthodoxy in the West, while at the same time maintaining a balanced vision of things and avoiding a premature pan-Orthodox decision.

Also affirmed by the Consultation was the fact that lunar tables for the Paschalia, which are still in use for the determination of the Paschal full moon, are lagging by five days; it was further noted that this discrepancy will increase in time.

It is obvious, I believe, from what has been previously noted that, by assigning the task of informing the churches of the date of Pascha to the Patriarch of Alexandria, the intent of the Fathers of the First Ecumenical Council was entirely clear: To employ the most accurate use of astronomical data available from the scientific community for a correct computation of the date of Pascha. This sense of dependency upon accurate scientific data was likewise accentuated by the 1977 Consultation:

> For this reason the Consultation unanimously recommends to the next Pan-orthodox Preconciliar Conference that a commission of astronomers be entrusted with the determination, for as long a period as possible, of the Sunday after the first full moon

following the vernal equinox. The Consultation sees in this initiative on the part of the Orthodox Church a contribution to the universal determination of the date of Pascha for all Christians.

At a Symposium of Orthodox theologians, held in Athens in 1969, to study the paschal problem and the growing concern of all Christians to find a solution for a common celebration of the feast, among other things discussed were: the problem of revising the Paschalia, interpretation of canon law, and various proposals for the institution of a chronological order setting a fixed and common date for Pascha. According to these proposals, the paschal Sunday would always fall within an established and defined seven-day period; such as April 8-14 (the proposal of Patriarch Athenagoras); April 15-21 (the proposal of the Athens Symposium); April 12-18, with the possibility in several instances of a later dating (the proposal of Professor D.P. Ogitsky of the Theological Academy of Moscow).

Similar, and other, proposals were brought before the World Council of Churches at its Fifth Assembly in Nairobi in 1975. However, the Orthodox Churches at this Assembly deferred any decision, declaring that they felt bound to calculate the date of Pascha in the traditional way until such time as all Orthodox Churches had expressly agreed on any change. The issue of a fixed common date was on the agenda of the 1977 Consultation as well. Regarding this issue, the Consultation arrived at the following decision:

> It is known that there have been proposals concerning the celebration of Easter on a fixed Sunday. The two noteworthy proposals have been those in favour of the Sunday following the second Saturday of April. Although some churches were in favour, pastoral concern has prevailed in dismissing this twofold proposal, which would risk provoking schism in certain Orthodox Churches, seeing that such a proposal betrays the letter of Nicea's intentions and the entire Orthodox tradition which maintains that Easter be celebrated on the Sunday following the first full moon after the vernal equinox.

Thus, for the Orthodox Church, the proposed suggestions for a fixed date, while noteworthy, are deemed in the final analysis unworkable and unacceptable. The Consultation of 1977, with its several recommendations to the Churches, appears to have defined Orthodoxy's future course of action in relating to the paschal question in broad, yet specific, terms. The focus of inquiry remains constant: the spirit and simplicity of the Council of Nicea's direct formula. The spirit of the Council is clear: the Church is obliged to calculate the time of Pascha precisely and correctly through the use of all available scientific data: its formula being clear enough, the dating of Pascha to be the Sunday after the full moon of the spring equinox. In consideration of this, two things need to be done. First, there is the need to settle at once a sustained pastoral effort to inform and edify the faithful. Second, there is the need to reform and adjust the Paschalia of both the East and the West, by canonists working in harmony with a commission of astronomers.

While doing this work, to paraphrase the communique of the 1977 Consultation, it is most desirable for the Church to study all the questions on the paschal feast in collaboration with all Christians who are interested in them.

NOTE

[1] E.g. in 1989 Pascha was celebrated on April 30 (which is the same as April 17 of the Old Calendar); in 1990 Pascha was on April 15 (which is the same as April 2 of the Old Calendar).

Local and Universal:
Uniatism as an Ecclesiological Issue

Kondothra M. George

Near the end of the first century Clement, then bishop of Rome, began a famous letter to Corinth in the East with touching words of greeting: "the pilgrim church of Rome writing to the church of God in Corinth, which is in pilgrimage..." The Greek word translated "pilgrim" *(paroikos)* can also be rendered as "alien", "sojourner", "exile". From the related word *paroikia* comes the English "parish" — a community of sojourners or pilgrims.

Clement's simple words of introduction reflected a self-understanding of the church shared by the burgeoning Christian communities everywhere from Rome to Jerusalem.

The Christian community in each particular place understood itself as a stranger to the world. With its sister communities, held together by a common faith in Christ, it was moving on to the ultimate destiny of life beyond history. Earthly rule, possessions and privileges were not primary for those Christian communities. Many of them were indeed under persecution, though some did face the temptations of power and wealth.

But over the years, theology took a different course from that reflected in Clement's salutation to the Corinthians.

Eleven centuries later, another bishop of Rome, Pope Innocent III (1198-1216), was to write that "kings rule each in his own kingdom; Peter rules over the whole earth. The Lord Jesus Christ has set up one order over all things. All should bow the knee to the Vicar of Christ".

The Christian East and the Christian West parted ways in their understanding of the Church (ecclesiology) long before any formal break occurred.

This difference in ecclesiological perceptions is at the root of the controversy which has flared around the "Eastern Catholic" or "uniate" churches in Eastern and Central Europe.[1] Ecclesiologically speaking, Eastern Orthodox churches see the presence among them of the "uniate" churches in communion with Rome as an anomaly and an affront to the true unity they seek with the churches of the West. From a Western Roman Catholic perspective, on the other hand, the creation and fostering of the "Eastern Catholic churches" is a missionary imperative fully in line with the ecclesiology of a universal church headed by the successor of Peter, the bishop of Rome.

The ecumenical implications of the inevitable conflict between these two positions go much wider than the current problems in Europe.

• Dr Kondothra George is a tutor at the Ecumenical Institute, Bossey, Geneva. This paper was first published in *One World*, No. 180, November 1992.

Universal and local

Generally speaking, the Eastern Christian tradition, both within and beyond the old borders of the Roman Empire, favoured the formation of local churches. "Local" in this sense is understood broadly. It may mean a parish, a nation with common ethnic roots, a large cultural grouping with the same linguistic and cultural heritage or a geographically distinct area like an island.

While fully recognizing diversity of expression, these churches essentially share a common apostolic faith, a common liturgical and spiritual ethos and a common understanding of the Church's nature and mission. They see their unity expressed locally in their communion in the one eucharist and in the one apostolic faith, together with the bishop, who is the focal point of unity.

At national, regional and global levels, councils of bishops express this eucharistic unity in their mutual consensus and in their common mind with the whole people of God. In their conciliar style of work these councils recognize the active presence of the Holy Spirit, who constantly guides the church.

From the parish to the global level, the principle of conciliarity, or the ongoing consensus of the whole body of the church, is pivotal. No primate or patriarch can stand against or above this conciliar character of the church.

In its eucharistic assembly the local church manifests the fullness of the church universal, the Body of Christ. The church's universality is not necessarily determined by geographical extension or number of faithful; rather, it is a "qualitative catholicity" of the Body of Christ manifesting "the fullness of him who fills all in all" (Eph. 1:23).

In the course of time, most of these local churches emerged as self-governing (autocephalous) national churches. They consider themselves as *sister churches* which share the same apostolic faith and tradition. While they recognize certain centres — Constantinople, Alexandria, Antioch, Jerusalem, and others — they have never accepted the idea of one universal structure or one universal pastor or patriarch for the world church.

Among Eastern Orthodox primates, the patriarch of Constantinople has a primacy of honour as "first among equals", but this does not imply any jurisdiction over other local churches.

In the self-understanding of the Western church, on the other hand, geographical or quantitative universality has played a crucial role, especially since the colonial expansion.

Claims of universal jurisdiction developed by the bishops of Rome since the fifth century have found concrete expression in many ways. The missionary dimension of this universalist vision is unquestionable. But the way it has been expressed has almost met with vehement disagreement from Eastern churches.

In the West, the idea of the universal church was integrally related to the "Petrine ministry" of the bishop of Rome as successor of Peter. As recently as June 1992, this was restated in the letter to Roman Catholic bishops by the Vatican Congregation for the Doctrine of the Faith: "The Roman pontiff as the successor of Peter is the perpetual and visible source and foundation" of the unity of the church. According to the letter, being in communion with the bishop of Rome is an essential condition for the ecclesial fullness of any Christian community or particular church. Introducing the document, Cardinal Ratzinger, prefect of the Congregation, emphasized "the need for a strong commitment to ecumenism, so that all may be able to recognize this primacy of Peter in his successors, the bishops of Rome".

The link between the universal dimension of salvation and the universal church headed by the Roman pontiff has always been strongly represented by the bishops of Rome.

Pope Boniface VIII (1294-1303) said that "it is altogether necessary to salvation for every human being to be subject to the bishop of Rome". That remains essentially true for this most recent Vatican document. It underlines "the unity of the eucharist and the unity of the episcopate *with Peter and under Peter*". Referring explicitly to the Orthodox churches, the document states that "their existence as particular churches is *wounded*", precisely because they "lack communion with the universal church, represented by Peter's successor".

In other ecclesial communities, which lack apostolic succession and valid eucharist, "the wound is even deeper". And the Roman Catholic Church is, of course, "injured" because of these wounds.

Political universalism

The Christian ecclesiastical universalism developed by the Western church had a strong basis in the structure of the Roman Empire. The term *oikoumene* — "the whole inhabited earth" — served as a synonym for the Empire, and the whole world was simply the Christian world in the Roman Empire.

"Ecumenical" councils were councils of bishops formally convened by Byzantine emperors for churches in this "whole world". But significant ancient Christian communities flourished on the fringes of or even outside the "ecumenical" Roman imperial borders — in Georgia, Persia, Ethiopia, Nubia, Armenia and India. They never entered the mainstream of Greek or Latin tradition within the Empire.

The famous patriarchal sees of Rome, Constantinople, Alexandria and Antioch developed within the imperial *oikoumene*. They gained ecclesiastical status as counterparts of the imperial protocol of chief cities. Rome took the chief place as the capital of the Empire. When the capital moved to Constantinople, it took the second rank as "the new Rome". Alexandria, originally second, became third, and so on. Jerusalem was a special case, because it was associated with the death and resurrection of Christ and was the first church. But it was assigned only a modest fifth rank and a titular honour.

Eastern churches within and outside the Roman Empire consistently maintained that Rome's rank was obviously due to its political status. Rome, however, affirmed that its church and bishops had primacy for *theological* reasons. The city was associated with the martyrdom of Peter, who, as the chief apostle, had primacy over others. The bishops of Rome, Peter's successors, thus have primacy over the universal church.

Because the Roman pontiffs consider Rome's primacy of divine origin, communion with the bishop of Rome is considered as the absolutely essential character of authentic ecclesiality of any church.

The Eastern Orthodox churches, respecting the decisions of the Council of Nicea (AD 325), concede a "primacy of honour" to the bishop of Rome in a united world church. But this primacy is as first among equals, with absolutely no jurisdiction over other churches and their bishops. The Oriental Orthodox Christian traditions, which grew up outside the ancient Roman borders, may also agree to this for the sake of harmony. But they insist that this title is of purely Roman imperial political origin and cannot be pushed beyond the simple primacy of honour. If any theological justification is possible for an historical primacy, they would argue, it should go to Jerusalem, not to Rome.

Uniatism outside Europe

"Uniate" churches exist in almost all Eastern and Oriental Orthodox churches. They have emerged at various points in history, but always through the active agency of Western Roman Catholic Christianity.

There were different reasons for this, among them imperial-colonial expansion, political-economic oppression, crusades, missionary initiatives, activity of Roman Catholic religious congregations like the Jesuits and the Franciscans, personal grievances against local clergy and poverty. But whatever the reasons, the important point is that Rome was always ready and eager to receive these Christians of Orthodox origin, and strongly supported their "reunion" with Rome, fostering their growth with financial and political aid and personnel.

The history of uniatism outside Europe is as complex as that within Europe. The relatively modern establishment next to the ancient Coptic Orthodox Church in Egypt of a Coptic Catholic Church (uniate) — to whom Pope Leo XIII gave a patriarch at the end of the nineteenth century — is an excellent example of the efficient realization of a universalist Roman Catholic ecclesiology through a combination of missionary, colonial, diplomatic and economic channels.

India offers another example of the growth of Oriental Catholic Churches outside Europe. When Portuguese colonizers landed in what is now the state of Kerala in 1498, they discovered an ancient Christian community which traced its origins to the preaching of St Thomas, one of the twelve apostles.

Jesuit missionaries accompanying them began a vigorous and aggressive mission among the Indian Christians. A forced synod in 1599 brought the whole church under Latin rule. Its Oriental character was suppressed and it was completely Latinized. In 1653 this led to a strong but peaceful revolt to liberate the Indian church. Though it was successful, one section of the church was gradually drawn to Portuguese Roman Catholic rule, thus constituting the first Uniate Catholic Church in Kerala (Malabar). This was obviously the result of the Portuguese colonial occupation. However, in the 1930s another smaller uniate church was constituted from among the remaining Orthodox by the "reunion" of one of the Orthodox bishops with Rome. In both cases financial support from Western Roman Catholic sources has been substantial.

Ecclesiologically, these two uniate churches accept the principle of communion with the bishop of Rome. However, while the older uniate church was almost totally Latinized and brought under foreign bishops for a long time, the younger one had to renounce such ancient traditions of the undivided church as the marriage of parish clergy and the election of bishops by the faithful.

A way out?

The growth of the Eastern Catholic bodies was a source of constant embarrassment for the Orthodox churches, as these bodies, while living with the latter in the same territory, went against the ecclesiological traditions of the Eastern church and engaged in active proselytism, often through dubious means.

There are Western Catholic theologians who acknowledge that the creation of Eastern Catholic churches constitutes an ecclesiological anomaly, a practical hindrance to good relations between Roman Catholic and Orthodox churches and a reversal of the ecumenical process of unity of all churches.

A joint communique from consultations between the Roman Catholic Church and the Oriental Orthodox churches in Vienna in 1978 clearly stated that "the Oriental

Catholic churches will not, even in the transitional period before full unity, be regarded as a device for bringing the Oriental Orthodox Churches inside the Roman communion. The role will be more in terms of collaborating in the restoration of eucharistic communion among the sister churches. The Oriental Orthodox Churches according to the principles of the Second Vatican Council and subsequent statements of the See of Rome cannot be fields of mission for other churches." The document encourages sister churches to work out local solutions in accordance with differing local situations with a view to a unified episcopate for each locality.

Several solutions have been proposed. Some suggest the return of the uniate churches to the mother bodies. Others say that a simple halt to proselytism would suffice, since what happened in history cannot easily be undone. Still others say that the only way out is for Rome to review its universalist ecclesiology in the light of the tradition of the undivided church.

The major difficulty is the tragic intertwining of ancient ecclesiological differences with contemporary political and economic realities.

Only a radical act of Christian love, humility and genuine respect for the freedom and diversity of God's churches can help us to re-enter the pilgrim path so powerfully evoked by Clement, bishop of Rome in the very first Christian century.

NOTE

[1] Cf. *One World*, no. 178, August-September 1992.

Eucharistic Hospitality:
Not a Question of Hospitality. A Comment

Paulos Mar Gregorios

An Oriental Orthodox theologian has great difficulty coming to terms with one of the new ecumenical slogans "eucharistic hospitality". It certainly does not occur in the ancient tradition of the Church. Even in the Western Church, it is a new concept.

I am not quite sure of its meaning. I presume that it refers to the custom of the Roman Catholic Church, which does not normally offer communion in the holy mass to non-Catholics, making a special dispensation during an ecumenical conference or other occasion and offering communion to those to whom it normally refuses communion. This could in theory be done also by other churches practising "closed communion", for example, the Orthodox and some Lutheran churches.

The puzzling questions for an Oriental Orthodox theologian are two: (1) Who is this generous host being so hospitable? and (2) What is the host offering and to whom?

The eucharist, as the Orthodox understand it, is the sacrifice of thanksgiving offered up to God, by the Church, in Christ, on behalf of the whole creation. Since the Church is offering it to God, the question of hospitality does not arise at that point. As far as offering communion to those who are not in communion, we do not think of the eucharist as kind of feast for the invited, to which the Church can hospitably invite some more people. It is the Church which offers itself to God through the body and blood of the Lord Jesus Christ. There is no hospitality question in administering the holy mysteries of the Church which the West calls sacraments.

The question of hospitality does not arise anywhere in that process. The Church is not withholding something from other people, which it then gives to them in a gesture of hospitality. In fact the term hospitality is quite offensive to us in this context, since it implies that those who do not do what some Western churches are now doing are being downright inhospitable. I personally feel offended by that implication and therefore by the term "eucharistic hospitality", which should be expunged from the ecumenical vocabulary for the sake of good relations.

The Orthodox have a principle of *oikonomia* or *economy*, which permits the canonical authorities to make exceptions to rules where such exception becomes pastorally necessary. But neither the term *intercommunion* nor the expression *eucharistic hospitality* make any theological sense to the Orthodox. In its place the Orthodox

● Metropolitan Paulos Mar Gregorios is metropolitan of the Malankara Orthodox Syrian Church for Delhi and the north, and head of the Delhi Orthodox Centre, New Delhi, India. This comment was published in *The Ecumenical Review*, vol. 44, no. 1, January 1992, pp.46-47.

would use the terms *communion* and *economy*, which for them make better theological sense.

So far I do not know of any instance in which the Orthodox have invoked the principle of economy to give communion to non-Orthodox at ecumenical meetings. Theoretically this seems possible, if the pastoral need was felt to be compelling. The principle of economy is usually used in situations of emergency, and a conference does not seem to be a situation of emergency. Economy is used usually in relation to persons rather than to groups, though there may be instances in which the principle is extended to groups as well.

Since I have not yet seen a positive argument for the term eucharistic hospitality, I can only confess failure in coming to terms with it. I shall of course be grateful for any further enlightenment on the subject.

Growing Together towards a Full Koinonia

Aram Keshishian

As moderator, it is my privilege and pleasure to welcome you to this forty-fourth meeting of the Central Committee in Geneva.

Since our last meeting in Geneva in September 1991, we have learned of the death of Dr Hans-Gernot Jung of Germany, who was a valued member of this Committee. We have also lost the Ecumenical Patriarch, His Holiness Dimitrios I, who played an important role in the ecumenical witness of Orthodoxy. In July we received news of the death of Son Eminence Diangienda-Kuntima, "chef spirituel" of the Kimbanguist Church in Zaire, and of Rev. Prof. John Meyendorff, a former moderator of the Faith and Order Commission. We thank God for these servants to the ecumenical cause.

We greet with joy the newly elected Ecumenical Patriarch, His Holiness Bartholomew I, who has been an active member of the Faith and Order Standing Commission as well as of the Central and Executive Committees. In his enthronement address he particularly emphasized the importance of the ecumenical movement and the commitment of the Orthodox churches to the World Council of Churches. May God strengthen him to carry on his pastoral and ecumenical role with renewed dynamism and vision. We also greet Patriarch Paulos of the Ethiopian Orthodox Church, the first patriarch to be elected in that country for many years, who was enthroned in July.

I. Introduction

1. For a number of reasons, my second report to the Central Committee will deal with communion/koinonia. Firstly, the Canberra assembly, in its major statement on church unity, described unity as koinonia. Second, in my first report to the Central Committee (September 1991), I considered the process of growing together towards a full koinonia as being one of the vital dimensions of the ecumenical vision for the post-Canberra period. Third, the forthcoming fifth world conference on Faith and Order (Santiago de Compostela, Spain, August 1993) will have as its major theme: "Towards Koinonia in Faith, Life and Witness". Fourth, the reflection process on the common understanding of the nature and vocation of the WCC inevitably touches on the question of koinonia. And fifth, the concern for koinonia — i.e. the sense of belonging to one world community — has become of crucial importance in the relationships of nations and societies.

2. For these reasons I believe that koinonia will henceforth occupy a pivotal place in ecumenical discussions, and it will provide an entry point to, and a challenging and

● Archbishop Aram Keshishian, archbishop of Lebanon in the Armenian Apostolic Church (Cilicia) and moderator of the WCC Central Committee, presented this report to the Central Committee meeting in Geneva in 1992. It was published in *The Ecumenical Review*, vol. 44, no. 4, October 1992.

promising perspective on, many issues that we are and will be facing in our common ecumenical pilgrimage. Thus, it is perfectly appropriate to make it the focus of our deliberations in this meeting.

3. My intention is not of course to treat the subject per se, nor to discuss it in extenso. I will attempt only to identify the ecclesiological and ecumenical implications of koinonia for some of the major aspects and dimensions of the life and work of the World Council at this point of our ecumenical fellowship.

4. Koinonia is not a new concept. It has been addressed at various periods of ecumenical history, and particularly at the time of the founding of the WCC. But it has never been the subject of a thorough and serious theological discussion. It has become a major item on the agenda of bilateral dialogues only in the last decade. Within several churches the understanding of church as koinonia has found special attention and increased acceptance. It emerged in Canberra as a vital issue.

5. I would like to look at koinonia from different perspectives and in different contexts: koinonia as the true nature of the church; as an appropriate model of the unity we seek; as a framework of the unity of humankind; and as the context for the common understanding of the nature of the WCC.

II. Koinonia: the true nature of the church

6. Koinonia belongs to the *esse* of the church. The church is *sancta communio*. The word koinonia comes from *koinos* meaning "common", and *koinoo* meaning "to put together". Koinonia, then, refers to the action of having something in common, sharing and participating in a common reality, acting together. It is rendered in Latin by *communio*. Koinonia has its roots in the Old Testament concept of covenant, which was an expression of the togetherness, partnership and mutual commitment that existed between God and his people (Jer. 24:7).

7. In the New Testament, koinonia is fundamental to the understanding of the reality of church. It ties together a number of basic concepts, such as life together (Acts 2:44,47), being of one heart and one spirit (Acts 4:32), holding everything in common (Acts 2:44), mutual sharing, etc. Koinonia refers to the "body of Christ" (1 Cor. 12) "being in" and "remaining in" Christ (John 14:20,23; 1 John 3:19-24). Other images given to the church, such as "people of God", "flock", "temple" of the Spirit and "bride" are various expressions of koinonia. Thus, koinonia means the participation of the people of God in the life of the Triune God as well as communion among the people who constitute the koinonia.

8. The following peculiar features of koinonia deserve our attention:

a) Koinonia is neither a Christological nor a pneumatological reality only. It is of the Trinitarian nature and basis, pointing to the quality of our common life in the Triune God and with each other. The life of the Triune God is the prototype and source of it. The church is, in fact, the icon of the inter-Trinitarian koinonia. Its being, life and mission are rooted in and sustained by the communion of the Father, the Son and the Holy Spirit. It is in virtue of this koinonia with God that we have unity among human beings, the bond of our fellowship with the Father being the Christ himself through the Holy Spirit. Without either of these, the church would not be the church.

b) Koinonia is not a human realization but a gift of the Holy Spirit. It is a "fellowship of the Holy Spirit" (2 Cor. 13:14). Koinonia with Christ is koinonia in the Spirit. We sometimes think we are achieving it when we attempt to create what is called "a new community". We are not. Koinonia is a given reality in Christ, once and for all, a living reality in the body of Christ. We must receive it, participate in it, grow in it, and remain one in it.

c) Baptism is the basis of koinonia and the source of its unity. Through baptism, human beings are incorporated into koinonia of the Trinity (Rom. 6:4-11). Baptism is unity "with Christ" (Rom. 6:8), incorporation "into Christ" (Gal. 3:27) and being "in Christ" (1 Pet. 5:14). Through it Christians are brought into union with Christ, with each other and with the church of all times and places.[1] Baptism creates and sustains koinonia. The church is a koinonia of the baptized. Our common recognition of baptism as incorporation into the common life in Christ is the basis of our koinonia. Therefore, baptism has an ecclesiological significance. We all share in the one koinonia through baptism. This fellowship based on baptism is the only ground on which unity in faith and eucharistic koinonia are established.

d) Koinonia is established through baptism and sustained by the eucharist. The church is both the body of Christ and the people of God. Together they point to a fellowship of a sacramental nature, i.e. eucharistic koinonia. The eucharist is the locus and supreme manifestation of koinonia. Through it the church becomes koinonia. Through the sharing of the body and blood of Christ we are united in him and to one another (1 Cor. 11:17-27). Koinonia is thus a "fellowship in the body and blood of the Lord" (1 Cor. 10:16). As the broken body is one, all those who share in it are formed into a single body.[2] Koinonia acquires its ecclesial fullness only through eucharistic communion which gathers the people together into the one body of Christ, transcending time and space and making the eucharistic gatherings (local churches) of all places and times part of one koinonia. Baptism, eucharist and the word of God are the constitutive elements of koinonia. They are manifested in their inter-relatedness through the eucharist. The church should therefore understand itself, its being and its mission in the light of the eucharist.

e) Koinonia means sharing in and reflecting the life of the Trinitarian God. It also means sharing the life of Christ in all its aspects within the community (Phil. 3:10; Rom. 8:17). The concept of koinonia holds together the vertical dimension, the divine source, and the horizontal dimension, the visible gathering of God's people. Mutual sharing of gifts, joy and sorrow (2 Cor. 16:7) is essential to koinonia. The church is a koinonia of common life, common diakonia and common witness (Rom. 15:26; 2 Cor. 9:13). In the early church koinonia was expressed through hospitality, visits, mutual material help (Rom. 12:13; 15:26) — in other words, through a common life of interdependence and sharing (2 Cor. 1:7; Rom. 12:13).[3]

f) Koinonia is never partial or incomplete. It embraces the wholeness of the church in all its aspects, dimensions and manifestations. It implies wholeness, fullness and catholicity. In koinonia all the people of God, irrespective of age, gender, time and place, share fully in "all the truth". A local church is not a part of koinonia: it is its full manifestation in a given place. In it the one, holy, catholic and apostolic church is present. Catholicity of koinonia does not refer only to its geographical extension but also to the manifold variety of the local churches and their participation in the one koinonia.

g) Koinonia is a concrete reality. The church is a koinonia in each and in all places and times. It has both a local and a universal manifestation. The church is a conciliar koinonia of local churches which has no geographical or administrative centre. Koinonia is rooted in history as well. Tensions, ambiguities, joy and despair of history in one way or another are echoed in its life and witness. In fact, koinonia helps us to understand the vertical and horizontal, the local and universal, the historical and spiritual dimensions of the church in their mutual challenges and close inter-relatedness.

h) Koinonia is a present reality here and now. It also has an eschatological dimension. Never fully realized in this world, our koinonia with God and with each other will reach its fulfilment in the eschaton, where we will all be united with God in glory (1 Cor. 9:23; 1 John 3:2). Hence, koinonia is always a growing reality.

9. Significantly, the concept of koinonia — or what is referred to in contemporary theology as "ecclesiology of communion" — has become a central theme and a nearly irreversible approach in all ecclesiologies. It was a corrective in Vatican II to a "pyramidal" understanding of the church; it emerged as a basic ecumenical perspective in bilateral dialogues; it came to the fore of theological discussions in Canberra. Koinonia should remain the heart of our ecumenical understanding of the church and a safe foundation on which we can build our continuing search for unity. Therefore, Unit I in general and Faith and Order in particular must take seriously the recommendation of Canberra to develop "ecumenical perspectives on ecclesiology"[4] in the light of an ecclesiology.of communion.

III. Koinonia: an appropriate model of unity

10. Koinonia describes not only the nature of the church but also the nature and model of the unity we seek. Canberra clearly stated: "The unity of the church to which we are called is a koinonia."[5] As koinonia, unity springs from the very essence of the Trinity which is a community of three distinct persons sharing one nature. Hence, koinonia helps us to understand the unity, the oneness, of the church in the multiplicity of local churches.

11. Koinonia is not monolithic. It is given with and in diversity, a diversity which is integral to the nature of koinonia (1 Cor. 12:4-6, 27-31): "L'unité sans diversité fait de l'Eglise un corps mort; le pluralisme sans unité en fait un corps dépecé."[6] As a gift of the Holy Spirit, diversity contributes to the richness and fullness of koinonia. Unity and diversity are inseparably inter-related dimensions of koinonia. Canberra warned us that "there are limits to diversity".[7] But how are we to determine the limits of acceptable diversity, since we have developed different criteria of diversity? Unlimited and uncontrolled diversities may threaten the unity of koinonia. We must distinguish "legitimate" diversities from "sinful divisions". This is indeed a crucial question facing the ecumenical movement.

12. A comprehensive description of unity as koinonia is provided by Canberra: "Koinonia [is] given and expressed in the common confession of the apostolic faith; a common sacramental life entered by the one baptism and celebrated together in one eucharistic fellowship; a common life in which members and ministries are mutually recognized and reconciled; and a common mission witnessing to the gospel of God's grace to all people and serving the whole of creation."[8]

13. In our quest for unity, where do we actually stand vis-à-vis these requirements?

1. Koinonia of faith

14. The ground of our koinonia in the Triune God is our common confession of the apostolic faith. Eucharistic koinonia is rooted in the koinonia of faith. Only those baptized and those who share the same faith are invited to participate and share the Lord's table. In the early church the eucharist was not a means to restore the broken unity: it was the sign of an existing unity of faith.

15. Christian faith has an apostolic origin. Apostolic faith does not refer to a fixed formula or to a specific phase in Christian history. It is the dynamic, historical reality of the Christian faith rooted in biblical witness, proclaimed, reinterpreted and transmitted in and by the church.[9] For some churches, confessing the common faith requires common acceptance of the same confessional text. For others, "pulpit and altar fellowship" is an essential requirement. Because of different histories and traditions, we also have different ways of expressing our common faith. The rich diversity of the apostolic faith incarnated in diverse contexts should not lead to conflict but to the enrichment of the catholic nature of the one apostolic faith.

16. In fact, the common confession of the one apostolic faith, which has been a permanent concern in the ecumenical movement, is an essential condition and concrete expression of the koinonia we seek. The Faith and Order study document on *Confessing the One Faith* helped us to identify the degree of convergence in the explication of the apostolic faith. This process should continue with a new dynamism. We need to establish together a common criterion to discern the One Tradition present and operative in all traditions, and to recognize the ecumenical creed of Nicea-Constantinople (381) as normative for a common confession of apostolic faith. Such an attempt will enable the churches to identify the common roots of apostolic faith, and will lead them to take concrete steps towards a common confession of the one faith.

2. Eucharistic koinonia

17. As I pointed out earlier, the eucharist is the source and supreme manifestation of koinonia. Koinonia is, in fact, participation in the body and blood of Christ (1 Cor. 10:16). Eucharist and koinonia were so closely identified with each other in the early church that it was common to refer to the eucharist as koinonia and vice versa. Eucharistic communion with Christ also implies communion within the body of Christ. These two dimensions of koinonia condition each other. Those who partake of the one bread become one body; this is what constitutes the koinonia. The eucharist creates koinonia, its catholicity and unity: "For we being many are one bread, and one body; for we are all partakers of that one bread" (1 Cor. 10:17).

18. There are still serious obstacles on the way of full eucharistic koinonia. For many churches eucharistic koinonia is the ultimate expression of unity in faith. For others, however, eucharistic koinonia is possible when there is already a "partial" communion or theological agreement. There are also churches which encourage "interim eucharistic communion", "progressive communion", or "eucharistic hospitality" as a way of preparing the faithful for full eucharistic communion. I believe that the eucharistic vision of unity — which was forcefully introduced into the ecumenical debate by the Vancouver assembly — needs to be deepened further. I also believe that the BEM process is crucial for the "unity we seek" as well as for the future of the ecumenical movement. It must be given a primordial importance by our churches.

3. Conciliar koinonia

19. The church is also a conciliar koinonia based on the eucharistic koinonia. The full koinonia of the churches will be expressed through conciliar forms of common life and action on local and universal levels.[10] The local church is not a self-sufficient reality; local churches are related to each other at every place and at all times. Koinonia implies inter-relatedness and interdependence. A local church maintains its ecclesiality and catholicity in conciliar relationship with other local churches. *Com-*

munio ecclesiarum is the description of the real nature of the church. The universal (catholic) church is not a worldwide organization but a koinonia of local churches truly united. The one, holy, catholic and apostolic church is a koinonia of local churches: "There can be no churches (in the plural) except as manifestations of the one true church (in the singular)."[11] The churches can exist only as the one people of God, as one koinonia spread all over the world. If we lose the sense of our common belonging to the one koinonia of the Triune God, the one true church, if we conceive ourselves as churches and act as such, and not as manifestation of the *una sancta*, we become merely a federation of churches. The conciliar koinonia in its fullness and wholeness is expressed both locally and universally. It has no geographical centre of worldwide structure. It must be noted, however, that such an understanding of conciliar koinonia is strongly challenged by the Roman Catholic Church, which considers the Petrine office as the locus and guarantee of the conciliar koinonia of local churches.

20. Unity is a koinonia. The icon of the Trinity is the icon of unity: "That they may be one, as we are one" (John 17:11). Unity is participation in the koinonia of the Holy Trinity. Our understanding of unity has undergone a significant development in the WCC. The New Delhi statement on unity provided the framework for it. It is rooted in the Trinitarian koinonia of the Father, Son and Holy Spirit. It has not been lost but obscured due to historical divisions. Unity is "God's gift and our task". The church is called to make visible its essential unity through fellowship, witness and service.[12] New Delhi put the emphasis on "all in each place", Uppsala on "in all places and times".[13] Nairobi clarified the goal of unity by describing it as a "conciliar fellowship of local churches".[14] Canberra referred to unity as being a koinonia which is both a gift and a calling. This is where the churches stand in their quest for unity, in other words, between the unity that is given and the unity that is lost and to be restored.

21. In our discussion of unity we have gone through various stages: "call to unity", "seeking unity", "models of unity", "nature of unity", "taking steps towards unity". Canberra's offer of "koinonia" as the vision of the unity we seek can surely provide a good basis for further steps towards full visible unity. The goal of visible unity is realized when all the churches are able to consider themselves as belonging to one koinonia. Koinonia is the origin and goal of all models of unity as well as the nature of the unity we seek. The unity of the church as koinonia must acquire central attention in the unity discussion. The logical sequence and theological interaction that exist between the assemblies of the WCC on the question of unity point in this direction.

22. As I stated earlier, koinonia is rooted in the Trinitarian communion of God. The churches, in one way or another, to a larger or smaller degree, do share in this koinonia through the power of the Holy Spirit. In fact, koinonia is "a promising way to explain and express the incomplete but real communion that already exists between [our churches]".[15] The vision of koinonia also challenges the co-existence of the churches in their division. It makes the churches look beyond themselves to *the* church, the koinonia, and consider themselves as being simply expressions of the one church.

23. The following are the requirements for full koinonia set by Canberra: mutual recognition of baptism, common confession of faith, eucharistic communion, mutual recognition of ministries, common diakonia and witness, establishment of decision-making structures.[16] The churches differ on whether all these are necessary for the full koinonia of the church. For the Roman Catholic Church, these requirements are conditioned by communion with the Petrine office. Others consider full fellowship of

word and sacraments essential to express koinonia, and yet others maintain unity in faith as the sine qua non for eucharistic communion.

24. The co-existence of the churches — even if it is a peaceful, fraternal, ecumenical one — contradicts the very nature of the church which is a koinonia, i.e. a shared life and witness of sacramental nature. Therefore, on the one hand, we must *manifest* concretely and visibly the koinonia which is given and which we still maintain to some degree, and on the other hand, we must together struggle to *restore* the koinonia that is broken. Koinonia does not grow only through theological convergence but also through our participation in the suffering and joy of other members of the same family (1 Cor. 12:26).

IV. Koinonia: framework for the unity of humankind

25. The catholic and missiological nature of the eucharist makes koinonia reject self-sufficiency and opens it to the world. Eucharistic koinonia does not possess its own being as a self-perfected community. It exists from God for the world. It incorporates the whole of humanity and creation within its sacramental being and existence. Hence, unity as koinonia is not a goal for its own sake. It must be located in the context of the saving purpose of God for all humanity. It must result in martyria and diakonia in and for the world.

1. Church, humanity and creation in the perspective of the kingdom of God

26. It is now a common ecumenical affirmation that, in the perspective of the kingdom of God, the church, humanity and creation belong together. The eucharist-centred (Eastern) and natural law-centred (Western) concepts of the world came together in the ecumenical movement which has seen church-world-kingdom in a dynamic and creative interaction and in an eschatological perspective. But church and world are not identical. The church is distinct from the world by its very nature and its intrinsic relation to God. It is a reality which transcends its historical expressions: a reality rooted in, and constantly sustained and shaped by, the communion of the Father, the Son and the Holy Spirit.[17] The church is in the world witnessing for the fulfilment of God's plan; but it is not of the world (John 15:19). Only in the perspective of the kingdom do the church and the world appear in their eschatological togetherness and fulfilment. The purpose of God is to gather, in the power of the Holy Spirit, the whole of humanity and creation in Jesus Christ. Being in koinonia with God implies working for the renewal and reconciliation of humanity and the sustainability and integrity of creation. In eucharistic koinonia, the church, humanity and creation are united with the Triune God.

27. The church is a koinonia which looks beyond itself and participates in the reality of God's kingdom of which it is called to be the firstfruit. It is in the context of the understanding of the church as koinonia that, in the ecumenical movement, we came to speak about the church as the "sacrament" of God's saving work. A sacrament is both a "sign" and an "instrument". Koinonia is a sign that God's purpose is being realized in the world through the Christ event. It is also an instrument for the full realization of God's salvific plan for the world.

28. Unity and mission are interconnected dimensions of koinonia. Mission is not merely a function of koinonia — it is its very raison d'etre. The church has no mission. It participates in the *missio Dei*. God's will revealed in Jesus Christ calls the churches to common witness and service for the renewal of the world from its brokenness. The church as the prophetic sign of the kingdom should reflect the

values of the kingdom, living the life of martyria. It should work for a renewed and transfigured world and humanity, towards a world in which there is justice, peace, just economic relationships, and a common responsibility towards the poor and the marginalized.

29. The whole life of the church is a continuing Pentecost through the epiclesis (invocation) of the Holy Spirit by which the church goes beyond its "boundaries" and becomes a foretaste of the kingdom, an effective instrument for the renewal of humanity and a sign for the unity of humanity: "The church is called to live as that force within humanity through which God's will for the renewal, justice, community and salvation of all people is witnessed to."[18]

2. Koinonia as ferment for the unity of humankind

30. Koinonia refers primarily to the church, since it is based on participation in the life of the Trinity. But in a broader sense it can also be related to the whole of humanity, since human beings are created in the image of God and are thus called into communion with God. The unity of the church as koinonia concerns the whole oikoumene, since unity is not for the church as such but ultimately for the whole of humanity and creation. This is a basic teaching both in the New Testament and in the early church. Uppsala stated that the church is "the sign of the coming unity of mankind".[19] The church as koinonia is the ferment and framework of the communion of humanity and creation with God. The church is called to break down barriers and reconcile a broken humanity, to manifest koinonia through diakonia and martyria, and to point to the eschatological fullness of koinonia. Thus the church as reconciled and reconciling koinonia should express in its own life and mission God's purpose for humanity and creation.

31. The church is the new koinonia sent to the world. Therefore it must live and witness as that reality within humanity through which the koinonia of all people is realized. It must participate as mystery and prophetic sign in God's saving work for the whole creation. It must proclaim in word and deed the kingdom in and for this broken world, becoming the foretaste of the transformation and reconciliation of the world.

32. As the body of Christ, the church participates in the divine koinonia and lives and reveals it for the world, becoming the mystery and the ferment of the new koinonia of humanity in a new creation. Already as a broken koinonia, it experiences the consequences of the brokenness of the world. But the church, the bearer of the koinonia of the Triune God, has "God's forgiveness accomplished in Christ and the unity already given by Christ".[20] It has also the God-given mandate to heal the brokenness of the world and re-establish it in its integrity, wholeness and unity. Koinonia is the new creation (kaine ktisis) which strives to make present in creation the new life of the kingdom. The church is the sign — i.e. God's pointer — to what God's intention is for the world: to unite "all things" and people in Christ to him (Eph. 1:10, 3:5). The church as prophetic sign and messenger of God is called to incarnate the gospel in all cultures, to announce God's judgment and salvation (John 16:8-11) in Jesus Christ and to become the visible koinonia of a renewed and reconciled humanity and creation in God (John 11:24-25). Through the church as living koinonia with God, the saving and uniting grace of God is constantly manifested to all humanity and creation. The church has a special function in relation to the unifying purpose of God for the world. As sacrament, sign and instrument, it should serve as an example and ferment of the unity of mankind.

33. Koinonia and its unity are, therefore, instruments of God's plan of salvation for all humankind in Jesus Christ, of the coming unity of humanity in God's kingdom, the transformation of creation and the fulfilment of "all things". The unity of koinonia and the unity of humanity are inseparably linked as two dimensions of one unique divine economy in history: God redeeming the brokenness of the creation and bringing back "all things" into koinonia with him.

34. The eucharistic koinonia is the focus and image of the redeemed brokenness of the world, the transformed and reconciled humanity and the recreated creation. It is also the source through which the grace of God flows to the whole of humankind and creation, to establish, in the power of the Holy Spirit, a personal relationship with the whole creation. Hence, through eucharistic koinonia, God becomes Emmanuel, God with us and for the whole of humankind. In the eucharist we offer to God the whole creation in its brokenness and receive "all things" back anew. There is no duality or opposition between the ecclesial koinonia and the created order. The koinonia we seek is God's koinonia which is his gift to the world. "All things" are created out of love of God and are related to God. Thus there exists continuity, interaction and interdependence between the church and the world. The one eucharistic koinonia should become a reality, anticipating the one human Christocentric koinonia.

V. Koinonia: the context for a common understanding of the nature of the WCC

35. Koinonia also has decisive ecumenical implications for the common understanding of the nature and vision of the WCC. Koinonia is the basis of the WCC. The first article of the WCC's constitution states: "The WCC is a fellowship of churches..." *(koinonia ton ekklesion)*. This basis indicates the WCC's very nature and provides a point of orientation for its work. It is significant to note that the well-known encyclical of 1920 of the Ecumenical Patriarchate, speaking about the necessity of creating a fellowship of churches, stated that "fellowship (koinonia) between them" (i.e. churches) "is not excluded by the doctrinal differences between them".[21] Koinonia was repeatedly used at the time of the founding of the WCC, and more or less in all its assemblies, in the words of Visser 't Hooft "to restore that consciousness of partnership, solidarity and fraternity which belongs to the very essence of the Christian faith and which had been lost to such a large extent during the history of the churches".[22] The WCC is a concrete reminder of the brokenness of koinonia. Paradoxically, it is also a fellowship that holds the churches together in the midst of disunity. In the ecumenical fellowship, through common worship, theological convergence, shared witness and joint diakonia, the churches were able "to recognize a certain degree of communion already existing between them".[23] What is the nature and scope of the churches' togetherness in the World Council? How can we move forward towards the fullness of koinonia?

1. The WCC: a broken koinonia

36. The Toronto statement (1950) clearly describes, in both a positive and negative way, the nature and scope of the churches' fellowship in the WCC. The statement still remains crucial for the self-understanding of the WCC. But after forty-four years of a growing fellowship sustained by common prayer, common reflection and common vision, we must raise fundamental questions: What is the WCC? How do we understand and express the reality of our fellowship in the WCC? What are the implications of a church's membership in the WCC for its self-understanding? In other words, to come to a common understanding of the nature and implications of our

togetherness in the fellowship of the WCC emerges as a challenge which we must face realistically, honestly and courageously.

37. It is a plain fact that the churches in the WCC are not yet in full koinonia. The WCC is not the council of the church: it is a council of churches. However, the WCC has become more than a framework of churches' common witness, more than an association of churches. It has become a family, enhancing the process of the churches' growing togetherness and making the ecumenical fellowship a kind of participatory koinonia. This has been most vividly expressed in common worship, the common affirmation of one baptism, common diakonia and witness. It is also certified and manifested by the Council's Trinitarian basis which undergirds its whole life, work and thought. The Council has become a mode of being together, a pattern of reflecting and acting together, and a way of looking forward together. The koinonia character of the WCC has strongly challenged parochialism and isolation, and has enhanced the sense of belonging, togetherness and universality. It has questioned the co-existence of the churches alongside each other and has encouraged pro-existence, participation, relationship, mutuality, sharing and accountability. The WCC has become for the churches a spiritual "house" where they challenge and confront each other, dialogue with each other, enter together into convergence processes with each other, and reach consensus on many vital issues together. We have not yet succeeded in breaking down all the barriers that divide us. We are still far away from full and visible unity. The koinonia we have in the WCC is not the full koinonia the church is meant to have.

38. Looking at the WCC in the perspective of koinonia, one may identify at least three problems facing the Council:

a) There are growing trends in the Council — such as the multiplication of programme priorities and structures, bureaucratization of working styles, etc. — that make the WCC an organization for operation rather than a koinonia of participation. Simply put, much energy, time and finance are spent on programmatic activities rather than on koinonia-building. The WCC, however, is not a centre for programmes but a koinonia of the people of God, which deals with relationship-building, enhances growth, encourages togetherness and builds up the body of Christ.

b) The question of the "ecclesial" character of the WCC is raised repeatedly in the Council and in ecumenical circles. It posed a problem in the early years of the WCC: "The main problem is how one can formulate the ecclesiological implications of a body in which so many different conceptions of the church are represented."[24] This is still a major problem. In fact, the "mutual recognition" of the "elements of the true church"[25] never implies mutual full recognition or ascribing an ecclesial nature to the Council. It is also true that a fellowship, though a broken one, committed to one vision cannot be void of any ecclesial significance. What is, then, the nature and degree of the Council's "ecclesiality"? This is a debatable issue. Some see it in the work of the Council, namely as a functional rather than as a static reality. Others identify it in the goal of the Council. There are also churches which do not attach any ecclesial significance to the WCC.

Nikos Nissiotis reacts to this issue in the following way: "Everything that Christians are doing together has ecclesiological significance, but it depends on what kind of 'significance' we mean. If we understand by it that a *new* church with a new confessional background is about to come into being through this koinonia, then I disagree completely. To my mind, this represents exactly the opposite of the nature and purpose of this fellowship. But if we think that by this fellowship and its ecumenical dialogue the churches are coming to the realization that there is one church in unbroken continuity, then I agree that the koinonia of the churches has an ecclesiological significance and fulfills its main God-given task of being the instrument of the local churches who are trying to restore church unity by living and praying together."[26]

c) Our ecumenical koinonia is not based on a common ecclesiology, but on a common commitment to grow together towards "visible unity in one faith and in one eucharistic fellowship".[27] But there are major obstacles on the way. As I pointed out earlier, the churches have not yet taken concrete steps on the BEM reception process. The text *Confessing One Faith* has not yet found a significant echo in the life of the churches. Although the ecumenical movement has paved the way for some churches to enter into different forms of koinonia, we are still quite far from eucharistic koinonia — the full and ultimate manifestation of koinonia. Nevertheless, our fellowship in the WCC has an ecclesiological bearing on the life and witness of the churches. In fact, the self-understanding of the WCC as a broken koinonia gives to the member churches a greater awareness of being intimately and inseparably inter-related in their very being, and of belonging to each other and to the one church of God.

2. Towards fullness of koinonia

39. Koinonia also depicts the goal of our pilgrimage together in the ecumenical movement. It is a false dichotomy to separate the nature of koinonia from the vision of it. The common vision of the WCC is the sustaining power of all that the WCC is and does. Its nature and work are conditioned by its vision. It is our common vision that brings about the koinonia and gives content and meaning to it. The WCC is a reminder of the brokenness of the body of Christ, and a challenge to grow towards full koinonia. The koinonia for which the Council stands is a unique koinonia in Jesus Christ and not an undefined conception of koinonia. The very nature of the WCC's vision, which is ecumenical, worldwide, reconciling and prophetic, makes it a growing koinonia. The reality of the WCC's being one family, one household, must remain the driving force of the Council's work. We must never be tempted to think of the WCC as a definite answer to the problem of disunity. The WCC is not the model of koinonia. It represents only "an emergency solution — a stage on the road".[28] It is still far from its goal. It is a provisional reality and still a pre-eucharistic and pre-conciliar koinonion on the road towards full koinonia.

40. The comprehensive and critical assessment of the nature of our ecumenical fellowship that we have started within the WCC should not be a one-time effort but an ongoing process. But "all these endeavours will remain fruitless unless every Christian community commits itself to live out the koinonia that has at its heart the mystery of the cross of Christ. This involves constant conversion to an authentic life in koinonia marked by acts of forgiveness and reconciliation."[29]

VI. Final remarks

41. There is now more or less common agreement that the key issue facing the ecumenical movement is ecclesiology.[30] Undoubtedly koinonia will emerge as a major and priority item on the agenda of the WCC in the years ahead. I fully agree with Cardinal Willebrands when he says that "the deepening... of an ecclesiology of

communion is... perhaps the greatest possibility for tomorrow's ecumenism".[31] I do hope that the fifth world conference on Faith and Order with its koinonia-centred theme will open new perspectives, provide new insights and give a new stimulus to the ecclesiology of communio.

42. But the question remains as valid as ever: How can the churches become an instrument of human koinonia when they cannot unite in eucharistic koinonia? How can they work for the renewal and reconciliation of humankind and anticipate the coming kingdom of God when they themselves are still divided? The Holy Spirit is the promoter of koinonia. He breaks down the barriers and creates, restores and sustains koinonia. He calls us to acknowledge, to live and to manifest the unity that exists among us. He "comforts us in pain, disturbs us when we are satisfied to remain in our division, leads us to repentance, and grants us joy when our communion flourishes".[32]

NOTES

[1] *Baptism, Eucharist and Ministry*, Geneva, WCC, 1982, pp.2-3.

[2] Cf. *ibid.*, *op. cit.*, pp.14-15; "Dogmatic Constitution on the Church", in *Documents of Vatican II*, ed. W.M. Abbott, New York, Geoffrey Chapman, 1966.

[3] It is worth reading the findings of the El Escorial consultation on sharing in this particular perspective. Cf. *Sharing Life*, ed. H. van Beek, Geneva, WCC, 1989.

[4] *Signs of the Spirit*, official report of WCC seventh assembly, Canberra, ed. M. Kinnamon, Geneva, WCC, and Grand Rapids, USA, Eerdmans, 1991, pp.97-98.

[5] *Ibid.*, p.173.

[6] J.M.R. Tillard, *Eglise d'Eglises*, Paris, Cerf, 1987, p.401.

[7] *Signs of the Spirit, op. cit.*, p.173.

[8] *Ibid.*

[9] *Confessing the One Faith*, Geneva, WCC, 1991, pp.2-3.

[10] *Signs of the Spirit, op. cit.*, p.173.

[11] *Gathered for Life*, official report of WCC sixth assembly, Vancouver, Canada, ed. D. Gill, Geneva, WCC, 1983, p.45.

[12] *A Documentary History of the Faith and Order Movement (1927-1963)*, ed. L. Vischer, St Louis, MI, Bethany Press, 1964, pp.144-150.

[13] *The Uppsala Report*, official report of WCC fourth assembly, ed. N. Goodall, Geneva, WCC, 1968, p.17.

[14] *Breaking Barriers: Nairobi 1975*, official report of WCC fifth assembly, ed. D.M. Paton, Geneva, WCC, 1976, p.60.

[15] *Joint Working Group between the Roman Catholic Church and the World Council of Churches: Sixth Report*, Geneva, WCC, 1990, p.30.

[16] *Signs of the Spirit, op. cit.*, p.174.

[17] *Church and World*, Geneva, WCC, 1990, p.26.

[18] *Ibid.*, p.23.

[19] *The Uppsala Report, op. cit.*, p.17.

[20] *Church and World, op. cit.*, p.25.

[21] *The Orthodox Church in the Ecumenical Movement*, ed. C.G. Patelos, Geneva, WCC, 1978, p.40.

[22] W.A. Visser 't Hooft, "The WCC as Koinonia and as Institution", *Mid-Stream*, vol. 23, 1984, p.146.

[23] *Signs of the Spirit, op. cit.*, p.173.

[24] "The Church, the Churches and the World Council of Churches", in *A Documentary History of the Faith and Order Movement (1927-1963), op. cit.*, pp.168-169.

[25] *Ibid.*, p.174.

[26] N. Nissiotis, "The Types and Problems of Ecumenical Dialogue", *The Ecumenical Review*, vol. XVIII, no. 1, 1966, p.48.

[27] "Constitution and Rules of the WCC", in *Signs of the Spirit, op. cit.*, p.358.

[28] W.A. Visser 't Hooft, *The Genesis and Formation of the World Council of Churches*, Geneva, WCC, 1982, p.90.

[29] "Towards Koinonia in Faith, Life and Witness", draft of a working document, WCC, Faith and Order, 1992, p.32.

[30] It was only after the completion of this report that I saw the recent "Letter to the Bishops of the Catholic Church on Some Aspects of the Church Understood as Communion" by the Vatican's Congregation for the Doctrine of the Faith. It is significant to note that this letter, which is to a large extent the reaffirmation of the teachings of Vatican II, considers the concept of koinonia as "a key to ecclesiology" and "at the heart of the church's self-understanding". However, its definitions of local-universal church and the Petrine office remain unacceptable to non-Catholics. Cf. *L'Osservatore Romano* (English version), 17 June 1992, pp.7-10.

[31] Cardinal J. Willebrands, "The Future of Ecumenism", *One in Christ*, vol. 11, 1975, p.323.

[32] *Signs of the Spirit, op. cit.*, p.174.

The Eucharist as the Sacrament of Sharing: An Orthodox Point of View

Gennadios Limouris

I. The eucharist as the sacrament in, for and through the church

As the locus of an ever-renewed Pentecost, the glorified humanity of Christ comes to us in the sacraments of the church — or rather the church is in the deepest sense nothing other than the sacrament of the risen Christ.[1] The church as eucharist is the hidden intention — "under a veil" — of the risen Christ drawing all things towards him in order to restore them to life permanently. At the same time, God expects a free and creative response by humankind: hence the veiled mystery of Easter can only be revealed through the cooperation (synergia) of the Holy Spirit and our freedom. Within each baptized person lies hidden the divine life, the "Spirit" (pneuma) at the "heart" of his or her personal existence that is the integrating centre of the total human person and hence the organ that permits a form of knowledge in the Spirit in which justice, beauty and love are inseparable. By a gradual process of acquiring roots both in communion with the One who alone is holy and with the communion of saints, this knowledge develops in the individual and he or she — instead of living in separateness and death — will live in the Spirit, for "that which is born of the Spirit is spirit" as Christ says in St John's Gospel (3:6).

The body of Christ is a "spiritual" body, i.e. one that is contained in the Holy Spirit, a body of light and fire: the eucharist is "fire and Spirit" in the words of an old Syriac saying. By a long process that will be identical with that of our life itself — in its underlying patterns of initiation, its "descents into hell" and "returns to paradise", its rejoicings, follies, ecstasies, sufferings, renunciations, transcendences, deaths and resurrections — we gradually unify our consciousness and our "heart", we gradually reconstitute in the grace of the Spirit that "understanding heart" in which there will be cross-fertilization and peace between soul and body and between the conscious and the unconscious, a heart that can faithfully reflect the true visage of one's neighbour as if superimposed on the image of the risen Christ. When it has looked down into the "abyss of the heart" this consciousness will expand — in the sphere of the Holy Spirit — to the utmost limits of humanity and of the universe and offer everything to God who is simultaneously the circumference and the centre and at the same time infinitely beyond them. This experience of the Spirit is not something extraordinary or reserved for mystics. It is offered to all. It is that hidden light, that opening to infinity in the opaqueness of daily life, of which everyone has a presentiment as soon as one's heart of stone begins to become a heart of the flesh. A mother smiling at her child, a genuine love that rends your heart, so that a face and a body make you aware of the immensity of life and death, the patient struggle to share bread and joy among all — all these

● This paper was published in *The Ecumenical Review*, vol. 38, no. 4, October 1986, when the Rev. Dr Gennadios Limouris was on the staff of the WCC's Commission on Faith and Order.

things are already experience of the Spirit. The very fact of existing, walking and breathing is, if we live with attention and gratitude, already an experience of the eucharistic mystery of sharing.

Every sacrament in the Orthodox Church is an event[2] *in* the church, *for* the church and *through* the church. It is incompatible with any atomization that would isolate the act and those who receive and share it.[3] Every sacrament has effects on the whole body and on all the faithful. Baptism is a new birth — a "rebirth"[4] — in the church which is enriched by every new member. Sacramental absolution "restores" the penitent to the church. The married couple above all accede to the ecclesiastical *synaxis* with the dignity of conjugal priesthood. The consecration of a bishop makes him the witness to the eucharist. And in the eucharist, all are united in the koinonia of one and the same Spirit. Thus, "every sacrament moves beyond the individual towards his or her catholic resonance, and the gifts conferred are made manifest for all since, ultimately, it is in the eucharist that the church bears witness to the descent of the Holy Spirit and to all the gifts received for sharing with others in the communion". This is the reason why, in the practice of the early church, every sacrament was an organic part of the eucharistic liturgy that set the final seal on what is given and what is received. According to Pseudo-Dionysius, transmitting a tradition already accepted during the first centuries of the church, the eucharist is not one sacrament among others but is the *sacrament of sacraments (teleton telete).*[5] This fundamental definition lies at the source of Orthodox ecclesiology. It means that the eucharist is not a sacrament *in the church* but is the sacrament *of the church* itself; it constitutes, manifests and expresses the essence of the church. Hence, in the East, the word "liturgy" by itself (joint work of the people) always refers to the eucharistic celebration.

As sacrament and worship, essence and expression of the church, communion and sharing, the eucharist has over the centuries exerted also a powerful refining and educational influence, above all by making men and women pre-eminently liturgical beings, the "new creature" who says with the Psalmist: "I will sing to the Lord as long as I live" (Ps. 104:33), a *living eucharist.* According to St Paul, the liturgy corresponds to God's wishes: the faithful are set apart according to the pre-established plan... (as) a people whom God has appointed "to live for the praise of his glory" (Eph. 1:11-14).

Moreover, the church fathers in their commentary on the passages of the Revelation of St John (4 and 5) see it as the image of the kingdom under the form of the eucharist of the future age. Hence, the constitution of the church on the day of Pentecost is immediately followed by the full revelation in the apostles' breaking of bread (Acts 2:46) so that in fact the very lives of the faithful immediately become eucharistic in character: "All who believed were together and had all things in common" (Acts 2:44). Through the Bread of Life — Christ — his disciples are changed into that same bread, that same love, into a particle of the "body of God" in the expression used by St John Chrysostom. And here, it may be said, is the essence of Christianity: the triune mystery of God's life becomes the mystery of human life, "so that they may all be one as we are one" (John 17:22). It is in the eucharist that this priestly prayer of Christ is received by the church, shared not only with his disciples but with all the faithful, men and women, down to our own day in our human, theological and fraternal relations within the movement of charity — ecumenism. The eucharist is thus a receiving and a doxological sharing of the Word made flesh (John 1:1): "Now the powers of heaven united with us adore invisibly. Here comes the King of Glory, here comes the mysterious sacrifice who offers himself. Let us draw near in faith and love, we are participants in eternal life."[6]

Everything is there: the fullness is such "that one can go no further nor add anything",[7] exclaims the great liturgist of the fourteenth century, Nicolas Cabasilas. The biblical sap of the Word, the definitions of dogma of the Councils, all the contemplative theology of the fathers are wonderfully synthesized and represented on the sacred stage of the temple: "the recapitulation of the whole economy of salvation" in the words of Theodore Studites,[8] "the cup of the synthesis" in the beautiful expression of St Irenaeus.[9]

II. The living eucharist

The ontological relation of the Logos to his humanity is matched by the dynamic relation of the Holy Spirit. The Spirit deifies the humanity of Jesus and alights upon him as unction and Dove. In a commentary on the epiklesis (invocation of the Spirit upon the faithful), St Maximus the Confessor takes the same dynamic approach: "All of us who share in the same bread and in the same cup are united with each other in communion with the one Holy Spirit." The communion with God is directly projected in the human sphere and that is what has been called the "sacrament of the brother". St Cyril of Alexandria stresses the physical unity produced by the "mystical blessing" as between the faithful, the *union of natures*.[10] One can even say that the eucharist is, as it were, a transcendent support for all social activity when the latter is directed towards the qualitative unity of all mankind.

The faithful are "Christified" and, according to St John Chrysostom,[11] the communicants are made "like lions" symbolic of invincible power. Cabasilas says that "by a veritable transfer of deifying energy the mud is transformed into the substance of the King".[12] The connaturality between Christ and those who partake of his "holy flesh" conditions the global efficiency of the eucharist, the somatic element being closely associated with the spiritual element. The communicants become "of one body and blood" with Christ, sharing in the divine nature according to St Cyril of Jerusalem,[13] and St Maximus emphasizes the theosis: "The eucharist transforms the faithful into itself and makes them like itself... so that the faithful may be called 'gods' because the whole of God wholly fills them."[14]

A eucharist communion prayer indicates the correct attitude: "I know that neither the magnitude of my faults nor the host of my transgressions surpass the infinite tenderness and immense love of my God for mankind.... In joy and trembling I receive the fire... as once the bush burned without being consumed." But the best form of thanksgiving — as St Ignatius of Antioch[15] reminds us — is the attitude of a martyr when the human being "ground between the teeth of the animals" is transformed into "the bread of Christ" agreeable to the Lord: "The heart absorbs the Lord and the Lord absorbs the heart".[16] "By partaking of the flesh of the Bridegroom and of his blood we enter the nuptial koinonia," says Theodoret of Cyrrhus.[17]

The communion established by the eucharist is with the whole of the body. In the case of the dead, it presupposes a very mysterious mode of participation by souls that are momentarily separated from their bodies. Here, nothing precise can be said and one can only quote the words of Cabasilas: "So there is nothing surprising if Christ enables souls freed from their bodies to participate. What is extraordinary and supernatural is that a human being living in corruption should be able to feed on incorruptible flesh. But what would be surprising about an immortal participating in immortal food in a way appropriate to him?"[18]

Nevertheless, the eucharistic communion embraces both the divine and the human, the living and the dead, the aeon of history. It guides the destiny of the world towards the glorious return of the Bride of the Lamb in the koinonia of the trinitarian love, a eucharist of the kingdom perpetuated world without end.

Thus, the world was created as a "dynamism" of celebration for participation in the grace of God and becoming eucharist through human offering. And this is what Christ, the definitive Adam, has brought about. Through his death and resurrection the universe has entered the realm of glory. It is this transfigured modality of the creation that is offered to us in the eucharist so that we too may be associated in the work of resurrection. "The bread of the communion", says St John Damascene, "is not mere bread but bread united with the divinity"[19] not through a new process of incarnation but through becoming part of the Body of Christ. The bread and the wine are transformed into the Body and Blood of Christ and thereby made complete, fulfilled and transfigured in accordance with their originally intended purpose.

III. The trinitarian existentiality of the eucharist

The eucharist in the Spirit through the Son is a theocentric movement that carries us upwards towards the unfathomable abyss of the Father. The liturgical worship is a call to participate in the epiphany.[20] Thus, we participate in God's boundless love for humanity and are given a genuine trinitarian existentiality.

Becoming one with Christ, the faithful become "members of one another". St Paul's expression *en soma*, one body, is clearly eucharistic in origin (1 Cor. 10:17). The members form a body in which God's life flows into humankind.

In Christ, Christians are not only united; they are ontologically one (consubstantial). The great Russian theologian, V. Lossky,[21] believes that, in the nuptial encounter with their Lord and the variety of flames of Pentecost, each of the human hypostases is an absolute, destined to give a single face to this Christified human nature: "The unity of the Body presupposes by reason of its completeness a harmonization of the human hypostases... The Pentecost story clearly indicates that the grace rested on each personally... Within the unity of Christ, the spirit diversifies... But the two are inseparable: Christ is manifested by the Holy Spirit and the Spirit communicates through Christ. 'Given drink by the Spirit, we drink Christ.'"[22]

Thus, the eucharist establishes the communion of saints in the communion of the consecrated bread and wine. Bypassing the difference between the individual and the collective, eucharistic existence is an existence in communion in which there is a correspondence between personal diversity and ontological unity reflecting that of the Trinity in accordance with an ontology of the mystery. "The triune mystery of the divine life becomes the mystery of human life: that they may be one even as we are one. It is in the eucharist that this priestly prayer of Christ is received by the Church."[23]

"Man is in the image of the triune God; in his nature the church-communion represents the ultimate truth. All men and women are called to gather around the one and only cup, to lift it up to the level of the sacred heart, to participate in the messianic meal and become one Temple-Lamb."[24]

The Christian East has too great a sense of mystery to try to "explain" the eucharist. The fathers of the church equate the bread with the body, the wine with the blood, referring always to the "pneumatic" humanity of Christ, to his body "transfigured and deified by the Holy Spirit". S. Boulgakov was particularly fond of saying that there is a eucharistic dogma in the theology of the eucharist.[25]

Moreover, the eucharistic miracle, the transformation *(metabole)* of the bread and wine into the Body and Blood of Christ is not "physical" like that at Cana but is in the full sense of the term "metaphysical". The bread and wine are "projected" beyond the bounds of this world, and the Body and Blood of Christ, as a "celestial" state of being, are solely an object of faith — the vision of the invisible — until the evidence of the "spiritual sense" develops in us.

The fathers of the church also speak, however, of a cosmology of the glorified body. The world was created as a "dynamism" of participation and sharing in order to become the eucharist in the offering of men and women. The world secretly transfigured is thus the body of the glory of the Lord — "a state in which the Spirit possesses the energies of the corporality".

IV. The eucharist as the centre of worship life

In human life there is no one moment that is capable of expressing the whole of a person's existence. One's life is a whole that has many aspects. The same is true of the life of the church. For human beings the fact of eating is as important as that of knowing others, communicating with them, reflecting on the past and future of this world and on what is happening, and wondering whether anything occurs after death. All that is part of life, and the same applies to the church. The life of the church cannot be envisaged from a single aspect. One cannot speak of its life without speaking of its worship and sacraments, its theology, spirituality and ethics. The only difference is that in the church, if one properly examines the different manifestations of its life, one finds that there is always a central element, a point of departure which is also a point of arrival, a centre that is the cause of its existence, namely the eucharist.

The fathers, and particularly St John Chrysostom, knew that the eucharistic communion involves the "sacrament of the poor", "the sacrament of the brother", which means sharing and pooling for the welfare of all, since the earth belongs to God and nobody, whether an individual, a nation or a culture, is the outright owner of its goods.[26] Hence the Christian is aware of the daily problems and solves them in accordance with what one lives in relation to the eucharist.

Worship, theology, spiritual and moral life are united at one point of the eucharist. If ever this link between the different domains of the church ceased to exist, the church would cease to exist. "The eucharist is the centre of all life in the church."[27] It is the essential item for the continued life of the church. Christ is present in the eucharist, and to abandon the eucharist would mean to lose the presence of Christ. A church without Christ cannot be a church. It is true that we have need of a plurality in the church but that must not lead us to forget the essential. Any "blindness" in the church can only lead to dangers that must be avoided at all costs. If the eucharist continues to be the true centre of the church's life, there are grounds for hope of a living church for the future.

Moreover, the communion (koinonia) is a vital element in the sacramental experience of the church. On this point Hans Küng's idea that the sacraments are the high points in the sanctification of Christian life seems extremely relevant. However, S. Boulgakov considered — long before Hans Küng — that all the sacraments (the importance of the precise number should not be exaggerated) are manifestations of a single sacrament of the church, the body of Christ. Similarly, Edouard Schillebeeckx considers that all the sacraments lead us towards Christ, who is the only true sacrament of God's presence in humanity.

Hence, the concept of koinonia with Christ and with the church which is his body, is present in all the church's ceremonies. If the latter are to be a true manifestation of the nature of the church, they must always be sacramental to some degree. If the eucharist unites humankind with its Creator, it is also true that it unites the communicant, the participant in this mystery, with his or her brothers and sisters. By drinking from the same cup and feeding on the same heavenly bread, the faithful become brothers and sisters in the same mystical family. On the one side, we have deification (theosis) as a result of the union of humanity with divinity, and on the other we have the fraternity or community of the eucharist. The spirit of fraternalization originates in baptism with our incorporation in the new Adam. The centre of this nucleus in which men and women consolidate the daring task of fraternal love (agape) and sharing in the same faith is pre-eminently in the eucharist.

The church fathers in their theology took every opportunity of developing the sacramental sense: the eucharist creates a bond in charity and love through the sharing of communion among the faithful. In their writings we find many profound expositions of the effects of that love in all facets of day-to-day social life. The role of the sacraments is not the performance of a ritual formality, and neither the church nor the faithful are entitled to see it in this way. By being promoted to one of the "faithful" a Christian must open his or her heart and possessions so that others may share.

Dionysius the Great writes: "Most of our brethren, inspired by an overflowing charity for their brothers, without thought of themselves, have devoted themselves entirely to others. Without fearing contagion, they have gone to visit the sick and served them with devotion, have cared for them in Jesus Christ and have died with them in joy. They have taken upon themselves the illness of their neighbours and voluntarily contracted their infirmity. And there have been many who, after caring for and healing others, have perished themselves taking on themselves the death destined for others."[28]

V. The eucharist as the bond of human fellowship

We regard the church as united by faith, as a union of all in one life, as a cosmic whole on the model of the union of the three Persons in the Holy Trinity. This union manifests itself *in* love and *through* love and is effected by taking part in the one holy life of the church. At celebrations of the eucharist, we see how moral practice is linked to dogma and vice versa. In the words of the church during the eucharist: "Let us love one another so that we can communicate in the same spirit."

To the eyes of faith, this unity of the church is not an external unity like that of secular unions found in all human communities, but the mysterious beginning of life. The whole of humanity is life in Christ, men and women are the bodies of a single vine, members of a single body. Each individual human life expands infinitely to become the life of others, as community of saints. Each human being in the church lives for the whole of humanity which has become a church. Each man and woman says like Terence: "I am a man and nothing human is alien to me."

As we know, the natural climate in which the faithful maintain and share their spirituality is by living *in* the church and *with* the church, life with brothers and sisters as in a real family. A Christian risks losing his or her integrity if he or she lives apart from this atmosphere of the mystical community. The epistle to the Hebrews already gave this warning: "Let us hold fast... not neglecting to meet together, as is the habit of some, but encouraging one another" (Heb. 10:23-25).

As long as we participate in the eucharistic assemblies, we preserve the mystery of the flock. When we neglect them, we are like the sheep wandering away from the others and expose ourselves to enemies setting pitfalls for us, as pastoral practice confirms. While the flock as a whole may be attacked, it will not be taken unawares and will resist more effectively. Participation in the eucharist does not require us to be perfect beforehand, since this would imply that salvation depends on the value of the individual and would no longer be a free gift of God. The only condition for receiving communion is faith in one holy catholic and apostolic church, and a conscious commitment to an unceasing struggle against the separatist forces of Satan in order to achieve a disinterested love of one's neighbour.

Hence, the communion is not a reward for pious feelings, a fast or any other circumstances giving rise to a degree of self-satisfaction. It is a true "gift" from God to the body of Christ whose members are assembled to meet him. It is not therefore a personal event: the body and blood of Christ are offered as an essential nourishment for us all and a defence against the separatist forces of the devil. "Let us all join together who have shared in the same bread and drunk from the same cup in a single communion of the Holy Spirit."[29] Hence, by the combined power of life and love, the destructive forces of death are held at bay far away from the body of Christ.

The boundaries of the body of Christ depend entirely on the eucharistic life. Outside that life, humanity is ruled by alien powers. Separation and destruction can only be averted by those who unite in Christ and prepare themselves for the joint assembly of the eucharist.

We find such "fraternization" in the mystical explanation of Pseudo-Dionysius where, in an analysis of the structure of the eucharist, he stresses its social significance and its influence on communicants: "This is why the term 'assembly' is used to refer to any liturgical practice which unites our separate lives in a unifying theosis and, by the godly gathering of the separated parts, gives us communion and union with the whole... Jesus has for our welfare brought about the union which is to bind us to him; he has raised our humble nature by mingling it with his divinity and associating us as members of his body in full accordance with his holy and pure life... If we rise towards union with him, we must ensure that our lives according to the flesh are raised towards his divine life by making it like his in innocence and achieving a way of behaving in conformity with God. This is the way in which we can bring about an all-round conformity with the divine model."[30]

In Hezychius of Jerusalem we find the other aspect, namely the elevation of human nature towards deification (theosis). Human perfection is attained in and through the liturgy according to its asceticism and eucharistic spirituality: "When we have, in spite of our unworthiness, been judged worthy of the pure and divine mysteries of Christ, our God and great and mighty King, let us display more temperance, more moderation of spirit and more strictness so that the divine fire (the Body of our Lord Jesus Christ) will forgive our faults and our blemishes great and small. When he enters us, he immediately drives out of our hearts the evil prompting of ill-naturedness, he forgives the sins that we have committed and the mind is undisturbed by bad thoughts. And since we then keep watch over our minds and hearts, when we are again judged worthy, he enlightens our minds increasingly and the divine body gives them the brilliance of the stars."[31]

The very hymns sung during matins (orthros) or the communion repeatedly emphasize our duty to love and regard our neighbour as brother or sister who, baptized in the same baptismal font and eating the same mystical food, deserves to be loved in the fullness of our hearts and to be treated as an image of God, a co-heir to the treasures of heaven.

The peak of this "fraternization" is in the Easter liturgy. All the chants exalt mutual love, the exchange of the holy kiss and the joy of sharing the great event of Easter. The Easter homily of St John Chrysostom calls for universal brotherhood: "Enter all of you into the joy of our Lord. Whether the first or the least, may ye receive your reward. Rich and poor, dance a round together... Let us embrace each other in joy."

VI. The eucharist as the mainspring of peace in a divided world

The ancient world too suffered from wars and the catastrophic consequences of war and disorder in human life. During the first centuries of the church, people were very conscious of the lack of peace, and the prayers reflected this and stressed peace. This is noticeable, for example, in the deacon's intercession in the Orthodox divine liturgy. At the beginning of the divine liturgy, we are asked to pray for peace or the coming and maintenance of peace. We are constantly reminded to be peaceful. The many exhortations and blessings of the priest emphasize peace. "May the peace of heaven reign among us." We are reminded again of peace in the people's offering (anaphora): "Let us stand up in respect and with fear; let us be attentive in offering in peace the holy oblation." So many times the deacon addresses us with a reference to peace: "Again and again let us pray to the Lord in peace... Let us beg the Lord to grant us an angel of peace... So that our lives may end in peace and repentance... May he grant us that our days may end in a Christian manner without shame, pain, reproach and in peace." Moreover, the deacon indicates the attitudes and deep feelings that should accompany the prayer. Peace is the primordial condition. "Peace be with you all." Firstly, towards God by reconciling oneself with God; to cease to be an enemy of God or a rebel, but to be a faithful child of the heavenly Father. Secondly, peace with one's neighbour near or far. This peace was a vital need in the volcanic ancient world. Peace was the dream, the longing in the broken hearts of that world, as expressed by Euripides. Peace is also our hope for today.

St Cyril of Alexandria tells us that Christians must be reminded of their duty to begin and end their prayers in a feeling of total peace in order to contribute to peace in this world: "In the holy assemblies especially — that is, in the eucharistic gatherings — from the moment when the mystery begins, we too say to each other the words: 'peace to all' (eirene pasin) with which Christ risen from the dead greeted his disciples, thus leaving a rule for the children of the Church."[32]

St Cyril of Jerusalem in his catechism gives a detailed analysis of the words "catholicity" and peace. "The Church is called 'catholic' because it extends everywhere to the ends of the earth; because it teaches catholically and exactly all the dogmas that mankind must know and that relate to things visible and invisible, heavenly and earthly; because it heals everywhere every sin committed in thought or act; because it has a deep understanding of virtue by its words, works and spiritual gifts."[33] In the light of these four statements of St Cyril we can measure the splendid generality of the term "catholic church".

From the beginning, the church has shown itself to be a universal, catholic church. We are all brothers and sisters. All human beings, of whatever colour or race, are called to worship God the Father and to be saved by God's Son. This is the foundation of the Christian feeling of human community and sharing.

The Christian is not and cannot be an isolated individual, nor can he or she escape responsibility towards others. A Christian must realize that he or she belongs to the great human family of which God is the Father. The destiny of the world, the fate of nations cannot be of indifference to a Christian.

Hence, we take responsibility for what happens in the world today and for what will happen tomorrow. We are responsible for our brothers and sisters. In our fragile hands we carry the future of the whole of humanity.

This solidarity will not be completely fulfilled until it has become deeply rooted in every Christian's consciousness, until we are all convinced of belonging to a "catholic" church, until we recognize that we are all members of one another so that if one is suffering the others are also suffering. This feeling of membership is not simply a characteristic of each individual, it is an eminently social characteristic applying to all: a Christian must realize that he or she belongs to others as others belong to him or her. St Maximus the Confessor says on this point: "The church transforms spiritually men, women and children who differ widely in their nature, language, culture, race and mode of living... It stamps all of them with the face of God. It gives to all without distinction a unique, indestructible value that obliterates the many, deep differences. Thus, all unite and develop in a genuinely catholic manner. In the church no one is separated from the community, all are so to speak amalgamated with each other through the single indivisible operation of the faith."[34]

St Augustine, profoundly struck by the great mystery of the church's universal unity that not only embraces all human beings but also unites them to form the people of God, exclaims: "Thou unitest citizens, nations and even the whole of humanity by faith in the unity of our origin so that all become brothers and sisters."[35]

The catholic character of the church is not a figure of speech. Apart from embracing all nations and all manifestations of life, the church embraces all times since it unites the faithful of all ages, past, present and future.

What is the real significance of this union of Christians of all times in the church? When we become members of the mystic body, we cease to be dependent on our own efforts as individuals in loving, understanding and serving God but are joined with those of others, from the Holy Mother of God to the most pitiable of lepers (adelphoi elachistoi) who in their disfigurement also praise God in the eucharist. The whole of the visible and invisible creation (kosmos), the whole of time (kairos) past, present and future, and the spiritual treasury of the saints — all this is ours. We are probably conscious of being the descendants of the martyrs, but we tend to forget that each of us has in the words of one of our great poets "the blood of heroes" in our veins. We should not forget that we are in communion with the apostles and with the early church whenever we share in the Mysteries. To believe otherwise would be a sad deviation. Since we live together, we must be saved together. As a modern writer has said: "A Christian is saved as part of a group." The traditional view is thus more up-to-date than it ever was.

A number of patristic writings have indicated the liturgical role of the congregation in communion with the Holy Spirit. In praising God, each individual is united with others in charity. It is the whole church that praises, worships and glorifies God. The proclamation of the faith is not, in this view, the expression of an intellectual formula but an act of mutual love. The kiss of peace as a rite in the eucharist has a profound meaning, as Cyril of Jerusalem pointed out: "Let us embrace and kiss each other. Do not imagine that this is like the kiss exchanged between friends who meet in the market-place. It is not that kind of kiss. It is a kiss that unites two souls and abolishes all resentment. It is the sign of a union of souls. That is why the Lord said: If you are offering your gift at the altar, and there remember that your brother has something against you, first be reconciled to your brother, and then come and offer your gift" (Matt. 5:23-24).[36]

This brings us to one of the most distinctive features of Orthodox spirituality. Its worship and liturgical ethos does not essentially consist of particular rites or a particular tradition. The whole liturgy expresses the anthropology and even the theology of Orthodoxy. This is apparent from the spirit of the ceremonies themselves. The gestures for the most part hinge on a fraternal attitude coupled with a display of frequently repeated ceremonial acts. Above all this is the unity of all that is visible — the cosmos — and invisible in a communion of love by the Holy Spirit.[37]

Therefore the eucharist gives particular emphasis to the transformation of the whole creation *(demiourgia)*. United with him, the first-born of many, the members of the mystic Body offer themselves with love and adoration to the Father "for all the world and on behalf of all the world".

A liturgy inspired by this spirit and possessing a captivating external form cannot fail to influence morals and produce radical change in daily social life. What is more, this spirit can become localized: it is backed up by "reception centres": the family home and the parish community. Each church is a home around Christ our brother, in the house of the heavenly Father. St Athanasius defines the church as "the act of coming together".[38]

VII. Sharing — intercommunion or eucharistic hospitality

To clear the ground for an objective study, the notion of sharing in its eucharistic meaning leads us to two other concepts that are currently much discussed within the ecumenical movement. In the first place, an obstacle that is psychological in character must be removed. Rather than having a positive desire to take communion outside their own church, many Christians today feel obliged to contest the canonical and doctrinal constraints which they feel to be arbitrary.

a) The dilemma

The insistence on interconfessional eucharistic communion puts one in a dilemma. By dissociating the witness of faith and the sacrament in the eucharistic action that is the hallmark of ecclesial unity, one tends either to devalue the witness of faith as an essential factor in unity or to devalue the sacramental action of the eucharist so that it loses its specific meaning which is essentially governed by the requirements of ecclesial unity.

Some will say that, if we can pray together and share communal love in joint prayer which is the communication between brothers and sisters, why could we not communicate sacramentally together? However, one wonders in this case why people are seeking to make the eucharist, which is the sign and the pledge of eschatological unity, into a mere symbol of ecumenical good will. Are not our prayers adequate to bring us together? They are prayers to our Father that unite us through sharing as God's people *(laos tou Theou)*. The love in our hearts manifests itself in prayer as expressing the union of our hearts in the same faith in him who suffered for our sake. This prayer of the heart becomes the cross and resurrection of our daily lives. But let us remember our brothers and sisters in Africa, the poor in Latin America, the martyrs in Cyprus and Lebanon, the quarrelling brothers and sisters in Northern Ireland and those resistance fighters in the birth-pangs of liberty for peace and justice. Our sharing in prayer becomes worldwide, it does not belong to us; it is without limits and frontiers. The poor in Latin America and the martyr in the Near East are associated with this *perichoresis* (coherence) of the prayer of the heart. It is the ecumenical instrument of our sharing, a sharing that is sometimes limited because of our ecclesial, social and political divisions.

Life in the church is of course an anticipated eschatology, but this fact does not relativize in any way the essential acts of the church. All our spiritual life, our life *in Christ*, is an anticipation of the *kingdom of God coming in power*. The theme of anticipation is a major theme in the Bible, the whole dialectics of the "already" and the "not yet". Anticipation is not opposed to the fullness of time but marks its stages in accordance with the seasons *(kairoi)* that God appoints in the course of history. The goal of the spiritual life is integral communion, but acceptance of all the demands of integral communion will not give access to the anticipated glory (in the eucharist) hidden in the faith in Christ which will appear in its fullness at his glorious return.

From the angle of Orthodox theology, the eucharist is not merely an individual act separate from the overall life in the church. It must be viewed in the wider setting of full, global and total communion which is the very nature of the church. Thinking members of the Orthodox Church cannot imagine a eucharist dissociated from the totality of the Orthodox Church, i.e. that one could receive the Body and Blood without fully accepting the community celebrating the mysteries and without total commitment to it, in the first place by faith.

In one sense, there is no separation between the church and the eucharist. This does not mean that Christians have no other occupation beyond the celebration of the eucharist but simply that the latter reveals the fullness of the church in that it is an efficacious "sign" because of the faith that it embodies. In the eucharist we take possession of the fullness of life in Christ — by anticipation, it is true, but not partially, and this is conditional on total commitment on our side. The mystery of the Body and Blood of Christ has meaning only in its fullness: the whole Christ and the whole of us individually and together, body and soul.

Orthodoxy does not regard *ecclesial unity* and *fullness* as conditions for the eucharist, nor as consequences of the eucharist — at least in a direct sense. It does not ask whether these must precede or follow sacramental communion. Unity and fullness are the very content of the ecclesial communion of which the eucharist is the sacramental sign, i.e., the eschatological sign in that it calls for and at the same time announces a reality that is coming and establishing itself in faith since "the Lord has begun his reign". Ecclesial unity and fullness of the faith are imperatives that one is not entitled to "bracket off" even provisionally.

One consequence of the eucharist as a sign of ecclesial unity and fullness is that the church "monitors" itself by monitoring its behaviour in relation to the eucharist. How can this attitude of a church be understood or tackled from the point of view of ecumenism?

If intercommunion is ruled out, at least as a norm, what else can be done? The answer surely is: to work for "full" communion at all levels and in all domains of ecclesial life with due regard to the stages and timing with respect to faith, while humbly and patiently awaiting God's decision, since the anticipation of the fullness[39] is dialectically related to the periods allowed by God's unlimited generosity and complete sovereignty. We are fully aware of the suffering among our brothers and sisters who cannot share the joy of the same ecclesial communion.

This suffering is one that sometimes leads us into polemics and useless confrontations, and to embarrassing situations. It is the ultimate aim of ecumenism to attain fullness of communion where the barriers and obstacles will not exist, the enmities of separation will be a thing of the past, and fraternal joy will be achieved in the mystery of the eucharist that is the symbol of the unity that we are seeking and hoping for.

For some years there has also been much talk about *eucharistic hospitality* as a kind of substitute for intercommunion, as a way of pointing towards visible unity.

The holy communion is an invitation to the faithful professing the faith and norms of a particular church. Eucharistic hospitality would mean a canonical *deviation*, an *economy* of dogma, or a sort of satisfaction in sharing joint prayer. However, at present we are at the basic level, seeking through our bilateral and multilateral discussions a coherent and vital theology, by going back to the common roots of our faith, and a new understanding of each other which will gradually eliminate the human and doctrinal obstacles, and may one day lead to visible unity of our churches. Hence, sharing in prayer, mutual love, are in a way incomplete as regards the joy of eucharistic communion. "Love one another" is the first stage on the way towards this goal "so that at last we confess the same faith". The way is long and difficult. The problem of ecclesial unity does not only involve human action; it also involves divine providence. We are at present at the stage of *promising signs* but the signs of such unity do not yet imply full unity.

b) Return and re-departure

It is true that ecumenical dialogue also as a "dialogue of charity" cannot bring us to visible unity unless we move together in a sound "dialogue of truth", one that is based on a return to the common roots of the apostolic faith of the one, holy, catholic and apostolic church. The participation of most of the churches in ecumenism is a reality full of promise from the point of view of "return and re-departure". At the theological level, the aim of the ecumenical movement is in the first place to overcome the long-standing alienation between Christians and create readiness for reunification in faith. Hence, the only realizable possibility of overcoming that age-old alienation and achieving full reunification in faith and sacramental community is best expressed as follows: in the truth revealed by God, liberty in case of doubt and love in all things *(in necessariis unitas, in dubiis libertas, in omnibus caritas)*.[40] The lack of *Caritas* has been a factor in the mass of ignorance, misunderstandings, resentments and rivalries between us, and propaganda and the memory of harsh treatment and persecutions have served only to increase them.

The Byzantine eucharist alludes to this *caritas* "as the essential condition and proper attitude for professing the common faith" when, before the Creed, the celebrant turns to the congregation and exhorts them in the following words: "Love one another so that we may in one spirit confess the Father, the Son and the Holy Spirit, the consubstantial and indivisible Trinity."

Conclusion

The eucharist is the heart of the liturgy, the expression of our present communion — in the Body and Blood of the risen Christ — with all humanity and the whole universe. In the eucharist we are suddenly aware of the cosmic dimension of the church, the unity of all creation, and the birth pangs of what is to become a new heaven and a new earth. So the discovery that the destiny of the world is in the church, the understanding of the church as the presence of Christ spreading to the ends of the world, are constituent elements of the church's meaning. For it is the whole world that rises up since matter is integrated in the glorious reality of the Lord. The efforts of humanity, the groanings of the creation, are taken up by Christ with a view to the ultimate triumph over death. The whole world thus becomes an immense diaspora needing to escape its solitude and isolation in order to become a world of love and sharing. We are to be an extension of the liturgy in the world, carrying the flame of the eucharist to the hearts of men and women. Our lives are given a direction to follow — not in order to "freeze" humankind in abstract certainties outside our experience, but to draw us towards a renewal in the radiance of the risen Christ. Hence, the eucharist seen as a sacrament of sharing makes us aware of our "catholicity". The horizontal plane on which we are linked by bonds of love meets a vertical plane where, through Christ, we enter the communion of the triune Love. Rublev's icon illustrates this point: the circle surrounding the three angels is not a closed one; it opens and makes a powerful appeal to humankind to join the eternal banquet of the "feast of love".

The unity of the church and of humanity is this task of perpetual becoming, a call to a universal "eucharistic" communion to which we are all united to collaborate at every moment in our divided and separated churches that are seeking to accomplish Christ's prayer so that "(they also) may be (one) in us" (John 17:21); but also in the offering of our whole being in response to the Son of God's sacrifice. In the face of the divided kingdom of Satan, this offering contributes to the building of the city of God; in a world doomed to *die*, it is an affirmation of *life*.

NOTES

[1] Cf. Gregory of Nazianzus, in *PG* XLVI, 581B: "Matter hitherto dead and without feeling is the medium for the great miracles and receives into itself the power of God"; cf. also O. Clément, *Questions sur l'homme*, Paris, Stock, 1972, p.158.

[2] O. Cullmann, *Les sacrements dans l'Eglise johannique*, Paris, 1951, pp.35-48, affirms: "The church's sacraments take the place of the miracles at the time of the incarnation"; see also *the Misunderstanding of the Church*, London, 1952.

[3] Cf. P. Evdokimov, "Eucharistie — mystère de l'Eglise", in *La Pensée orthodoxe*, 2/3, Paris, 1968, p.53.

[4] N. Cabasilas, *The Life in Christ*, in *PG*, 150 524 CD; 525 CD; N. Cabasilas, *The Life in Christ*, NY, St Vladimir's Seminary Press, 1974 trans. C.J. deCatanzaro (English edition).

[5] *Eccl. Hier.* III, 1, in *PG* 3, 424C.

[6] *Cherubic Hymn* from the Presanctified Divine Liturgy (which is celebrated only during the Great Lenten period).

[7] Cf. G. Limouris, *Nicolas Cabasilas et le rayonnement spirituel de sa pensée*, Strasbourg, Université de Sciences Humaines de Strasbourg, 1983, p.427.

[8] *Antirrh* 8, in *PG* 99, 340C.

[9] *Adv. Haeres.* III, 16, 7.

[10] *In Joa...* XI, in *PG* 74,557.

[11] *Homily on St John's Gospel*, 46.

[12] S. Broussaleux, "La vie en Christ", in *Irénikon* 9, 1932, pp.99-100.

[13] *Catechism*, 22,3.

[14] *Mystagogia* 21, in *PG* 90, 697 A; see also L. Thunberg, *Man and the Cosmos: the Vision of St Maximus the Confessor*, St Vladimir's Seminary Press, NY, 1985, pp.155-156.

[15] *Ad Rom.* 4, 1.

[16] Spiritual text of an anonymous person from Philokalia.

[17] *De Sacr.*, 5,11, 5-6; in *PL* 16 447C; see also J. Daniélou, "Eucharistie du cantique des cantiques", in *Irénikon*, 23, 1950, p.174; "Les repas de la Bible et leur signification", in *Maison-Dieu*, 18, 1949, p.8ff.

[18] *A Commentary on the Divine Liturgy* XLII, 13, in *PG* 150,460C; see also Nicolas Cabasilas, *A Commentary on the Divine Liturgy*, trans. J.M. Hussey and P.A. McNulty, London, SPCK, 1978.

[19] *De fide Orth.* IV, 13.

[20] Cf. P. Evdokimov, *L'adoration liturgique dans l'Eglise d'Orient*, IV in *Verbum Caro*, 35, 1955, p.170.

[21] *Essai sur la théologie mystique de l'Eglise d'Orient*, Paris, Aubier, 1944, pp.178ff.

[22] Athanasius of Alexandria, *Epist. I ad Serapionem*, in *PG* 26, 576A; see also P. Evdokimov, *L'Orthodoxie*, Paris-Neuchâtel, Delachaux et Niestlé, 1945, p.145.

[23] P. Evdokimov, *La prière de l'Eglise d'Orient: la liturgie de St Jean Chrysostome*, Paris, 1966, p.54.

[24] *Ibid., L'art de l'icône: Théologie de la beauté*, Paris, Desclée de Brouwer, 1970, p.216.

[25] *Le dogme eucharistique*, in *Put.* 20 and 21, 1930, p.3 (in Russian).

[26] Cf. O. Clément, "L'eucharistie dans la pensée de P. Evdokimov", in *Kleronomia*, 6, 1964, p.393.

[27] G. Konidaris, *The Historian, the Church and the Nature of the Tradition*, Athens, 1961, p.8 (in Greek).

[28] *Letter XII, 3 to Alexandrians* in *PG* 10,1337.

[29] Cf. *The Divine Liturgy of St Basil*.

[30] *Hier. Eccl.* IV, 1, C in *PG* 3,424.

[31] *De Temperentia et Virtute*, I, 100, in *PG* 93,1512.

[32] *Comm. and Johan. XII*, in *PG* 74,708.

[33] *Catechism XVIII*.

[34] *Mystagogia* I.

[35] *De monibus Ecclesiae Catholicae*, Lib. I, 30.

[36] *Catechism XXXIII*, III,2A.

[37] Cf. Theodosius of Mopsueste, *Liturgical Homily* VIth (according to the Latin translation), ed. Ad. Rücker, *Opuscule et Textus*, series *Liturgica* f.2; Monasterii 1933, p.33; *Hom. in Ps. XXVIII*, 3, in *PG* 29, 288.

[38] *Commentary to the Parables* XXXVIII, in *PG* 28,724.

[39] H. Schüte, *Um die Wiedervereinigung im Glauben*, Essen, 1961, p.178, 4th ed.

[40] Augustin Cardinal Bea, *Einheit in Freiheit*, Stuttgart, 1965, pp.177-188.

Eucharistic Hospitality:
Implications for the Ecumenical Movement

Robert G. Stephanopoulos

It was a privilege for me to be at the WCC assembly in Canberra. Like others who worshipped there, the celebration of the Orthodox divine liturgy became a painful reminder of our ecumenical dilemma. Many people were pointedly excluded from participating in the eucharistic communion. They left, no doubt feeling less than "eucharistic" about their exclusion, and perhaps confused about why. It was, after all, an ecumenical celebration and a worldwide assembly of Christians who are dedicated to the principle that we are people of prayer and one in our desire for visible unity!

Valerie Zahirsky, an Orthodox observer from the USA, captured the embarrassment of the moment when she wrote:

> For most Orthodox, the burden of this eucharistic division is a real *martyria*. It often calls forth such accusations against the Orthodox, and in trying to answer them we realize that the whole ecclesiological understanding of Orthodoxy is being called into question. How is it possible to explain that the eucharist is another thing the Church does together, as one body, "with one mind" as the divine liturgy puts it? How do we show that our attitude is not one of intransigence but of attempted faithfulness to God's own revelation? How do we help people see that when the day comes that we really are all of one mind, it will be manifested by the fact that we are all in the same church? And when that day comes, the shared eucharist will be the crown of our unity. But until it comes, we must hash out our differences, so that it *can* come.[1]

My own frustration in attempting to explain the answers to Valerie's questions was compounded by the disagreeable fact that upon emerging from the worship tent we were all met by a small and determined group of Greek Orthodox (Old-Calendarist) demonstrators from Australia who were there to protest the very presence of Orthodox in the WCC and in the "ecumenical heresy". Indeed, Orthodox ecumenists, like all good Christians who are seeking unity in Christ's Church, are having a hard time of it!

These anti-ecumenical Orthodox fundamentalists are a vivid reminder to us all of one of the inevitable difficulties connected to worship at ecumenical gatherings. Is the eucharist an "end" or the "means" to an end? We are divided in conscience over the issue. However, only ill-informed and ill-willed Christians, both those against and those who favour some form of "intercommunion" among divided Christians, which is not at the same time a communion in the fullness of the una sancta — faith, word, sacrament, ministry — will prevent us from arriving at the true goal of our ecumenical endeavours. The truth is to be found in our efforts to discover it. In the words of a distinguished Orthodox participant at Canberra, Nicholas Lossky:

● The Rev. Robert Stephanopoulos is dean of the Greek Orthodox Archdiocesan Cathedral of the Holy Trinity in New York, USA. This paper was published in *The Ecumenical Review*, vol. 44, no. 1, January 1992.

...so long as [the ill-informed] are not brought to accept and *receive* that what the ecumenical movement is doing is not a betrayal of the gospel of Jesus Christ but a proclamation thereof, Orthodox participation in "intercommunion" would result in a multiplication of schisms, not in a contribution to the unity of Christians or of humankind...

All those who have any knowledge of the Orthodox are aware of their insistence on the necessity to be able to confess together the apostolic faith in order to be able to restore the unity of communion. Hence the importance in the eyes of the Orthodox of the ongoing apostolic faith study in the Faith and Order Commission.[2]

Once again, therefore, we must address the problems of eucharistic sharing and somehow "give an account of the hope that is in us". It is part of our continuing task to arrive at being one in the fullness of the divine life and truth. Deeply-felt convictions must be shared in charity and truth since the stakes affect my salvation and yours, both *orthodoxia* (right faith) and *orthopraxia* (right action), and eternal life itself.

I

As a formal term "eucharistic hospitality" can only be understood in the context of the modern ecumenical movement. It is one of the many terms often used to describe the possibility of sharing the Lord's supper in our divided state as Christians.[3] Many Christians believe that this is possible, either in principle or as an interim measure leading to deeper unity. However, for many others it *may not* refer to the practice of sharing in the eucharist with others who do not belong formally to their own faith community, either as a normal practice or in exceptional circumstances. The issue has divided us and pains us. It is commonplace to speak of our divisions as we gather in prayer, mutual support, study and mission. At the point of the core "mystery" we are truly scandalized. Our separation at the Lord's table is a sign of our spiritual alienation and of its tragic aftermaths. Indeed, it challenges the very meaning of what the una sancta is and does "for the sake of the world".

For the Orthodox, the very nature of the Church, of its unity and catholicity and mission, are addressed when we approach the eucharist. Indeed, the ecumenical problem is raised in all its fullness. Since membership in the Church is tantamount to communion with the holy things of the ekklesia *(ta hagia tois hagiois)* and since the eucharist is the very manifestation of the Church in its fullness

...it is impossible to allow any approach to divine communion by way of "hospitality", or in [the] case of need, because *admitting one to communion and to church membership are identical; to what church one belongs is manifested where he receives communion, or where he is admitted to communion.* So the concept of intercommunion is unknown to the ancient Church, as it is to the NT also: there is only communion and non-communion.[4]

Moreover, in spite of the fact that schisms and formal separations existed from the earliest times, the normative Eastern tradition does not speak of "eucharistic hospitality" or relationships of "intercommunion" between *separated* churches. The undivided church only knew of the terms of *full* communion between ecclesial communities, identical with one another in the essentials and norms of the apostolic faith, sacramental life and ministerial order. A review of the patristic teaching and practice leads us to conclude that:

(a) In principle, heretics are not in any way members of the Church. Their sacraments are vehemently rejected. (b) Also in principle, schismatics may be considered as members of the Church. Their baptism and priesthood are accepted, especially when they return to the Church. (c) Leniency (oikonomia) may be applied according to the specific needs of certain groups of people, in order to facilitate their return to the Church.[5]

II

In the wider context of the ecumenical movement the issue takes on a problematic importance unforeseen in the past. Representatives from the churches have pursued vigorously rapprochement and a deeper understanding of the issues that both unite and divide us after centuries of mutual isolation and open hostility. Reflecting on their experiences, they have devised inventive and innovative ways to facilitate a convergence of views, which may even hopefully lead towards a consensus to be "received" by all. The vision is best described in the constitution of the WCC:

> To call the churches to the goal of visible unity in one faith and in one eucharistic fellowship expressed in worship and in common life in Christ, and to advance towards that unity in order that the world may believe.[6]

Orthodox theologians have participated actively in this effort from its formal beginnings at the turn of this century. They have "agonized" along with the others over fundamental Christian issues, e.g. unity, ecclesiology, the apostolic faith, baptism, eucharist, ministry, conciliarity, authority, renewal, mission, etc. In a solemn way Orthodox have affirmed this progress and its results. A report of a consultation of Orthodox theologians took into account the advances of the ecumenical movement which

> constitutes another attempt, like those made in the patristic period, to apply the apostolic faith to new historical situations and existential demands. What is in a sense new today is the fact that this attempt is being made together with other Christian bodies with whom there is no full unity. It is here that the difficulties arise, but it is precisely here that there also are many signs of real hope for growing fellowship, understanding and cooperation.[7]

Particular stress is placed on the meaning of church and its unity in the eucharist which would imply "a reorientation of the ecumenical problematic as a whole".

> This means basically that the unity which we seek in the ecumenical movement cannot be the product of theological agreements, such as a common signing of a *confessio fidei*. Theological work is certainly needed and should be of a serious kind and high quality. But its aim should be directed towards the understanding of the existential significance of the community of the church, particularly of her visible structure which provides man with the possibility of entering into new and saving relationships with God and the world.[8]

III

Throughout these discussions, Orthodox ecumenical policies have been based upon an experience of the one church, fully and concretely evident in their own historic communion. No doubt is entertained that all the criteria for church and the apostolic tradition are found in the visible Orthodox Church of today, which is in a direct continuity with the historic early church. In faithfulness to our ecclesiological self-understanding, Orthodox reject the confessional or denominational identities which are commonplace in the conciliar ecumenical movement. The so-called Toronto Statement (1950) of the WCC is regarded as a constitutional guarantee of ecclesiological neutrality in the ecumenical enterprise and is a pre-condition to Orthodox participation in all ecumenical activities.

The sense of a lively and infallible Tradition is what sustains the Orthodox Church. Tradition is much greater than adherence to past historic forms alone or merely a conservative attitude towards antiquity and the fundamentals. It is alive, Spirit-led and Spirit-blessed, dynamic and integral. It implies a direct continuity of vision and purpose with the apostolic foundations of the Church of God, expressed in the historic creeds, councils and liturgy.

Officially the Orthodox Church has taken the position that ecumenical participation and dialogue on issues of unity are conditioned by two principles which were forged in their present form out of its experience in the ecumenical movement and its perspective on the dialectic unity-division-reunion. One can find these expressed in a series of documents beginning already in 1920. It is evident from these that the foundations of Orthodox ecumenical theory and practice are both *doctrinal* and *ecclesiological*. On the one hand, an unswerving adherence to the apostolic witness as the basis for ecclesial unity, and on the other hand, allegiance to the one visible church called into being by God and historically present in the Orthodox Church. Thus, it is our claim that the Orthodox Church is *the Church*, preserving the truth of Christianity in an unbroken continuity with the original apostolic community. Disunity, where it exists, requires that we work for reunion and reconciliation through renewal, dialogue, common prayer, service and witness.

The two principles, basic to our understanding of the ecumenical quest for Christian unity, were clearly presented in 1957:

> We begin with a clear conception of the Church's unity which we believe has been embodied and realized in the age-long history of the Orthodox Church, without any change or break since the times when the visible unity of Christendom was an obvious fact and was attested and witnessed to by an ecumenical unanimity, in the age of the ecumenical councils.
>
> This unity in faith, worship and life is the foundation of the Church's unity and continuity. Unity in doctrine is absolutely essential to the constitution of the Church and presupposes any sharing in the Lord's table and in the sacramental life of the Church. Therefore the ecumenical problem for Orthodoxy is not the *unity* of the Church, which is given and preserved essentially by God in the historical Orthodox communion. The ecumenical problem for us is the problem of the *disunity of Christendom* and the necessity of the recovery of the biblical-patristic synthesis of faith which is constitutive of the one Church. For Orthodoxy, theology and worship do not express the thought and life of one particular denomination, but of the Church of Christ.[9]

Thus, Orthodox ecumenical policy is consistent in its insistence that the conditions for (re)union include a formal acceptance of the *Tradition of the Church* in its fullness. Specifically, Orthodox objections to the current notions about the advisability of eucharistic hospitality are not based, in our view at least, on a contrary spirit, lack of ecumenical concern, or some negative criticisms, but on a *positive view* of the Church, its faith, ministry and unity as revealed in the eucharist.

Gradually, the implications of this perspective on the ecumenical enterprise have guided the discussions. Our most serious difficulties revolve around the central issue of the nature of the Church itself. The late Georges Florovsky, soon after the WCC Amsterdam assembly (1948), asserted that:

> ...the doctrine of the Church is in its pre-theological phase [and that] the true interpretation of the antinomy of the Christian schism can be reached only in the context of a balanced doctrine of the Church.[10]

Progressively the ecumenical discussions have led to the discovery of the Church as the central theme of all our theological and ecclesial efforts. Much theology today is self-consciously an interpretation of the experience of God as lived in the community of the Church.[11]

The Orthodox especially are probing more deeply into this appreciation of the Church,

> firstly, by indicating the presence of those dimensions for which the contemporary ecumenical perspective is searching, and secondly, by pointing out that these dimensions represent potentialities that could in fact be realized in a form adapted to the Church's contemporary mode of understanding, and thus become the expression of a united Christianity.[12]

IV

Historical studies often show that bilateral and multilateral conversations were among the first examples of reunion efforts between divided Christians. Sometimes these methods failed because they tended to create artificial dilemmas (e.g. between Chalcedonian and non-Chalcedonian, Greek and Latin, Reformation and counter-Reformation). The more generalized, even holistic, methodology adopted by the WCC appears to be preferable, although certainly more complex and time-consuming. The recent return to bilaterals has proven to be invaluable in providing significant understandings and even breakthroughs in specialized and limited areas. Agreements in ecclesiology, conciliar fellowship, the apostolic faith, ministry, authority, etc., when taken in isolation are clearly remarkable.[13] Added together, they seem to be pointing in the general direction of visible, ecclesial unity, with one apostolic faith, one eucharistic communion and one ministry.[14] The Orthodox appreciation of the dialogue process is favourable and its achievements are recognized as important to the final goal of ecumenism.[15]

Convergence on the eucharist is a result of both bilateral and multilateral conversations. Ecumenical teams, inclusive of significant Roman Catholic participation, have marked real progress. The Roman Catholic ecumenist John Hotchkin has summarized many of these agreements of recent years. He discerns a pattern of convergence from diverse dialogues on such eucharistic points as sacrifice, memorial, real presence, eucharistic change, epiclesis, and a host of subsidiary questions, both theoretical and practical. His conclusion is very hopeful:

> Such is the record of our agreements. They are deep and encompassing as together we reflect upon the gift of the eucharist. They are not only substantial, I believe, taken all together, they are full and complete... In the light of what our past history has been, they are clear and compelling evidence the Christian people have crossed over into an unmistakably new era in their life together.[16]

Hotchkin's article was updated by J. Robert Nelson who confirms the widespread conviction about agreement in the bilaterals over the eucharist. He concludes that

> ...for all the churches in the ecumenical dialogue there has been both an ascending interest in the practice and theology of the eucharist as well as a converging movement towards common understanding and compatibility. In fact, when considered and weighed in light of past centuries of alienation, disputation, and polemics, this convergence is utterly astounding, although it is by no means completed in full unity.[17]

The Lima statement, *Baptism, Eucharist and Ministry* (BEM), represents a crowning achievement of multilateral dialogue. It is certainly no exaggeration to state, as Georges Tsetsis does, that BEM is:

> ...the most serious WCC contribution to the ecumenical movement and probably the most inclusive ecumenical theological statement ever produced by the Faith and Order Commission.[18]

The section on the eucharist reveals many points of convergence with which the Orthodox are comfortable, especially because they appear to conform to the teaching and witness of the early Church.

On the issue of eucharistic sharing, however, there is no agreement. Fr Tsetsis, in a synthesis of Orthodox responses to BEM, concludes the following:

> The growing unanimity concerning the eucharistic theology and practice is not sufficient reason for establishing intercommunion between the churches. Most certainly the increased mutual understanding as described in the Lima text might allow some churches to attain a greater measure of eucharistic communion among themselves; however, it is a strong belief of the Orthodox that this eucharistic communion will be achieved only on a basis of the unity of faith. This eucharistic communion with the believers of other Christian confessions will be the climax and the crown, the conclusion and fullness of the unity of all churches and of all Christians.[19]

This viewpoint is illustrated in the bilaterals of Orthodox with both Roman Catholics and Anglicans. In an agreed statement on BEM the Eastern Orthodox-Roman Catholic consultation in the USA speaks favourably about the section on the eucharist and lifts up several points that require further clarification and development. On the specific issue of eucharistic sharing, they concluded:

> We do not find that growing consensus on eucharistic theology and practice is, of itself, sufficient for such sharing among our churches. The resolution of questions connected with ministry and the nature of faith of the Church are also important...[20]

Similar conclusions were drawn by the Orthodox-Anglican theological consultation in the USA in its agreed statements on the eucharist. It expressed its fundamental agreement with the Moscow (1976) and Dublin (1984) international dialogues which concluded that the issues concerning the relationship of eucharist and church unity, eucharist and ministry, communion and intercommunion, are not resolved and will be addressed in the future and at greater depth.[21]

The official position of the Orthodox in ecumenical dialogue has remained remarkably consistent in rejecting not only the practice but also the very idea of eucharistic sharing without a clear ecclesial unity in doctrine, ministry and sacramental life. Every statement on the matter has followed the reasoning of the early church in affirming the intimate connection between church and eucharist, between the fullness of truth and the fullness of communion with the Catholic tradition.[22] This was affirmed once again in the aftermath of the Canberra assembly at a special meeting of Orthodox

(Chalcedonian and non-Chalcedonian) at Chambésy in September 1991. The conference report noted that one of the outstanding problems of Orthodox participation in the WCC is the issue of "intercommunion". It restates once again our understanding of the ecumenical task which is to overcome real differences in doctrine, order and liturgy before there can be a communion in the eucharist.

> Thus, in view of our continuing division, it is not permitted for the Orthodox in conscience to invite others to "eucharistic hospitality" nor to reciprocate a similar invitation from others. We look forward to the day when our common faith, ecclesiastical order and communion will require and permit us to share in the common cup as the supreme expression of our unity.[23]

V

The way towards resolving our impasse is by theological dialogue which proceeds towards a vision of the one church, visibly one and unified in its eucharistic, doctrinal and ecclesial dimensions, concretely manifesting the mystery of sharing in the divine life which sanctifies the world and reveals to the world a new mode of existence. For the Orthodox this clearly points to an ecclesiology of communion rather than intercommunion. The worship, faith, spiritual and moral life of the Church are fully expressed in the eucharist. As Gennadios Limouris states:

> The insistence on interconfessional eucharistic communion puts one in a dilemma. By dissociating the witness of faith and the sacrament in the eucharistic action that is the hallmark of ecclesial unity, one tends either to devalue the witness of faith as an essential factor in unity or to devalue the sacramental action of the eucharist so that it loses its specific meaning which is essentially governed by the requirements of ecclesial unity... If intercommunion is ruled out, at least as a norm, what else can be done? The answer surely is: to work for "full" communion at all levels and in all domains of ecclesial life with due regard to the stages and timing with respect to faith, while humbly and patiently awaiting God's decision, since the anticipation of the fullness is dialectically related to the periods allowed by God's unlimited generosity and complete sovereignty.[24]

Some Orthodox theologians have called for a review of the matter. As early as 1933 Sergius Bulgakov had called for "partial" reunion of a small group of Orthodox and Anglicans who would enter into occasional intercommunion as a prophetic witness to the future reunion of the whole church. This experiment soon failed, although others continued to express this notion with variations.[25] Still others elaborated a type of "eucharistic ecclesiology" which recognizes that the eucharist creates the unity of the Church and that sharing in it will bring us to a real unity of faith and life. The main exponents of recent Orthodox eucharistic ecclesiology, however, do not accept this conclusion. In the wake of Vatican Council II, some Orthodox prelates and synods have advocated limited admission to the eucharist of non-Orthodox Christians in special circumstances. These, however, were countered by numerous statements and actions which effectively nullified these tentative suggestions.[26]

Another line of inquiry which had led some Orthodox theologians to review the present policy is based on the principle of "economy" by which the Church can exercise a certain leniency or pastoral clemency to correct certain abnormalities. They argue that issues like the boundaries of the Church and the validity of non-Orthodox sacraments are still open questions in Orthodox ecclesiology and that the *economy* of the Church which imitates the philanthropy of God in anomalous situations has been extended at various times for healing and overcoming divisions. Although it has no specific creative power of its own and may not violate the essential unity of doctrine of the Church, *economy* has proven helpful in the desire of the Church to reconcile dissidents and to determine the primary reality of sacramental actions celebrated outside its canonical boundaries. It is a way of allowing the Church to recognize itself and to accept what properly belongs to it from *outside* its normal structures of life. Since, in fact, the Orthodox Church has permitted "partial intercommunion" at the level of prayer and the sacraments in some cases

> it appears clearly that there is a possibility that the Orthodox Church will recognize, through *economy*, not only the sacraments of Christians outside her institutional boundaries, but also these Christians themselves are her members in "diaspora".[27]

Perhaps it is to read too much into an economic approach to sacramental theology. Recent studies in the principle of economy

> ...suggest the need for greater precision in the use of this term. In Byzantium at least, *oikonomia* was not understood as a limitless power to make what otherwise is invalid to be valid should that be expedient, as so many presentations have claimed. Rather, *oikonomia* was seen above all as prudent pastoral administration on the basis of the canons and the example of the fathers. By definition it was expected to operate within certain universally recognized limits and according to certain well-defined patterns.[28]

Validity or non-validity of sacraments may be related to the question of intercommunion, but they are not exactly the same. It is possible to consider eucharistic hospitality as a violation of the relationship between church-faith-eucharist without at the same time dismissing the validity of sacraments of other ecclesial bodies.[29]

VI

Our disagreement about the advisability of eucharistic sharing need not keep us out of each other's prayers and thoughts. Rather it should keep in the forefront of our efforts the deep tragedy of our separation and the pain and anger it sometimes engenders. Our inability to share together the grace of God in the eucharist should be a constant reminder of the blessings we enjoy in the traditions which are ours and of our constant task to reconcile these in conciliar fellowship. It should remind us of the work that still lies ahead as we move out of our self-exclusion and isolation. To quote Gennadios Limouris:

> The holy communion is an invitation to the faithful professing the faith and norms of a particular church. Eucharistic hospitality would mean a canonical *deviation*, an *economy* of dogma, or a sort of satisfaction in sharing joint prayer. However, at present we are at the basic level, seeking through our bilateral and multilateral discussions a coherent and vital theology, by going back to the common roots of our faith, and a new understanding of each other which will gradually eliminate the human and doctrinal obstacles, and may one day lead to visible unity of our churches. Hence, sharing in prayer, mutual love, are in a way incomplete as regards the joy of eucharistic communion. "Love one another" is the first stage on the way towards this goal "so that at last we confess the same faith". The way is long and difficult. The problem of ecclesial unity does not only involve human action, it also involves divine providence. We are at

present at the stage of *promising signs* but the signs of such unity do not yet fully imply unity.[30]

Intercommunion is too limited and isolated an act to achieve unity. The late Nikos Nissiotis called for a vision of the continuation of the work on the unity of the Church which would correlate the three current interdependent notions of the unity we seek: (1) "organic union", (2) "unity in reconciled diversity", and (3) "conciliar fellowship of churches".

> In the near future we have to enter into more detailed clarification of the necessary steps to be taken for pointing out this kind of coherence of the three trends of conceptualized unity. We now need badly the exchange of Catholic-Orthodox with Protestant-Evangelical models of unity. We have to declare clearly whether or not we do work for a visible unity in faith and order and propose the necessary elements of achieving it.[31]

The schemes of reunion between churches, re-establishing ecclesial communion, as is currently under way between the Orthodox and non-Chalcedonian churches, are realistic and achievable goals in the near-term. As these begin to happen, a trend can be established which will have long-term effects as well.

Since Orthodox stand virtually alone in their resistance to eucharistic sharing as an ecumenical means to unity, it is imperative that they make its case for the integrity of church-faith-eucharist all the more clear and credible. The image of Orthodoxy, its internal unity and its authentic witness to the world should resonate the truth of the apostolic community itself. As Ion Bria concludes:

> In the interests of a more authentic witness, we should reinforce the pan-Orthodox structures and institutions, and shape an Orthodox "symphony" in a new, contemporary and creative form... Since the Orthodox claim to be the *leaven* in the universal, undivided church, they should agree to stay right in the midstream of the ecumenical movement. Moreover, as we prepare for a new era of faith, they should assume the continuity of the apostolic church and search for new expressions of common witness and prayer.[32]

NOTES

[1] *The Ecumenical Review*, Vol. 43, No. 2, April 1991, p.224.

[2] *Ibid.*, p.213.

[3] Cf. "Beyond Intercommunion", in *Study Encounter*, Vol. 5, No. 3, 1969, pp.94-114; and Vilmos Vajta, "'Intercommunion': A Terminological Problem", in *The Ecumenical Review*, Vol. 22, No. 2, April 1970, pp.125-132.

[4] George Galitis, *The Problem of Intercommunion from the Orthodox Point of View. A Biblical and Ecclesiological Study*, Athens, 1968 (in Greek), pp.24-25.

[5] Maximos Aghiorgoussis, "The Holy Eucharist in Ecumenical Dialogue: An Orthodox View", in *Journal of Ecumenical Studies*, Vol. 13, No. 2, spring 1976, p.206. Contrast the findings of Geoffrey Wainwright, "Conciliarity and Eucharist", in *Mid-Stream*, Vol. XVII, No. 2, April 1978, pp.135-53, who argues that "the modern ecumenical movement sets a context of non-hostility, in which Christian unity is actively being sought by partners committed to a common search for a common goal" (p.147), and that "our human striving needs the grace of God which has the possibility of coming to us through eucharistic sharing" (p.153).

[6] Constitution III,1, in *Breaking Barriers: Nairobi 1975*, ed. D.M. Paton, London, SPCK, 1976, pp.317ff.

[7] "The Ecumenical Nature of the Orthodox Witness", in *Apostolic Faith Today: A Handbook for Study*, ed. H.-G. Link, Faith and Order Paper No. 124, Geneva, WCC, 1985, p.178.

[8] *Ibid.*

[9] Statement of the representatives of the Eastern Orthodox churches in the USA (North American Faith and Order Conference, Oberlin, OH, 1957), in *Guidelines for Orthodox Christians in Ecumenical Relations*, ed. R.G. Stephanopoulos, New York, SCOBA, 1972, pp.48-49.

[10] Cf. *The Ecumenical Review*, Vol. II, No. 2, 1950, pp.152-162.

[11] Cf. Lukas Vischer, "The Church — One People in Many Places", in *What Unity Implies*, Geneva, WCC, 1969, pp.65-101.

[12] Dumitru Staniloae, "Trinitarian Relations and the Life of the Church", in *Theology and the Church*, St Vladimir's Seminary Press, 1980, p.12. See also the brilliant ecclesiological studies of John Zizioulas, e.g. *Being as Communion*, Crestwood, NY, St Vladimir's Press, 1984; and Gennadios Limouris, "The Eucharist as the Sacrament of Sharing", *The Ecumenical Review*, Vol. 38, No. 4, October 1986, pp.401-415 (reprinted in this volume).

[13] Cf. *Fourth Forum on Bilateral Conversations Report*, Faith and Order Paper No. 125, Geneva, WCC, 1985.

[14] See the articles of Paul Crow, Nikos Nissiotis, Lukas Vischer, William Lazareth et al. in *Mid-Stream*, Vol. XVIII, No. 1, January 1979, in the aftermath of the Bangalore Faith and Order Commission meeting.

[15] "Final texts-resolutions of the Third Pan-Orthodox Pre-Conciliar Conference (28 October-6 November 1986)", in *Episkepsis*, 17/369, 15 December 1986.

[16] "Christian Dialogue and the Eucharist", in *Mid-Stream*, Vol. XVI, No. 3, July 1977, pp.271-93. See also the special issue of the *Journal of Ecumenical Studies*, Vol. 13, No. 2, spring 1976, ed. L. Swidler, with numerous articles on the eucharist in ecumenical dialogue.

[17] "The Holy Eucharist as Considered in Bilateral Conversations", in *Journal of Ecumenical Studies*, Vol. 23, No. 3, summer 1986, pp.449-61. The articles of C.J. Schreck and J. Erickson in the same issue are important.

[18] "A Synthesis of the Responses of Orthodox Churches to the Lima Document on 'Baptism, Eucharist and Ministry'", in *Orthodoxes Forum*, Zeitschrift des Instituts für Orthodoxe Theologie der Universität München, 1987, p.100.

[19] *Ibid.*, p.107. Also G. Wainwright, "The Eucharist in the Churches' Responses to the Lima Text", *One in Christ*, No. 1, 1989, pp.53-63.

[20] The complete statement in *Greek Orthodox Theological Review*, 29/3, autumn 1984, pp.283-88.

[21] "Agreed Statement on the Eucharist", 16 January 1988, New York. See also *Anglican-Orthodox Dialogue: The Dublin Agreed Statement 1984*, Crestwood, NY, St Vladimir's Seminary Press, 1985.

[22] Cf. *The Orthodox Church in the Ecumenical Movement: Documents and Statements 1902-1975*, ed. C.G. Patelos, Geneva, WCC, 1978, *passim*; and *Orthodox Thought: Reports of Orthodox Consultations Organized by the WCC, 1975-1982*, ed. G. Tsetsis, Geneva, WCC, 1983.

[23] "The Orthodox Churches and the WCC", in *Enemerosis* Z-1991/9-10, pp.10-16 (my translation). Obviously this same reasoning applies to the Orthodox objections to Vatican II and its extension of intercommunion to the Orthodox. See e.g. Camillus Hay, "Intercommunion: a Roman Catholic Approach", in *One in Christ*, Vol. V, No. 4, 1969, pp.355-78.

[24] *Op. cit.*, pp.412-13.

[25] P.M. McDonald, *Approaches to Intercommunion*, Durban, Unity Publications, 1967, pp.16-25. See also Henry Hill, "Father Sergius Bulgakov and Intercommunion", in *Sobornost*, 5/4, 1966, pp.272-76.

[26] For a full discussion cf. Kallistos Ware, "Church and Eucharist, Communion and Intercommunion", in *Sobornost*, 7/7, 1978, pp.550-67; and Paul N. Evdokimov, "Communicatio in Sacris: A Possibility?", in *Diakonia*, 2/4, 1967, pp.352-66.

[27] Liviu Stan, "Economy and Intercommunion", in *Diakonia*, 6/3, 1971, p.218. See also Emilianos Timiadis, "Possibilities and Limitations of Eucharistic Communion", in *The Patristic and Byzantine Review*, 5/3, 1986, pp.165-84.

[28] John Erickson, "Reception of Non-Orthodox Clergy into the Orthodox Church", in *St Vladimir's Theological Quarterly*, 29/2, 1985, p. 128, and related articles of his. See also "Orthodox-Roman Catholic Consultation on Unity and Divine Economy", in *Diakonia*, 11/3, 1976, pp. 296-97, and Michael Fahey, "Ecclesiastical Economy and Mutual Recognition of Faith: A Roman Catholic Perspective", *ibid.*, pp. 204-23.

[29] Erickson, *op. cit.*, pp. 131-32, and Ware, *op. cit.*, p. 560.

[30] *Op. cit.*, p. 414.

[31] "Visions of the Future of Ecumenism", in *Greek Orthodox Theological Review*, 26/4, winter 1981, pp. 295-296.

[32] "Ecclesial Unity in the Ecumenical Movement: Theology and Expectations", in *Greek Orthodox Theological Review*, 26/4, winter 1981, p. 323.

The Meaning of the Orthodox Presence in the Ecumenical Movement

Georges Tsetsis

In many church circles, Orthodox and non-Orthodox alike, there is a widespread impression that the ecumenical movement emerged from within the Protestant world, as a result of its internal situation and in an endeavour to find solutions to the existential problems the churches of the Reformation were facing in their daily life and witness. Thus many Orthodox wonder about the Orthodox presence in the ecumenical movement and the active participation of the Orthodox churches in the World Council of Churches, while not a few Protestants, who joined the movement midway through the ecumenical pilgrimage and are unfamiliar with Eastern Christianity, are tempted to consider the Orthodox as a body belonging to a different "world" and culture, alien to the concerns of the ecumenical movement and often constituting a stumbling block in the march towards Christian unity.

The history of Orthodox presence

It is a fact, however, that the history of the ecumenical movement, and more particularly of the WCC, is very closely linked with the Orthodox Church. It should be remembered that the first concrete proposal "without precedent in Church history",[1] to establish a "koinonia of churches", was made by an Orthodox church, the Ecumenical Patriarchate, which in its well-known 1920 Encyclical[2] expressed the conviction that the coming together of the churches and their fellowship and cooperation were not excluded by the doctrinal differences between them. As W.A. Visser 't Hooft once pointed out, "the church of Constantinople was among the first in modern history to remind us that world Christendom would be disobedient to the will of its Lord and Saviour if it did not seek to manifest in the world the unity of the people of God and of the body of Christ. With its 1920 Encyclical, Constantinople rang the bell of our assembling."[3]

Seen therefore from an Orthodox perspective, the foundation of the World Council of Churches at the 1948 inaugural Assembly at Amsterdam could be considered in a way as the fulfilment of the proposal made by Constantinople 28 years earlier. The more so because most of the eleven models of cooperation projected by the above Encyclical eventually became the basis of the programmatic concerns of the WCC, at least in the first decade of its life and activity.

It is true that at the inaugural Assembly only three Eastern Orthodox churches — the Ecumenical Patriarchate, the Church of Cyprus and the Church of Greece — and

● Grand Protopresbyter Dr Georges Tsetsis is permanent representative of the Ecumenical Patriarchate to the World Council of Churches. This paper, written on the occasion of the 40th anniversary of the WCC, appeared in *The Ecumenical Review*, vol. 40, nos 3-4, 1988.

the Romanian Orthodox Episcopate of USA, were represented. The rest of the Orthodox churches, which actively participated both in the Faith and Order and Life and Work movements between 1920 and 1938 (with the exception of the Russian Orthodox Church, living under precarious conditions during the post-Revolutionary period), did not attend the Assembly, as a result of the recommendations of the Moscow conference held just one month before which decided against the participation of the Orthodox.[4] That was more due to the tensions of the cold war and the East-West relationships at that time than to any theological or ecclesiological reasons. Soon, however, the misunderstandings were cleared up and between 1961 and 1965 all autocephalous and autonomous Eastern Orthodox churches became members of the WCC.

As the third Pan-Orthodox Preconciliar Conference (Chambésy, November 1986) pointed out: "The Orthodox participation in the ecumenical movement today is not strange to the history of the Orthodox Church. It constitutes another attempt to express the Apostolic Faith in new historical situations and to respond to new existential demands."[5] What is new however is the fact that this attempt today is being made together with other churches and Christian bodies with whom there is no full unity. Of course it is here that difficulties arise. But it is precisely here that there are also many signs of real hope for growing fellowship, understanding and cooperation.[6]

The past forty years in the life of the WCC demonstrated that the Orthodox Church as a whole, consistent with the attitude of openness she adopted from the very beginning, has offered herself wholeheartedly to the ecumenical movement and to the WCC. First, she shared her doctrine and beliefs with Faith and Order. Secondly, she gave her particular input in terms of her moral and social concepts within the framework of Life and Work. Thirdly, she highlighted the role and meaning of worship, and particularly of the eucharist, in the life of the church. Fourthly, she expressed the mystical and ascetic concepts of Christian experience which are discernible in the lives of Orthodox faithful. And lastly she made a unique contribution to the ongoing debate on the unity of the church, as it is understood theologically and historically.[7] Thus, as the late George Florovsky remarked, the role of the Orthodox in the development of the ecumenical movement was considerable and at times even decisive.[8]

For the Orthodox Church itself, these have been years of enrichment, both in the field of ecclesiastical and theological experiences and in the area of Christian love and solidarity. The WCC has deployed considerable resources in many parts of the world in the fields of diakonia, theological education and social service, and these have been of great help to Orthodox churches as to others. What is even more significant is the fact that this has provided unique opportunities for a broader encounter and deeper dialogue between the Orthodox and Protestant churches.

A problematic presence?

It should be added, however, that the Orthodox presence in the WCC has often been problematic, both for the WCC and the Orthodox churches themselves. The specificity of Orthodox ecclesiology and theology, the Orthodox vision of the world, some historical misgivings the Orthodox have vis-à-vis Western Christendom were, and to some extent still are, the main factors giving the impression that Orthodoxy remains on the fringe of the Council's work and does not fully participate in its activities which appear to be "Western" in emphasis.

If this is true to a certain extent, it is equally true that in the course of all these years of the life of the WCC, the Orthodox churches fully identified themselves with the ongoing struggles of the Council, in an effort to jointly respond to the aspirations and the existential needs of the people of God around the world. This was the outcome of the belief that the church above everything else is the manifestation of the presence of God in the world, the sign of the continuous intervention of the love of God in our life, and that therefore the responsibility of the church is to bring to the world of today, torn apart by hatred, conflict, material and spiritual poverty, the liberating action of God. In this respect, during the past four decades the churches belonging to the WCC reflected and acted together, convinced that the council "as an instrument of the churches engaged not only in theological dialogue but also in love and mutual solidarity, should persist in its efforts towards a broader and even more positive encounter with humankind, which suffers today in so many ways".[9]

It is beyond doubt that the manifold activities in the fields of evangelism, service, development, health, theological education, peace and justice, the struggle against racism, and interfaith dialogue, which have been developed during the past four decades of the Council's life, "respond to particular needs of the churches and of the world today and provide an opportunity for common witness and action".[10] The whole spectrum of the programmatic activities of the WCC and their periodical re-adjustment, Assembly after Assembly, are the natural consequence of the fact that the ecumenical movement is not only a continuing challenge to the churches but also the mirror reflecting the situations in which the churches live, act and witness.

The convergence statement

One of the major achievements of the WCC in the past forty years has been the extraordinary breakthrough in the move towards the visible unity of the churches of Christ, something unthinkable four decades ago. It is generally admitted that the convergence document on baptism, eucharist and ministry, elaborated with the active participation of many outstanding Orthodox scholars, in spite of its weaknesses, especially in its section on Ministry, is so far the most serious contribution of the WCC to the ecumenical movement and without doubt a major step towards Christian unity. It is a significant advance towards the recovery of the apostolic tradition and of the faith and practice of the early church.[11]

This explains in the clearest possible way the ecumenical motivation of the Orthodox and the raison d'être of their presence in the WCC. The third Pan-Orthodox Preconciliar Conference [1986] stressed it when it said: "The Orthodox Church by her inner conviction and ecclesial consciousness that she is the bearer of and the witness to the Faith and Tradition of the One, Holy, Catholic and Apostolic Church, deeply believes that she has a central and unique position in the Christian world today in order to further the unity of the Church."[12]

In this framework, the presence of the Orthodox Church in the WCC has been, and I think will remain, a constant reminder that in addition to any joint action and witness dictated by the world's agenda today, the main objective of the churches in their common ecumenical search is the reintegration for the Christian mind, the recovery of the apostolic tradition, the fullness of Christian vision and belief "in agreement with all ages". The Orthodox delegates at the New Delhi Assembly (1961) put it quite explicitly when they advocated an "ecumenism in time". For "the common ground, or rather the common background of existing denominations can be found, and must be sought in the past, in their common history, in that common ancient and Apostolic Tradition, from which all of them derive their existence".[13]

This was the stand of the Orthodox Church already in the 1927 Faith and Order World Conference. In their declaration, the Orthodox delegates at Lausanne reminded participants "that reunion can take place only on the basis of the common faith and confession of the ancient, undivided Church of the seven ecumenical Councils and of the first eight centuries".[14]

The importance of the study of the Apostolic Faith

The Orthodox firmly believe that the Christian faith is one indivisible unity. All doctrines formulated by the Ecumenical Councils, as well as the totality of the teachings of the early undivided church, must be accepted by all, for one cannot be satisfied with teachings and doctrines which are isolated from the life, witness and experiences of the early church. "The Church is one Body whose historical continuity and unity is safeguarded by the common faith arising spontaneously out of the fullness of the Church."[15] No doubt that on this particular point the Orthodox have been consistent through the years and they have never changed their line in regard to the nature of the unity we seek within the WCC. In that respect the position recently taken by the third Pre-Conciliar Pan-Orthodox Conference is quite explicit:

> The Orthodox Church, faithful to her ecclesiology, to the identity of her inner structure and to the teaching of the undivided church, in participating in the fellowship of the WCC, does not accept the idea of a parity of denominations and cannot accept Church unity as an interdenominational adjustment. In that respect the unity which is sought in the WCC cannot be the product of theological agreements only. God calls us to the living unity in the Mystery and the Tradition of the faith, as experience in the Orthodox Church.[16]

This attitude most probably shocks the ecumenical partner. It is a reminder however that ecumenism should not be confused with doctrinal relativism. Visser 't Hooft very pertinently pointed out: "Ecumenical dialogue, which for reasons of politeness or opportunism conceals the real issues, does far more harm than good. We need maximum ecumenism, in which each church brings the fullness of its conviction, not minimum ecumenism in which we are left with a meagre common denominator."[17] In this Visser 't Hooft joins his old-time friend and ecumenical companion Patriarch Athenagoras I who, during his visit to the WCC in November 1967, underlined that "the more a church has the consciousness that she possesses the truth and remains faithful to the word of Christ, the tradition and the mission of the one ancient and undivided Church, so much the more has [she] the obligation to enter into dialogue and collaboration with all other Christian denominations, in a spirit of love, humility and service".[18]

The above considerations lead me to underline the utmost importance of the ongoing debate on the apostolic faith for the future of the ecumenical movement and of the WCC. Undoubtedly, the next decade leading towards the fiftieth anniversary of the WCC, just two years before the third millennium starts, will be crucial. Therefore the study undertaken by Faith and Order "to interpret the Apostolic Faith as expressed in the Nicene-Constantinopolitan Creed" is of primary importance, for it will lead to a positive explanation of many basic tenets of the one prevailing faith in the church for centuries and will on the other hand give a definite answer to the question: "How can the faith handed down by the apostles to the undivided Church be interpreted today amid the problems and anxieties of people of our times."[19] This interpretation however presupposes a faithfulness to our common Christian roots and a sense of being part of the same Christian family. Any attempt to reject or even to minimize our belonging to the same roots, for ideological, cultural, regional or national considerations, will be detrimental to the ecumenical cause and to the future of the WCC.

Philip Potter once pertinently pointed out that "the WCC is not an end in itself, but represents a fellowship of the pilgrim people of God on the way to the visible realization of the universal Church of Jesus Christ... The future depends on God's blessing and on our common obedience to Jesus Christ and his call to unity."[20] It could be said that obedient to this call, the Orthodox members of the WCC, together with the other sister churches engaged in the same struggle, have taken part and will certainly continue to participate in the ecumenical pilgrimage.

This common march and dialogue will inevitably go on, as long as we continue using a theology which separates the divine from the human and places God behind history, instead of putting God right in the middle of today's world. Let us remember that the fathers of the early church never made a distinction between the vertical and the horizontal because they had a holistic vision of the world's realities. They developed a theology of the whole creation, a theology of cosmic dimension.

Could it be said that in its forty years life, the WCC has followed the path shown by the early fathers? Such an affirmation would probably be an exaggeration! It is true nevertheless that the WCC never tried to make a real distinction between the vertical and horizontal dimensions of its work. It tried to combine its socio-political activities with an in-depth theological reflection with regard to Christian unity, although such theological positions did not always agree with the traditional Orthodox stand. It is a fact however that even its most "horizontal" and much-disputed activities were not without a vertical reference to God, as they sought the diakonia of the human being created in God's image and likeness.

NOTES

[1] W.A. Visser 't Hooft, *The Genesis and Formation of the World Council of Churches*, Geneva, WCC, 1982, p.1.

[2] Encyclical of the Ecumenical Patriarchate, 1920, in *The Ecumenical Review*, vol. XII, October 1959, pp.79-82.

[3] "Celui qui n'assemble pas avec moi disperse", sermon at St Peter's Cathedral, 8 November 1967, on the occasion of the visit of the Ecumenical Patriarch Athenagoras. See G. Tsetsis, "L'Eglise orthodoxe et le mouvement oecuménique", in *Le monde religieux*, vol. 32, L'oecuménisme, 1975, p.152.

[4] Actes de la Conférence des Eglises autocéphales orthodoxes, vol. II, Moscow, 1952, p.450.

[5] Eglise orthodoxe et mouvement oecuménique, in *Episkepsis*, no. 369, December 1986, pp.14-17.

[6] *The Ecumenical Nature of the Orthodox Witness*, report of the New Valamo consultation, WCC, Geneva, 1977, p.19.

[7] Archbishop Iakovos, "The Contribution of Eastern Orthodoxy to the Ecumenical Movement", in *The Ecumenical Review*, Vol. XXI, July 1959, pp.394-404.

[8] Constantin Patelos ed., *The Orthodox Church in the Ecumenical Movement*, Geneva, WCC, 1978, p.213.

[9] Declaration of the Ecumenical Patriarchate on the occasion of the 25th anniversary of the WCC, ed. Patriarchal Institute for Patristic Studies, Thessaloniki, 1973, p.33.

[10] See *Episkepsis*, No. 369, December 1986, p.15.

[11] Response of the Moscow Patriarchate to the Lima document; see Georges Tsetsis, "A Synthesis of Responses of Orthodox Churches to the Lima Document", in *Orthodoxes Forum*, I, 1987, p.110.

[12] See *Episkepsis*, No. 369, December 1986, p.14.

[13] C. Patelos, *op. cit.*, p.98.

[14] H.N. Bate ed., *Faith and Order, Proceedings of the Lausanne Conference*, London, SCM, 1927, p.384.

[15] See statement of Orthodox delegates at the Second Assembly in Evanston (1954), in Patelos, *op. cit.*, p.95.

[16] See *Episkepsis*, No. 369, December 1986, p.15.

17 "The Ecumenical Movement, from Amsterdam to Geneva (1948-1966)", in *The Welcome and the Speeches of Dr Visser 't Hooft and E.C. Blake at the University of Athens*, Athens, 1967, p.33.

18 Address by His Holiness Athenagoras I, Ecumenical Patriarch of Constantinople, in *The Ecumenical Review*, Vol. XX, January 1968, p.87.

19 Reply of His All Holiness the Ecumenical Patriarch Dimitrios I during his official visit to the WCC, December 1987.

20 Todor Sabev ed., *The Sofia Consultation*, Geneva, WCC, 1982, p.41.

Bibliography

CONTRIBUTIONS TO "THE ECUMENICAL REVIEW"

ABRAMIDES, E.C., "Ethical Aspects of Climate Changes", 44 (1992), 333-338.

AGOURIDES, S., "Salvation according to the Orthodox Tradition", 21 (1969), 190-203.

ALIVISATOS, H., "The Ecumenical Movement and the Orthodox Church", 1 (1948-1949), 267-276.

ALIVISATOS, H., "The Roman Catholic Church as a Member of the World Council of Churches", 21 (1969), 3-6.

ARIGA, T., "Christian Tradition in a Non-Christian Land", 12 (1959-1960), 199-205.

BASDEKIS, A., "Between Partnership and Separation", 29 (1977), 52-61.

BEBAWI, G., "The Crown of Life: An Orthodox Perspective", 34 (1982), 263-270.

BELOPOPSKY, A., "Youth as Part of the People of God", 45 (1993), 421-426.

BOBRINSKOY, B., "The Continuity of the Church and Orthodoxy", 16 (1963-1964), 512-529.

BOBRINSKOY, B., "The Holy Spirit in the Bible and the Church", 41 (1989), 357-362.

BONIS, K., "The Orthodox Conception of the Spirituality of the Church in Relation to Daily Life", 15 (1962-1963), 303-310.

BOROVOY, V., "The Ecclesiastical Significance of the WCC: The Legacy and Promise of Toronto", 40 (1988), 504-518.

BOZABALIAN, N., "Life in the Oikoumene: A New Way for the Church", 36 (1984), 177-178.

BRATSIOTIS, P., "The Fundamental Principles and Main Characteristics of the Orthodox Church", 12 (1959-1960), 154-163.

BRIA, I., "Creative Vision of D. Staniloae", 33 (1981), 53-59.

BRIA, I., "The Eastern Orthodox in the Ecumenical Movement", 38 (1986), 216-227.

BRIA, I., "Unity and Mission", 39 (1987), 265-270.

BRIA, I., "A Fresh Breath of Spirituality", 44 (1992), 429-432.

CHIRBAN, J.T., "Healing and Orthodox Spirituality", 45 (1993), 337-344.

CHRYSOSTOMOS, Metropolitan (Konstantinidis), "Life in Christ", 35 (1983), 277-281.

CHRYSSAVGIS, J., "Acquisition of the Spirit as the Aim of Life", 42 (1990), 298-300.

CLAPSIS, E., "The Holy Spirit in the Church", 41 (1989), 339-347.

CLAPSIS, E., "Naming God: An Orthodox View", 42 (1990), 100-112.

CLEMENT, O., "Athenagoras I", 25 (1973), 310-328.

DAMASKINOS, Metropolitan (Papandreou), "Reformation and the Reformed Churches", 39 (1987), 96-97.

DANIEL, Metropolitan (Ciobotea), "Challenges for Orthodoxy in a Changing World", 44 (1992), 204-208.

FITZGERALD, T., "Eastern Orthodox-Roman Catholic Statement on Apostolicity", 39 (1987), 485-487.

FLOROVSKY, G., "The Doctrine of the Church and the Ecumenical Movement", 2 (1950), 152-161.

FLOROVSKY, G., "The Ethos of the Orthodox Church", 12 (1960), 183-198.

GEORGE, K.M., "Gospel, Culture and Theological Education", 42 (1990), 459-464.

GEORGE, K.M., "Looking beyond Doctrinal Agreements", 44 (1992), 1-5.

GREGORIOS Mar, G. (Metropolitan), "The Witness of the Churches: Ecumenical Statements on Mission and Evangelism", 40 (1988), 359-366.

GREGORIOS Mar, G. (Metropolitan), "Not a Question of Hospitality: A Comment", 42 (1990), 46-47.

HADDAD, F., "Orthodox Spirituality", 38 (1986), 64-70.

HARAKAS, S., "The Local Church", 29 (1977), 182-195.

HARAKAS, S., "Must God Remain Greek?", 43 (1991), 194-199.

HUTTUNEN, H., "For the Life of the World: Orthodox Unity". Syndesmos IVth International Orthodox Youth Festival, 44 (1992), 198-204.

IAKOVOS, Archbishop, "The Contribution of Eastern Orthodoxy to the Ecumenical Movement", 11 (1958-1959), 394-404.

IAKOVOS, Archbishop, "The True Nature of the World Council", 13 (1960-1961), 463-468.

IGNATIOS IV (Patriarch of Antioch), "Behold, I Make All Things New", 42 (1990), 122-130.

ISTAVRIDIS, V., "The Work of Germanos Strenopoulos in the Field of Inter-Orthodox and Inter-Christian Relations", 11 (1958-1959), 291-299.

ISTAVRIDIS, V., "The Ecumenicity of Orthodoxy", 29 (1977), 182-195.

JIVI, A., "Life in the Oikoumene: Orthodox Participation at Vancouver", 36 (1984), 174-177.

KARMIRIS, J., "The Second Ecumenical Council", 33 (1981), 244-248.

KARTACHOFF, A., "Orthodox Theology and the Ecumenical Movement", 8 (1955-1956), 30-35.

KESHISHIAN, A., "The Assembly Theme: More Orthodox Perspectives", 42 (1990), 197-207.

KESHISHIAN, A., "Growing Together in the Ecumenical Vision", 42 (1990), 113-120.

KESHISHIAN, A., "Reflections on the Future", 43 (1991), 259-261.

KESHISHIAN, A., "Towards a Self-Understanding of the World Council of Churches", 43 (1991), 11-21.

KESHISHIAN, A., "Growing Together towards a Full Koinonia", 44 (1992), 491-500.

KRIKORIAN, M.K. (Bishop), "The Armenian Church and the WCC: A Personal View", 40 (1988), 411-416.

LARENTZAKIS, G., "The Unity of the Church as Koinonia: Some Reflections from an Orthodox Standpoint", 45 (1993), 69-71.

LEMOPOULOS, G., "The Prophetic Mission of Orthodoxy", 40 (1988), 169-177.

LEMOPOULOS, G., "Come, Holy Spirit", 41 (1989), 461-467.

LEMOPOULOS, G., "The Icon of Pentecost: A Liturgical Bible Study on Acts 2:1-4", 42 (1990), 92-97.

LIMOURIS, G., "The Eucharist as the Sacrament of Sharing", 38 (1986), 401-415.

LIMOURIS, G., "The Sanctifying Grace of the Holy Spirit", 42 (1990), 301-312.

LIMOURIS, G., "Orthodoxy Facing Contemporary Social Ethical Concerns", 43 (1991), 420-429.

LIMOURIS, G., "Being as Koinonia in Faith: Challenges, Visions and Hopes for the Unity of the Church Today", 45 (1993), 78-92.

LOSSKY, N., "The Promise and the Outcome", 43 (1991), 211-216.

MASSOUD, E, "Life in the Oikoumene: Comments by an Orthodox Youth Delegate", 36 (1984), 171-172.

MATSOUKAS, N., "The Economy of the Holy Spirit: The Standpoint of Orthodox Theology", 41 (1989), 398-405.

MELITA, M., "The Significance of the World Council of Churches for the Older Churches", 9 (1956-1957), 16-18.

MELITON, Metropolitan, "The Re-Encounter between the Eastern Church and the Western Church", 17 (1965), 301-320.

NIKODIM, Metropolitan, "The Russian Orthodox Church and the Ecumenical Movement", 21 (1969), 116-129.

NISSIOTIS, N., "Interpreting Orthodoxy", 14 (1961-1962), 4-28.

NISSIOTIS, N., "The Witness and the Service of Eastern Orthodoxy to the One Undivided Church", 14 (1961-1962), 192-202.

NISSIOTIS, N., "Eastern and Western Theologians Study together Spirituality", 15 (1962-1963), 245-251.

NISSIOTIS, N., "Conversion and the Church", 19 (1967), 261-270.

NISSIOTIS, N., "The Theology of the Church and Its Accomplishment", 29 (1977), 62-76.

NISSIOTIS, N., "Faith and Order as a Witnessing Event", 34 (1982), 124-131.

NISSIOTIS, N., "Towards a New Ecumenical Era", 37 (1985), 326-335.

"Orthodox Perspectives on Justice and Peace", 41 (1989), 582-590.

"Orthodox Reflections on the Assembly Theme", 42 (1990), 301-312.

OSTHATHIOS MAR, G., "The Ground of Hope: The Ground of Faith", 31 (1979), 26-28.

PANCHOVSKI, I. & SABEV, T., "An Orthodox Comment" [on the study document "Common Witness and Proselytism" of the Joint Working Group], 23 (1971), 25-29.

PAPADEROS, A., "Baptism, Eucharist and Ministry", 36 (1984), 193-203.

PHILIPOS, K., "The Malabar Church: South India", 11 (1958-1959), 300-306.

SABEV, T., "The Joint Working Group Twenty-Five Years in Service of Unity", 42 (1990), 17-23.

SABEV, T., "The Nature and Mission of Councils in the Light of the Theology of Sobornost", 45 (1993), 261-270.

SCOUTERIS, C., "The Ecclesiastical Significance of the WCC: the Fusion of Doctrine and Life", 40 (1988), 519-527.

SCOUTERIS, C., "Christian Europe: An Orthodox Perspective", 45 (1993), 151-157.

STEPHANOPOULOS, R.G., "Implications for the Ecumenical Movement" [of Eucharistic Hospitality], 44 (1992), 18-28.

STYLIANOPOULOS, Th., "Jesus Christ — the Life of the World. Creation, Incarnation and Sanctification", 35 (1983), 364-370.

TARASAR, C., "Worship, Spirituality and Biblical Reflections: Their Significance for the Churches' Search for Koinonia", 45 (1993), 99-104.

TIMIADIS, Metropolitan (Emilianos), "Disregarded Causes of Disunity", 21 (1969), 299-309.

TIMIADIS, Metropolitan (Emilianos), "From the Margin to the Forefront", 27 (1977), 52-61.

TIMIADIS, Metropolitan (Emilianos), "Common and Uncommon Faith", 32 (1980), 396-409.

TSETSIS, G., "The Meaning of the Orthodox Presence", 40 (1988), 440-445.

TSETSIS, G., "What Is the World Council's Oikoumene?", 43 (1991), 86-89.

VALENTIN, F., "Ecumenism in Parish of the Russian Orthodox Emigration", 8 (1955-1956), 276-280.

VERGHESE, P., "Aggiornamento and the Unity of All", 15 (1962-1963), 377-384.

YEGSAW, L., "Life in the Oikoumene: A Reflection from the Delegation of the Ethiopian Orthodox Church", 36 (1984), 173-174.

ZAHIRSKY, V., "Are the Orthodox that Far Apart?", 42 (1991), 222-225.

ZANDER, L., "The Ecumenical Movement and the Orthodox Church", 1 (1948), 267-276.

ZIZIOULAS, Metropolitan (John), "Reflections of an Orthodox" [on the study document "Common Witness and Proselytism" of the Joint Working Group], 23 (1971), 30-34.

CONTRIBUTIONS TO THE
DICTIONARY OF THE ECUMENICAL MOVEMENT

ed. by N. Lossky, J. Miguez Bonino, J. Pobee, T. Stransky, G. Wainwright, P. Webb, WCC Publications, Geneva, and William B. Eerdmans Publ. Company, Grand Rapids, 1991

BOBRINSKOY, B., "Holy Spirit", 470-473.

BRIA, I., "Mysticism", 706-708; "Saints", 890-892; "Witness", 1067-1069.

BRIERE, E., "Fellowship of St Alban and St Sergius", 419-420.

CIOBOTEA, D., "Trinity", 1020-1023.

CLAPSIS, E., "Eschatology", 361-364.

CLEMENT, O., "Athenagoras I" (Ecumenical Patriarch), 63-65.

FITZGERALD, T., "Encyclicals, Orthodox", 354-355.

GEORGE, K.M., "Oriental Orthodox-Orthodox Dialogue", 757-759.

GREGORIOS MAR, P., "Nature", 715-718.

HACKEL, S., "Sobornost", 924-926.

HUTTUNEN, H., "Syndesmos", 966-967.

ITTY, C.I., "Just, Participatory and Sustainable Society", 550-552.

KNIAZEFF, A., "Apostasy", 39-40; "Heresy", 453-454; "Schism", 901-902.

L'HUILLIER, P., "Economy (Oikonomia)", 320-322; "Excommunication", 401-402.

LIMOURIS, G., "Constantinople, First Ecumenical Council", 226-227; "Nicea", 726-727; "Nicene Creed", 727-728.

LOSSKY, A., "Epiclesis", 358-359.

LOSSKY, N., "Eastern Orthodoxy", 311-313; "Icon/Image", 495-498; "Vl. Lossky", 633; "Orthodoxy", 764-768; "Theology, Ecumenical", 986-988.

MEYENDORFF, J., "Patristics", 781-784.

MEYENDORFF, P., "Liturgy", 623-626.

OSSORGUINE, N., "Church Calendar", 178-179.

OSTHATHIOS MAR, G., "Oriental Orthodox Churches", 755-757.

TSETSIS, G., "Pan-Orthodox Conferences", 774-775.

WARE, K., "Ethnicity", 373; "Tradition and Traditions", 1013-1017.

PUBLICATIONS

relating to programmes and projects of the WCC,
inter-Orthodox consultations, and Orthodox subjects related to ecumenism

BRIA, I., *Martyria "Mission". The Witness of the Orthodox Churches Today*, WCC, Geneva, 1980.

BRIA, I. (ed.), *Jesus Christ, the Life of the World: An Orthodox Contribution to the Vancouver Theme*, WCC, Geneva, 1982.

BRIA, I. (ed.), *The Witness of St Methodius: Orthodox Mission in the 9th Century*, WCC, Geneva, 1985.

BRIA, I. (ed.), *Go Forth in Peace. Orthodox Perspectives on Mission*, WCC Mission Series, Geneva, 1986.

BRIA, I. (ed.), *People Hunger to Be Near to God. Common Convictions about Renewal, Spirituality, Community*, WCC, Geneva, 1990.

BRIA, I., *The Sense of Ecumenical Tradition: The Ecumenical Witness and Vision of the Orthodox Church*, WCC, Geneva, 1991.

BRIA, I. & PATELOS, C. (eds), *Orthodox Contributions to Nairobi*, WCC, Geneva, 1975.

KESHISHIAN, Aram (Archbishop), *Conciliar Fellowship: A Common Goal*, WCC, Geneva, 1992.

KESHISHIAN, Aram (Archbishop), *Orthodox Perspectives on Mission*, Regnum Lynx, Oxford, 1992.

LEMOPOULOS, G., *Your Will Be Done. Orthodoxy in Mission*, Tertios, Katerini/Greece, and WCC, Geneva, 1989.

LEMOPOULOS, G., *Come, Holy Spirit — Renew the Whole Creation*, Tertios, Katerini/Greece, 1991 (in Greek).

LEMOPOULOS, G., *The Seventh Assembly of the World Council of Churches*, Canberra, Australia, February 1991, Tertios, Katerini/Greece, 1991 (in Greek).

LIMOURIS, G. & VAPORIS, M. (eds), *Orthodox Perspectives on Baptism, Eucharist and Ministry*, Holy Cross Orthodox Press, Brookline/MA, USA, 1985.

LIMOURIS, G. (ed.), *Church — Kingdom — World. The Church as Mystery and Prophetic Sign*, Faith and Order Paper No. 130, WCC, Geneva, 1986.

LIMOURIS, G. (ed.), *Icons — Windows on Eternity. Theology and Spirituality in Colour*, Faith and Order Paper No. 147, WCC, Geneva 1990.

LIMOURIS, G. (ed.), *Justice, Peace and the Integrity of Creation: Insights from Orthodoxy*, WCC, Geneva, 1990.

LIMOURIS, G. (ed.), *Come, Holy Spirit — Renew the Whole Creation: An Orthodox Approach for the Seventh Assembly of the World Council of Churches, Canberra, Australia, 6-21 February 1991*, Holy Cross Orthodox Press, Brookline/MA, USA, 1990.

LIMOURIS, G. (ed.), *The Place of the Woman in the Orthodox Church and the Question of the Ordination of Women*, Tertios, Katerini/Greece, 1992.

PAPADEROS, A. (ed.), *Liturgical Diakonia: The Social Mission of the Church in the Contemporary World*, Acts of the WCC Inter-Orthodox Consultation, 20-25 November 1978, published by Orthodox Academy of Crete, Chania/Greece, 1981 (in Greek).

PATELOS, C. (ed.), *The Orthodox Church in the Ecumenical Movement*, WCC, Geneva, 1978.

SABEV, T. (ed.), *The Sofia Consultation: Orthodox Involvement in the World Council of Churches*, WCC, Geneva, 1982.

TSETSIS, G. (ed.), *The Ecumenical Nature of the Orthodox Witness: The New Valamo Consultation, Finland (24-30 September 1977)*, WCC, Geneva, 1977.

TSETSIS, G. (ed.), *An Orthodox Approach to Diaconia*. Consultation on Church and Service, Orthodox Academy of Crete (20-25 November 1978), WCC, Geneva, 1978.

TSETSIS, G., *Orthodox Thought: Reports of Orthodox Consultations Organized by the World Council of Churches 1975-1982*, WCC, Geneva, 1983.

TSETSIS, G., *Ecumenical Analecta: Contribution in the History of the World Council of Churches*, Tertios, Katerini/Greece 1987 (in Greek).

TSETSIS, G., *The Contribution of the Ecumenical Patriarchate in the Foundation of the World Council of Churches*, Tertios, Katerini/Greece, 1988 (in Greek).